THE ENEMY ON TRIAL

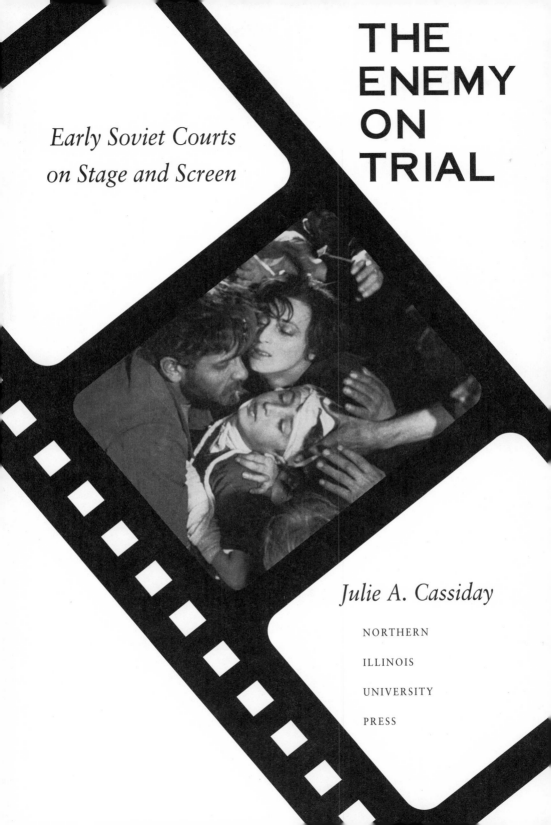

THE ENEMY ON TRIAL

Early Soviet Courts on Stage and Screen

Julie A. Cassiday

NORTHERN

ILLINOIS

UNIVERSITY

PRESS

© 2000 by Northern Illinois University Press

Published by the Northern Illinois University Press,

DeKalb, Illinois 60115

Manufactured in the United States using acid-free paper

All Rights Reserved

Design by Julia Fauci

Library of Congress Cataloging-in-Publication Data

Cassiday, Julie A.

The enemy on trial : early Soviet courts on stage and screen / Julie A. Cassiday.

    p. cm.

Includes bibliographical references and index.

ISBN 0-87580-266-4 (alk. paper)

    1. Moscow Trials, Moscow, Russia, 1936–1937. 2. Courts—Soviet

Union—History. 3. Socialism and theater—Soviet Union—History. 4. Socialism

and motion pictures—Soviet Union—History. 5. Culture and law. I. Title.

KLA40.P64 C37 2000

347.47'01'09—dc21   00-025544

For Leyla

CONTENTS

Acknowledgments   ix

Introduction   3

1 Imperial Precedents and the First Bolshevik Show Trials   28

2 The Mock Trial: Mythopoetic Justice I   51

3 Trials on Film: Mythopoetic Justice II   81

4 Marble Columns and Jupiter Lights in the Shakhty Affair   110

5 The Redounding Rhetoric of Legal Satire   134

6 For Each Enemy, Another Trial   161

Conclusion   189

Notes   197

Selected Bibliography   233

Index   255

ACKNOWLEDGMENTS

I received the original impetus for this book approximately ten years ago, in the office of Professor Gregory Freidin of Stanford University. For his seemingly casual suggestion that I investigate the "show" in show trials, I am enormously indebted. His sharply posed questions and vast knowledge of Russian literature and culture were invaluable in formulating, writing, and preparing the dissertation out of which this book grew. My appreciation also extends to the other members of my dissertation reading committee—Lazar Fleishman, Marjorie Perloff, and Andrew Wachtel—who brought great expertise and patience to the aid of my work. I owe a special debt of gratitude to the late Professor Edward Brown for encouraging my ideas during his last year of teaching at Stanford University.

I would like to thank the many friends and colleagues who have read various versions of my work and have offered invaluable suggestions for its improvement. Darra Goldstein's intelligent and sensitive commentary not only renewed my enthusiasm for my research but also taught me the true meaning of collegial support. The recommendations of Denise Young-blood helped me to define the body of films discussed in the chapters that follow. To Eric Naiman and Anne Nesbit I owe a special debt for introducing me to Kalatozov's lost film, *Gvozd' v sapoge (A Nail in the Boot)*. I am also obliged to Choi Chatterjee and Karen Petrone, who organized an outstanding conference on ideology in early Soviet culture in November 1997 at the University of Indiana. I would like to thank Joan Neuberger, Louise McReynolds, and Lars Lih, who have helped me to articulate the sections of this book devoted to melodrama. I am likewise grateful to the many historians whose work has urged me toward ever greater historical accuracy, including Michael David-Fox, Nikolai Krementsev, Elizabeth Wood, and Matt Lenoe. In addition, I would like to thank the two reviewers for Northern Illinois University Press, who provided the helpful comments and scholarly support necessary for revising my manuscript. To Mary Lincoln at Northern Illinois University Press, I would like to extend my gratitude for her courtesy, promptness, and professionalism.

In addition to the individuals who have generously advised me, a number of organizations have provided funds for my research and travel over the last eight years. I would like to acknowledge the Stanford Humanities Center, the Mabelle McCleod Lewis Foundation, the Social Science Research Council, the American Council of Teachers of Russian, the Kennan Institute of the Woodrow Wilson Center, the Oakley Center for the Humanities and Social Sciences of Williams College, and the Dean of the Faculty at Williams College, all of whom have provided me with the financial assistance necessary to research, write, and complete this book.

I owe a significant debt of gratitude to the organizations that have provided me access to much needed scholarly materials, as well as to their considerate staffs. I would like to thank the Pacific Film Archives, in particular Nancy Goldman and Jason Sanders of the PFA library, who allowed me to use their magnificent collection of early Soviet film. To Heidi Bliss of Harvard's Carpenter Center, I am grateful for viewing a copy of *A Nail in the Boot*. I also thank the faculty and staff of the All-State Institute of Cinematography, as well as those at the Central State Archive of Art and Literature. The workers at the Central State Archive of Film and Photographic Documents and Gosfil'mofond deserve my special appreciation for helping me to obtain the illustrations and for providing me with the permission necessary to reproduce them. I must also extend my appreciation to Allison O'Grady and her assistants in the Interlibrary Loan Department at the Sawyer Library of Williams College, who proved that there was no book too obscure to travel to rural New England. Needless to say, the views expressed in the chapters that follow are entirely my own, and none of the individuals or organizations listed above bears any responsibility for the opinions expressed in this book.

Finally, I would like to perform the impossible task of thanking my family and friends, whose patience, support, and humor have made this book possible. I dedicate the pages that follow to my partner, in projects academic and otherwise, Leyla Rouhi.

Earlier versions of portions of this book have appeared in the following journal articles:

"Marble Columns and Jupiter Lights: Theatrical and Cinematic Modeling of the Soviet Show Trial in the 1920s." *Slavic and East European Journal* 42, no. 4 (winter 1998): 640–60.

"Flash Floods, Bedbugs, and Saunas: Social Hygiene in Maiakovskii's Theatrical Satires of the Twenties." *Slavonic and East European Review* 76, no. 4 (October 1998): 643–57.

THE ENEMY ON TRIAL

Most honored guests, we're tragedians ourselves, and our tragedy is the finest and best we can create. At any rate, our entire state has been constructed so as to be a "representation" of the finest and noblest life—the very thing we maintain is most genuinely a tragedy. So we are poets like yourselves, composing in the same *genre,* and your competitors as artists and actors in the finest drama, which true law alone has the natural powers to "produce" to perfection (of that we're quite confident). So don't run away with the idea that we shall ever blithely allow you to set up stage in the market-place and bring on your actors whose fine voices will carry further than ours. Don't think we'll let you declaim to women and children and the general public, and talk about the same practices as we do but treat them differently—indeed, more often than not, so as virtually to contradict us. We should be absolutely daft, and so would any state as a whole, to let you go ahead as we've described before the authorities had decided whether your work was fit to be recited and suitable for public performance or not.

—Plato, *The Laws* VII.817

INTRODUCTION

Historians of Stalin's Great Terror, Western journalists assigned to the Soviet beat, and political dissidents ordinarily describe the public trials that punctuated the first two decades of Soviet history as highly theatrical spectacles. Using terminology borrowed from the stage, they label these *pokazatel'nyi protsessy* (show trials) bad drama and expand some part of the theatrical metaphor to support their claim. Some writers express their outrage at the hand-picked audiences, the defendants' memorized scripts for confession, or rehearsals that took the form of grueling interrogation or torture. Others denounce what happened behind the scenes, the tyrannical direction of the state's prosecutor Nikolai Krylenko, and the fatal consequences of bringing down the curtain on the accused. In all of these cases, the theatrical metaphor helps to discredit show trials as legal procedure and ultimately to critique the legitimacy of the Soviet regime. Such writers downplay the denotation of the adjective *pokazatel'nyi* (model or exemplary) and instead focus on its connotations of *na pokaz* or *pokazukha* (just for show). They have equated the theater with fiction and presume that any intrusion of theatrical fiction into the realm of truth and justice makes the courtroom incapable of producing either.[1]

Nonetheless, an examination of trials outside of the Soviet Union shows that drama and the law have been longtime partners in the Western legal tradition. Phenomena as diverse as the Nuremberg trials and the Scopes monkey trial show that, even in the twentieth century, adversarial law has relied heavily on drama in its determination of justice. The theatrical nature of jurisprudence alone does not undermine the legitimacy of the court, and to condemn Soviet show trials for their theatricality simply states the obvious. The use of the theatrical metaphor to denounce Soviet jurisprudence becomes even more problematic in light of the frequency with which this particular trope appears in more general discussions of the first two decades of the country's history. It has become commonplace to refer to the "tragic" events of the civil war and collectivization, "dramatic" shifts in political alliances and associations, and the "director" behind the scenes of various Party congresses. Theater as metaphor and as cultural model has developed into what is arguably the most widespread interpretive tool not only of Soviet studies but also of cultural studies as a whole.[2] The ubiquity of the theatrical metaphor would seem to diminish its heuristic capacity and to take the sting out of the accusation that Soviet show trials were theatrical. If, to borrow from William Shakespeare, all the world is a stage, how can we express indignation that the Soviet courts were too?

In order to give this accusation meaning, we must stop using the theater as an archetype exempt from the vicissitudes of history and the peculiarities of culture.[3] We must reconnect Soviet show trials, which indeed constituted illegitimate legal procedure, with the actual dramatic practice on stages and screens of the early Soviet period. During the first three decades of the twentieth century, the proliferation of theatrical and cinematic theories and the intense vitality of stage and screen suggest a more concrete link between public trials and the theatrical terminology used to describe them. As historians have repeatedly noted, Russian culture at the time of the 1917 revolution was highly theatrical in both the literal and the figurative senses of the word.[4] Hence, we must try to understand theater and cinema, and their respective relationships to life outside the auditorium, just as those who created the institution of the Soviet show trial did in their day. By examining the dramatic means of representation on stage and screen specific to the early Soviet period, we can see what elements of theater and cinema entered the Soviet courtroom, how they functioned in a legal setting, and why they made Soviet show trials arguably the kangaroo courts of the twentieth century.

The semiotician Iurii Lotman employs a similar approach in his studies devoted to the theatricality of the early nineteenth-century Russian gentry.[5] Although his discussion treats neither law nor the courts, Lotman connects the diversity of theatrical activity in the first quarter of the nineteenth century to an expansion in the range of possible modes of behavior among members of the Russian upper class. In his analysis of the Decembrist uprising of 1825, Lotman shows that the interpenetration of theater and life allowed noblemen to assume a succession of social roles and to view themselves as actors on the stage of history, capable of revolutionary social change. Lotman never turns his attention to the Bolshevik revolution approximately one hundred years later; nonetheless, the 1917 coup d'état presents itself as a logical candidate for this type of analysis because of the fusion of the dramatic and political spheres that made the earlier period worthy of discussion. However, whereas Lotman correctly defines the theatricality of the early nineteenth century as an essentially liberating force, the present study contends that post-revolutionary theatricality, as seen in the Soviet show trial, functioned in a contrary manner and actually diminished the number and fluidity of roles available to Soviet citizens in the 1920s and 1930s. The radically different understanding of drama on stage and screen after 1917, as well as the Soviet state's use of this understanding to achieve specific ideological ends, gave post-revolutionary theatricality a form and function opposite of that of the century before.

The theater and cinema that came into public trials after the revolution were part of a larger modernist movement in which art did not merely reflect or comment upon life but actually helped to reform, to redirect, and ultimately to revolutionize the lives of artists and spectators alike. Within this broad, modernist agenda, drama had particular importance, since theater did not privilege language as a semiotic system and, as a result, allowed for the reordering of all semiotic systems, which language had traditionally dominated in Western culture. Upsetting the apple cart of artistic representation, the theater at the turn of the century created a new relationship between the subject and object of perception and cognition, effectively destroying the dualism that had characterized this relationship previously.[6] First theater and then cinema opened up the possibility of interaction between art and its audience, making drama the ideal means of mythopoesis, that is, the creation of myth with the power to revolutionize life. Bringing drama into public trials after 1917 was not intended to discredit the Soviet courtroom but rather to transform it into a powerful arena for propaganda, education, and legal mythopoesis.

Representatives of the Soviet state left an indelible ideological imprint on the fundamentally modernist conception of the drama in the show trials of the 1920s and 1930s, however. Elements from stage and screen were used to strengthen the state's case against those it deemed criminal, politically dangerous, counter-revolutionary, or some combination of all three. These enemies of the people had little or no freedom to use drama in their defense. Unlike O. J. Simpson or the Chicago Seven, the defendants in *pokazatel'nye protsessy* found themselves the victims of a totalizing script that allowed for no outcome other than guilty as charged. Originally, the avant-garde theatrical and cinematic techniques brought into the show trial were peripheral to ideological and moral concerns, but the manner in which these techniques were implemented in the Soviet courtroom resulted in an all-encompassing and ever expanding script for confession that culminated in Stalin's Great Terror. The illegitimacy of the Soviet show trial arose not merely from its theatricality but from the severe imbalance in access to the dramatic means of representation, an imbalance that figured as one of the show trial's constituent parts from its earliest instances.

Because this study analyzes the convergence of theatrical and cinematic paradigms in show trials of the early Soviet period, it addresses neither the individual psychology of confession (as Arthur Koestler does in his novel *Darkness at Noon*) nor the vast body of archival material on individual trials that has come into the hands of scholars since 1992.[7] Although both of these topics provide rich material for the cultural historian, they do not necessarily reveal the origins of the show trial's totalizing legal discourse and only confirm the efficacy of this discourse once it was put into place. The present study looks for the patterns that anticipated the show trial's totalizing script in a variety of popular media from the 1920s, including the Soviet and foreign press, propaganda and professional theaters, and documentary and feature films. Each of these media had its own unique form, function, and message in Soviet culture of the time; and those organizing early show trials transferred the patterns of legal propaganda from print, stage, and screen into the courtroom to make show trials comprehensible to their intended audience of millions of Soviet citizens.

An examination of legal propaganda on stage and screen reveals that theater and cinema developed overlapping models of confession, repentance, and reintegration into society during the 1920s. Propaganda theater in the form of the *agitsud* (mock trial) initially codified this tripartite paradigm, focusing on the defendant's almost religious conversion to the new way of life. Popular films and documentaries of the decade placed the threefold pattern in a specifically melodramatic context that emphasized the events preceding and following the conversion of the accused. When these two models of confession came together in actual courtroom practice, they allowed trial organizers to create a script with roles not only for court officials and defendants, but also for spectators of the trial, as we see in the first show trial of Stalin's era, the Shakhty Affair of 1928. By the end of the 1920s, the show trial had become a legal melodrama that unmasked the regime's internal, hidden enemies and hoped to compel its spectators to replicate the *samokritika* (self-criticism) of defendants on trial.

After the paradigm for confession, repentance, and reintegration into society coalesced in the Soviet courtroom, the very media that originally generated this formula were prohibited from its further elaboration. The legal melodrama of samokritika belonged exclusively in the actual courtroom, and commentaries on or alterations to the rigid script of the Soviet show trial were in effect banned from the stage and screen. By the 1930s, the show trial had been firmly institutionalized, and theater and cinema could only depict the personal, emotional drama of defendants who replicated the threefold paradigm without fail, even if reintegration into society had become entirely impossible in actual trials of the day. After the Soviet court seized the dramatic means of representation and learned to wield them effectively in public trials of the 1920s and 1930s, it obscured the dramatic origins of the show trial's script and made the stage and screen return to the courtroom to regain only the smallest fraction of the mythopoetic power they had once given the Soviet show trial.

DRAMA AND THE LAW

If drama's connection to the law is not unique to the Soviet show trial, neither is it solely the property of the other twentieth-century trials mentioned above. During the last one hundred years, print and electronic media have broadcast the dramatic modeling of public trials to an audience immeasurably greater than that of any previous century. However, the connection between courtroom and stage reaches back to the very foundations of Western civilization—as this book's epigraph, taken from Plato's *Laws*, attests. Since fifth-century Greece, manuals of rhetoric have taught that the art of the lawyer is, in essence, that of the actor.[8] In addition, the canon of western European drama, built on the foundation of Attic tragedy, regularly turns to the courtroom for its setting, to legal testimony for its dialogue, and to a trial's verdict for its dénouement. Aeschylus's *Eumenides*, Shakespeare's *Merchant of Venice*, Kleist's *The Broken Pitcher*, Shaw's *St. Joan*, and Brecht's *Caucasian Chalk Circle*, all demonstrate the remarkable frequency with which Western dramatists have turned to the law for thematic and structural purposes. As an eastern sibling in the same dramatic tradition, the Russian theatrical repertoire displays the same tendency: Kapnist's *Iabeda (Chicanery)*, Tolstoi's *The Living Corpse*, Sukhovo-Kobylin's *Trilogy*, and Voinovich's *Tribunal* set part or all of their action in a courtroom. Whether one questions, as Plato does, or praises the theater's use of legal material, the fact remains that drama and the law share common roots and overlapping territory in Western culture.

Given this close tie between drama and the law, it is surprising that scholars of both jurisprudence and the theater have paid little attention to this relationship during an era of growing interest in cultural studies. Over the past twenty years, academia has created a small industry out of the study of popular legal culture and literature and the law.[9] But only a fraction of this scholarly attention has focused on drama's relationship to the law, and usually this discussion treats great works of dramatic literature, such as Euripides or Shakespeare's tragedies, to the exclusion of dramatic performance.[10] The legal establishment tends to use an ahistorical, acultural model of the theater, whose dangers were noted above, in the discussion of drama's utility in the courtroom.[11] Only a handful of scholars, all of whom address highly specific areas of inquiry, have noted the tense and fluctuating relationship between dramatic practice and the law.[12] In spite of recent interest in the field of law and literature in both law schools and the literary establishment, the study of drama and the law has found no theoretician as its advocate in the last few decades.

We can better understand the shape and significance of the Soviet show trial's particular fusion of drama and the law if we place it within the larger context of Western legal and dramatic development dating back to ancient Greece. Law courts and the theater evolved at the same time in Athenian society and shared striking procedural, administrative, formal, rhetorical, and religious similarities.[13] As a number of influential scholars (including Jacob Burckhardt, Johan Huizinga, and Walter Benjamin) have noted, drama and the law in ancient Greek society were both instances of agon, that is, the "contest bound by fixed rules and sacred in form, where the two contending parties invoked the decision of an arbiter."[14] Like its successors in Western culture, Attic law used agon in the form of specific rhetorical strategies to determine *dike* or justice in the courts. However, ancient Greek drama both represented agon in the action of individual plays and was itself a type of agon, much like the law. A large number of surviving Greek tragedies—including Aeschylus's *Oresteia,* Sophocles' *Antigone* and *Ajax,* and the majority of Euripides' plays—contain scenes of rhetorical agon, which "consist of a pair of opposing set speeches of substantial, and about equal, length," and "evoke the lawcourts not only in their structure but also in their style."[15] In addition to this structural and stylistic affinity between Athenian drama and law, the renowned competitions between playwrights for the feast of Dionysus were in the form of a contest using religious, moral, and rhetorical criteria to determine the best tragedies and comedies in any given year. Needless to say, the court and the theater were separate institutions in ancient Greek society; but the fundamentally agonistic nature of each made them kindred in both form and in function. The fixed rules and sacred structure of dramatic representation and competition were easily transported into the law, which, in its turn, gave ancient Greek tragedy its essentially forensic structure.[16]

Cementing the bond between these two institutions, Athens's theatergoing public and her juries included the same group of people, whose responsibility it was, in both the theater and the courts of law, to judge the spectacle and decide the fate of those represented on stage.[17] The presence and participation of an adjudicating audience firmly united drama and the law in ancient Greece, as it did in the European Middle Ages and continues to do to the present day. In order to understand the complex and ever changing relationship between drama and the law in Western civilization, we must focus our attention on the nature of the audience in the theater and court, as well as on the forms its participation could and did take either in ancient Greece or in the Soviet Union. The constantly shifting possibilities for theatrical and legal spectatorship become visible on the background of the law's continuous secularization in Western society. As sociologists and legal anthropologists have described, Western law has evolved from its initial identification with religious morality in ancient society toward an abstract concept of secularized justice.[18] Putting the theatrical and legal spectator back into this evolutionary schema allows us to discern the distinctive form of the relationship between drama and the law in a given time and place and, consequently, to describe the nature of justice in a particular society.

The generally smooth pattern of legal evolution in Western society has been twisted by totalitarian states, such as Hitler's Germany and Stalin's Russia. Although National Socialism and communism represent clearly antagonistic ideologies, the two regimes implemented remarkably similar judicial practices: "justice was moralized; the law was instrumentalized; and the judiciary was politicized." Rather than continuing the process of legal evolution that had pushed the law and morality farther apart, Nazi Germany and Stalinist Russia deliberately devolved the law, placing political ideology where religion had once been.[19] In spite of this devolutionary similarity, Nazi courts used the available theatrical and cinematic models to figure the legal spectator in ways that distinguish German trials from their Soviet counterparts of approximately the same era. The courts of both regimes claimed to stand for the interests of a collective consciousness; however, the racial definition of the German *volk* resulted in dramatic paradigms and a legal audience that differed radically from those in the class-defined Soviet Union.[20]

As this book argues, the devolution of law in the Soviet Union coincided with a deliberate attempt to devolve the Russian theater. At the same time that Soviet legal theorists began to write the new laws that embodied proletarian morality, directors in the Russian theater and cinema were consciously attempting to return drama to its collective, religious origins in ancient Greek tragedy. In both cases, those creating change made deliberate efforts to bring the drama on stage and screen into contact with the law, in order to effect the greatest social change possible. Rather than forcefully expelling the actor from the polity for distracting his audience from the serious discussion of the law, as Plato advised, Bolshevik culture of the 1920s brought the actor into the heart of the legal sphere to complement and augment the new law's impact. Even more important than the actor, the spectator—that is, the recipient of these edifying performances—became an integral part of drama in both the theater and the court. In order to understand how audiences were intended to watch and to participate in Soviet show trials, we must investigate the modernist theories of theater and cinema circulating in Russia at the time of the 1917 revolution. Although our overview of these theories begins by necessity with Russia's avant-garde theater, it ends with revolutionary cinema's redefinition of spectatorship during the era of silent film.

REVOLUTIONARY THEATRICALITY

The professional and amateur theaters that developed after October 1917 were particularly well adapted to mixing art with life in institutions such as the show trial. Russia took part in the pan-European renovation of the theater at the turn of the century, which focused not simply on expanding the materials that constituted drama but, more important, on the fusion of real life with the theater, that is to say, theatricality.[21] However, Soviet Russia was in a unique position to realize the usually abstract and utopian portents of the avant-garde theater because of a series of actual, political revolutions during the first two decades of the twentieth century. Unlike their western European counterparts, Russian theorists of the new drama could connect the revolutionary agenda of modernist theatricality to real events taking place in the streets, and the promises of the revolutions of 1905 and 1917 became inextricably linked to those of the new theater. For the first time, the much anticipated revolution in the theater—first prophesied in the nineteenth century by Richard Wagner and Friedrich Nietzsche—took physical and political shape. Russians interested in the new theater owed a great intellectual debt to their allies on the western side of the continent; nonetheless, the peculiarly Russian realization of these originally western European ideas proved the potential and power of revolutionary theatricality.

Some fifty years earlier, in an 1848 article entitled "Art and Revolution," Wagner had described a revitalized German stage that returned drama to the religious form and function it once had in ancient Greek society. Twenty-four years later, Nietzsche amended and expanded this vision in *The Birth of Tragedy* (1872), placing emphasis on the inevitable triumph of Dionysian ecstasy over Apollonian reason in the revitalized theater.[22] Their redefinition of drama as a synthesis of many art forms capable of forging the spirit of a modern nation (as they assumed tragedy had forged the spirit of the ancient Greeks) entered Russia and was adapted to the contours of Russian society by the turn of the century: the period between the failed 1905 revolution and the October revolution of 1917 generated countless books and articles treating the "crisis" or "revolution" in the contemporary theater and connecting it to the turbulent events taking place in the country's politics.[23] In addition to the ideas of Wagner and Nietzsche, Russian theorists of the new theater also read the latest western European works such as Romain Rolland's *The People's Theater* (1903), Gordon Craig's *The Art of the Theatre* (1905), and Georg Fuchs's *Revolution in the Theatre* (1909).[24] The active engagement of Russians in the pan-European discussion of the resurrection of ancient Greek drama arose out of the internationalism of avant-garde art, which allowed Russians at the turn of the century to be both the recipients and the donors of cultural exchange.

In spite of continual contact with western European treatises on the new theater and with foreign touring companies that demonstrated its practice on the stages of St. Petersburg and Moscow, the Russian version of the new theater exhibited its own peculiarities. Even in its populist and socialist incarnations, the new drama in Russia tended toward the ambitious goal of not merely forging the spirit of the Russian nation but transforming the very foundations of human society as a whole. This universal scope arose from the dramatic theories of the symbolist poet and philosopher Viacheslav Ivanov, who had first adapted Wagner and Nietzsche to the Russian scene. Before the works of Fuchs, Craig, and Rolland reached a Russian audience, Ivanov combined the country's native populism and Orthodox Christianity with Wagner's vision of the *gesamtkunstwerk* of music-drama and Nietzsche's appeal to the Dionysian spirit. Ivanov's synthesis of Russian and western European elements irrevocably affected the reception in Russia of the two German theorists, as well as the western European reformers following in their footsteps. Thanks to Ivanov, the theater's vital role in transforming the human spirit quickly became a maxim that every theorist of drama in Russia during the first three decades of the twentieth century was obliged either to proclaim or to denounce before he offered his own solution to the crisis in the theater.

Unlike his German predecessors, Ivanov explained and justified the call back to Greek tragedy using the philosophical underpinnings of Russian symbolism. Strongly influenced by the philosopher Vladimir Solov'ev, Ivanov based his prescriptions for the new theater on a Neoplatonic view of art, in which a fundamental duality characterizes all of existence. Ivanov defined two types of reality: a higher spiritual reality called *realiora,* and its pale reflection in everyday life called *realia*.[25] Through the act of artistic creation, the artist moves *realia* ever closer to the ideal *realiora*, and the artistic process functions as an act of communication between the artist and his audience as they strive to make material reality conform to the spiritual ideal through collective mythopoesis. Although his Neoplatonic explanation applied equally to all the arts, Ivanov's aesthetic philosophy was particularly well suited to the theater since, for Ivanov, artistic creation was essentially a transcendental form of theatricality. Through symbolic representation in poetry, dance, sculpture, or drama, the artist tries to transform the representation of *realia* into *realiora*—that is, to transform reality into the vision of a mystical, Platonic ideal.

Drawing on his own studies of the ancient Greek cult of Dionysus, Ivanov labeled catharsis, which he claimed had left the modern theater long ago, the key ingredient for realizing collective mythopoesis in the theater. Restoring the cathartic effect of ancient Greek drama promised to make the theater "an active factor in our spiritual life" and to "throw a bridge from individualism to the principle of universal collectivity."[26] According to Ivanov, catharsis would assume its proper place in the theater only when the other arts that originally created drama's unique synthesis also returned to the stage. The reintegration of song and dance into drama would resurrect the ancient Greek chorus and ultimately make "The spectator . . . an actor, a participant in the action. The audience should merge into the choral body, like the mystical community of ancient 'orgies' and 'mysteries'" (206–7). Ivanov never described the practical mechanics of returning techniques that had left the theater some two thousand years ago to Russian stages at the turn of the century. Nonetheless, his compelling description of a Dionysian theater, characterized by collective action, audience participation, and erasing the boundary between the stage and real life, attracted not only fellow symbolists but also contemporaries working in all branches of culture.

For those writing and working in the theater, the most exciting element of Ivanov's Dionysian theater was not its resurrection of long extinct theatrical techniques but its promise to aid in the creation of a new social order. As he described, the loss of individuality in the Dionysian theater would parallel and actually stimulate a similar evaporation of social divisions outside the auditorium (196). A revitalized, synthetic drama would bring about an entirely new, organic era in human history, characterized by complete artistic and political freedom and the reintegration of cultural and social forces (195). The *narod* (people) of this era would constitute and express its identity in the new drama:

the organization of future choral action is the organization of national art [*vsenarodnoe iskusstvo*], and this latter—the organization of the people's soul [*narodnaia dusha*]. . . . And only then, we will add, when actual political freedom comes to be, then, will the choral voice of such societies be the genuine referendum of the true will of the people [*volia narodnaia*]. (218–19)

In his description of this future epoch in human history, Ivanov repeatedly used terminology tied to a national agenda, for example, *narodnaia dusha* or *volia narodnaia*. However, the subtle ambiguity of the word *vsenarodnoe* (an adjective meaning, literally, "all people") reveals that his agenda was not intended simply for all the Russian people but rather for all the peoples of the world. Ivanov's vision reached deep into the human psyche but simultaneously strove for the heavens: he and those who followed him believed the theater would play a leading role in a universal transformation of the human spirit.

The poet philosopher never succeeded in realizing this Dionysian vision in his own plays; even his fellow symbolists, who had practical experience in the theater, sarcastically asked, "But are we really Greeks? Should we really be eating olives and dancing around a goat?"[27] Nevertheless, Ivanov's heady combination of art, philosophy, religion, and revolution found advocates in a number of different movements outside Russian symbolism that wanted to restore the theater's ability to interact with the social sphere. Although Ivanov's theories were justifiably criticized as anachronistic, overly abstract, altogether divorced from the country's professional stage, they allowed Russians to look at the theater as a means for radical social transformation for the first time. Without exception, every theatrical movement that emerged in the first three decades of the twentieth century reacted in some way to the universal revolutionary mission of Ivanov's Dionysian theater, either rejecting it or adapting it to its own purposes.[28]

Those working in Russia's professional theaters during the pre-revolutionary decades fought over the viability of Ivanov's theories in actual dramatic practice, dividing themselves roughly into two opposing camps. On the one hand, advocates of a blatantly antitheatrical naturalism such as Konstantin Stanislavskii, the director of the Moscow Art Theater, modeled dramatic art on real life and tried to re-create genuine emotion in the actor on stage. Theatrical naturalism won great success with audiences in Russia and abroad, but it confined drama to a small group of highly trained actors, whom the spectator could admire but with whom he dared not interact. On the other hand, supporters of conventionalized theatricality, such as Nikolai Evreinov, reversed this formula entirely. According to Evreinov, theatricality was a deeply rooted human instinct that made the efforts of naturalists to bring real life onto the stage entirely meaningless, because theater already saturated all areas of human life. Evreinov supported neither Ivanov's theories nor the symbolist theater as a whole.[29] Nevertheless, his extreme advocacy of theatricality illustrates the vital connection between drama and everyday life, which had become a dramatic axiom in the wake of Ivanov's Dionysian theater.[30]

The term "theatricality," as Evreinov employed it over the course of several decades, remains virtually indefinable: he sampled biology, aesthetics, psychology, philosophy, and religion in the effort to delimit the source, significance, and function of drama. As he himself admitted, theatricality defies rational explanation; we must retrace his eclectic and eccentric line of reasoning in order to grasp the term's meaning.[31] Drawing on the works of Nietzsche and Schopenhauer, Evreinov called the theatrical instinct the "will to theater" or the "instinct of transformation." Such descriptions allowed him to assert that theatricality was an inherently prehistoric, presocial, and pre-aesthetic drive (30–32). As a fundamental component of the human psyche, theatricality provided the foundation of both artistic creation and primitive social institutions as diverse as war, religion, and the law (37). Although his proof lacked scientific rigor, Evreinov's belief in the theater as the foundation of human society gained a certain veracity by the sheer dint of the biological, philosophical, and religious examples he amassed.

Evreinov's search for the origins of theatricality resulted in a number of fascinating dramatic experiments, such as the staging of medieval mystery plays and Spanish Golden Age drama in St. Petersburg's Starinnyi or Ancient Theater, and the development of the concept of monodrama.[32] Evreinov's constantly evolving theories and experiments culminated in what he called the theater-for-oneself (or -itself), which took drama out of the physical confines of the theater and thrust it out into real life. Echoing Ivanov's goal of human and social transfiguration, Evreinov advocated the complete theatricalization of all facets of human existence, so that the individual could "become oneself a work of art!" (55). This desire to aestheticize everyday life led to a stunning diversity of ways in which theatricality could be applied. Evreinov styled himself the apostle of theatricality in a religious cult led by the god Theatrarch (8).[33] He advocated "theater therapy," which promised to heal the actor, the individual, and society as a whole through catharsis, as he demonstrated in his most famous play *Samoe glavnoe (The Main Thing)*.[34] Evreinov also believed in the utility of the stage for creating propaganda, as illustrated by his staging of the 1920 mass spectacle *Vziatie zimnego dvortsa (The Storming of the Winter Palace)*.[35] He even sounded the call for more theatrical heads of state, who could do for Russia what Napoleon had done for France: "The theater will be the new teacher. To make life theatrical—this will become the duty of every artist. A new breed of directors will appear—directors of life. Pericles, Nero, Napoleon, Louis XIV" (12). Evreinov's choice of ambivalent historical examples, as well as the fact that *The Storming of the Winter Palace* distorted history for propaganda purposes, betrays the moral indifference of theatricality as he conceived it. Much like Dostoevskii's narrator in *Notes from Underground,* Evreinov asserted that "On the stage, 2 x 2 can equal 3 or 5, depending on a greater or lesser degree of theatricality" (110). Since theatricality existed wherever there was man, drama could provide either a healing tool for the well-meaning psychologist or a political weapon for the tyrannically minded dictator.

Given the myriad uses of theatricality, it is hardly surprising that Evreinov also addressed its application to the law. In fact, Evreinov began his career in the theater after completing a legal education and publishing a thesis devoted to the history of corporal punishment and the theatrical aspects of execution in Russia. He recognized that "in legal and administrative practice . . . the success of speeches by the prosecution and defense often depend on the theatrical and oratorical hypnosis of those giving testimony." In 1921 Evreinov suggested that the theater could be used to train policemen, lawyers, and secret investigators in the young Soviet state.[36] This application of theatricality to Soviet security must have been, at least in part, a concession to the political powers of Evreinov's day. Nonetheless, his own dramatization of the Stalinist show trials, *Shagi Nemezidy (The Steps of Nemesis*—written in 1938 during exile in Paris), shows Evreinov's understanding that what he had recommended had in fact occurred and that although theatricality might be amoral in the abstract, its application had profoundly immoral ramifications in the Soviet courtroom.[37]

Evreinov's understanding of theatricality was oddly suited to a variety of dramatic spectacles that propagated the victory of socialism in the Soviet Union. Nonetheless, only a single Bolshevik theater critic, Ia. B. Brukzon, embraced Evreinov's theories after the revolution, giving them a Kantian and Marxist lineage that Evreinov himself had never imagined.[38] Workers in the post-revolutionary theater were reluctant to take up the ideas of a director so closely associated with pre-revolutionary theatrical "decadence," an association that Evreinov could not escape in spite of efforts to integrate himself into the revolutionary theater. But if his religious, philosophical, and biological theories were too exotic to be adopted directly, the practices they implied proved entirely suitable to the drama that developed on the stage and in political life after the 1917 revolution.

In spite of the clear ideological hostility between Evreinov's theater-for-oneself and Ivanov's Dionysian theater, these two visions of dramatic art came together in both theory and practice on the post-revolutionary stage. The work of Platon Kerzhentsev, the self-styled spokesman on theatrical affairs in the proletarian culture movement (appropriately called Proletkul't), performed the almost unimaginable task of melding these differing views of drama into a practical amalgam.[39] Kerzhentsev explained the significance of a distinctly proletarian theater in his book titled *Tvorcheskii teatr (The Creative Theater)*, which came out in five editions from 1918 to 1923 (an astonishing fact given the serious paper shortage that crippled the Soviet publishing industry throughout the 1920s).[40] By mixing the many currents flowing in the Russian world of theater at the time of the revolution, Kerzhentsev managed to merge the collective mythopoesis of Ivanov with Evreinov's theatricality, and to give concrete advice for building a theater capable of political as well as artistic revolution.

As Kerzhentsev's largest contribution to revolutionary theatricality, *The Creative Theater* filled the gap between utopian theory and dramatic practice by modeling the revolution in the theater on the revolution that had just taken place in Russia's streets. Other writers—such as the playwright and first commissar of enlightenment Anatolii Lunacharskii, whose theatrical writings had influenced Kerzhentsev—had described a socialist theater whose connection to actual political events was abstract and tenuous at best.[41] On the contrary, Kerzhentsev wrote about a proletarian theater that was the logical product of the dictatorship of the proletariat in the new country. Just like the Soviet state, Kerzhentsev's creative theater would be built and staffed by the working class, and it would address the artistic tastes and creative needs of the proletariat. In Kerzhentsev's opinion, the cultural superstructure should reflect the new economic conditions of the first-ever socialist society, and the new theater, which so many theorists had described and praised, would finally fulfill its revolutionary promise under the dictatorship of the proletariat.

In order to purify dramatic art, Kerzhentsev rejected everything associated with what he called the decadent, commercial, and bourgeois theaters of western Europe and the United States. He discarded the entire history of the Western professional theater and, instead, turned to that of the *narodnyi teatr* (people's theater) in search of precedents for proletarian drama. Repeating the catchwords of his day, Kerzhentsev listed ancient Greek tragedy, Roman spectacle, medieval mystery plays, spectacles of the French Revolution, and Japanese Noh drama as the proletarian theater's legitimate forerunners. He proudly admitted his debt to Rolland's *The People's Theater* in this constructed heritage; nonetheless, Kerzhentsev ultimately repeated Ivanov's axiom that theatrical art must return to its religious roots with its corollaries of collective action, audience participation, and erasing the boundary between the stage and real life.

Kerzhentsev also argued that the theater provided the ideal means for educating the proletarian and peasant masses since it exploited their "own theatrical instinct." His use of this phrase drastically truncated Evreinov's understanding of the will to theater; still Kerzhentsev referred to Evreinov directly in his own explanation of the incredible strength of "the theatrical instinct in man, the thirst 'to play a role,' to create scenic images." Needless to say, the "aristocrat" Evreinov and his egocentric theater-for-oneself elicited nothing but Kerzhentsev's scorn.[42] His desire to give credit to Rolland notwithstanding, the description of the foundations of proletarian drama demonstrates the mixture of Ivanov's collective mythopoesis with Evreinov's all-encompassing theatricality, which constitutes the creative theater.

Kerzhentsev departed from the work of Ivanov and Evreinov not only in his specifically political program but also in his patronizing attitude toward the proletariat who would supposedly make and enjoy the new theater. Like many of the shapers of early Bolshevik culture, Kerzhentsev assumed that the proletarian and peasant masses were little more than wet clay waiting to be formed by the first person astute enough to take advantage of their theatrical naiveté. For this paternalistic attitude, Kerzhentsev indeed found support in Rolland's *The People's Theater*, which argued, "a people is feminine; it is guided not solely by reason: more by instinct and by the passions; it is necessary to nourish and to direct these." Adopting Rolland's belief in the masses' extreme receptivity to theatrical representation allowed Kerzhentsev to maintain a remarkably primitive view of the theater and theatricality as pure mimesis.[43] He assumed, unlike Ivanov and Evreinov, that simply putting the right role models on the stage would induce spectators to replicate revolutionary behavior in their lives. Although the creative theater brought together elements of the Dionysian theater and theater-for-oneself, Kerzhentsev's adaptation of his predecessors to a political agenda entailed simplifying the relationship between the action on stage and the theater's spectators.

His overwhelming faith in the proletariat's almost childlike desire to participate in drama led Kerzhentsev to stress collectivity and spontaneity in his vision of a proletarian theater. Shunning any type of professionalism as not merely superfluous but actually harmful, Kerzhentsev stated that actors, designers, and directors must be amateurs who volunteered their spare time away from factories to put on shows in local clubs (53–55, 78–79).[44] In the hope of fostering theatrical literacy, Kerzhentsev suggested that the audience practice watching plays just as actors rehearse their roles. As a result, spectators would become "co-actors" and would "co-act" with those on stage (48). As Ivanov, Evreinov, and countless other advocates of dramatic reform had already stated, the new theater needed not only to make the passive, bourgeois spectator active but also "to turn the spectators into actors" (47). Such a theater would teach the masses the rudiments of drama so that they could create the ultimate expression of the creative theater—that is, spontaneous, improvised, collective, open-air, mass spectacles portraying important moments in labor history. Clearly, no scripts that fit Kerzhentsev's bill existed at the time of the revolution, and the most important task of the creative theater in the area of repertoire was to adapt old plays to new, proletarian purposes. In a Bolshevik variation of the late eighteenth-century Russian theater's "adaptation to our tastes," Kerzhentsev treated plays as mere scenarios, from which politically offensive sections were cut and to which new scenes of revolutionary import were added, according to the needs of the working class. Kerzhentsev even provided an example of the possibilities of proletarian repertoire in his 1921 play devoted to labor's ongoing struggle to liberate itself, *Sredi plameni (Amid the Flames)*.[45] Unlike those who had formulated utopian visions of the theater previously, Kerzhentsev brought the creative theater within reach of his readers by describing the workers, spectators, techniques, and repertoire of the proletarian theater in copious and concrete detail.

The educational value of the creative theater pushed drama beyond the stages of academic and amateur theaters in early Soviet Russia and into every area of daily life. Kerzhentsev gave Evreinov's list of the applications of theatricality a Bolshevik twist and stated that proletarian theater would prove useful in primary schooling, in increasing efficiency in the workplace, in the battle against religious superstition, and in fostering self-control among proletarian youth.[46] He advocated the complete theatricalization of life to instill Bolshevik values in the Soviet populace and to inspire the conduct that such values implied. In vocabulary highly reminiscent of Ivanov's Dionysian theater, Kerzhentsev proclaimed: "The new theater will become a majestic creator of the unity of all arts, the creator of a grandiose synthesis. It will again, as in its heyday, unite poets and artists, musicians and writers, artists of all types, in creative work" (49). As the first expression of revolutionary theatricality, the creative theater promised to liberate humanity from the confines of bourgeois life and art and to effect political, economic, and social transformation in its empowering synthesis.

As Kerzhentsev's blend of avant-garde theatrical theories suggests, revolutionary theatricality was intended to reach far beyond the national borders of Russia and to engage the theatrical instinct of the proletariat around the world. Russia's unique historical path had made her the world's political vanguard; hence, her theater should blaze a trail toward new art, the new man, and a new, global society. However, as the decade after 1917 proved, innumerable practical problems inside the Soviet Union required immediate attention on the part of the government. Before implementing any plan for worldwide revolution, the Soviet state had to consolidate its support, secure economic stability, define its own ideology, and form the consciousness of the inchoate peasant and proletarian masses in whose name it ruled. Rather than following the demands of revolutionary theatricality to expand beyond the new country's borders, the Soviet state in the 1920s looked inward and applied the lessons and techniques of the avant-garde theater to the new social institutions taking shape. Revolutionary theatricality indeed helped to modernize agriculture, reconstruct factories, teach the new socialist morality, and educate the populace on any number of practical concerns. Such a theatrical crucible of revolution provided the ideal means for reuniting drama with the law and making the Soviet courtroom a venue for legal mythopoesis.

REVOLUTIONARY CINEMATICALITY

Russia's avant-garde theater did not provide the only means for reconnecting the spectator to the spectacle in early Soviet Russia. The cinema, which according to legend Lenin called "the most important of the arts," played an equally important role in defining the possibilities of spectatorship for the Soviet show trial.[47] Throughout the 1920s, film was a highly touted medium for Soviet propaganda, legal and otherwise, largely because of the particular advantages that those making and critiquing movies ascribed to cinema as an art form. Despite the confident and optimistic statements concerning the uses of film in the project of enlightenment, however, the actual production of Soviet films during the decade limped along under the crippling effects of a severe shortage of film stock and camera equipment, a dearth of suitable revolutionary screenplays, and fierce competition with foreign, especially American, movies.[48]

In spite of these painful realities, enthusiasm for cinema and its educational potential was so strong and grew so rapidly that it threatened to erode support for film's closest artistic relative, the theater. Although avant-garde theatrical directors such as Vsevolod Meyerhold, Evgenii Vakhtangov, Aleksandr Tairov, and their cohorts had radically changed the terms of the pre-revolutionary debate on the "crisis" in the theater, the discussion of film's existence as an independent art form, capable of educating the Soviet masses, revived questions of the theater's utility and viability in the society of the future. Bold declarations of film's superiority to the theater came hand in hand with statements of extreme skepticism toward the need for theater in the modern socialist state. Ironically enough, the troubling question of stage drama's survival arose at the very time when theaters across the Soviet Union, professional and amateur alike, were experiencing unparalleled growth. A massive and well-documented theatricalization of public and everyday life took place in Soviet society during the 1920s, in spite of the gloomy predictions of many filmmakers and theorists regarding the stage. Debates around the cinema as a medium of entertainment and enlightenment during the 1920s invariably mapped out terrain for an imaginary battle between film and stage drama that never materialized in actuality.[49]

In fact, cinema and theater relied largely on the same cadre of workers, the same group of critics and commentators, and many of the same directors and stars throughout the 1920s. Many of the ground-breaking discoveries in cinematic montage and techniques of screen acting were first tried in the revolutionary theater, which responded, in its turn, with a cinematification of the professional stage. Sergei Eisenstein's initial (1923) declaration of "Montazh attraktsionov" (A montage of attractions) arose out of his work as a director in Moscow's Proletkul't theater; Lev Kuleshov conducted his first experiments in cinematic acting in his famed "films without film"; and Meyerhold's renowned experiments in the episodic staging of Russian stage classics such as Gogol's *Inspector General* (1926) and Griboedov's *Woe to Wit* (1928) adapted cinematic techniques to the theatrical stage.[50] If the actual relationship between cinema and the theater during the 1920s was one of relative harmony, cooperation, and shared theoretical and practical concerns, why did the discussion of the cinema as a medium of enlightenment develop such a hostile and even condescending attitude toward the theater?

Pragmatic considerations, such as the real competition between theater and cinema for scarce funding and the same audience during the 1920s, might help to explain the antitheatrical stance of those promoting film as an art form and as propaganda. But discussion of the cinema clearly distorted the actual association between these two media at the time. The definition of cinema as an art form—superior to the theater in its ability to entertain, educate, and enlighten the masses—sounded as if it had turned the clock back to pre-revolutionary debates on the "crisis" in the theater, because in fact it reproduced this debate, placing the term "cinematography" where such formulae as "new theater," "people's theater," or "revolutionary theater" had once been. References to the technological innovations of film and the use of Bolshevik rhetoric brought the pre-revolutionary discussion into the present day, yet many of the hottest points of contention, such as audience participation and the relationship of the work of art to real life, were no different than they had been two decades before in the writings of Ivanov, Evreinov, Kerzhentsev, and their followers. Advocates of "Cinematography, that powerful agitator, a silent propagandist, a book for the illiterate," answered the "crisis" in the theater with film, thereby modifying and augmenting the concept of revolutionary theatricality with a new way of modeling life on art and art on life based on cinema, that is, revolutionary cinematicality.[51]

Certainly, the great practitioners and theorists of early Soviet cinema such as Kuleshov and Eisenstein quickly left the question of theater versus cinema behind, in the wake of experiments in montage and screen acting that became increasingly sophisticated during the 1920s.[52] Yet those evaluating cinema as a means of propaganda from outside the film studio cast their discussion largely in terms of the earlier struggle for a new theater, which determined the premises of the debate and made revolutionary cinematicality an extension and refinement of earlier notions of theatricality, rather than an overall revision. The repetition of the already-twenty-year-old controversy betrayed the fact that revolutionary theatricality had ultimately failed in its bold promises to stimulate the creative energies of the masses and thereby to constitute Soviet society's new collective identity. The magical combination of collective action, audience participation, and erasing the boundary between the stage and real life had not revolutionized the social landscape of the Soviet Union to the degree it initially promised, in spite of the spread of theatrical circles across the country much like bacteria (to quote Viktor Shklovskii).[53] Revolutionary theatricality left too much to the whim of the spectator, whose spontaneous participation during a theatrical performance was no less troubling than his revolutionary behavior once he left the theater. Placing film in the same debate literally moved the difficult question of how the work of art transformed spectators into another medium, where terms such as "audience participation" and "collective action" had entirely different meanings.

In order to oust the theater from the debate that originally proclaimed it the art work of the future, advocates of cinema as a means of enlightenment had to prove that the screen possessed the same qualities that had initially been ascribed to the stage, but in greater quantity. In part, Soviet advocates of film propaganda continued the lively debate that had arisen in the Russian press before the revolution, in which the futurist Vladimir

Maiakovskii and others had discussed the competition between cinema and the theater.[54] Soviet theorists copied their pre-revolutionary predecessors by touting film as a more democratic medium of art than the theater, primarily because of its greater appeal to the unschooled masses as a form of popular entertainment. After 1917 even the creative theater's inventor and spokesman, Platon Kerzhentsev, admitted that cinema had outstripped theater in its attraction and popularity with the broad masses. This assertion arose from cinema's promise to deliver a variety of easily comprehensible messages to millions of citizens across the Soviet Union as a mechanically reproducible art form.[55] If the enormous popularity of foreign films during the 1920s provided any indication of the potential of cinema to reach the masses, then the case for the superiority of the movie screen over the stage was clear in this regard. When placed alongside critics' very selective descriptions of the theater as an outmoded bourgeois art form, such claims for the movies' greater democracy and potential impact made cinema—and not theater—the art form for the socialist, machine-age future.[56]

Linked to the notion of cinema's greater audience appeal was its allegedly higher degree of realism. Realism during the 1920s was an ideologically loaded term, most easily defined in the realm of propaganda as a crude combination of verisimilitude and audience impact, concepts that theorists assumed depended on each other. Advocates of revolutionary cinema claimed greater realism for film than for the theater because of the camera's ability to capture and reproduce certain privileged aspects of revolutionary life, for example, massive crowd scenes and rapid leaps through time and space, both of which, according to critics, theater was incapable of realistically depicting. According to one theorist, "this ability [to make leaps through time and space] makes cinematography, which is devoid of color, sounds, relief, and words, the art form most perfect for the reproduction of life."[57] But beyond such technical specificities, the fact that cinema photographically reproduced actual human movement led most advocates of film propaganda to assert that cinema had greater proximity to reality than any other medium of art.

This assertion fueled an ongoing and passionate debate between proponents of fiction films and believers in documentary film, which found its most outspoken supporter in Dziga Vertov in the 1920s.[58] Many of the claims of those taking part in the debate tended toward amusing hyperbole. For example, Brukzon, the same critic who had given Evreinov's theatricality a Marxist twist, inexplicably wrote only a few years later that "the film reel reflects life as it is, that is, in its movement, which no theater can do." Another theorist, in the grips of a virtual cinema fever, was moved to call Pushkin's novel in verse *Eugene Onegin* "the perfect cinema-poem." These extravagant exclamations indicate the importance of propaganda's realism in the aesthetic canon of the 1920s and hold the key to cinema's alleged superiority over the theater as a medium of propaganda.[59]

Film's supposedly closer tie to reality meant that cinema would have a stronger "reaction on the viewer" than would the theater. Theorists assumed the same patronizing position toward the proletarian and peasant spectator in the movie house as they had in the theater: film viewers "simpleheartedly believe [what they see], they take a fantasy and illusion for truth."[60] The apparently childlike simplicity of the masses to which film appealed meant that spectators in the movie house would believe any story presented to them; as a result, they needed protection and guidance in the form of film censorship and propaganda. The belief in the cinema's powerful and dangerous influence on children, so strong it could draw them into vice, crime, and premature sexual development, led several Soviet cities to pass laws prohibiting children under the age of sixteen from watching films not approved for their consumption.[61] In the discussion of cinema as a means of enlightenment, the proletariat and peasantry were figured essentially as vulnerable children, who needed not only defense against the decadent, alluring, and ultimately corrupting images of foreign cinema but also indoctrination with revolutionary images to develop their class consciousness. Although everyone acknowledged that film could not educate without entertaining, revolutionary cinema was "not an end in itself, but a very strong weapon in the battle for communist culture," as the 1919 manifesto for the Association of Revolutionary Cinema (ARK) stated.[62] When taken with its mass appeal and heightened realism, the innocence and vulnerability of the cinematic spectator seemed to promise that film would provide better propaganda than the theater ever had.

Even if we grant that cinema had broader appeal and was somehow more realistic than the theater, we have not yet addressed the issue of spectator participation, which had given the new theater its greatest claim to creating social change. Advocates of revolutionary theater believed that drama transformed the spectator through direct participation in the action on stage, making theater the ideal venue for collective mythopoesis. Through the seemingly simple act of mimesis, the theatrical spectator observed revolution on stage, took part in its dramatic representation, and imitated it in real life once he left the theater. The boundary between art and life was entirely erased, allowing the art form to have a tangible impact on reality. By the standards of revolutionary theatricality, silent film regardless of its content took the active, spectating collective of the theater and divided it into passive, silent, viewing individuals, when the lights came down in a movie house at the beginning of a film.

What in theory was a simple act of mimesis, however, had proved in practice to be very complex and highly problematic because of the unpredictability of what an audience member might or might not do in a given production of the propaganda theater. Some theorists stated that revolutionary cinema stimulated mimesis just like the theater, simply eliminating spectator participation altogether from the formula for successful propaganda.[63] Others kept audience involvement in the formula but explained that the participation of movie viewers took another form. The decade's ground-breaking experiments in film editing, or montage, addressed this issue head-on and proved that the cinematic viewer was not passive, as those who spoke on behalf of the revolutionary theater might suggest. Whether one preferred Kuleshov's experiments in film continuity or Eisenstein's colliding images, the cinematic spectator participated in the production of meaning by creating logical connections between individual shots in a given segment of edited film. By creatively editing raw images on film, cinema directors forced viewers to make new, hitherto unthinkable connections between images, challenging and ultimately altering the viewer's means of perception. Such participation in the production of meaning in film promised to do no less than fundamentally reshape the viewer's consciousness.

Participation in the cinema was not as easily monitored as its counterpart in the theater; yet it fulfilled the requirements of revolutionary theatricality as it simultaneously transformed them. The process of filling in the gaps between edited images constituted not only the individual viewer's participation in cinema but also that of the collective audience, joined in a common artistic act: "During the happy seances, the entire room is aroused, it creates, let us suppose, and a single general current is united by a general rhythm of the heart. The picture is only a pretext, only an illusion; and truth is brought to it by those who watch it in fascination." In this euphoric vision of cinematic enchantment, film theorists asserted that such passive group participation allowed the great masses of peasants and proletarians to take part in collective artistic creation for the first time.[64] According to this view, the cinema had finally answered the call for a revolutionary people's theater, since it alone reached a mass audience and allowed for collective mythopoesis. As far as cinema was from Ivanov's original plans for a Dionysian theater, it nonetheless fit his utopian mold during the 1920s when it was conceived as a means of Bolshevik education and enlightenment.[65] If cinema was capable of fulfilling the promises of revolutionary theatricality so much better than the theater, it seemed only reasonable to assert, as some theorists did, that the theater would wither away and be replaced by the cinema as an art form.

The very passivity of cinematic participation constituted a major alteration in the paradigm of revolutionary theatricality from the perspective of Soviet propagandists. Theatrical participation could and indeed was checked in the propaganda theater, and often it was found severely lacking. Cinematic participation, on the other hand, neither could be readily monitored nor depended on conscious decisions or activity by the mass spectator. The viewer's mere presence in the movie house guaranteed his enlightenment, and the fact that films could be more carefully produced, controlled, and distributed guaranteed a unity of message and effect that the theater could never achieve. Although the idea of actively and consciously involved spectators had galvanized Soviet propagandists in the theater during the first years after the revolution, the problematic and chaotic reality of the 1920s made the passive and unconscious participation of the movie spectator more appealing and ultimately more useful for ideological indoctrination.

Of course, actually delivering revolutionary images to the masses in need of enlightenment proved difficult since theater was still more widespread as an art form in the Soviet Union during the 1920s, and the clubs where edifying films would be shown rarely had functioning film projectors.[66] In addition, the tremendous gulf separating avant-garde films by directors such as Eisenstein, Vertov, Vsevolod Pudovkin, and Kuleshov from popular films that drew mass audiences meant that many of the truly revolutionary images on early Soviet film were never seen by their targeted audience. To make the situation even worse, the extreme popularity of foreign films such as Douglas Fairbanks's *The Thief of Baghdad*, which was the decade's biggest box-office hit, suggested that the same passive participation that promised to raise class consciousness was actually poisoning a large part of the Soviet populace.[67] These problems led to the removal of foreign films from Soviet screens by the end of the decade, but they did not diminish the enthusiasm for film propaganda or alter the formula of revolutionary cinematicality.

With the addition of sound to Soviet films in the following decade, revolutionary theatricality was entirely subsumed by its cinematic extension. As theater and film historians have documented, both media returned in the 1930s to more traditional and explicitly theatrical modes of representation with the institution of socialist realism as the country's official aesthetic doctrine in 1934. Nonetheless, the relationship between drama (either on stage or on screen) and its audience followed a cinematic model, in which viewers no longer expressed any active participation in the action of a given movie or play. Film provided the model of the relationship between art and life, a model in which spectators passively absorbed images and sounds manufactured for mass consumption. Although the film- or theatergoer of the 1930s was intended to participate in a collective act of creation, this act was intended to be unconscious and to eliminate any freedom in its determination or direction. This cinematic mode of cultural modeling functioned not only to discipline the Soviet spectator but also to place the burden of self-discipline on the audience's shoulders. While a theatrical mode of cultural modeling continued to inform many public spectacles of Stalin's time including the show trial, such theatricality was, in fact, theatrical only in its internal aesthetic structure and cinematic in its reception. By the end of the 1920s the many spectacles—on the Soviet stage, screen, and in the court—presented theatrical sets, costumes, props, and actors to a passive but attentive cinematic audience.

The shift from theater to cinema in theories of early Soviet spectatorship had a profound impact not only on the development of the performing arts in the Soviet Union but also on the emerging institution of the Soviet show trial. Theorists of drama and film articulated increasingly narrow possibilities for spectator involvement, moving from the utopian vision of spontaneous participation to a pragmatic notion of passive absorption. Similarly, those organizing show trials during the first decade of Soviet power created legal spectacles that initially demanded the active involvement of the Soviet Union's viewing public but subsequently forced the public into the passive position of a movie audience. Although the catchphrase of spectator participation would play an important role in Soviet show trials throughout the 1920s and 1930s, the possibilities for and reality of this participation changed markedly from the first public trials held after the October revolution to the Great Terror of 1936–1938.

By realizing the theories of spectatorship in vogue in Russian theater and film, early Soviet show trials pushed both drama and the law backward on their respective evolutionary paths, in the hopes that they would collide with one another and regain a portion of the mythopoetic power they once had as primitive religious and moral institutions. This simultaneous devolution and fusion of theater and jurisprudence was intended to return agon to the Soviet court and to give revolutionary law the authority to distinguish good from evil, friend from foe, and the power to punish on the basis of such distinctions. The alliance of film with revolutionary theatricality promised to form a receptive audience for the edifying messages of the show trials, and to broadcast legal mythopoesis to the proletarian and peasant masses it was meant to shape.

By examining the Soviet show trial in light of the theater and cinema of that time, we can effectively recuperate the theatrical metaphor and reinvest it with the heuristic power it has lost in the condemnations of historians, journalists, and dissidents mentioned above. Contrary to expectations, the theatricality of the Soviet courtroom did not undermine the justice handed down to Stalin's enemies of the people. Instead, this theatricality constituted the gruesome justice of the Soviet show trial, giving it a distinctive form, function, and undeniable force. The unique configuration of judge, criminal, and spectator in the Soviet courtroom allowed the institution of the show trial to reach across the entire country and to penetrate the highest tier of the Soviet elite by the time of the Bukharin and Rykov trials in the late 1930s. The institution of the Soviet show trial not only had its roots in Russia's theatrical avant-garde but also provided a grim realization of the avant-garde's goal of a universal transformation of the human spirit.

CHAPTER ONE

IMPERIAL PRECEDENTS
AND THE FIRST BOLSHEVIK
SHOW TRIALS

Those in charge of creating the Soviet Union's law courts and formulating its law codes were particularly aware of the dramatic and educational potential of political trials. Many of the radicals who became leading functionaries in the Soviet government during the 1920s had themselves witnessed or been prosecuted in pre-1917 political trials, which served as rites of passage for Russian revolutionaries. As a consequence of Alexander II's sweeping legal reforms of 1864, political radicals could take advantage of the newly introduced institution of the public trial, as well as representation by legal counsel—for the first time in Russian history. Although public trials before 1917 were intended to condemn and punish the activities of populists and socialists, the tsarist court unwittingly provided tremendous publicity for the accused and the causes they espoused. Initially, the October revolution did little to change the relatively new practice of publicly trying the ruling regime's political enemies. The events of 1917 simply placed the Bolsheviks on the other side of the gavel, allowing them to suppress opposition to their government as the courts of the tsar had tried to suppress them.[1]

Although the system of public trials appropriated by the Bolsheviks was relatively young, their experience in postreform tsarist courts convinced them of the judiciary's unique educational potential. Widely hailed as the most successful of Alexander II's great reforms, the judicial statutes of 1864 introduced the western European traditions of an independent judiciary, a professional class of jurists, trial by jury, and open legal proceedings into a country that had previously lacked all of these.[2] Emphasizing the equality of citizens before the law and procedural uniformity, the legal reforms transformed Russia's notoriously draconian judicial system into the country's sole venue for free speech.[3] This sudden change in the possibilities for public discourse took place in a particularly tense political climate, and those interested either in quelling or in fomenting social unrest hoped to exploit the new space for free expression created in the courts to benefit their respective causes. On one hand, the legal experts who originally drafted the 1864 reforms—including minister of justice Count K. I. Palen whose job it was to put the reforms into action—believed that publicizing political trials (which even under the new statutes could be held in camera) would undermine the radical movements gaining support in Russia in the second half of the nineteenth century.[4] On the other hand, revolutionary agitators apprehended by the tsar's police in the 1870s effectively used their right to testify publicly in court to disseminate incendiary ideas and to construct a self-image that cast them in the role of revolutionary martyrs in a great drama of social progress. With the final demise of imperial Russia in 1917, the courts promised to become an even stronger and more effective means of broadcasting revolutionary ideology and politicizing the country's populace.

In addition, the particular form of theatricalized justice in postreform Russia taught the Bolsheviks that publicized political trials could function as not only an extremely powerful but also a readily adaptable weapon in the revolutionary's arsenal of propaganda. Political radicals subjected to trial by jury in Russia could expect a more sympathetic audience than their counterparts in western Europe, as evidenced by Russia's higher rate of acquittal. This greater degree of leniency arose, in part, because Russian juries had the option of exonerating a criminal, even when he was found guilty as charged. More important, Russian juries tended to use this option because they were composed disproportionately of peasants and other members of the lower classes, who had no means to escape the often onerous burden of jury duty and who often judged cases by the norms of customary law rather than by legal statute. Those who framed the 1864 reforms intended for all classes of society to serve on juries and hoped that the participation of the populace in the process of justice would help "to wean the people from the amorphous and variable customary law and to teach them the new, uniform, statute law."[5] However, the weight of jury duty fell overwhelmingly on the shoulders of those in the lowest layers of Russian society, who frequently disregarded the statutes they had been instructed to apply and acquitted confessed criminals on the basis of long-standing custom.[6] As a result, political radicals put on public trial and their defenders learned to appeal to the jury's and the public's sense of customary justice in their efforts to denounce the statutes the radicals had indeed violated, as well as the regime that these statutes upheld.

The reformers themselves had allowed customary law to penetrate the new judicial system in their efforts to make the legal reforms accessible and comprehensible to Russia's populace as a whole. But contrary to expectations, the hybrid system of justice the reformers framed did not result in the elimination of customary law from Russia's courts. Instead, juries, spectators, and journalists alike judged the highly publicized political cases of the 1870s using such customary criteria as the defendant's perceived status in the community, his apparent moral character, and his stated intent in committing the crime under examination. Lawyers defending political radicals regularly called juries to judge the accused not only *po zakonu* (according to the law) but also *po sovesti* (according to one's conscience).[7]

Postreform political cases tried by jury applied customary law in a manner similar to that of the *samosud* (self-trial or self-adjudication). The samosud encompassed a diverse and complex variety of popular justice in the Russian countryside through the end of the 1920s, including vigilante justice, "rough music," and upon occasion socially sanctioned murder.[8] As historians have documented, manifestations of the samosud shared a common function in rural Russian society: regardless of the form taken, *samosudy* all responded to the threat of invasion or disintegration in the community and thus involved communal administration of justice and public humiliation as deterrents to repeated crime.[9] While legal reformers hoped to usurp and eventually to replace customary justice as seen in the samosud, revolutionaries on trial succeeded in identifying themselves as oppressed members of the same community to which jurors and trial spectators belonged. Rather than dividing and humiliating the regime's political enemies, political trials in the late nineteenth century created a new sense of community among jurors, spectators, and the accused, as well as among the different factions of Russian revolutionaries. By effectively manipulating this type of customary law, radicals and their lawyers inverted the intended justice of such political trials, humiliating the tsarist court and government by portraying them as the actual villains threatening the community.[10]

The political trials of the postreform era provided the ideal venue for Russian radicals to express their ideology openly and to garner the support of the peasant and working masses in whose name they acted. In the trial of Nechaev's followers in 1871, the case of the 50 in 1877, and the enormous trial of the 193 in 1877–1878, the new judicial system created highly publicized legal spectacles that spread the ideas of Russian radicalism even as they condemned the radicals themselves to imprisonment, exile, hard labor, civil death, or execution.[11] Throughout the 1870s, indicted revolutionaries learned to turn the tables on their accusers by rehearsing their impassioned defense before testifying in court and denouncing the tsarist legal system as "a hollow comedy." By the end of the decade, public trials had become an important source of popular entertainment, attended by large responsive audiences and publicized in extensive newspaper articles and on broadsheets.[12] The last of these legal spectacles in the postreform era, the trial of Vera Zasulich in 1878, provided the culmination of the invasion of customary justice into postreform public trials and illustrates the dynamic form and function of theatricalized justice that the Bolsheviks learned before 1917. The Bolsheviks' own efforts to organize political trials immediately after the October Revolution seem much less revolutionary against the backdrop of the Zasulich case. The 1878 trial helps us to understand both the successes and the failures of the first highly publicized legal spectacle of the new era, the trial of the Socialist Revolutionaries (SRs) in 1922.

THE TRIAL OF VERA ZASULICH

In the public trial by jury of Vera Zasulich, the Ministry of Justice committed the same mistake it had made in previous cases during the 1870s by attempting to handle obviously political litigation without fully acknowledging its political dimensions.[13] The public furor in the wake of the Zasulich case could have been diminished, if not averted, by placing the trial either in a closed court-martial or under the jurisdiction of the Senate, as mandated by law in such clearly political cases. Nonetheless, Minister of Justice Palen deliberately chose to ignore the political nature of Zasulich's offense, to prosecute Zasulich as a common criminal, and to leave her judgment in the hands of a jury. In his belief that a public hearing would inevitably find Zasulich guilty and thereby show the loyalty of Russia's people to their tsar, Palen created the very conditions that allowed the 1878 trial to render a verdict and aftereffect diametrically opposed to those he had anticipated. The case of Vera Zasulich undermined and usurped the legitimacy of the tsarist court to an even greater extent than the trials of the 50 and of the 193—using the postreform system of trial by jury to draw Russia's public into the case's legal drama long before audience participation became the catchphrase of avant-garde theater and Soviet show trials.[14]

Although Zasulich was formally charged with attempted murder, the crime to which she confessed had an undeniable political motivation and intent. In response to the illegal flogging of an imprisoned protester named A. S. Bogoliubov, Zasulich decided to shoot the official responsible for the incident, F. F. Trepov, the governor-general of St. Petersburg. Bogoliubov had allegedly shown disrespect by neglecting to remove his hat in the governor's presence. Zasulich waited until the conclusion of the infamous trial of the 193 before putting into action her plan to avenge Bogoliubov, fearing that if she moved too soon her scheme would have a detrimental effect on the verdicts in this case. The day after the sentences were announced in the trial of the 193, Zasulich went to Trepov's office, posing as a petitioner to gain entrance, and wounded the governor by shooting him in the left side. Zasulich neither attempted to escape from Trepov's office after the shooting nor hid her reason for committing a terrorist act: "For Bogoliubov."[15] In light of Zasulich's obvious political motive of avenging a fellow radical, we must marvel at Palen's decision to allow her a public trial by jury and at his inability to see—as did the famous jurist A. F. Koni, who presided over the Zasulich proceedings—the dangerous possibilities for political martyrdom created by such trials (46).

Palen attempted to control the outcome of the Zasulich case in two ways, both of which failed. First, he had the job of selecting the chief prosecuting attorney; he quickly discovered that both his first and second choices refused to accept the job on the terms he required. Palen finally gave the duty to K. I. Kessel, described as a "colorless personality," who was commonly considered unsuited for the job.[16] Second, Palen tried to pressure Koni, the president of the court, into guaranteeing the guilty verdict the government so desperately wanted. Both a liberal and an impassioned advocate of impartial justice, Koni flatly refused to show any bias during the trial and did a remarkable job, by all accounts, of giving both prosecution and defense a fair hearing. Koni describes Palen's efforts to secure a guarantee of the trial's outcome in his memoirs (72–74, 85–88). The lawyer for Zasulich's defense, P. A. Aleksandrov, was a gifted orator who displayed considerable talent in swaying both public opinion and the jury's decision in his concluding speech. In the unfavorable light shed by the trial of the 193 on the government's policies toward political prisoners, Palen's attempts to manipulate the instruments of justice and to create a legal spectacle to glorify the ruling regime clearly backfired.

The trial took place on March 31, 1878, and attracted large crowds both in the courtroom and in the streets around the St. Petersburg circuit court, where a crowd of about fifteen hundred or two thousand people awaited the jury's decision. The jury was composed of educated city dwellers and low-level bureaucrats, displaying Aleksandrov's successful efforts to impanel jurors sympathetic to Zasulich's cause.[17] Eager to watch the trial, the public gained entrance into the courtroom only by tickets, which officials of the court had previously distributed and which some spectators tried to counterfeit. Those who filled the circuit court to overflowing represented all ranks of society and included such celebrities as the foreign minister A. M. Gorchakov, the minister of war D. A. Miliutin, the future minister of finance A. A. Abaza, and the novelist F. M. Dostoevskii who would later incorporate his impressions of that day into Dmitrii's trial in *The Brothers Karamazov*.[18] The strong interest in the Zasulich case shown by the government, journalists, and the St. Petersburg public intensified the theatrical elements already present in the postreform courts and made appeals to a sense of customary justice especially important for both the prosecution and the defense.

As those familiar with the rhetorical skills of Kessel and Aleksandrov had foreseen, the battle between the two sides in the case was one in name only. The indictment Kessel delivered to the jury and public built a sound case for the defendant's guilt, which she herself confessed at the trial's start. Notwithstanding the rationality of his argument, Kessel's delivery proved "insipid, feeble, and wishy-washy," demonstrating, as Koni had predicted, that Palen's choice for a prosecuting attorney was "an entirely insignificant adversary for Aleksandrov" (84, 87). By contrast, Aleksandrov's eloquent and fervent defense effectively overwhelmed all rational proof of Zasulich's culpability and portrayed the confessed criminal on trial as a revolutionary martyr. Aleksandrov carefully described the bitter experience that had formed Zasulich's youth as a political radical, as well as the moral conviction that had motivated her to shoot Trepov. Zasulich's entire defense rested on rhetorical strategies that shifted attention away from her actual crime onto what Aleksandrov described as her attempt to protect her fellow citizens and to ameliorate their social lot: "What was considered a state crime yesterday becomes a highly esteemed feat of civic valor today or tomorrow" (143).

The most heartrending moments of Aleksandrov's closing speech focused on the extreme self-sacrifice implied by Zasulich's undeniably illegal actions, as well as her willingness to continue this self-sacrifice, if the jury deemed it necessary:

> When she crossed the threshold of the governor-general's office with the decisive intent of laying to rest the idea that had tormented her, she knew and understood that she was sacrificing everything—her freedom, the remains of her broken life, what little fate had allotted as her portion. . . . Gentlemen of the jury! This is not the first time that a woman appears before the court of the people's conscience on this bench of crime and severe spiritual suffering . . . if legal retribution must be called upon for the general good, for the triumph of law, for public safety, then—let your chastising justice be carried out! (155–56)

Such skillfully delivered purple passages moved members of the trial's audience to applaud Aleksandrov, to shout "Bravo!" and to weep openly, as Zasulich herself did, during his closing speech.[19] Koni responded to such public outcries by reminding spectators that "A court is not a theater; approval or disapproval is forbidden here. If this is repeated again, I will be forced to clear the room" (148). In spite of this warning, Aleksandrov produced a visible impression on both the jury and the public at the 1878 trial, successfully transforming the ruling on Zasulich's crime into a judgment of her personality.

The personality of the revolutionary martyr described by Aleksandrov in his speech had lost its individual characteristics and acquired more generalized traits, which allowed the public at large to empathize and ultimately to identify with Zasulich. In a famous article devoted to the trial, the journalist G. K. Gradovskii describes his own reaction to the trial, which illustrates this process of identification: "The longer the session goes on, the more broadly and minutely the drama of the court develops, the more the personality of the accused disappears. Some kind of hallucination is happening to me. . . . It seems to me that not she, but I, all of us—society—is being judged!"[20] In a similarly lofty gesture, the young radical I. P. Iuvachev asked his friends for "a photograph of Vera Ivanovna—I'll hang it in my room in place of the icon!" (17). Such simultaneously personalizing and sanctifying reactions to the image of Zasulich created by her defense were complemented by comparisons to the French Revolution. In spite of the blatant inaccuracy of such comparisons, Zasulich received the epithet of "the Russian Charlotte Corday" and her trial was likened to the taking of the Bastille (69, 180).[21] Aleksandrov's stirring argument and rhetorical polish elevated the accused Zasulich, as well as her criminal actions, in the eyes of the trial's audience and of the Russian public as a whole.

However great Aleksandrov's theatrical skills as a lawyer, his charismatic speech would probably have fallen on deaf ears had it not been for Zasulich's ability and insistence that she fulfill the role of the revolutionary martyr. Aleksandrov described her as a typical member of the younger generation of Russian radicals, but Zasulich looked, spoke, and carried herself like the stereotypical young *nigilistka* (female nihilist), as depicted in and inspired by N. G. Chernyshevskii's novel *What Is to Be Done?*[22] In his memoirs, Koni describes her distinctly awkward figure, whom he first saw only hours after the fateful shooting:

> There, in [Trepov's] receiving room, behind a long table . . . sat a young woman of medium height, with an oblong, pale, unhealthy face and smoothly

combed hair. She nervously shrugged her shoulders, on which a long, gray burnoose with scalloped edges awkwardly sat, and looking straight ahead of herself, even when she was asked questions, she lifted her light gray eyes up as if examining something on the ceiling. This gaze, expressing "grief" from under her scowling brows, her compressed, thin lips over a sharp, prominent chin, and the entire behavior of the young woman bore the imprint of decisiveness and perhaps a certain impassioned *acting*. (65)

Although Koni detected falseness in Zasulich's nigilistka image, generally the Russian public interpreted the deliberate lack of grace he described as a rejection of the cultivated manners of the Russian gentry and a sign of authenticity. Indeed Aleksandrov suggested that Zasulich dress more respectably for her trial, hoping to downplay her revolutionary affiliations. Zasulich refused to take her lawyer's advice, but she did agree to refrain from biting her fingernails at the trial, a common attribute of male and female nihilists alike.[23] Zasulich spoke plainly, directly, and with such emotion she found herself almost unable to complete her brief testimony (120). Although the jury and audience at the trial had already been swayed by her lawyer's charismatic defense, it was Zasulich—costumed and acting as the plain, self-sacrificing nigilistka—that authenticated Aleksandrov's theatrical oratory. Zasulich's antitheatrical brand of theatricality provided a strong contrast to that of her lawyer and gave both her and his statements the veracity necessary for her defense.

The contrast between the refined and eloquent lawyer and his homely and unassuming client made Aleksandrov's pleas to judge Zasulich by customary criteria particularly compelling. Throughout his closing statement, Aleksandrov referred to her downtrodden status in Russian society, her rectitude and integrity, her sincere desire to better the lot of her fellow Russians by violating a legal statute. Aleksandrov asked repeatedly that the jurors heed their conscience, making an appeal that even Koni echoed in his opening and closing remarks at the trial (93, 168). Kessel on the contrary tried to use the concept of customary justice to condemn Zasulich's actions, describing them as *proizvol* (taking the law into one's own hands), or what Koni called "a bloody samosud" (69).[24] Kessel argued:

> And what right did Zasulich have to consider her own personal decision anything like the sentence of a court? What right did she have to give her own views those consequences, which only a court's sentence has? . . . Zasulich considered it possible to make some kind of a secret judgment [*tainyi sud*] of the person who gave the aforementioned orders [to flog Bogoliubov]. Having made her secret judgment, she considered it possible to unite in her

own person the prosecutor, defense, and judge; she considered it possible to decree a death sentence. . . . I am entirely sure you will agree with me that every public figure, whoever he is, has the right to a trial by law [*sud zakonnyi*] and not to a trial by Zasulich [*sud Zasulich*]. (131, 134–35)

Despite the logic of Kessel's reasoning, neither his interpretation of Zasulich's actions nor his negative attitudes toward proizvol or samosud prevailed at the trial. Instead, the jury and the vast majority of spectators agreed with Aleksandrov that Zasulich had rightly taken the law into her own hands, thus turning the entire Zasulich case into a samosud of the tsarist regime.[25]

After a mere ten minutes of deliberation, the jury at the trial announced its verdict to an enthusiastic audience, finding Zasulich not guilty of the very crimes to which she had confessed only a few hours before. Conservatives in the crowd complained of the obvious theatricality of the trial and compared the popular support that greeted Zasulich's acquittal to "the end of a drama in the Mikhailovskii theatre."[26] However, both opponents and supporters of the jury's decision experienced the verdict as "an electric shock," which passed through the courtroom and was quickly followed by shouts of "Bravo! Hooray! Well done! Vera! Verochka! Verochka!" (71–72). When Zasulich and her lawyer left the courthouse and greeted the crowds in the streets, they were lifted into the air and carried in a spontaneous demonstration through the city. In the days and weeks that followed the trial, newspapers across Russia and western Europe publicized the events of March 31, 1878, broadening the support for Zasulich herself and the revolutionary cause in Russia.[27]

The Senate predictably overturned the verdict of not guilty and eventually referred the Zasulich case to the Novgorod circuit court for retrial. However, in the confusion that followed her trial, Zasulich managed to elude the tsarist police and escaped to Switzerland where she lived in exile until the general amnesty of 1905. Hence, in the short term, the results of the Zasulich case were felt most acutely in the Ministry of Justice: Count Palen was relieved of his post for his incompetence; Koni was denied promotion for the impartial hearing he provided; the regulations for conducting political trials out of the public eye became more numerous and more stringent. The tsarist regime, in allowing the Zasulich case an open hearing, had mistakenly banked on the tractability of the Russian public and had miscalculated the degree to which legal custom outweighed legal statute among the Russian populace.[28]

In the long term, the Zasulich case helped to validate terrorism as a political act and was seen by many, including L. N. Tolstoi, as "a harbinger of revolution." The moral ruling handed down by the Zasulich jury, as well as the popular support this verdict received, illustrated to other Russian radicals how the tsarist court could function as a tool for the cause of social change. Like the politically aware but entirely unschooled son in Maksim Gor'kii's 1906 novel *Mat' (Mother)*, political prisoners put on trial before 1917 used the courtroom to denounce the tsarist government and broadcast their intent to fight to the death, regardless of the judge's verdict.[29]

EARLY BOLSHEVIK SHOW TRIALS

Experience in pre-revolutionary trials such as the Zasulich case allowed those in charge of the courts after 1917 to appreciate the power of using the judiciary as a means of propaganda. Lenin himself expounded the need for "the compulsory staging of a number of *model* trials [*obrazovye protsessy*] (as regards speed and force of repression, and *explanation* of their significance to the masses of people through the courts and the press)." What he called "the educational role of trials" was just as self-evident and important as the judiciary's function of rendering proletarian justice.[30] A strong emphasis was placed on making justice available to the people, especially in the form of demonstration trials that occurred outside the actual courtroom and stressed spectator participation. Those organizing demonstration trials and the model trials urged by Lenin were free to generate a wide variety of legal propaganda including books, pamphlets, articles, and lectures, which made these legal spectacles comprehensible and accessible to the masses they were intended to educate.[31]

When October 1917 brought the Bolsheviks to power, the judges and legal experts working in the first proletarian courts did not embrace the rhetorically polished theatricality of legal professionals such as Aleksandrov, schooled in Western adversarial law. Instead, those holding the gavel after 1917 continued the pre-revolutionary tradition of a deliberately unsophisticated theatricality exemplified by Zasulich and by the son in Gor'kii's novel.[32] Even though such authenticity was, in fact, no less theatrical than the rhetorical brilliance of the professional lawyer, members of the new revolutionary courts continued to use the seemingly simple speech, plain clothing, and nontheatrical diction that had previously served to undermine the tsarist regime. This expansion of antitheatrical theatricality into all areas of the early Bolshevik court brought with it a corresponding increase in the importance of customary criteria for the determination of revolutionary justice. The proletarian court proudly declared its reliance on "revolutionary conscience," which served as the sole criterion for judging and sentencing in the first trials after 1917, and re-nounced all claims to objectivity, which legal specialists of the time labeled bourgeois falsification.[33]

Implementing a proletarian version of customary law in the early Bol-shevik courts required the same spontaneity, improvisation, and spectator participation as most theorists of avant-garde theater recommended for the stage. Nonetheless, the first Soviet courts were consciously modeled not on the new theater of the preceding decades but, rather, on the public trials and executions of revolutionary France, which in fact provided the Soviet law court with the name Revolutionary Tribunal. Leaders of the Bolshevik Revolution, such as Lenin and Trotskii, styled themselves as the direct and legitimate descendants of the French Revolution. The Red Ter-ror intentionally copied that of approximately 130 years before, and the revolutionary tribunals were designed, as the French courts of 1794 had been, to function as the terror's administrative arm.[34] Much as public tri-als, festivals, and parades in revolutionary France had helped to constitute the Republic's body politic, the revolutionary tribunal was meant to aid in the process of forming and politicizing the Soviet Union's peasant and proletarian masses.[35] Witnessing and participating in the judgments of the revolutionary tribunals promised to be a reliable means of accelerating the development of spectators' revolutionary consciousness.

Correspondent for the *San Francisco Bulletin* Bessie Beatty attended the first trials of the Petrograd Revolutionary Tribunal and noted that the Bolshevik court relied heavily on a French archetype, in every aspect except the bloody excesses of the guillotine.[36] Beatty's description of the trial of Countess Panina, the minister of public welfare under Kerenskii, on November 28, 1918, shows the nascent theatricality of the Bolshevik law court, as well as the consciousness of judges and spectators alike of the revolutionary tribunal's debt to the French model. Panina was brought to trial for her refusal to hand over to Bolshevik authorities ninety-three thousand rubles belonging to the Ministry of Education. In the absence of a Bolshevik courtroom and even a civil law code, her trial took place in

> the music-room in the Grand Duke's palace, where the favorites of other days entertained their royal patrons. . . . It was a big, square auditorium paneled in rarest wood and roofed with delicately tinted glass. . . . Into this setting the revolutionists had introduced a semicircular table covered with shiny red leather and skirted with a flouncing of turkey red cloth. The elec-tric lights had gone out, and the room was lit by two garish red glass lamps with green shades. (295)

On this pre-revolutionary stage decorated with Bolshevik props, the spectators at the trial could literally see how the new regime had co-opted the old, leaving little doubt as to who would eventually take possession of the money under question. The costuming of the members of the court reinforced the impression of a proletarian confiscation of the imperial stage, as another spectator at Panina's trial described:

> The court filed in: the president, Zhukov, clean-shaven, with a lean intelligent face and distinctly at ease, and the six judges—two peasants, two soldiers, two workers. The president's white shirt and collar stood out among the black blouses and peasant shirts with cross-stitched work. . . . The commandant, who stood at one end of the table, interested me most. His padded brown canvas coat was in itself a symbol of proletarian dictatorship; his high sheepskin hat was like that worn by the soldiers, but worn jauntily.[37]

Zhukov opened the trial with a direct reference to "the part played by military revolutionary courts during the French Revolution," and spectators in the audience quietly discussed the possibility of terror and the guillotine suggested by historical precedent (296).

True to the pre-revolutionary tradition of political trials, the six judges presiding over Panina's case replicated the antitheatrical theatricality of authenticity in their uneasy behavior and casual conduct. Although they no longer occupied the bench of the accused, "Most of [the court members] sat stiffly on the edges of green-brocaded silk chairs, and looked as thoroughly uncomfortable as if they were prisoners instead of the judges" (295). Another observer of early trials sarcastically remarked that the Bolsheviks had "turned the Tribunal into a tavern," where it became permissible "to sit during the court's sessions in a cap; both the judges and the public smoked and chewed sunflower seeds." As part of this deliberately nonformal atmosphere, legal ceremony at Panina's trial was reduced to a minimum and trained legal specialists were kept out of the court: "There were no lawyers. Prosecutors and defenders both came from the crowd" (302). The antitheatrical authenticity that had characterized defendants alone in political trials before 1917 now characterized all areas of the new revolutionary tribunal.[38]

Actual spontaneity and spectator participation characterized Panina's trial, in which the court's prosecutor, the defendant, and the audience had equal access to theatrical means of representation. Beatty's description of the rather chaotic testimony by Panina and her allies shows that there was no predetermined script for this 1918 case, even if the audience could easily predict the outcome. In spite of the anticipated verdict, the actual drama and sentence in Panina's case was determined largely by the crowd of friends who rallied to her support and persuaded the Bolshevik court merely "to holding Citizeness Panina up to the reprehension of society" (300–301). While Beatty expressed her approval of the new court's ability to bypass the river of blood unleashed by the guillotine in France, other observers of these first Bolshevik trials saw such light sentencing as a sign of the court's impotence and an admission that the revolutionary tribunal was little more than "a theater where the most cheerful farces are staged."[39]

Panina's trial was indeed public; nonetheless, her case took place on a relatively small scale, with no more than several hundred spectators and a handful of journalists in attendance. In addition, the outcome of Panina's trial showed the relative mercy of the revolutionary tribunal's justice. Other defendants received much harsher sentences that demonstrated "the speed and force of repression," which Lenin demanded for early Soviet show trials. The first case heard by the Moscow Revolutionary Tribunal, that of Admiral Shchastnyi in 1918, illustrates the atmosphere of retribution that often prevailed in Soviet courts of the time.[40] Shchastnyi was accused of high treason for having disregarded orders from Commissar of War Trotskii. The Moscow tribunal permitted only a single defense lawyer in the courtroom, V. A. Zhdanov, who had a history of defending political radicals in the tsarist court before the revolution. Coincidentally, one of the Moscow judges, a worker named Galkin, had been saved from the death sentence by Zhdanov's advocacy several years previously. During the tribunal's closed deliberations of the Shchastnyi affair, Galkin argued vehemently not only for the admiral's guilt but also for his death, showing how little leniency most political defendants could expect from the Bolsheviks. That Shchastnyi was executed before a firing squad within twenty-four hours proved the power of the revolutionary tribunal and set a terrifying precedent.

In order to propagate these lessons of mercy or reprisal, newsreels of the era often featured short segments devoted to the earliest show trials and the new Soviet court. In 1918 Dziga Vertov began producing the newsreel *Kino-Nedelia*, which covered a number of trials, including the case of P. E. Dybenko in Moscow, the trial of Kulikov and Basov (accused of murdering F. Kokoshkin and A. Shingarev) in Petrograd, and the case of F. K. Mironov in the city of Balashov.[41] The brevity of these subjects (typically no longer than a few minutes in length) and the difficult conditions under which filming took place mean that Vertov's coverage merely identifies the most important people, places, and events in each trial. His depiction of the 1919 Mironov case, for example, is comprised primarily of static close-ups of the accused Cossack commander and brief shots of various courtroom officials speaking.[42] Without the detailed and rather lengthy intertitles that identify the faces on the screen and notify the viewer of the trial's accusation, outcome, death sentence, and ultimate pardon, there would be no story line to this short segment. Although film coverage did little to enhance or modify the fundamental message of the earliest show trials, it increased the Soviet populace's awareness of the existence and functioning of the revolutionary tribunal.

Those who advocated highly publicized, model trials for the purposes of mass education, such as Lenin and Trotskii, hoped to adhere more closely to the model provided by the French Revolution, replete with highly prominent defendants from the old regime who would perish in the modern equivalent of execution by guillotine. The symbolic importance of such a legal spectacle would depend on locating a defendant sufficiently famous, one who symbolized and embodied the old order, that is, the Russian counterpart of Louis XVI. For this reason plans for the first highly publicized show trial focused on the former tsar, Nicholas II, as attested by an article from a provincial paper in April 1918: "the Supreme Investigatory Commission has prepared a series of trials of prominent figures of the old regime. The trial of Nicholas II will be held first."[43] Nonetheless, the former tsar never sat in a revolutionary tribunal, since he and the entire imperial family were executed without trial while under arrest in Yekaterinburg in 1918.

Trotskii was perhaps the most vocal advocate of a public trial for Nicholas II. He too had passed through the imperial court system as a young political radical, and he used his own trial in 1906 as a platform for denouncing the tsarist government. His experience in the imperial courts and his own detailed study of the French Revolution led him to conceive of the former tsar's trial as a coordinated media spectacle that would educate the peasant and proletarian masses about the injustice of the old regime:

> I proposed that we hold an open court trial which would reveal a picture of the whole reign, with its peasant policy, labor policy, national minority and cultural policies, its two wars, etc. The proceedings of the trial would be broadcast throughout the country by radio; in the *volosts,* accounts of the proceedings would be read and commented upon every day. Lenin replied to the effect that it would be very good if it were feasible.

Trotskii described this plan at a meeting of the Politburo in which he urged that the former tsar be brought to justice quickly, because of difficult circumstances in the Urals, where the imperial family was being held captive. According to Trotskii, the tense political situation and the fact that judicial procedure of the time would actually preclude executing the tsar and his family eventually compelled the Politburo to order their execution without trial. In spite of the educational promise of the anticipated trial of Nicholas II, the clear and brutal message of regicide proved more powerful and important in 1918 than courtroom testimony revealing the old regime's injustice.[44]

The unstable position of the Bolsheviks immediately after October 1917 required the use of terror not only "to frighten, horrify, and dishearten the enemy, but also to shake up our own ranks, to show them that there was no turning back, that ahead lay either complete victory or complete ruin." In addition, truncating the model of trial and execution set by the French Revolution allowed Bolsheviks to distinguish themselves from their bourgeois predecessors as "authentically proletarian—ruthlessly efficient and aggressively unromantic."[45] The revolutionary tribunal functioned on a lower level, as the cases of Panina, Shchastnyi, and Mironov illustrate, to replicate the theatricalized justice of the French Revolution in a Russian setting. Yet the highly publicized show trials that would periodically dominate newspaper, radio, and film coverage across the country during the next two decades proved impossible to stage in 1918. The lack of formal, legal institutions of Bolshevik justice, such as a fully developed court system and written legal codes, and also the fact that the country was literally torn by war made such courtroom battles impractical and diminished their possible educational impact. In order for the courts to function as the theatricalized venue for defining right and wrong and for distinguishing friend from foe, the competing venue of the theater of war would have to recede from view.

THE TRIAL OF THE SOCIALIST REVOLUTIONARIES

In spite of its failure to bring Nicholas II to trial, the Soviet government tried and found a number of visible individuals and groups guilty of counter-revolutionary opposition during the civil war. The editor of the newspaper *Russkie vedomosti*, several prominent representatives of the Orthodox Church, and the so-called Tactical Center, all occupied the defendant's chair in highly publicized trials exposing the enemies of the new proletarian state.[46] Among these, the trial of the SRs in 1922 proves interesting—not because of its primacy, since it certainly was not the first of its kind, but because of its phenomenal visibility both within and outside the Soviet Union.

The celebrity of the defendants and the timing of their indictment allowed Bolshevik legal experts to make the trial a synthesis of the first five years of revolutionary justice.[47] The SRs had posed a serious threat to the consolidation of Bolshevik support at the time of the revolution, and the 1922 trial gave those who had won the battles of 1917–1921 a chance to distinguish themselves from their former allies by labeling them enemies of the new state.[48] In addition, the trial of the SRs took place immediately after the adoption on June 1, 1922, of a new criminal code that instituted the legal foundation of the New Economic Policy (NEP). A lawsuit abiding by the new code's articles would demonstrate to the world the Soviet Union's fundamental legality, as well as the lengths to which the new government would go in suppressing opposition. The massive propaganda campaign surrounding "Lenin's show trial" broadcast for the first time to a worldwide audience the theatrical and cinematic methods of constituting justice that would dominate later trials of the 1930s, even if the outcome of the 1922 trial actually resembled that of its pre-revolutionary precursors more than its Stalinist successors.[49]

Preparations for this international media spectacle began long before the two months of public hearings that lasted from June 8 to August 7, 1922. The twelve most prominent leaders of the SR Party had already been arrested by August 1921; and as soon as the Soviet government announced its intention to try the incarcerated SRs, it became immediately embroiled in negotiations with the three Socialist Internationals that claimed a right to monitor any legal proceedings conducted against their members. After meeting in Berlin with the Soviet spokesman Karl Radek, representatives of the three Internationals obtained permission to defend the SRs and a guarantee from the Soviet government that those on trial would be spared capital punishment.

Two alleged ex-members of the SR Party, G. I. Semenov and L. V. Konopleva, provided evidence that its Central Committee had conducted an armed struggle against the Soviet state, which included two attempts to assassinate prominent Soviet statesmen (Volodarskii, who indeed had been murdered, and Lenin), and treasonous contacts with hostile foreign powers. The SRs vehemently denied both their participation in these activities and the allegation that such actions constituted a crime, resting their defense on two points. First, indictments against the SRs were based on the new criminal code instituted almost a year after the accused were deprived of the liberty to commit any crime; hence, the Bolshevik court violated a basic tenet of Western law by applying its laws retroactively. Second, the Soviet government contradicted the general amnesty it had granted the SRs in February 1919.[50] The prosecution at the trial disregarded these objections, forcing both the Soviet and the foreign defenders—including Emile Vandervelde and Arthur Wauters of the Belgian Labor Party and Kurt Rosenfeld and Theodore Liebknecht of the German Independent Socialist Party—to abandon their advocacy of the SRs as futile.

A public protest took place in Moscow on June 20, 1922, supporting the proletarian court and demanding the execution of the accused SRs. After passionate denunciations of the Soviet court, the ten men and two women on trial were found guilty of membership in an anti-Soviet organization under Article 60 of the new penal code. In spite of Radek's earlier assurances to the contrary, the proletarian court sentenced the defendants to death. However, under strong pressure from the international socialist movement, the Soviet court commuted the death sentence to life imprisonment, which would keep the SR Central Committee hostage in Soviet prisons as a guarantee for the good behavior of the few SRs still at large within the country. In spite of the international controversy caused by the 1922 trial, the case against the SRs demonstrated graphically Nikolai Bukharin's statement that, in the Soviet Union, "one party is in power and all the others are in prison."[51]

The SR trial publicized this message effectively because of the revolutionary theatricality put into courtroom practice in the 1922 case. The use of the French Revolution as a model in the early show trials allowed and even encouraged the incorporation of avant-garde theatrical theories into Bolshevik legal spectacles. Beginning with the 1922 case, Soviet show trials were constructed with a new emphasis on the role of the spectator, which included the same calls to spontaneity, audience participation, and eliminating the boundary between the stage and real life recommended by Ivanov, Evreinov, and Kerzhentsev in their descriptions of the new theater. To achieve these ends, the courtroom of the SR trial was modeled on a theatrical stage. Foreign press correspondents quickly noted the set pieces, props, costumes, and dramatis personae of the trial, calling it "as dramatic an event as ever was staged, even in Russia."[52] The correspondent for the *Nation,* Paxton Hibben, gives an eloquent description of the theatrical design of the 1922 courtroom:

> The room is lofty; twenty-eight immense marble pillars surround it, and from a high balcony there hang between these pillars twenty-six enormous chandeliers, with twenty-eight smaller ones hanging from the ceiling to light the balcony, all like conical bird cages of scintillating crystal, in strings and pendants, on a framework of wrought bronze, like dull gold. But none of these are lighted—this is no ball of nobles. But in each of four small chandeliers, a business-like, high candle-power electric light bulb has been thrust

between the strings of crystal, and burns there like a glowing bird in its cage.

The court sits on a slightly elevated platform at one end of the great hall, once the concert stage of the Club of the Nobles. Above the heads of the five judges, stretched across four of the pillars, is a band of red bunting, like a banner while from one pillar hangs a poster representing a worker at an anvil, against a red, rising sun, holding aloft in one hand a placard on which is the inevitable "Workers of the world, unite!"[53]

As Hibben's description points out, the stage for the trial—an elegant vaulted concert hall in the Moscow Nobles Club—visually represented the pre-revolutionary regime. The addition of red bunting and the ubiquitous icons of Soviet power placed a distinctly Soviet set on the tsarist stage. In the replacement of the once glittering candle-lit chandeliers with four stark electric light bulbs, the audience of the trial literally saw the opulent imperial stage in a new light. The high-wattage bulbs shed the glaring light of modern technological truth on the proceedings of the trial, illuminating the contrast between pre-revolutionary decadence and proletarian justice.

On such a stage of contrasts, we would expect the dramatis personae to costume themselves in typical proletarian or Bolshevik garb, that is, to place themselves in clothes that complemented the banners and lights of the trial's set. On the contrary, neither court officials nor the accused donned working clothes and leather jackets, as Hibben describes later in the same article:

> Piaterkov [sic], the president of the tribunal, in a dark blue blouse with white polka dots, and a black coat over it, occupies the center . . . N. Bukharin, in shirt sleeves, his collar unbuttoned, his hair rumpled, his trousers unbelted and constantly slipping down as he darts here and there. . . . Most of the accused are in their shirt sleeves, though no one else in the court is save Bukharin. . . . Most of the men are lean-faced, with soft shirts open at the throat and hair brushed back to resemble André Chénier or Lamartine or Shelley.[54]

Rather than copy the Bolshevik soldier or Soviet worker, both the prosecution and the defense at the SR trial took stereotypical images of the pre-revolutionary political radical as the model for their costume. Although the ruling power had changed, all the participants in the SR case used stock images they had learned from experience in tsarist courts. Imitating the antitheatrical theatricality of pre-revolutionary defendants, court officials and defendants alike tried to build sympathy in the audience by casting themselves in the role of the unsophisticated and un-schooled revolutionary martyr.

The accused SRs found themselves at a disadvantage in garnering such sympathy since those organizing the 1922 case had chosen the trial's audi-ence just as carefully as its set and costumes. Foreign press correspondents who obtained tickets to the trial were scrutinized multiple times before en-tering the courtroom. Common Soviet citizens interested in attending the trial found it impossible to get tickets if their names did not appear on a predetermined list of audience members. Tickets to public hearings—ap-proximately twelve hundred for each day of the trial—were distributed through the workplace, and attendance was compulsory for loyal trade union and Party members.[55] The need for the correct expression of audi-ence participation at the trial proved so great that agents of the State Po-litical Administration (GPU) even sat among the trial's spectators to pro-voke appropriate responses to testimony and to the final verdict. By carefully assembling spectators, trial organizers hoped to control their re-action and to create an ideal audience that would carry the trial's message from the courtroom into the streets. Accounts of the actual attentiveness and enthusiasm of the hand-picked audience vary widely; nonetheless, the selection of audience members for the SR trial amounted to no less than

A close-up of the three judges presiding at the trial of the S.R.s. Court president Piatakov is seated in the middle. From D. Vertov, *Kinopravda* no. 4, 1922.

the scripting of the spectators' role in the unfolding legal drama.[56]

The ultimate expression of scripted audience participation in the SR trial was the mass demonstration of June 20, 1922, on the fourth anniversary of Volodarskii's death. An estimated 150,000–300,000 people marched through Red Square, led by members of the Soviet court.[57] After prolonged speeches by workers and officials, the demonstration crowd burst into the courtroom to voice support for the proletarian court and to demand the heads of the accused SRs. As in the case of ticket distribution, people's genuine participation in the June 20 demonstration has been seriously questioned.[58] The international press strongly censured Soviet authorities for allowing the public to breach the sanctity of the courtroom; still, the court willingly risked rendering its verdict invalid by encouraging and even simulating (if the accounts cited above are accurate) the interference of the Soviet masses in the SR Trial. Following the model of revolutionary theatricality, the June 20 demonstration demolished the barrier separating the stage of the court from its audience, allowing the trial's spectators to take part in the legal drama.

In spite of their ability to control the participation of the audience in the SR Trial, court officials found themselves incapable of scripting the testimony of the men they had indicted. In 1922 the accused SRs and the Western socialists defending them could still use the trial as a platform for condemning Soviet excesses and preaching their own brand of socialism. The defendants denied their guilt and even managed to stage a number of their own dramatic moments, such as a hunger strike and the publication in the West of vitriolic letters denouncing the Soviet court, in an attempt to sway public opinion in their favor. The final statements of the accused SRs were striking in their refusal to confess and their complete lack of repentance. Instead, they declared: "If death awaits us, we will accept it without fear, and if we are to remain among the living, then we will conduct our battle with you after our liberation just we have conducted it to this day." Such defiance copied the statements of political radicals tried in tsarist courts before the revolution and earned the praise of socialists in the West. But the accused SRs grossly miscalculated the potential impact of their actions if they believed that such statements would aid in their acquittal.[59] Although the theatrical means of representation still lay within reach, the Soviet authorities' complete control over the national media—especially newspapers and the cinema—made the SR defendants' dramatic gestures, as well as those of their foreign defenders, entirely in vain.

As Dziga Vertov's coverage of the trial in *Kinopravda* shows, it proved a simple task of editing to delete the SRs' denunciations from newsreels distributed to movie houses across the Soviet Union.[60] Interestingly

Smiling stenographers and distracted audience members at the trial of the S.R.s. From D. Vertov, *Kinopravda* no. 8, 1922.

enough, Vertov's portrayal of the trial in *Kinopravda* and a short documentary that recycled this footage did not focus upon the counter-revolutionary nature of the accused SRs; the massive barrage of propaganda that preceded the trial had already explained at great length that the defendants were enemies of the Soviet state by the time the trial opened.[61] Instead, the 1922 newsreels and the 1923 film show a semicircle of weather-beaten tables that stand on approximately the same level as the trial's audience and behind which court officials casually shuffle through heaps of legal documents pertinent to the case. This arrangement gave the courtroom a surprisingly intimate atmosphere, one in which spectators occupied the same space as the members of the court, who dressed, smoked, and even sat in the same circle of chairs as they did. Vertov's films not only cut testimony unflattering to the Soviet government from records of the trial but also communicated to their viewers that those attending the hearings participated in passing judgment.

To intensify the message of spectator participation that created contact between the courtroom and real life, Vertov inserted a short fictional passage into the final edition (no. 8) of *Kinopravda* devoted to the trial.[62]

Most of the newsreel depicts courtroom testimony by the accused, their defenders, and members of the proletarian court. In the final minutes of the film, a legal stenographer transcribes the words of Commissar of Enlightenment Lunacharskii, to be printed on a flier within the hour and distributed to the crowds outside the courtroom. The flier then becomes a newspaper, which pedestrians on the street buy and read. One copy of the newspaper is pasted on the wall, a second is handed to a passenger on a moving trolley, a third is given to the driver of a motorcar, all of whom read and discuss the news with great interest. Curiously enough, Vertov cast himself in the role of the trolley passenger to show how spectator participation propagated the lessons of the 1922 trial. Thus, even if the SR defendants still had access to the theatrical means of representation, the Soviet state monopolized the cinematic means of representation, corrected any shortcomings in the dramatic spectacle of the 1922 trial, and disseminated the message they deemed appropriate to citizens of the Soviet Union.

Organizers of the SR trial implemented an avant-garde theatrical paradigm that brought spectators into the 1922 legal drama, thereby erasing the boundary between the courtroom and real life. This combination of theater and the law in the *pokazatel'nyi protsess* promised to make Soviet jurisprudence into a flexible venue for proletarian justice, as well as a powerful medium for Bolshevik propaganda. Already in 1922, Soviet court officials had learned the importance of concentrating not only the theatrical but also the cinematic means of representation in their own hands to create exemplary moral messages that served their ideological needs.

During the next six years, enemies of the Soviet state, including Boris Savinkov, the Provocateur Okladskii, and Patriarch Tikhon, were tried in much the same way as the SRs.[63] These trials copied the theatrical and cinematic modeling that characterized the early paradigm of the Soviet show trial. After October 1917, the antitheatrical theatricality of prerevolutionary radicals typified the Soviet court as a whole, which made explicit its appeal to customary criteria in rendering proletarian justice. The defendants in these early Soviet show trials rarely confessed their guilt; when they did, they showed no signs of remorse for their crimes and no desire to return to Soviet society. From the perspective of the accused, show trials of the mid-1920s were examples of dangerously bad drama. From the point of view of the Soviet state, the court that labeled and condemned these enemies of the people had created theater at its most effective and, hence, at its best.

Early Bolshevik show trials had a number of different precedents, including native Russian legal customs such as the samosud, pre-revolutionary political trials like that of Vera Zasulich, and the tribunals of the French

The director Dziga Vertov receives a newspaper with coverage of the S.R. trial while on a moving trolley car. From D. Vertov, *Kinopravda* no. 8, 1922.

Revolution. These precedents taught those organizing the first Bolshevik legal spectacles to use in their favor the inherent theatricality of the court, and to shape their own political trials using an explicitly avant-garde understanding of drama. Nonetheless, show trials during the first decade of Soviet power enjoyed only limited success compared with those of the 1930s. All the cases described so far lacked the most important component of Stalin's Great Terror: the contrite confession of the accused enemy of the people. Although the audience of the 1920s played an integral part in the legal spectacle staged in early Soviet courts, the totalizing script that characterized trials of the 1930s had yet to emerge and to encompass both defendants and spectators. The courtroom that denounced the accused SRs indeed contained the theatrical and cinematic elements that would characterize later Stalinist show trials; however, it still lacked the means to fuse these elements into legal mythopoesis.

CHAPTER TWO

THE MOCK TRIAL

Mythopoetic Justice I

Show trials of the early 1920s proved successful in teaching the Soviet populace several lessons of great importance to the country's ruling regime. Through the *pokazatel'nyi protsess,* the Bolsheviks effectively communicated that theirs was a law-abiding country and that its citizens played a crucial role in determining proletarian justice. In addition, early show trials confirmed that Soviet power was besieged by a panoply of political enemies, who used terrorism and espionage to impede the construction of Socialism. Nonetheless, early show trials modeled on the SR case failed to bring their revolutionary lessons into the minds and everyday lives of those who watched and participated in them. Their sporadic occurrence, massive public demonstrations, and high-profile media campaigns made early show trials instances of revolutionary carnival, which signaled a departure from the quotidian realm that trial organizers ultimately hoped to affect.[1] This failure to penetrate the psyche of the masses also arose from the fact that all the defendants in trials of the early and mid-1920s were well-known, outspoken opponents of Bolshevism, who did nothing to deny or to diminish their crimes. The Soviet public was hardly surprised when longtime opponents of the Bolshevik regime such as the SRs, the Patriarch of the Russian Orthodox Church, or a professional spy such as Okladskii denounced both the Soviet Union and its courts. Although early show trials brought the new government's enemies to the attention of the Soviet public and international media, the educational impact of trials such as that of the SRs was intrinsically limited because of the defendants' defiance of the Soviet court.

To increase the propaganda value of the public trial, it proved necessary to shift from the Soviet state's self-proclaimed external enemies such as the SRs to internal enemies, who respected the Soviet court and were not simply willing but eager to abide by its decisions. The dramatic unmasking of the secret enemies of Bolshevism would take the form of the most popular theatrical and cinematic genre of the era—melodrama, which cultural authorities such as Anatolii Lunacharskii and Maksim Gor'kii recommended for its appeal to the unschooled masses. Melodrama's roots in the French Revolution, which Bolsheviks consciously strove to imitate in both their courts and their theaters, recommended it as an appropriate means for remodeling trial testimony to achieve greater audience impact.[2] The genre's use of manichaean oppositions, its privileging of social conflict over psychic drama, and the accelerated consciousness-raising of melodramatic characters all promised to overcome the limitations of show trials. In addition, the cast of stock characters (the noble hero, the hidden villain, the innocent and vulnerable heroine, and so on), caught in the struggle between good and evil, provided an accurate aesthetic model for Russia's Marxist revolution, even though it was at odds with Marxism itself.[3]

Melodrama's underlying principle of enantiodromia (commonly called poetic justice) fortuitously overlapped the Marxist historical dialectic, providing a popular teleology for the Bolshevik revolution: the evil capitalists got their just deserts and relinquished power to the innocent and long-suffering proletariat.[4] With the introduction of the melodramatic mode into public trials, their lessons would become more comprehensible and more appealing to their audience, and hence, more effective in forming the consciousness of the Soviet Union's peasant and proletarian masses.

By conflating melodrama's poetic justice with the proletarian justice rendered in the courtroom, the show trial promised to reach into the everyday lives of spectators and increase their vigilance in uncovering counter-revolutionary activities and attitudes. Replacing the self-proclaimed foe with his hidden counterpart from melodrama also allowed for the reconnection of justice with morality, making the show trial not simply a moral but almost a religious institution in a country whose official creed was atheism. That the enemy of the people hides his crimes, for whatever reason, until prosecuted shows his fundamental acceptance of and belief in the morality of the social order that judges him. The enemy's unmasking during his trial leads to confession and repentance, which replicate religious rituals of Russian Orthodoxy in the law court's secular setting. Having confessed his crime and repented of all wrongdoing, the enemy begs for reintegration into the social order from which his transgressions separated him. As was the case in the Orthodox Church and under the ancien régime, the Bolsheviks hoped to use "repentance [as] an unavoidable ritual for including the individual in totalitarian structures, which produce a distinctive procedure of coercive, compulsory repentance for those trying to avoid it."[5] By subjecting the internal enemies of Bolshevism to this threefold pattern of confession, repentance, and reintegration into society, Soviet propagandists hoped to transform show trials into yet another venue for creating the new Soviet man and defining the contours of the new proletarian society.

Try as they might, however, those organizing actual show trials in the early 1920s failed to turn their stubborn real-life opponents into melodramatic enemies of the Soviet people. Instead, the internal enemy of Bolshevism was first successfully indicted in fictional trials that took place on the stages of the country's growing propaganda theater. These mock trials—or *agitsudy*—could compress and tailor the legal narrative to suit a wide variety of purposes. Mock trials had greater versatility as propaganda than the nonfictional trials of the early 1920s, their initial model. By taking the rigid legal form of the Soviet court and filling it with flexible fictional content, propagandists manufactured the enemies they needed to expose problems in areas as disparate as agriculture, sex education, heavy industry, and political enlightenment. This new type of fictional defendant could be molded to fit the needs of the day and would reproduce, without fail, the paradigm of confession, repentance, and reintegration into the community in his testimony. Like other genres of theatrical propaganda evolving alongside it, the mock trial took the utopian goals of avant-garde theatrical theory and put them into revolutionary action.[6]

As a genre of both theater and law, the mock trial had an extensive prerevolutionary history, unlike living newspapers and Blue Blouse theater groups, two kinds of propaganda theater the Bolsheviks themselves invented and introduced. The agitsud bore a closer resemblance to Soviet adaptations of pre-1917 vaudeville and Petrushka puppet shows, which had roots in both western European and popular Russian traditions, than to the new varieties of theatrical agitation.[7] Staged trials had originally entered Russia in the second half of the nineteenth century during the influx of western European legal practices that came on the heels of the sweeping legal reforms of 1864. Moot courts originally trained a new class of professional lawyers studying in the law faculties of Russian universities. Soon afterward, teachers in secondary schools began to stage trials for their own pedagogical purposes and created the first theatrical trials based on nineteenth-century Russian literature.[8]

These literary trials spread from the gymnasiums to clubs patronized by the Russian upper classes where the morally ambiguous attitudes and actions of the Russian novel's most popular protagonists were regularly discussed in the form of fictional litigation.[9] As the audience of prerevolutionary staged trials grew, the scope of the genre's subject matter expanded from purely fictional characters and situations to the burning social and political issues in Russia at the turn of the century. Greater social relevancy brought a predictable increase in the fictional trial's controversy, as well as closer adherence to actual legal procedure of the day. By the time the Bolsheviks adopted the genre as their own, the mock trial had already proved itself capable of attracting a relatively broad audience and discussing the thorniest issues of Russian society on the brink of revolution.

In addition to its academic lineage, the agitsud also had a popular heritage that gave it special appeal as a genre of Bolshevik propaganda. Soviet mock trials did not simply put the Western bourgeois institution of the moot court into proletarian clothing; rather, the inclusion of elements from popular dramatic games and the samosud fundamentally altered the mock trial's pre-revolutionary academic forerunner. Dramatic games, such as *Sud atamana Buri (The Court of Ataman Buria)*, often depicted the judgment by leaders and chieftains of those who maltreated the community and usually took a half-improvised, half-scripted form.[10] The samosud, in spite of its varied types, functioned through the collective judgment and sentencing of those who transgressed the rules in a given community and served to preserve the integrity of the community in this way. Bolshevik theorists of the agitsud might have preferred to deny the genre's roots in pre-revolutionary academic and popular culture; nonetheless, the formal constraints of the moot court and the social function of dramatic games and the samosud converged in the creation of the mock trial after 1917. In the words of the mock trial's Bolshevik historian I. V. Rebel'skii, dramatized trials were no longer intended merely "to amuse for a while, to kill time . . . to obtain pleasure." Instead, mock trials should "try to spur listeners on to Revolutionary action, to draw them into the general revolutionary flow, to move unconditionally ahead."[11] By using readily recognizable popular dramatic and legal forms, Bolshevik propagandists brought the enemies of Bolshevism under the scrutiny of the masses and recast their testimony in a melodramatic mode. The convergence of diverse currents of avant-garde theater, popular melodrama, revolutionary law, customary justice, and Orthodox repentance in the mock trial gave this modest genre of theatrical propaganda the ability to shape the community it represented in a way earlier trials never had.

MASS FESTIVALS AND THE AGITSUD

The earliest agitsudy combining the academic legal tradition with popular justice appeared immediately after the October Revolution. The majority of mock trials staged during the civil war (1917–1921) took the form of mass spectacles incorporating several hundreds and even thousands of spectator/participants.[12] At the same time as the famous May Day parades of 1918 and 1919 and *The Storming of the Winter Palace,* mass trials of the enemies of Bolshevism were staged in Moscow, Petrograd, and the outlying provinces.[13] Since organizers of mass mock trials placed great emphasis on improvisation and spontaneity, formal scripts were rarely used; consequently, little documentation exists from the genre's earliest days. Indeed no complete scripts survive, if any ever existed, and contemporary press coverage of the mass mock trial gives fragmentary descriptions of these productions at best. Nonetheless, theater historians provide extensive lists of the titles of mass agitsudy:

"Trial of Vrangel', who attempted to put the Revolutionary workers and peasants back into the chains of slavery,"

"Trial of a former factory owner, who thirsts for the return of his nationalized factory,"

"Trial of the Second and the Second-and-a-half Internationals, that deceived the working class of Western Europe,"

"Trial of Poincaré and Wilson, who aided the White Guards in hanging and executing the workers of our Revolutionary outskirts,"

"Trial of a deserter, who weakens the fighting efficiency of our Army," and alongside

"Trial of the Red Army, that defends the dictatorship of the proletariat,"

"Trial of the working class, that carried out the October coup d'état."

"Trial of the party of communists-Bolsheviks,"

"Trial of an atheist, who agitates against God and his lackeys," etc., etc.[14]

As this list illustrates, the defendants in mass mock trials were not limited to individuals hostile to Bolshevik power; in fact, they could include groups of people, ardent supporters of the revolution, and enemies alike. During this early period of the mock trial, producers preferred highly visible public figures (Kolchak, Iudenich, Vrangel'); large classes of people (the Red Army, the illiterate, the working class); and abstractions (capital, drunkenness, feudal Poland) to the more individualized workers and peasants who sat on the defendant's bench in later agitsudy.[15]

The preceding list also demonstrates the topicality of the mass agitsud. Subject matter came directly from the current events and daily concerns of war communism and usually focused on some issue of specific local concern. Typical of this trend was "the prosecution of the enemies of the books," as witnessed by René Fülöp-Miller in Petrograd in 1919. Counter-revolutionary forces had destroyed a great number of Bolshevik publications during the attack on and subsequent retreat from the city. In response Soviet authorities decided to conduct a solemn procession of "the melancholy remnants of these burnt and torn writings." The funeral procession and burial of massacred Bolshevik books lasted several days and culminated in a mass mock trial, as Fülöp-Miller describes:

> A "prosecution of the enemies of the books" was also held. The buyers of stolen books, the bibliophiles who exported rare works abroad, and other similar dangers to the book market, were indicted. Here, too, all the accused were represented by actors. In connection with this trial, a petition was forwarded to the authorities asking that the crimes dealt with in this case should be made liable to actual legal penalties.[16]

Like other mass festivals of the time the prosecution of the enemies of the book embraced the populace at large, in the streets and on the stages of Petrograd. Yet Fülöp-Miller's description points to an unusual and new outcome of this particular mass agitsud: the petition forwarded to the authorities asked that the dramatized legal proceedings be taken as actual legal precedent. Thus, even in the earliest days of the agitsud's development, the line between the fictional and the nonfictional was diminished to invisibility, allowing life to spill onto the stage and the theater to enter into real life.

Theorists of Russia's growing propaganda theater agreed that this highly desirable interpenetration of art and life resulted from the extreme realism of the mass mock trial. Certainly, an orchestrated theatrical spectacle using hundreds, sometimes thousands, of actors and occupying entire city squares fell well outside any definition of theatrical realism in common usage at the time. Nonetheless, this so-called realism distinguished the mass agitsud from competing genres of propaganda and gave it a special claim to effectiveness. The ability of fictionalized legal testimony to disguise precisely its fictional nature provided the key to the realism of the mass mock trial, as Platon Kerzhentsev describes in an agitsud titled *Delo o Krazhe (A Case of Theft)*:

> The calm, confident tone of the president, the heated speeches of the public prosecutor and defender, the sullen appearance of the accused—all this forced us to forget somehow for a minute that we are not in the building of the people's court on Revolution Square but in the first socialist club.[17]

As Kerzhentsev's description indicates, the mass agitsud had certain elements from a more traditional understanding of theatrical realism that contributed to the genre's interpenetration of art and life. First, the mass agitsud copied actual courtroom setting, characters, testimony, and props, encouraging spectators to confuse the staged trial with its real-life counterpart. Second, the mass mock trial tended to depict types instead of individuals: "The characters are typical and permanent, the 'bourgeoisie, intellectuals, generals, workers, Red Army Soldiers'—always in new combinations, but with constant unvarying characteristics." The typicality of both positive and negative characters in the mock trial reflected the Bolshevik interpretation of the political reality outside the theater and encouraged spectators to accept this interpretation as their own. In short, the mass agitsud earned its label of realism because it reflected salient features of revolutionary daily life, and more important, because this reflection served to catalyze revolution in the thoughts and actions of the genre's viewing public.[18]

In order to fulfill the mass mock trial's promise to revolutionize its spectators, theorists believed that audience participation, the axiom of Russia's theatrical avant-garde, was absolutely indispensable. The hundreds of spectators attending a mass agitsud were expected to express their support or disdain for the accused by voting on the trial's verdict and shouting out their opinion during the course of testimony. *Pravda*'s review of the 1920 *Sud nag Leninyn (Trial of Lenin)* explained this peculiar ability of the mock trial to draw its audience into the action on stage:

> The benefit of these trials is enormous: we've grown tired of mass meetings, lectures and discussions do not interest the entire audience. But at a trial, from the dead audience that expresses its participation in the discussion only by voting, is made a living, thinking audience. Stimulating the interest of non-party members, trials are also extremely useful to communists: appearing as witnesses, defenders, and prosecutors, they are learning to state their views not only in general terms of the present moment but also in polemics, which forces them to contemplate issues deeply and seriously.[19]

Apparently, the revolutionary rhetoric of public speeches and mass meetings was already falling on deaf ears by 1920. The agitsud remedied this situation by transforming political lecture into dramatic conflict between sharply opposed factions on the stage. Although Lenin was predictably acquitted in this 1920 play, the over three hundred people in attendance apparently learned elementary lessons in communism through participation in the action on stage.

Accounts of the most famous mass agitsud—*Sud nad Vrangelem (Trial of Vrangel')*, also from 1920—provide similar justification of the genre's effectiveness as theatrical propaganda.[20] One eyewitness described how ten thousand soldiers took part in passing sentence against Baron Vrangel', from whose hands the Red Army had just wrested significant portions of Ukraine. The reviewer of *Trial of Vrangel'* states that traditional agitation, in this instance the political lecture, "has become completely obsolete and no longer achieves the goal of propaganda." The closeness of the mock trial to the real events that provided its script earned the reviewer's highest praise: "All of the trial's participants received only the outline of their role, and each one improvised the rest, guided by that which he had just seen and lived through. All the participants wore makeup and the appropriate costumes. The entire viewing mass was spontaneously drawn into the action."[21]

The script of *Trial of Vrangel'* grew out of an actual battle, in which the ten thousand mock trial participants had just risked their lives routing enemy forces. In fact, the hatred for Baron Vrangel' displayed by the mock trial's mass of spectator-participants was so strong that the actor who played the title role feared physical harm at the hands of the enraged audience. True to its strange brand of realism, *Trial of Vrangel'* returned to life that which provided its impetus: "The performance turns into a trial. The trial turns into life."[22]

The reviewer of *Trial of Vrangel'* lauded this "improvisation that combined elements of theatricality with elements of agitation and propaganda," because it followed directly on the heels of the battle in which the mock trial's participants drove the real Baron Vrangel' from the train station where the performance took place.[23] The improvisational nature of the spectacle, its tie to actual events, and the sheer number of its participants impressed the reviewer. Oddly absent from his critique of *Trial of Vrangel'* is the journalist's evaluation of the specifically legal form of the performance he witnessed. At this early stage in the genre's development, the internal enemy of the people had yet to be unmasked in the witness stand, and the mass mock trial's peculiar realism and audience participation were the genre's most salient features. In fact, the mass agitsud had more in common with other forms of theatrical propaganda popular during the civil war than it had with its successor, the scripted mock trial of the NEP. Like early agitational films and Meyerhold's experimentation under the rubric of Theatrical October, the mass mock trial figured as one of many ways to stimulate the creative potential of the masses immediately after 1917. Only after the mass agitsud moved to the smaller stages of workers' and peasants' clubs did the hidden enemy of the people join the cast of characters and the threefold paradigm of confession, repentance, and reintegration into the community become the mock trial's script.

SCRIPTING THE AGITSUD

Organizers of mass agitsudy left little documentation behind from the genre's early days, but their successors during the NEP created a rapidly expanding corpus of literature. The burgeoning body of scripts, instructional tracts, and reviews in periodicals defined the genre and described its form, content, and function in explicit detail. The publication of mock trials and how-to manuals for those interested in staging an agitsud not only propagated the genre across the Soviet Union but also changed the nature of the agitsud itself. Knowing the popularity and success of the mock trial's earlier renditions, writers in the agitational theater continued to tout the agitsud as an especially effective means of political propaganda, regardless of the label they gave the genre in their work. The agitsud, *politsud, pokazatel'nyi sud, bytovoi sud, sansud,* and *agrosud* (abbreviations for agitational trial, political trial, show trial, everyday trial, sanitary trial, and agricultural trial) each addressed a different sector of Soviet life; nonetheless, they all promised to educate and revolutionize their viewers by combining a rigid legal form with a wide variety of agitational contents.[24] The increasingly numerous writings on the agitsud helped those composing and staging their own mock trials in the mid-1920s to refine their methodology and to create spectacles infused with melodrama.

A survey of approximately 130 scripts of mock trials published during the 1920s shows that the scripted agitsud exhibited remarkable consistency as a genre. Rather than using the diverse dramatic techniques for which the decade is usually known, authors of agitsudy seem to have actively avoided artistic innovation. As specialists in public health, agronomy, personal hygiene, and industry, they clearly felt more comfortable writing the long explanatory speeches of expert witnesses than they did tampering with the dramatic formula of the agitsud.[25] In addition, those composing mock trials believed that the largely illiterate masses, to whom the agitsud was addressed, would understand little more than the simplest of theatrical touches. For these reasons, the genre exhibited a uniform master narrative that normally entailed an equally uniform performance practice. One proponent of the genre, writing in the journal *Derevenskii teatr (Rural Theater)* in 1925, encapsulated this master plot in a thirteen-point outline intended to aid those interested in writing or staging an agitsud of their own.[26] The vast majority of scripted mock trials abided by this strict ordering of stage action, as well as the production recommendations that accompanied it.

To illustrate the agitsud's rigidity of form, as well as the variety of contents that this fixed form accommodated, it is instructive to examine two mock trials by the genre's most prolific author, Doctor B. S. Sigal. Responsible for some thirteen agitsudy written between 1924 and 1930, Sigal wrote in a style characterized, in the evaluation of one Glavrepertkom censor, by "dryness, heaviness, and verbosity . . . defects [from which] all the numerous sanitary *agitki* of the present author suffer."[27] In spite of the censor's apt criticism that Sigal in particular and the mock trial in general "adhere excessively to the theme and style of an actual trial," Sigal's plays devoted to public health were regularly approved for publication. In addition, his agitsudy received print runs of anywhere from five to one hundred thousand copies and often went into second and third editions.[28] Notwithstanding its many faults, Sigal's writing was typical of the agitsud and exerted a noticeable influence on those composing and staging mock trials during the NEP. If we briefly examine two of Sigal's mock trials— *Sud nad Stepanom Korolevym (Posledstviia p'ianstva) (Trial of Stepan Korolev [as a Result of Drunkenness]),* from 1924, and *Sud nad mater'iu, vinovnoi v plokhom ukhode za det'mi, povlekshem za soboi smert' rebenka (Trial of a Mother, Guilty of the Poor Care of Her Children, Which Entailed the Death of a Child),* from 1926—we will see the striking similarity of works bearing plainly dissimilar titles.[29]

Like all agitsudy, *Trial of Stepan Korolev* draws a clear line between the friends and enemies of Soviet life during the very first moments of the play. The action begins as the court is called to order and the sergeant at arms announces those who have appeared to testify in the case of the accused drunk Stepan Korolev. The ensuing dialog between members of the court and various witnesses portrays a standard newspaper story of inebriate violence and is the typical stuff of melodrama, as the mock court's opening indictment of the defendant shows: "The citizen of Leningrad, Stepan Korolev, 34 years of age, is handed over to the court under accusations of systematic drunkenness, the theft of factory goods and materials, battering his wife and children, assault with a knife, and the attempted murder of a policeman."[30] Although each witness has his own perspective on Korolev's activities, their testimony corroborates the court's accusation and paints a vivid picture of the defendant's crimes. An upstanding Party member and worker from the factory where Korolev was formerly employed describes how the once industrious and upright Korolev succumbed to the pressure of an alcoholic friend and began to drink in the establishment of a local bootlegger. In spite of his awareness that such a slippery path could lead only downward, Korolev became addicted to drink, began stealing from the factory where he worked, was fired from his job, sold his wife's clothes and child's schoolbooks to finance his drinking bouts, and ended up consoling himself by beating his family, cavorting with a woman of loose virtue, and lashing out in violent attacks against local law enforcers. Korolev is not only the victim of temptation, alcohol, and bootleggers but also the perpetrator of multiple crimes against his family and society.

As the testimonies of his elderly neighbor and his wife prove, Korolev's family has sustained the most damage from his bouts of dipsomania. His beleaguered wife has been reduced to providing for her family by washing and ironing the clothes of others, an activity dangerously close to destitution in actual life and to prostitution in the popular imagination. Korolev's bruised and battered son was compelled to buy back his schoolbooks in secret at the local bazaar in order to continue his studies. The improbability of Korolev's accelerated spiral downward—which began with a single night of drunken fun but ends in a broken home, unemployment, murderous violence, and dangerously weak health—points to the melodramatic modeling of the defendant's crime. Such undermotivated chains of events, in which "There is an *excess* of effect over cause," characterize melodrama and contribute to the teleology of its poetic justice.[31]

In the case of Stepan Korolev, the accumulation of crimes proves to the audience, beyond any shadow of a doubt, that it is not the defendant but, more important, "Alcohol is our old enemy." By the end of Korolev's trial, the retribution of the court has turned from the defendant to one of the witnesses—the bootlegger and bar-owner Pavlenko, who embodies all the evils of alcohol. Pavlenko turns out to be the true villain in Sigal's play, and the court promptly arrests and imprisons this "spider that drinks in the worker's body and sucks his blood"—for trial at a later date. While Korolev's combined villain/victim status allows for his eventual rehabilitation, "For Pavlenko there is severe retribution ahead."[32]

In spite of the lifeless dialogue of witnesses and almost ten pages of testimony by an expert on the effects—medical, social, and hereditary—of alcohol, Sigal's *Trial of Stepan Korolev* was meant to move its spectators to indignation and compassion. The anger-provoking facts of Korolev's crimes were relieved by the copious tears shed on stage by the defendant's elderly neighbor, his wife, and himself in his final confession. Sigal's careful placement of not only tearful but also tear-jerking testimony throughout the play suggests a gradual buildup toward the spectator's own tears: the old woman next door is the third to testify at the trial; Korolev's wife takes the stand immediately before the last witness, the medical expert; and Korolev's own lachrymose final statement falls at the play's end. In his last burst of weeping, the poetic justice demanded of Korolev's many crimes by the narrative meets actual justice in the court as Korolev accepts his guilt:

> Now I see that I have hurt my wife and children, and yes, they have reason to reproach me. I am guilty before them. Forgive me, citizen judges, and I won't do this anymore. I see that this leads a person to misfortune, I want to become a person again, I ask you to have mercy on me. . . . So many miseries because of me. Let me make up for my guilt, acquit me (he cries). I will do everything so I won't give in anymore.[33]

In the coda to his tearful confession, Korolev is reunited with his wife, who weeps once again when she hears that the court's sentence of three years of hard labor has been suspended because of her husband's proletarian background and his sincere promise to abstain. By the end of Sigal's play, the repeated weeping of characters on stage has found its reflection in the merciful sentence of the mock court, which benevolently grants the renegade worker Korolev the opportunity to be reunited with his family as well as his fellow proletarians. By recognizing the villain within himself, Korolev validates his status as a victim of the bottle and merits the mercy the court shows him in its final sentence. Although Korolev entered the mock court as a criminal and an outsider, his frank confession and sincere repentance earn him the privilege of being reintegrated into the Soviet Union's populace of conscious workers and peasants.

As different as a trial devoted to child abuse might seem to be at first glance, closer examination reveals the resemblance of the trial of the negligent mother to that of Stepan Korolev. Similar to the earlier agitsud, *Trial of a Mother* begins as the court is brought to order and the various witnesses in Akulina Artem'eva's case are called to testify. Once again, the defendant's crime has both familial and social ramifications, as the emphasis on Artem'eva's consciousness of her transgressions in the court's indictment shows: "the citizeness of Leningrad, Akulina Artem'eva, 39 years of age, is handed over to the court under the accusation that her consciously bad care for her child resulted in his death."[34] Although the ensuing testimony occupies only half the number of pages as in its counterpart *Trial of Stepan Korolev*, the statements made by witnesses to Artem'eva's crime paint an appalling picture of neglect and abuse: of the seven children born to the illiterate Artem'eva, only three have survived, and of these three, one was blinded by venereal disease in infancy and another is mentally deficient. The last of her children to perish (and of whose death Artem'eva stands accused in court) was a six-month-old infant, who died because of the defendant's refusal to feed him correctly. The testimony of Artem'eva's indifferent and alcoholic husband adds even blacker tones to an already darkened canvas: rather than urging Artem'eva to consult the newly instituted centers for maternity and childcare, he beat his family and encouraged his wife and children to join him in his drinking binges. As was true in *Trial of Stepan Korolev,* an excess of effect over cause characterizes Artem'eva's crimes and gives her trial its distinctly melodramatic shape.

The most credible voice describing Artem'eva's many misdeeds as a mother comes from her young neighbor, who also has a small child. Much like the upstanding Party member in the Korolev case, this virtuous and responsible mother represents the antithesis of Artem'eva and provides a positive example against which the defendant is judged. The young neighbor, whose child was born out of wedlock, confirms the efficacy of Soviet doctors and childcare, simultaneously illustrating the new regime's acceptance of women who were previously abandoned and abused before 1917. The neighbor also points out that Artem'eva, much like Korolev, is not entirely guilty of the crimes she has committed and that she is a victim of the ignorance in which the old way of life held people of her gender and social class. Artem'eva's simple speech, her frequent mispronunciation of the Russian word for doctor *(dokhtor* instead of *doktor),* and her superstitious belief that an illness called "dog's old age" took her infant's life, all betray the backwardness at the root of her offense. The true enemy in Artem'eva's case turns out to be ignorance; the actual villain, who took advantage of this ignorance, is the old woman and quack Fedorovna, who treated all of Artem'eva's children and diagnosed the specious ailment of "dog's old age." Much like the bootlegger Pavlenko, the aged Fedorovna embodies the evils of the old regime. She is, predictably, placed under arrest—for "crippling the health of women and children"—to stand trial at a later date.[35]

Artem'eva's combined status as criminal and victim becomes more evident in the closing statements of the prosecution and defense. When Artem'eva hears the convincing argumentation of the two lawyers, she confesses with tears in her eyes, much like Stepan Korolev: "Now I see— I've done badly. Maybe it's so that Kol'ka [my son] died because of me. Only I didn't want this, God knows, I didn't want this. Don't judge me harshly. Let my other children grow up. Now I'll do everything the right way." On the heels of her confession and repentance, the court decides not to punish Artem'eva for her ignorance, but "to enlighten the Artem'evas and then they themselves will understand their mistakes committed due to backwardness."[36] In its mercy, the court suspends its sentence of one year of imprisonment, requiring instead that Artem'eva take courses on the proper care of children. Rather than excluding the degenerate mother Artem'eva from the social order, the court rewards her contrition and repentance with the chance to join the Soviet way of life and become a better parent.

Typical of the genre as a whole, these two mock trials by Sigal reproduced with striking accuracy the paraphernalia of an actual Soviet court. As Sigal's stage directions show, the theater sets copied a contemporary courtroom, including special tables covered with red cloth for court officials, pitchers of water for speakers at the trial, and agitational posters broadcasting slogans pertinent to the case.[37] Their casts of characters comprised a court president (or judge), secretary, guards, prosecution and defense attorneys, expert witnesses, as well as defendants, plaintiffs, and witnesses to the crime. Like defendants and witnesses in real trials, when the agitsud began, those in a mock trial signed a solemn oath to tell the truth in court.[38]

The division into acts and scenes in the typical script also duplicated the proceedings of a contemporary court case. In act 1 of both mock trials, the court was called to order and the basic facts of the case came to light in the statements of the defendant, the witnesses, and a legal expert, each within a scene devoted to his testimony. In act 2, lawyers for the prosecution and defense presented their cases, and then the newly exposed criminal confessed his wrongdoing and penitently received the verdict of the court. Breaks between acts or scenes were styled as court recesses, and characters' speeches often quoted detailed passages from the country's civil and legal codes. In spite of the fictional nature of the criminal and his crime, the court on stage simulated the Soviet Union's actual legal organs to the greatest extent possible.

In spite of such strict adherence to contemporary courtroom practice, almost anyone or anything could figure as the defendant in a scripted mock trial, as Sigal's plays on drunkenness and child abuse confirm. Prostitutes, pimps, syphilitics, alcoholics, bootleggers, midwives, doctors, Komsomol members, young Pioneers, the illiterate, lazy workers and peasants, anti-Semites, thieves, murderers, hooligans, arsonists, and fascists all confessed and received their just deserts in agitsudy. Among the genre's more unusual defendants appeared cows, pigs, mosquitoes, the three-field system of crop rotation, a plow, Henry Ford, Imperial Russia, the Holy Trinity, and even God himself. A mock court might indict or acquit the accused, and often, the criminal who confessed at the trial's end was not the original defendant but some other person called to testify during the agitsud. Regardless of its verdict, the mock trial presented the audience with a heated and carefully staged debate in which Bolshevik interests clearly triumphed. The melodrama of unmasking the internal, hidden enemies of Soviet power created a legal justification for the new regime and compelled viewers to apply the verdict they watched on the stage to their own lives. As had been the case in earlier mass mock trials, the fictional courtroom spilled from the stage into real life. However, the incorporation of a clandestine foe made the scripted mock trial vastly more effective than its predecessor in creating a theatrical spectacle intended to change the lives of its audience. If the mass mock trial stimulated the creative potential of its spectator-participants, the scripted mock trial directed this potential and manufactured the mythopoetic justice of Bolshevism.

A deep chasm separated mock trials by writers such as Sigal from productions directed by Meyerhold, Eisenstein, Vakhtangov, and their peers in the professional theater of the 1920s. A comparison between the amateur productions of propaganda trials and the greatest instances of Theatrical October and constructivism seems patently absurd at first glance. Nonetheless, the agitsud developed out of the same milieu as the work of early Soviet Russia's greatest directors and shared with it common roots in Ivanov's vision of a Dionysian theater. Just as Ivanov had recommended for the symbolist theater, Evreinov for theater-for-oneself, and Kerzhentsev for the proletarian theater, the mock trial used spontaneity, improvisation, amateur actors, and collective participation to transform the lives of its spectators and of society as a whole. The agitsud was drama by, for, and about the proletarian and peasant masses; it portrayed individual skirmishes within a larger, ongoing social battle.[39] In spite of its formal predictability and stridently plebeian nature, the agitsud took the utopian theatrical theories of its day and put them into practice to effect a revolution on the stage and in everyday life.

HODGEPODGE REALISM

The introduction of the melodramatic unmasking of the enemy decisively separated the scripted mock trial from its predecessor during the civil war; yet the genre continued to claim legitimacy as propaganda because of its realism. For the most part, those who wrote mock trials and the instructional literature supporting them had little formal theatrical training, if any at all; hence, their use of the term "realism" had nothing to do with the plays of Ostrovskii, the theater of Stanislavskii, or any other previously articulated definition of theatrical realism. Many writers simply used the term to describe the mock trial's faithful reproduction of the contemporary Soviet courtroom, as had been the case in reviews of mass agitsudy. Others amassed such a bizarre collection of theatrical techniques and effects under the banner of realism that the capaciousness of the term became utterly baffling during the mock trial's heyday in 1925–1926.

In order to fathom the curious logic of the agitsud's realism, we must realize that writers such as Sigal used the term in two different ways at the same time, both to describe what should happen on the stage during a mock trial and to prescribe what effect the agitsud should have on its audience. In the mass mock trial, the descriptive use of the term "realism" had led to a prescriptive definition of the genre as realistic: real-life courtroom setting and testimony resulted in the interpenetration of stage and life. In the scripted mock trial, the descriptive use of realism still led to such prescriptive definitions. However, the opposite became much more common, bringing a host of clearly nonrealistic theatrical techniques under the label "realistic." Theorists prescribed that the mock trial affect the actual lives of its spectators, and retrospectively, any technique that furthered this aim fell under the rubric of realism.

A large part of the mock trial's hodgepodge realism was the result of the agitsud itself being a melange of other genres of propaganda. Although the mock trial contained elements of lectures and *agitki* (both forms of propaganda already recognized as severely limited in their ability to induce people to change their attitudes and behavior), it allegedly suffered the limitations of neither.[40] On the one hand, lectures were said to appeal only to the rational faculty of the audience; they presented the plain truth of everyday phenomena and frequently bored the listener. On the other hand, entirely fictional *agitki* were thought to affect the unpredictable and amorphous realm of the spectator's imagination and emotions. The agitsud straddled the boundary between these two genres: it presented the rational point of view on a given issue but used dramatic means and emotional leverage to persuade the audience to share this viewpoint.[41] By crossing the boundaries of other genres of propaganda, the agitsud amassed a larger arsenal of "realistic" techniques and supposedly produced a more profound impact upon its spectators than the genres it subsumed.

The most important of these realistic techniques in the agitsud, which guaranteed the interpenetration of theater and life, was spectator participation. Although Ivanov's original template had undergone significant revision by the time it entered the mock trial, we nonetheless recognize the initially symbolist prescription to break through the stage's fourth wall by means of audience involvement, to eliminate the distinction between spectator and actor, as well as between auditorium and stage.[42] However, moving this rather abstract and utopian theory into practice presented a number of very concrete problems. The spontaneous participation of audience members in the mock trial sometimes did not take place at all, and even when it did, it often produced less than revolutionary results. As the genre matured, those writing mock trials and how-to manuals suggested ever more detailed scripts for actors, in order to control more closely the audience's involvement in and reception of a given performance. The genuine spontaneity of the Red Army soldiers who threatened to dismember the leading actor of *Trial of Vrangel'* gradually gave way to a narrower range of programmed responses, spontaneous in name only. Even in the latest examples of the agitsud from the end of the 1920s, the desire to orchestrate precisely spectators' involvement betrays the overwhelming importance theorists placed on audience participation.

Authors and commentators elucidated four ways of encouraging, stimulating, inducing, and eventually forcing the audience to take part in a given mock trial. First, rather than addressing issues of global or even national concern as the mass mock trial had often done, the scripted agitsud turned to specifically local topics that had a direct bearing on the lives of spectators. A village falling behind in grain production might decide to stage a mock trial of a peasant who refused to convert from three-field to multiple-field crop rotation; a factory with a high rate of work-related accidents might try a worker who repeatedly showed up for his shift under the influence of alcohol. A Komsomol drama club might indict a young man for infecting his wife with syphilis; a pioneer club might accuse one of its members of abusing his body through the use of tobacco. In addition, any script chosen by a given club or dramatic circle as being applicable to its own situation would be subjected to an overall adaptation to the specific locale. Such revisions could include adding witnesses and deleting others, changing characters' names, even altering the final sentence. Invariably, the script that provided the basis of any performance was liberally splashed with local color to attract and hold the audience's attention.[43] By choosing a topic of local interest and peppering the script with references to the local scene, dramatic clubs could allegedly increase the size of their agitsud's audience and encourage spectators to take part in the fictional trial on stage.

Second, audience members actually did take part in scripted agitsudy in a way that the spectators of mass mock trials never had. At the beginning of the typical agitsud of 1922–1928, just as in actual courts of the time, two to three audience members were elected as *narodnye zasedateli* (people's assessors) who actually passed sentence on the accused, as part of the mock court.[44] The fictional judge of *Sud nad pionerom-kuril'shchikom (Trial of a Pioneer-Smoker)*, another play by Sigal from 1927, explained the function of these representatives from the audience in the fictional court: "Since the deed [that the accused] have committed shames us all, you yourselves must take part in hearing this case and passing sentence. Therefore, I am asking you to elect two comrades from among yourselves who will take part in hearing this case."[45] These elected representatives occupied seats on stage, in full view of the audience, and provided a constant visual reminder of the audience's role in the legal spectacle. If the act of electing people's assessors compelled the audience to take part in the scripted mock trial, theorists of the genre hoped that the continued presence on stage of such representatives from the audience would encourage participation throughout the play.

Occasionally, rather than electing spectators as people's assessors, the entire audience was asked to deliberate the fate of the accused and come to a consensus as to what punishment should or should not be doled out.[46] The 1927 *Sud nad polovoi raspushchennost'iu (Trial of Sexual Promiscuity)* by E. B. Demidovich provides a good example of this technique: "the decision of Citizen Vasel'ev's guilt or innocence will be carried out not by the assembly's presidium but by means of counting the votes of the entire assembly for and against his guilt. This is why each of us must be an active and conscious judge in hearing this case."[47] Either through the election of people's assessors or through actual deliberation of the case at hand, spectators of the scripted agitsud were compelled to take part in the mock legal proceedings and to act as the jury.

Third, question and answer periods incorporated into the legal testimony of the scripted mock trial created a conversation between individual actors and spectators. The breaks between acts and scenes, styled as court recesses, often included informative slide shows or minilectures on the topic under discussion. Spectators could pose their own questions to actors who took part in the trial as witnesses, experts, prosecutors, or defenders, and maintained the illusion of their stage roles during such entr'actes. For example, at the end of the first act of Sigal's *Trial of a Mother,* the court president urges the audience, "Citizens, if you have questions about the care of your children, you are allowed to pose them to the doctor-expert during the recess. The doctor has kindly agreed to answer them."[48] Organizers of mock trials hoped that spectators would take such opportunities to query the actors and thereby incorporate the mythopoetic justice presented on stage into their own lives.

Fourth, to guarantee that all these measures designed to induce spectator involvement would work, organizers planted actors in the audience who cued the participation of the spectators and even simulated it if need be.[49] Sometimes, actors merely played the role of vociferous audience members who responded energetically to the action on stage. Other times, witnesses were planted in the audience so that their testimony would seem more credible and spontaneous than that of the actors sitting on stage from the start.[50] Such planted witnesses usually played the role of a victim too frightened or ashamed to testify that he had been injured by the criminal under indictment. Once the true nature of the crime and the criminal himself came to light during the agitsud's testimony, the planted witness jumped up to add his voice to the angry chorus of injured citizens. One mock trial author even recommended the use of spies and instigators both before and during the agitsud. He suggested that incognito club members could effectively arouse interest in an upcoming mock trial by discussing the play with friends and family as if it were a real court case. Such recommendations betray a growing lack of trust in the spontaneity of the mock trial's audience. As the genre matured in the mid-1920s, theorists of the agitsud felt the need not simply to prompt but to script the audience's participation in and reaction to the mock trial.

Distrust of spectator participation in the mock trial came hand in hand with a belief in the extreme naiveté of the Russian viewing public. The vast majority of the workers and peasants attending agitsudy were illiterate, had never tasted the fruits of culture, and had never set foot inside a professional theater. In this virgin state, so theorists argued, the Russian peasant or worker was extremely malleable, and very likely to take as true coin the counterfeit reality on stage. Authors of mock trials tried to capitalize on the spectators' theatrical innocence by casting actors in roles that fell as closely as possible to their real-life occupations, so that the actors in fact did not need to act during the agitsud. In particular, responsible members of the community were encouraged to play the roles of court president, public prosecutor, and reliable witnesses; consequently, the innocent spectator would identify the moral and political integrity of the actor with that of the character he portrayed. Casting from real life eliminated the need for stage makeup and fancy costumes, both of which smacked of teatral'nost', or the conventionality of the professional theater that might undermine the illusion of reality in the mock trial. Whether intentionally or unconsciously, theorists of the mock trial who suggested such casting from real life were once again relying on the notion of antitheatrical theatricality, which had proved to be the key to authenticity in actual political trials of the preceding decades.[51]

Given the assumed gullibility of the genre's audience, a well-performed agitsud could achieve what writers of and on the mock trial considered the pinnacle of its realism; that is, the "realistic" agitsud would be mistaken for a real-life trial. Newspaper reporters actually mistook A. I.

Akkerman's 1923 *Sud nad prostitutkoi (Trial of a Prostitute)* for a real criminal case. *Pravda's* initial coverage of this particular mock trial never refers to the play's title, set, or actors but instead describes how "a very typical case was heard by the people's court; Citizeness Z. was accused of practicing prostitution and of infecting the Red Army soldier K. with syphilis." Five days later, *Pravda* published a correction of the earlier article, which pointed out: "Due to the oversight of the contributor in charge of the section, the report placed in *Pravda* No. 179 about the dramatization of the case of Citizeness Z. was mistakenly placed in the legal section instead of the local events section."[52]

The oversight of the *Pravda* editor gave the *Trial of a Prostitute* the serious reception that theatrical propagandists felt the agitsud deserved and shows the similarity between the mock trials and the real criminal cases that newspapers and magazines of the day covered as part of their standard reporting. After abbreviating the defendant's speaking name, Zaborova (Hedge-roller), the reporter could easily confuse the staged *Trial of a Prostitute* with real trials of the same type. Perhaps theorists' belief in the theatrical innocence of Russian peasants and workers was not as patronizing as it might seem at first, if a paid reporter for the nation's largest and most influential newspaper was capable of making the same mistake that organizers of the agitsud counted on in their audience.

Reviewers of agitsudy hailed the genre as "the least theatricalized form [of theater], standing on the border between life and the stage," and spectators developed similarly high expectations for the genre's verisimilitude.[53] One audience member, who attended a performance of *Sud nad bezbozhnikom (Trial of a Godless Person)* from approximately 1924, chastised the actors for not adhering closely enough to contemporary courtroom practice.[54] This desire by authors, reviewers, and spectators alike to confuse fictional trials with their nonfictional counterparts was so strong by the mid-1920s that theorists even denied the fundamental theatricality of the mock trial, that is, the very feature that had attracted them to this particular genre of legal propaganda in the first place. The agitsud had proved itself highly effective in manufacturing the internal, hidden enemy of the people because the means of representation in the fictional court lay entirely in the hands of Bolshevik propagandists. Unlike the legal authorities in charge of actual trials of the time, the authors and directors of mock trials had the power to create the internal enemy they wanted, to unmask him, and then make him confess. Nonetheless, in order for the mock trial to have sufficient impact on its audience, spectators needed somehow to forget or never know that the spectacle before them was indeed theater. Rather than hoping for the willing suspension of the audience's disbelief, theorists of the mock trial wanted to guarantee spectators' belief in the mock trial by disclaiming the genre's inherently theatrical nature. A judge in the 1923 *Sud nad samogonshchikami (Trial of Bootleggers),* by the husband and wife team of L. M. and L. A. Vasilevskii, illustrates this paradox. Repeating almost verbatim the admonition of court president Koni at the Zasulich trial, the fictional judge in the 1923 play shouts out during a humorous moment, "Please do not laugh! This is not a theater."[55] The judge's antitheatrical statement is itself a highly theatrical gesture and reveals the contradictory currents that converged in the mock trial's so-called realism.

The contradiction of a theatrical genre that covered up its own theatricality created a host of paradoxical elements in the scripted agitsud in the mid-1920s. In particular, improvisation elicited copious advice from authors and theorists alike, although it eventually ended in the same dead end of orchestrated spontaneity as audience involvement. Under the influence of Ivanov's template for a Dionysian theater, authors stressed the importance of improvised lines in enhancing the effectiveness of the scripted agitsud, to the extent of forbidding actors to memorize the script or to rehearse a mock trial in its entirety.[56] Many early scripts provided little more than a synopsis of the mock trial's action and did not even contain complete speeches for the various characters, in the hopes that improvisation would give actors' performances the ring of real legal testimony.[57] In spite of such advice, the same authors wrote increasingly lengthy and detailed plays, provided ever greater amounts of character description and stage direction, and reduced the actor's capacity to improvise. By the late 1920s, in the waning days of the genre, the call for improvisation in the agitsud was little more than a hollow phrase.

The highly conventionalized theatrical techniques used in a genre so "realistic" as to be confused with real life were just as paradoxical as the mock trial's scripted improvisation. For example, many of the characters in agitsudy had speaking names, a feature that had fallen out of dramatic fashion with the waning of neoclassicism in the early nineteenth century. The priest Ikonostasov (Icon-stand), the slovenly boy Korovin (Cowman), the illiterate peasant Nevezha (Ignoramus), and the philandering husband Guliaev (Walk-about), all appear in various mock trials as typical expressions of the etymological roots of their names.[58] Akkerman's *Trial of a Prostitute* presents an especially vivid example of such speaking names. The cast of characters includes one Zaborova (from *zabor,* or fence, behind which the accused "rolls" her clients), Krest'ianov (the *krest'ianin,* or peasant, recently arrived in the city where he falls prey to the infectious embraces of Zaborova), Kazakov (the conscious Red Army soldier, from the word *kazak,* or Cossack), and Boev (the student who tries to elevate Zaborova's place in life, from the word *boi* for battle or combat).⁵⁹ Each agitsud presented a small slice of Soviet life in which archetypal characters bearing emblematic names exhibited the traits peculiar to their class: the kulak was always greedy, the priest always superstitious, the ex-noble resentful and nostalgic, the proletarian hardworking and hungry for enlightenment. The obviously contrived names of such characters pointed to their respective virtues and vices, providing the audience with signposts it could use to navigate its way through the moral melodrama of the agitsud.⁶⁰

In addition to speaking names from eighteenth-century Russian theater, the mock trial borrowed farcical interludes from the pre-revolutionary popular theater to give comic relief. Often, a single character who represented the old way of life—an illiterate old woman or perhaps an uneducated priest—gave humorous and self-damning testimony. Such diverting testimony used slapstick comedy and humorously garbled words to show the character's ignorance of the new way of life. Comic characters typically misunderstood and therefore misused expressions associated with post-revolutionary society and culture. To a much greater degree than in the case of the accused Artem'eva in Sigal's *Trial of a Mother,* popular mispronunciations—such as *sekhlitar'* for *sekretar'* (secretary) and *liniversitet* for *universitet* (university)—abounded in the testimony of such comic foils. According to the genre's instructional literature, comedy provided an especially effective means of keeping the audience's attention, which, theorists assumed, would flag during the tedious testimony of witnesses and experts. Occasionally, entire mock trials took the form of vaudevilles or comic courts, as in three brief sketches by Viktor Ardov, called *Alimenty (Alimony), Poltinnik pogubil (A Fifty-kopeck Piece Ruined Me),* and *Delo o prokhodnoi komnate (The Affair of the Connecting Room).*⁶¹

At first glance, both speaking names and comedy seem at cross-purposes with avant-garde dramatic techniques meant to enhance the mock trial's realism. However, the features of pre-revolutionary popular drama imported into the agitsud were no more or less realistic than the elements of the avant-garde introduced into the genre for the same purpose. Neither comic interludes, speaking names, improvisation, nor audience participation fell under any descriptive definition of realism in the mock trial; rather, they resulted from the genre's prescription to revolutionize the spectators by taking drama from the stage and thrusting it into real life. If audiences were truly as innocent as commentators believed, speaking names and hearty laughter could only help guide the naive viewer to a correct interpretation, which ultimately was just as important as improvisation and participation in the agitsud. The mock trial's realism presented a hodgepodge of staging methods borrowed from different dramatic schools, none of which ever received the label of realism in its own day. Nevertheless, these disparate theatrical techniques worked in concert to take the melodrama of unmasking the country's internal enemy and make it part of the spectators' lives outside the theater.

COMPELLING CONFESSION

Even if we accept the unusual definition of realism in the mock trial and agree that its disparate elements successfully brought the theater into real life, it is still puzzling how these fictional trials could have a greater impact than their nonfictional counterparts in actual courtrooms of the mid-1920s. Could a simple shift from an external to an internal enemy truly revolutionize the genre's audience? In the actual courtroom, such a change might make little difference to those watching trials; but in the theater, which demanded audience participation, indeed this shift significantly altered the possibilities for spectatorship in trials of all types and created the paradigm of mythopoetic justice.

The mock trial compelled spectators to play the role of the jury, to pass judgment on the enemy of the people. At the same time, the audience identified with the accused, turning the censure of the enemy of the people into the condemnation of oneself. Since the defendant bore only the most general of personality traits and described only the roughest outline of his crime, each and every audience member could identify with him and his tale of vice, as how-to manuals explicitly stated:

> Clearly, we are judging not the club member who is sitting on the stage as the accused. In his person, we are judging one of those who will be watching our trial. This means that the accused should resemble those citizens who are seated not on the defendant's bench, but on the spectators' bench, but whose activities we are actually evaluating in our agitsud. These citizens should recognize themselves in the defendant. They should see that the trial is being conducted precisely against them.[62]

The shift from an external to an internal enemy gained meaning in the mock trial because the genre's peculiar realism made the compelling confession of the defendant compulsory for the spectator.

When spectators identified with the criminal on trial, they replicated his confession, repentance, and pleas for reintegration into society, which provided the dénouement of the agitsud. The lengthy testimony of witnesses and experts was predictable and made the court's final verdict and sentencing easy to anticipate long before their announcement. The defendant's reaction to the court's decision proved more exciting and aroused a complex blend of indignation and sympathy in those watching the play. Just like Korolev and Artem'eva in Sigal's plays, the typical defendant in an agitsud did not know he had committed a crime or had counter-revolutionary tendencies. Only as the action on stage unfolded did he come to the sudden realization that he was unknowingly an enemy of the people and had hindered the building of socialism. His coming to consciousness took the form of a violent religious conversion, and the defendant's belief in the Soviet regime at the end of the mock trial was just as fervent as the denial of his crimes had been at its beginning. The underlying assumption was that spectators who identified with the accused found the same unwitting criminal potential in themselves and replicated his *samokritika* (self-criticism) as they watched the mock trial.[63]

In these formulaic confessions, the accused routinely refused to defend his previous actions and asked only to be punished so that he might have the opportunity to correct his evil ways. The defendant in the *Trial of Sexual Promiscuity* offers a fine example of such samokritika addressed directly to the mock trial's audience:

> Comrades! You will now judge me and my actions. I'll tell you honestly that only here in the courtroom has the evil that I've done been revealed to me in all its extent. The defense is right—there is much I've never thought about in the confusion of my life, and chiefly, I really didn't know much that I know now. . . . Of course, I'll stop being socially dangerous. Judge so that your judgment will help me to take the healthy path.[64]

The average defendant confessed his guilt and dutifully swore to raise his consciousness through education or active involvement in his trade union, the Red Army, agricultural innovations, the Komsomol, and so on. Theoretically, each audience member of an agitsud underwent a similar but silent confession of guilt so that he too could leave the old way of life and join the defendant on the healthy path toward socialism.[65]

To avoid any ambiguity as to where such a path would go, authors of mock trials put positive role models for rehabilitation alongside the criminals who confessed. As in both *Trial of Stepan Korolev* and *Trial of a Mother,* the agitsud's cast of characters often included the ideal proletarian, peasant, housewife, or pioneer so that the defendant's crime would be revealed during testimony by means of contrast. In another good example of this technique found in N. Glebova's 1924 *Sud nad delegatkoi (Trial of a Delegate),* part of the testimony against a factory trade union representative comes from the woman who took up the defendant's neglected responsibilities. For every fault of the negligent delegate described by witnesses, the audience also hears of the diligence and hard work with which the model delegate applied herself to correcting these faults. The good delegate even describes her own consciousness-raising, a condensed version of which the audience sees in the person of her negligent counterpart. The model delegate ends her story with an exclamation of heartfelt gratitude: "I'll say thank you to Soviet power for opening my eyes."[66] Since the mock trial ended abruptly after indictment and sentencing, spectators never had the opportunity to see the moral regeneration promised in the defendant's confession and repentance. In order to depict the continued moral growth of the new convert, authors of the agitsud included such exemplary characters whose conversion to Bolshevism had taken place long before the mock court was called to order.

The religious and moral nature of this conversion becomes even more evident in the types of crimes staged and the means of sentencing that prevailed in the vast majority of agitsudy. Actual breaches of the civil and criminal codes often appear in mock trials, including theft, murder, treason, bootlegging, and pimping. However, such clear cases of trespassing the letter of the law were usually left to the actual criminal courts of the day. More typically the mock trial attacked some personal quality or attitude far beyond the jurisdiction of the law that resulted or might someday result in socially questionable behavior. Such deviations from the moral and social code included inefficiency in the workplace, sexual promiscuity, greed, sexism, anti-Semitism, being overly fond of alcohol or tobacco, general ignorance, illiteracy, reluctance to use new farming or industrial technology, and social or cultural backwardness. Holding any of these attitudes is certainly of questionable utility to society; yet none of these vices alone would make the individual liable to criminal proceedings. Even in the presence of an actual crime, the agitsud emphasized the ideological implications of the breach in the law and the moral state of the defendant who committed such an offense. While the actual courtroom dealt with illegal actions and their consequences, the fictional courtroom of the agitsud concerned itself with the creation and maintenance of socialist morality.

Passing sentence on moral backwardness required compassion and even leniency on the part of the mock court, in contrast to real-life demonstration trials of the time.[67] Although judges usually found the accused guilty of holding a morally and socially dangerous point of view, they nonetheless determined that the defendant was only marginally culpable, as seen in the cases of Sigal's defendants Korolev and Artem'eva. Illiteracy, malnutrition, childhood beatings, pre-revolutionary living conditions, sexual discrimination, or any number of extenuating circumstances lessened the personal guilt of the accused. The past social order and not the defendant bore ultimate responsibility for any illegal actions or questionable attitudes put on trial in the agitsud. Since the revolution had already removed the oppressive influence of these extenuating circumstances, it was the job of the mock court not to punish the proletarian or peasant defendant but to urge him to adopt the fundamentally sound values of his social class without fear of further oppression. Given the defendant's promise to mend his once counter-revolutionary ways, sentencing in the agitsud was usually quite lenient and was rarely carried out. After threatening to imprison the accused or to confiscate his personal property, the court often suspended its sentence in favor of some combination of reeducation and socially useful work. The remarkable leniency of the mock court not only showed the compassion of the Soviet legal system but also urged spectators toward samokritika so that they might experience the same clemency as the mock trial's defendant.

Sometimes the court's leniency was contrasted with the audience's demand for severe punishment, as Walter Benjamin describes in his *Moscow Diary*. At a mock trial of a midwife, which Benjamin attended in December 1926, "a Komsomol appeared on stage and made a plea for the harshest possible punishment. Then the court retired for deliberation—a pause ensued. Everybody stood to hear the verdict read. Two years' imprisonment with recognition of mitigating circumstance."[68] The reduction of the midwife's sentence from possible execution to two years of imprisonment illustrates the court's clemency and shows the agitsud's ability to harness and direct the wrath of indignant spectators.

At other times, the court's leniency even depended on the participation of the audience in the sentencing. In a 1924 agitsud devoted to the fight against venereal disease, the judge promised to lessen the defendant's punishment on the condition that audience members solemnly swear to take concrete measures to avoid syphilis in their own lives:

> The sentence can be suspended, in regard to the matter under consideration, if no fewer than ten people from the citizens present swear in writing before the court not to enter matrimony without a thorough examination by a doctor and without requesting fulfillment of the same from the person with whom they will be entering into matrimony.[69]

The identification of the audience with the accused extended beyond confession and repentance to the actions that would allow for reintegration into society. Having heard the judgment of the mock court, the defendant,

as well as the audience members he represented, acknowledged and confessed the error of the old way of life and joyously embraced the duties
and privileges of a conscious worker or peasant.

The ideal conversion to Bolshevism included an enthusiastic and sometimes ecstatic expression of gratitude to the Soviet authorities. Like the
model delegate mentioned above, defendants on the path to rehabilitation
expressed joy at the opportunity to change their ways and to become productive members of the Soviet workforce. Although hardened criminals
appeared rarely as defendants in the agitsud, exclusion from society and
physical punishment always threatened a recalcitrant one. Any reluctance
to reform on the part of either the defendant or the audience had clearly
dangerous consequences: "You must confess that you are all criminals before yourselves, before your family and the state. Think about this and
take measures before it's too late."[70] Authors of the agitsud preferred to
depict voluntary participation in mechanized seed-sorting, the local Komsomol, and eradicating bootleg liquor, that is, in transforming Soviet society through the reeducation of its citizens. Yet, the legal form of the agitsud always contained the threat of imprisonment, exile, even execution, to
give an additional persuasive push to the defendants' and the audience's
confessions.

Since the accused inevitably confessed and his personal guilt was usually minimal, defense attorneys in agitsudy did not actually need to defend
their clients. Instead, the council for the defense helped to soften the final
sentence by fully explicating the extenuating circumstances that had a
bearing on the case. Revealing such mitigating circumstances did not get
the defendant off the hook, as explained in the stage directions for Boris
Andreev's 1926 *Sud nad starym bytom (Trial of the Old Way of Life)*:

> The defense strives in each of the aforementioned questions to find mitigat-
> ing circumstances—the accused's ignorance and his past—that of a country
> boy, who had scarcely become literate in the city, his view of women as
> "skirts," formed in the backwaters of society, and also the fact that he didn't
> beat his wife while sober and that the instances of beating always occurred
> during "a drinking binge." . . . But in any event, regardless of the questions
> and answers, the weakness of the justifications of the accused—entirely in
> the power of the old way of life that is dying away—becomes clear.[71]

The typical defense actually began with an implicit admission of the defendant's guilt, such as, "I don't intend to defend Ivanov." Defenders then
described their client's transgressions not as acts of individual volition, but
as physical defects that arose out of the old way of life: "Since we can't

pass judgment on a blind person because he doesn't see, we can't try an ignorant person because he's ignorant." Defenders blamed the transitional character of the period for their client's failure to adapt successfully to the new way of life. In short, the counsel for the defense merely repeated and elaborated the arguments of the prosecution in the agitsud.[72]

The accused's only true defense lay in his social class. As was the case for Korolev and Artem'eva in the two agitsudy by Sigal, any member of the proletariat or peasantry could be rehabilitated and reintegrated into the new society regardless of the severity of his crime. Conversely, any member of the leftover social classes—such as the bootlegger Pavlenko in the *Trial of Stepan Korolev* and the old woman Fedorovna in the *Trial of a Mother*—was beyond redemption even if his crime were trivial. Akkerman's 1925 *Sud nad prostitutkoi i svodnitsei (Trial of a Prostitute and Procuress)* illustrates the overwhelming importance of social class in determining the defendant's innocence or guilt. Although the prostitute of the play's title is found guilty of infecting a Red Army soldier with syphilis, she receives a reduced sentence because she is a daughter of the proletariat. The procuress Sviridova, whom the prosecution describes as a "dangerous social element," has an entirely different fate as a member of the petite bourgeoisie:

> In the old, bourgeois court, the defender only defended, defended at all costs. And he did not enjoy the workers' respect.
>
> In the worker and peasants' court, the defender is the judge's helper, dispassionately revealing the essence and details of the case under investigation. And therefore with respect to the defendant Sviridova, I have to agree with the public prosecutor. . . .
>
> The Sviridovas of this world can not be reeducated.[73]

As these examples show, the council for the defense argued neither for his client's innocence nor for his legal rights but defended the potential for reeducating and reintegrating the accused into the new Soviet order. The defendant's social class formed his moral character and hence determined whether the new society would accept him with open arms or expel him ruthlessly. Working in concert with the genre's peculiar realism, forced audience participation, and religious means of persuasion, the absence of defense in the agitsud compelled spectators to reproduce in themselves the defendant's confession on the witness stand. By making spectators identify simultaneously with the accusers and with the accused, the mock trial realized the vast potential of legal propaganda and constituted the mythopoetic justice of Bolshevism.

According to accounts from the time, mock trials often achieved their goals and had a measurable impact on the lives of their spectators. One advocate of agricultural mock trials recommended them on the basis of the progress they had already fostered in various regions of the country: "In the Serpukhovskoi county of the Nikolaevskaia region, a trial of the system of three-field crop rotation was held. The result of this trial was a massive switch to multiple-field crop rotation and to wide fields in the named region."[74] The movement away from the mass mock trials of the civil war era to the more humble productions of the mid-1920s gave the agitsud greater efficacy and brought the genre closer to the actual show trials of the late 1930s. Infamous protagonists who vehemently denounced Soviet power gave way to more modest proletarians and peasants who compliantly and enthusiastically confessed to their counter-revolutionary crimes. The spontaneous expression of the people's creative potential in the mass agitsud proved too unpredictable to go unchecked and was eventually channeled into the rigid formula of confession, repentance, and reintegration into society in the scripted agitsud.[75] A paradoxical blend of legal, theatrical, and religious elements gave the genre the ability to manufacture the melodramatic enemy needed by the Soviet state, so that the hidden foe could be unmasked and made to confess before the mock trial's audience. Although the genre denied the elements it borrowed from Ivanov's plan for a Dionysian theater, as well as its very theatricality, the mock trial realized the utopian goals of Russia's avant-garde theater in its creation of mythopoetic justice.[76]

If the mock trial successfully constructed the legal melodrama necessary to manufacture the New Soviet Man, why did it disappear from the repertoire of amateur theaters at the end of the 1920s? Did the amalgam of theater, jurisprudence, and religion constituting the agitsud disintegrate by 1929? Before answering these questions, we must acknowledge that although the mock trial indeed disappeared, the fictional trial lived on in movies, debates, and theatrical trials derived from the agitsud.[77] Literary disputes, in particular, continued to take the form of a fictional trial throughout the Soviet period, as Andrei Sinyavsky attests in his description of a mock trial of Il'f and Petrov's comic hero Ostap Bender in the 1950s.[78] The mock trial even returned to the Russian stage during the age of Glasnost. Mikhail Shatrov reinterpreted the 1920 *Trial of Lenin* in his play *Diktatura soresti (Dictatorship of Conscience),* standing the genre on its head in the mid-1980s. At the same time, members of a student circle at the Moscow State Historico-Archival Institute created a moot court that tried a series of famous figures from medieval and ancient history, in effect resurrecting the pre-revolutionary tradition of the mock trial. In short, the agitsud did not vanish from Russian culture, but from the Russian stage, at the end of the NEP.[79]

The reason for this disappearance from the stage lies in the dramatic upping of the ideological ante that took place toward the end of the 1920s. With the introduction of the first five-year plan, the weakest link in the mock trial's paradigm of mythopoetic justice became all too evident. The spectator in all his naiveté and malleability could still elude the compulsion to confess and repent, in spite of attempts to script his response as completely as the testimony of the fictional enemy he was supposed to emulate. The need to guarantee the audience's compliance and to mobilize all of Soviet society toward the ambitious goals of the planned economy required that legal propaganda amass even more means of representation, that it incorporate more media into the mythopoetic justice initially created on the stage. The mock trial created the paradigm of legal mythopoesis that lay at the foundation of the Stalinist show trial, but it remained for the cinema and the courtroom to take this tripartite formula, to adapt it, and to realize the utopian goals that ultimately proved too ambitious for the theater to realize alone.

CHAPTER THREE

TRIALS ON FILM

Mythopoetic Justice II

T he agitsud's decline in popularity began at the same time that fictional trials gained new importance in movie houses across the Soviet Union in the second half of 1920s. Feature films of the early Soviet period consistently depicted a wide variety of fictional courtrooms, including pre-revolutionary imperial trials, western European "bourgeois" courts, and contemporary Soviet tribunals. Directors of agitational films even made a small number of cinematic agitsudy, which took the generic formula of the theatrical mock trial and translated it onto film. The agitfilms *Abort. Sud nad akusherkoi Zaitsevoi (Abortion: The Trial of Midwife Zaitseva)* by G. Lemberg (1924) and *Prestuplenie konovala Matova (The Crime of the Horse-doctor Matov)* by Ia. Posel'skii (1925) brought a popular theme from the stage of the agitsud to the movie screen, the theme of Soviet science's struggle to eradicate traditional medical practices.[1] Yet both these films strayed from the rigid legal structure of their theatrical counterparts. *Abortion* featured animated sequences that illustrated the testimony of the expert witness. The incorporation of flashbacks, which cut from the witness stand to the scene of the crime, pushed the legal drama far beyond the confines of the Soviet courtroom and into the homes and workplaces of the films' witnesses and defendants. Transporting the mock trial from theater to cinema entailed giving up many of the fixed rules that theorists had promoted to increase the genre's effectiveness in the propaganda theater, as well as expanding the narrative that took place outside of the court. Although the changes that appeared in the fictional trial as it moved from stage to screen meant that no distinct genre of filmed mock trials ever existed per se, these revisions allowed the agitsud's threefold formula of mythopoetic justice to enter a surprisingly wide variety of feature films and prepared it for entry into the real-life court.

The melodrama of confession, contrition, and reintegration into society found its fullest cinematic expression in films that depicted the contemporary Soviet court, before which the viewer in the movie house might someday find himself accountable. Popular features such as *Tiazhelye gody (The Difficult Years)* by Razumnyi (1925), *Don Diego i Pelegaia. Delo Pelegai Deminoi (Don Diego and Pelegaia: The Affair of Pelegaia Demina)* by Ia. Protazanov (1927), *Parizhskii sapozhnik (The Parisian Cobbler)* by F. Ermler (1927), *Saba* by M. Chiaureli (1929), *Prestuplenie Ivana Karavaeva (The Crime of Ivan Karavaev)* by T. Lukashevich (1929), *Gosudarstvennyi chinovnik (The Government Bureaucrat)* by I. Pyr'ev (1930), and *Sekret rapida (The Secret of the Rapid)* by P. Dolina (1930), all placed their dénouement in a contemporary courtroom. Similar to the agitsud, each of these films focused on the commission of a social crime— such as drunkenness, bureaucratic red-tape, or slacking on the job—and showed the injurious effects on the collective and on Soviet society as a whole. In the trial scene that provided the climax, the accused initially denied his responsibility for a breach in the social code—only to recognize, at the film's end, the criminal nature of an activity that once seemed harmless to him. Before a large audience of his peers, the defendant confessed his transgression, repented his wrongdoing, and had the opportunity to be welcomed back into society with open arms. Films with trials before a Soviet court broke the generic restrictions of the agitsud; nonetheless, they replicated on the screen the most distinctive features of the theatrical genre, namely, the samokritika (self-criticism) of the internal enemy and the tripartite formula for conversion to Bolshevism.

The significance of these movies' depiction of legal mythopoesis comes into focus only against the background of the many films of the era that portrayed unjust legal procedure in tsarist or bourgeois courts. Features containing pre-revolutionary or non-Soviet trials provided not simply a contrast to but more important the context for the Soviet courts on film. On the one hand, cinematic portrayals of pre-revolutionary imperial courts glorified the formative experiences of Russian radicals subjected to public trial, exile, and execution before 1917. The viewer of these movies was meant to experience a complex blend of righteous indignation at the injustice of the tsarist court, immense relief that such injustice was rapidly receding into the historical past, and heartfelt gratitude that would inspire the viewer to repeat the great sacrifices made by pre-revolutionary radicals on his behalf. Such films include the comic short *Son Tarasa (The Dream of Taras)* by Iu. Zheliabuzhskii (1919); two screen adaptations of Gor'kii's novel *Mat' (Mother)*, by A. Razumnyi (1919) and by V. Pudovkin (1926); *Stepan Khalturin* by A. Ivanovskii (1925); *Katorga (Penal Colony)* by Iu. Raizman (1928); an adaptation of Tolstoi's play *Zhivoi trup (The Living*

Corpse) by F. Otsep (1929); and *Dvadtsat' shest' komissarov (Twenty-six Commissars)* by N. Shengelaia (1932). On the other hand, films culminating in bourgeois trials showed the oppressive devices of foreign courts and provided the Soviet viewer with another opportunity to feel indignation and relief that he would never fall victim to supposedly histrionic, bourgeois justice. *Teni bel'vedera (The Shadows of Belvedere)* by A. Anoshchenko (1926), the popular hit *Protsess o trekh millionakh (The Trial of the Three Million)* by Protazanov (1926), and *Prividenie, kotoroe ne vozvrashchaetsia (The Ghost that Doesn't Return)* by A. Room (1929), all portrayed the dangerous theatricality of foreign courts, in which eloquent Western lawyers presented a case that, more often than not, landed an innocent proletarian in jail. Although a small number of films with non-Soviet trials painted an ambiguous picture of the workings of justice (as we will find later in the work of Lev Kuleshov), the majority of these movies illuminated by contrast the compassionate nature of Soviet justice and created a context in which the personal drama of converting to Bolshevism had global implications.

Against this background of bourgeois injustice, the many fictional Soviet courts on film not only reproduced the agitsud's paradigm of mythopoetic justice but also altered it in accordance with the perceived requirements and possibilities of the medium of film. The privileged status of cinema during the 1920s made this medium the logical means to overcome the limitations of theatrical mock trials and thereby to augment their impact. Cinema's allegedly greater realism and its appeal to a mass audience allowed those filming fictional trials in the late 1920s to ignore the hodgepodge of rules, restrictions, and recommendations that had constituted the theatrical realism of the agitsud. As a result fictional trials on film were only a part of a larger legal drama that encompassed the psychology of the criminal, the commission of his crime, and most important, the immediate and long-term consequences of samokritika. Moving the threefold pattern of the mock trial from the theater to the cinema shifted the emphasis of the legal drama from confession and repentance to the final element, reintegration into the socialist community.

This shift in importance allowed legal propaganda on film to realize the potential of the mock trial's essentially melodramatic structure. With its unmasking of the internal villain, the agitsud put melodrama into courtroom testimony. Films depicting Soviet tribunals reversed this pattern by placing the Soviet court right in the middle of a melodrama, replete with stock characters fighting in a battle of good versus evil. Fictional legal drama on film closely followed the recommendation of cultural authorities, headed by Commissar of Enlightenment Anatolii Lunacharskii, who advocated melodrama as the most comprehensible and hence the most appropriate genre for proletarian and peasant spectators. Moving the fictional trial from the stage of the agitsud to the melodramatic movie screen promised to create more effective propaganda and helped to bring greater variety to fictional trials, which on the whole reflected more accurately their counterparts in real-life courts. Legal propaganda on stage and screen was not written with an eye to performance in the actual courtroom. Nonetheless, first theater and then cinema asserted the power of mythopoetic justice to shape audience attitudes and behavior, and together, they paved the way for the introduction of the threefold formula into actual show trials. Although fictional trials on films did not create the pattern of confession, repentance, and reintegration into society, they amplified the agitsud's model of legal mythopoesis and prepared the model for its next and most important venue, the real-life Soviet court.

LUNACHARSKII'S CALL TO MELODRAMA

The ongoing quest to find the ideal medium for Bolshevik propaganda resulted in cinema's victory over the theater by the end of the 1920s. At the same time that theorists weighed the respective virtues of the stage and screen, they actively sought the most appropriate genre—comedy, tragedy, satire, or melodrama—that these media should employ. Since mass appeal played a significant role in film's status as the "most important of the arts," cinematic genres that had already demonstrated their attraction to the proletariat and peasantry provided logical avenues for film propaganda. Taking their cue from foreign silent films, whose titles and stars dominated the marquees of Russian movie houses, filmmakers interested in a popular audience turned to revolutionary melodrama as a recipe for success. Just as in western Europe, a host of negative connotations surrounded melodrama in the Soviet Union, and the most prominent experimental Soviet filmmakers were loath to stoop to what they perceived as the lowest common denominator of the new country's viewing public. Nonetheless, directors with an eye on box office receipts, especially those with experience in the pre-revolutionary Russian film industry, anticipated that revitalized and revolutionized melodrama would perform the minor miracle of simultaneously fulfilling a popular audience's demands for lively entertainment and the Soviet state's mandate for suitable content on the country's movie screens.

In light of the well-known experiments in documentary film and movies with mass heroes during the decade, melodrama seems an oddly conventional and surprisingly bourgeois genre to preach a revolutionary message.

Its associations with bathos and overacting would seem to weaken the serious messages Bolshevik propagandists sought to deliver to Soviet audiences. Nevertheless, the genre's long democratic history, which began on the late eighteenth-century stage of post-revolutionary France, suggested it would deliver politically attuned messages of direct relevance to the lives of Soviet workers and peasants. Melodrama presented a condensed and engaging story of consciousness raising, as George Bernard Shaw, who reviewed melodramas in London's Adelphia Theater for many years, described:

> A really good Adelphia melodrama is very hard to get. It should be a simple and sincere drama of action and feeling, kept well within that vast tract of passion and motive which is common to the philosopher and the labourer, relieved by plenty of fun, and depending for variety of human character, not on the high comedy idiosyncrasies which individualize people in spite of the closest similarity of age, sex and circumstances, but on broad contrasts between types of youth and age, sympathy and selfishness, the masculine and the feminine, the serious and the frivolous, the sublime and the ridiculous, and so on. The whole character of the piece must be allegorical, idealistic, full of generalizations and moral lessons. It must represent conduct as producing swiftly and certainly on the individual the results which in actual life it produces on the race in the course of many centuries.[2]

Shaw's pithy definition of melodrama characterizes a dramatic genre whose poetic justice was unusually suited to Russia's revolutionary stage and screen during the 1920s. It is understandable that cultural authorities such as Lunacharskii and Maksim Gor'kii found the persuasive moral message of melodrama highly attractive and ardently advocated its inclusion in revolutionary culture after 1917.

Although Lunacharskii sounded the call "Back to Ostrovskii!" much louder and with far greater results in professional theaters of the 1920s, the Soviet Union's first commissar of enlightenment believed in the utility of melodrama for the revolutionary stage just as passionately as in that of the Russian theater's classical repertoire.[3] Lunacharskii had espoused melodrama as the means of creating a genuinely popular theater with socialist inclinations long before Bolshevism became the country's dominant ideology.[4] His belief in melodrama's serviceability for social and political goals drew directly on the French socialist Romain Rolland's highly influential book *The People's Theater* (1903), in which an entire chapter provided a manifesto of melodrama as the genre most suited for revitalizing the theater at the turn of the century.[5] Rolland's expansive yet critical definition of melodrama as a theatrical genre motivated Lunacharskii to adopt his position and to encourage a renaissance of melodrama on the Russian revolutionary stage.

As part of his declaration of the need to return theater to the masses, Rolland rewrote the history of melodrama and retraced the genre's aesthetic lineage. Rather than describing melodrama's genesis in the plays of René Charles Guilbert Pixerécourt, Rolland looked back from modern-day popular playhouses to the amphitheaters of ancient Greece. Reacting against the snobbery of theater critics of his own day, Rolland turned accusations of melodrama in the plays of Aeschylus, Sophocles, and Shakespeare on their head, claiming that the alleged shortfalls of these great Western dramatists were in fact the surest sign of their genius. Careful to contrast the cheap melodrama of the boulevards with *Oresteia, Oedipus Rex,* and *Macbeth,* Rolland asserted that the greatest playwrights, regardless of time and place, all incorporated melodrama in their tragedies as well as in their comedies.[6] In his description of the intersection of tragedy and melodrama, Rolland in effect re-created both genres as a single hybrid theatrical form: the lofty language and finely crafted dramatic action of Sophocles or Shakespeare came together with the social relevancy and emotional effect of Pixerécourt. In essence, Rolland's vision of revitalized melodrama placed the Western theater's rich history of tragedy in the modern revolutionary context of melodrama.[7]

After granting this distinguished heritage to the popular theater of his day, Rolland listed the four most important qualities for a successful melodrama: varied emotions, "true realism," a simple moral, and getting your money's worth. All these terms described actual melodramatic productions of Rolland's day, which indeed combined laughter with tears, depicted realistic scenarios, delivered a simple moral message, and were compelled to give their audiences something for their money. Yet Rolland followed his list with a call to apply these rules with artistic integrity, urging playwrights to purify an admittedly popular genre, to raise it from lowbrow to highbrow tastes, and to infuse it with a noble, moral aim. The fact that large popular audiences, on a regular basis, already watched and enjoyed "the simple emotions, the simple pleasures" of melodrama encouraged Rolland to refine the genre for his vision of a people's theater.[8] Rather than invent some new and untried type of dramatic spectacle that would bridge the gap between popular and intellectual audiences, Rolland preferred to nominate a melodramatic reading of tragedy as the reincarnation of ancient Greek drama for the theater of the future.

Lunacharskii unabashedly expressed his debt to Rolland's vision in post-revolutionary calls for melodrama on the Soviet stage. The commissar for enlightenment copied Rolland's somewhat fanciful family tree, which traced the connection between melodrama and Attic tragedy, as well as the assertion that the genre had the greatest appeal, and hence the most utility, for the mass audience.[9] Like Rolland, Lunacharskii coupled the need to entertain the popular spectator with the desire to teach a simple yet noble, moral message; and he elaborated his own set of defining characteristics, similar to those of Rolland, that culminated in "the ability to stimulate undivided and total emotional reactions of compassion and indignation; the connection of action with simple and hence majestic, ethical tenets, with simple and clear ideas." Lunacharskii even duplicated Rolland's recommendation that the melodramatic playwright learn from his audience before he composes plays intended to teach the masses.[10] Lunacharskii's only substantive alteration of Rolland's plan was the rather predictable addition of a proletarian worldview as the foundation of melodrama on the revolutionary stage, an addition that promised to create the propaganda messages needed in the 1920s.[11] Lunacharskii's decision to adopt Rolland's view of melodrama shows the first commissar of enlightenment's unusually practical and synthetic view of dramatic art after 1917. Many directors in the theater conducted radical experiments that tossed old dramatic genres and techniques off the steamship of theatrical modernity; yet Lunacharskii understood the need to renew prerevolutionary melodrama, as it appeared both in popular, fairground booths or *balagany* and on the stage of Russia's nineteenth-century professional theater, if revolutionary art ever hoped to reach its intended audience.[12]

Echoing Lunacharskii's ideas, Gor'kii also declared the need "to return to a clarity of emotion, even to a primitiveness . . . [of the] 'grand' emotions, on which the greatest experts of the human soul—the Greek tragedians, Shakespeare, Schiller, Goethe, and so on—constructed their dramas." A handful of prominent members of the Soviet Union's theatrical avant-garde responded to these appeals for melodrama in the first half of the decade. In 1920, theater critic Pavel Markov wrote that melodrama was the genre most capable of realizing and synthesizing the "left" theatrical experiments of the previous decade and of putting them to revolutionary work. The director responsible for much of the "left" theater, Meyerhold, declared in a lecture devoted to his production of *Uchitel' Bubus (Teacher Bubus)* (1925) that melodrama, in its purest form, indeed constituted a revival of ancient Greek drama. On the other end of the artistic spectrum, the director Aleksandr Tairov applied melodrama's poetic justice, in which good is promptly rewarded and evil inexorably punished, to his production of *Rosita* (1925).[13]

In spite of this enthusiasm, the professional theater never brought about what Lunacharskii and Gor'kii had hoped would be a rebirth of melodrama on the Soviet stage. A number of directors produced revivals of nineteenth-century French melodramas; a handful of new Soviet melodramas also appeared; but the two Moscow theaters that devoted their entire repertoire to the genre, the Free and the Romanesque, both collapsed after only a single season.[14] A 1919 playwriting contest, which Lunacharskii and Gor'kii cosponsored to encourage the composition of revolutionary melodramas, presaged the genre's failure on the Soviet Union's professional stage. Not one of the forty-one submissions merited a first prize, and the only entry that was widely produced, Aleksandr Vermishev's *Krasnaia pravda (Red Truth),* failed to meet the jury's definition of melodrama.[15]

In great contrast, popular Soviet cinema heeded the call to melodrama and implemented Lunacharskii and Gor'kii's recommendations in films that hoped to diminish Soviet viewers' adoration of Western stars such as Mary Pickford, Harry Piel, and Harold Lloyd. Although Lunacharskii initially sounded the call to melodrama expressly for the stage, by the mid-1920s he had shifted his attention to the screen, which he ultimately believed was better suited than the theater to melodrama and mass propaganda: "Our films must be just as attractive and just as entertaining as bourgeois films. The melodramatic form is the best form for cinema in the appropriate treatment, of course, because in this respect cinema is 'in all its facets' considerably richer than the theater." Adapting the bourgeois genre of cinematic melodrama to Soviet purposes would allow film to function "as an instrument of intelligent propaganda and as a purveyor of intelligent entertainment and also as a source of revenue."[16] Ambitious as this formula sounds, Lunacharskii himself proved the ability of film melodrama at least to entertain and to turn a considerable profit by co-authoring the screenplay of the decade's largest domestic box-office hit, a distinctly un-Soviet melodrama titled *Medvezh'ia svad'ba (The Bear's Wedding)* by Eggert (1925). Rather than producing a script with a simple Soviet moral, Lunacharskii rewrote Prosper Mérimée's tale of vampirism and perversion, which revolves around the marriage of an innocent girl to a sinister count, who ravages his young bride on their wedding night when he is transformed into a predatory demon during a supernatural seizure.[17] In this and other melodramatic screenplays, Lunacharskii proved the popularity and viability of melodrama for cinema. However, this lurid movie, whose flimsy political message had clearly been tacked on at the last moment, failed to meet the high standards that Lunacharskii himself had set for the genre and supported critics such as Adrian Piotrovskii who saw melodrama as inherently bourgeois, individualistic, and hence unsuited for Soviet film.[18]

Both Piotrovskii's hatred for and Lunacharskii's attraction to melodrama on film undoubtedly arose in part from the country's already established tradition of cinematic melodrama, which constituted the most popular genre of domestic and imported films in Russian movie houses before 1917.[19] As critics pointed out, Lunacharskii's screenplay had much in common with pre-revolutionary blockbusters that, like Russian stage melodramas of the previous century, emphasized protagonists' internal emotional states, static acting and camera work, and quintessentially tragic "Russian endings."[20] However, not all post-revolutionary melodramas on film followed the model of their pre-revolutionary predecessors. Instead, many film directors after 1917, looking to educate as well as to entertain, focused on the social conflict, fast-paced action, and contrived but happy endings for which Hollywood melodramas were better known.[21] Although the Hollywood model of moviemaking was not brought into Soviet films without serious reservations about Americanization, the convergence of Soviet cinema with Hollywood melodrama promised to create propaganda with tremendous audience appeal, undeniable emotional impact, and clear revolutionary values.

The American version of melodrama on film provided a good means to rework the agitsud and to overcome the many shortcomings of theatrical mock trials. First, melodrama's poetic justice overlapped conveniently with the fictional justice of the mock court, thereby shaping and enhancing the moral of the agitsud. As a result, developing the melodramatic core of the agitsud into full-blown screen melodrama in a legal setting intensified the already strong, social conflict between right and wrong in the mock trial. Second, the ability of screen melodrama to elicit spectators' tears increased the indignation and compassion that viewers would allegedly experience during the agitsud, which had always been hampered in this regard by its rigid legal structure and bureaucratic jargon.[22] Third, the perplexing issue of audience participation in theatrical mock trials was laid to rest once and for all by the passive spectatorship required by melodrama on film. By shifting legal drama from the propaganda stage to the melodramatic screen, its entertainment and educational merits increased; the moral values on trial gained even greater clarity; and the thorny question of spectator involvement entirely disappeared. In short, the movement from stage to screen changed the very nature of the legal drama in the agitsud, allowing it to reach and to affect a significantly larger audience even as it signaled the theatrical genre's demise.

M. Chiaureli's film *Saba: Melodarama v 6 chastiakh (Saba: A*

Melodrama in 6 Parts) provides a good illustration of how adaptation to the melodramatic screen fundamentally altered both the intended message and the anticipated reception of Soviet legal drama. This 1929 movie proves particularly interesting for our analysis because of its likeness to B. S. Sigal's *Trial of Stepan Korolev*. Although the action in Sigal's play takes place in the Leningrad of approximately 1924 and Chiaureli's film is set in Tbilisi at the decade's end, the two tales of the dangers of drink bear a striking resemblance from their shared roots in the well-established sub-genre of the temperance melodrama.[23] The most obvious difference between these two works is *Saba*'s greater narrative breadth: in contrast to the agitsud, which took place entirely within the confines of a contemporary courtroom, only the last of *Saba*'s eight reels depicts "The Show Trial of the Former Trolley Conductor Saba Dzhaliadshvili." The preceding seven reels show Saba's crimes in all their despicable and colorful detail, which viewers of the film could actually see in great contrast to the mere narration of Korolev's crimes in Sigal's play.

The moviegoer himself witnesses Saba's slide into alcohol abuse, wife battering, child neglect, unemployment, theft, drunken brawls, and homelessness, which only ends when Saba nearly kills his son in a drunken trolley-driving accident. In addition to the chain of Saba's many misdeeds, the viewer sees the appalling consequences of intemperance in the lives of his wife and their son, rather than simply hearing about them at the trial. Like Korolev's wife in the earlier agitsud, Saba's wife must make her living washing clothes, and his young son cannot participate in Pioneer activities at school since the dissolute father has given him a black eye and made him the target of the other Pioneers' ridicule. Saba's wife and son vividly bear the marks of his misdeeds, which the movie viewer witnesses as he anticipates the poetic justice that will punish Saba and reward his beleaguered family. As a filmed legal melodrama, *Saba* replaced the spoken testimony of defendants and witnesses in the agitsud with compelling images of crime and its personal, familial, and social consequences.

By the time Saba comes to trial, the audience in the movie theater is intended to have already reached the same conclusion that it does while watching Sigal's play: "Alcohol is our class enemy." Nonetheless, the testimony of Saba himself and that of the leader of his son's Pioneer circle are interspersed with flashbacks that repeat Saba's crimes and reinforce the inescapable connection between them and the trial in progress. The flashbacks of his own debauchery and cruelty to his family prompt Saba to recognize his dual status as both victim and villain and to beg the court to judge his actions: "It's true, I was the undoing of my own son. . . . Judge me." Yet these flashbacks do not function exclusively on an individual level to activate Saba's long-dormant conscience. In addition, they remind the spectator at the trial and in the movie house of the rips in the social fabric of Saba's home and at his workplace.

The broad social implications of Saba's transgressions become clear in the intertitles and clips from documentary films that support the testimony of expert witnesses. Much like officials and experts in a typical agitsud, the court's president states, "We are not judging only [Saba]. The old way of life, with its drinking binges and debauchery, is at the defendant's dock." At this point in the film, we see grotesque images of several men disfigured by the effects of chronic alcohol abuse (most probably taken from medical films of the time). These images prove the judge's contention and warn Saba, the trial's spectators, and the film's audience of the fate awaiting those who drink to excess. Although the trial constitutes only a fraction of the film's plot, the use of images from earlier in the narrative and from outside *Saba*'s fictional world give this scene greater visual persuasion than its theatrical counterpart. The flashbacks connect the fictional trial on film to the world of its viewers, urging the desired response of moviegoers who might have missed *Saba*'s didactic message in earlier episodes of the film.

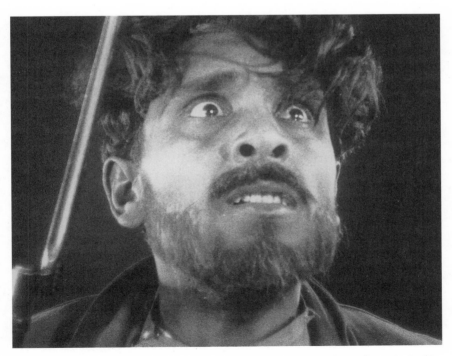

Saba looks on anxiously at his trial. From the last reel of *Saba*, M. Chiaureli, 1929, Goskinprom Gruzii.

As Saba's compliant confession shows, defendants in filmed mock trials unmasked their enemy status with just as much regret and just as many tears as they did in theatrical agitsudy. But unlike its theatrical predecessor, the fictional trial on film could actually depict reintegration into society, something that lay beyond the narrative confines of the agitsud. The collective nature of Saba's crimes dictated that the social networks that sustained damage, namely his family and the cadre at the factory, determine his punishment and decide if he can be invited back. Like Stepan Korolev, Saba's initial fall from sobriety took place when he buckled under the pressures of his alcoholic working-class peers and spent his entire paycheck on drink. Correspondingly, the collective that pressured him into crime must discipline not only Saba but also itself, before he can be welcomed back. After Saba's confession and the harsh words of the prosecution, the cadre of workers from which Saba was expelled states: "He alone shouldn't be judged . . . but our entire collective." First, they point their collective finger at the true villains in the film, those who sell alcohol to innocent men such as Saba. After demanding that bars in working-class neighborhoods, such as the one where Saba met his downfall, be closed, they then ask for leniency in Saba's sentencing. After these requests, Saba's wife and son take the witness stand, where they weep and beg to be reunited with the head of their family. After these two pleas for clemency, no official sentence is ever read by the court's president or appears in intertitles at the end of the trial scene. In spite of the number and gravity of Saba's crimes, the film ends on a happy note, with the title character cured of his alcoholic tendencies, reunited with his wife and son, and working once again as a trolley conductor. Moviegoers could actually see the rehabilitation of the defendant, which was only discussed as the future outcome of sentencing during the closing moments of Sigal's *Trial of Stepan Korolev*. Fictional trials on film reproduced the theatrical mock trial's formula for conversion to Bolshevism but actually represented the final moment of reintegration into the socialist community.

In addition, a new character appeared in mock trials on film, one whose composition and position were so similar to those of the film's actual viewing public that it promised to stimulate spectators' indignation and compassion, as every good melodrama should. This new character was none other than the audience of Saba's trial, which constituted the collective reaction to and judgment of the testimony at the trial, much like a melodramatic revision of an ancient Greek tragic chorus. In *Saba*, the audience in the courtroom is comprised of a mixed crowd of men, women, and children, who attentively follow the testimony of Saba's case and react with tremendous emotion and heartfelt compassion. After Saba's

Saba is reunited with his wife and injured son at the end of his trial. From the last reel of *Saba*, M. Chiaureli, 1929, Goskinprom Gruzii.

wife and son plead for his release, the camera pans across the audience and shows that several of its members have been moved to tears by their own empathic reaction to the weeping of the wife and son. Although the viewer outside the film could not hear the words that accompanied the audience's tears, the visual signs of feeling in the viewer inside the film were intended to trigger an identical display of emotion in his real-life counterpart. This correspondence between the audience inside and that outside the film continues as *Saba* comes to its end: the actual moviegoer was meant to experience the same joy that he saw on the faces of the happy crowd leaving the courtroom for the streets, as a mock funeral of alcohol made its way through Tbilisi. Additional, documentary shots of young members of the local Komsomol and trade union, to whom Saba's now cheerful son lectured on the evils of drink, reinforced the tie between the audience of Saba's trial and the spectator in the movie house. The unpredictable participation of those who watched agitsudy had been replaced by the entirely scripted response of the audience in the film, which not only cued the audience outside the film as to its own reaction but also provides a good approximation of the response that organizers of theatrical mock trials had hoped agitsudy would elicit.

The movement from stage to screen changed the nature of Soviet courtroom drama in the agitsud, expanding its melodramatic modeling and allowing it to reach a significantly larger audience. By turning the rigidly realistic theatrical mock trial into a cinematic melodrama with a legal setting, both the entertainment value and educational impact of Soviet courtroom drama were considerably increased. The Soviet state's greater control over cinema as an art form, the ability to reproduce mechanically and to distribute such films throughout the entire country, and the elimination of active, spectator participation in the theater in favor of passive spectator reception in the movie house, all made film the preferred medium for courtroom drama by the end of the decade. When he sounded the call to revolutionize melodrama, Lunacharskii probably did not have a film as tendentious as *Saba* in mind, since he hoped "wherever possible [to] avoid tendentious films—that is, large-scale films in which a didactic theme is unraveled rather obviously."[24] Nonetheless, in the very year in which Stalin relieved Lunacharskii of his post as commissar of enlightenment, dogmatic film propaganda like *Saba* realized the formula for melodrama that he first described ten years before.

Filmed legal propaganda such as *Saba* translated much of the spoken drama of the agitsud into forceful melodramatic images. Yet for all their visual persuasion, fictional trials on film struggled to compensate for the loss of orality that came with moving the agitsud to the silent screen. The need to communicate the precise details of crime and the legal technicalities of its consequences meant that directors often used an unusually large number of intertitles to guarantee that spectators would correctly understand the film's action. In particular, trial scenes such as *Saba*'s relied on frequent and sometimes lengthy intertitles to gloss the film's images. Although the oral component was lost when Soviet trials came to the movies, a strong verbal component, which had been a distinguishing feature of pre-revolutionary Russian films, remained to complement and reinforce the visual construction of the battle between good and evil.[25]

F. Ermler's 1927 film *The Parisian Cobbler* provides a good example of this pointed and polemical use of intertitles in a cinematic mock trial. Much like *Saba*, Ermler's film takes an approved agitsud theme, in this case the problem of sexual promiscuity among members of the Komsomol, and translates it into film melodrama.[26] Unlike theatrical mock trials that simply described the complications arising from relaxed sexual relations, the spectator of *The Parisian Cobbler* has the opportunity to see the deceitful and entangled associations that have developed among sexually active *komsomol'tsy* in a rural paper factory. The film's cast of characters is comprised solely of melodramatic stereotypes, such as the unwed mother (Katia), the irresponsible yet culpable father (Andrei), the humble, deaf-mute cobbler of the film's title (Kirik), the jilted gypsy girl in search of revenge, and "Mot'ka Tundel'—a rowdy and an enemy." Intertitles help the viewer sort the good characters from the bad during the first moments of the film, even though the action of *The Parisian Cobbler* is so fast-paced and involved as to defy such easy classifications. Intertitles also help the viewer understand the nature of the crime that takes place in the film: as Andrei's friends laugh over their attempts to sexually harass Katia in the hopes that she will stop pestering their friend and perhaps have a miscarriage, they happen to read the section of the Penal Code of the Russian Federation that addresses rape and the extortion of sex "through the use of deception." Without such written signposts, the viewer of *The Parisian Cobbler* might get lost in the tangled web of sex and retribution out of which Ermler builds his story.

Yet the film's two trial scenes take this use of verbal material in a nonverbal art form to a metatextual level. In the first trial, a Komsomol court attempts to evaluate Katia's claim that Andrei fathered her son and is now using his friends to harass her. Only Kirik, the deaf-mute cobbler has witnessed the crime, and although he cannot hear or speak, he must provide testimony to the Komsomol judges. Kirik gives his statement in mime, which the court has great difficulty in deciphering and ultimately does not know how to interpret or incorporate into their judgment. Only after Andrei is caught by other witnesses, who are capable of orally describing his physical abuse of Katia, does the Komsomol court finally pass its judgment: "We have decided: To acknowledge the behavior of Andrei Goriunov as unworthy of a member of the Komsomol and a Soviet citizen. As a consequence, the case should be handed over to the Central Committee." In the film, the cobbler's sincere love and compassion for Katia are clearly depicted, as are his honesty and unswerving devotion to the truth. Yet the young *komsomol'sty* at Andrei's trial cannot believe the gestures that constitute Kirik's testimony, unaccompanied as they are by any verbal expression. Only the oral testimony of other eyewitnesses to Andrei's brutality (translated into intertitles in the film) can give Kirik's evidence sufficient weight to expel Andrei from the Komsomol. In cinema that itself had no spoken words to communicate its message, Kirik's utter impotence to protect Katia betrays the court's incompetence in arriving at its judgment.

As this metatextual wrinkle in Ermler's story suggests, the poetic justice of *The Parisian Cobbler* is unusually open-ended in spite of the copious

Kirik, the deaf-mute "Parisian cobbler," tries to testify before the Komsomol court. From reel 3 of *Parizhskii sapozhnik (The Parisian Cobbler)*, F. Ermler, 1927/1928, Sovkino.

intertitles that direct viewers in the movie house to appropriate opinions and conclusions. Although by the film's end the Komsomol court has indicted Andrei, almost all of the other characters, including the seemingly innocent Katia and Kirik, have crossed the line of the law to redress personal vendettas. Neither the paper-pushing Party secretary nor the Komsomol court is able to break the cycle of retribution in the film, which ends in Andrei's sullen removal of his Komsomol pin and Mot'ka's near death at the hands of an enraged Kirik. The final moments of *The Parisian Cobbler* place this very melodramatic preponderance of effect over cause in all its severity: the film's final intertitle poses the famous and oft-repeated question, first asked in Russian social criticism by Aleksandr Herzen: Who is to blame? Ermler provides no easy answer to this question in the film, and although *The Parisian Cobbler* has much in common with *Saba*, Ermler's work comes closer to pre-revolutionary Russian melodrama with its tragic overtones and lack of closure than it does to the agitsud whose ending was always a foregone conclusion.[27]

Nonetheless, the highly polemical question Who is to blame? must have sparked debate among viewers of the film and encouraged audience involvement in a manner quite similar to that of the agitsud. In addition, Ermler's chosen topic for the film—sexual promiscuity among the Komsomol—helped spectators to answer this question with little hesitation, since Soviet propagandists had for a number of years already described the alleged sexual license of this particular group.[28] The moviegoer of 1927 could readily see that everybody in *The Parisian Cobbler* bore part of the blame for the libertinism that destroyed social bonds and disabled the Komsomol collective.

The positive reviews elicited by *Saba* and *The Parisian Cobbler* from Soviet film critics of the time revolved primarily around the films' accurate portrayal of troubling social issues. Ermler's film earned praise for its use of "living material," whereas Chiaureli was reproached by some members of the Association of Revolutionary Cinematographers (ARK) for having produced an excessively realistic story.[29] Despite such statements of the films' relationship to contemporary life outside the movie theater, the underlying messages of the two films were virtually identical to that of the agitsud, which unmasked the country's unwitting hidden enemies so they could confess and take an active part in the building of socialism. Both directors had found a suitable combination of entertainment and enlightenment, which other Soviet filmmakers of the time were struggling to accomplish. In order to create propaganda on film, *Saba* and *The Parisian Cobbler* relied on melodramatic characters, codes, and paradigms, which had become part of the Russian moviegoer's vocabulary before the revolution and which bore a suspicious similarity to those of Hollywood melodramas also being shown on Soviet screens. That such "living material" became propaganda by virtue of its translation into cinematic melodrama indicates the importance and power of poetic justice in modeling actual justice beyond the movie screen.

LOCATING THE FICTIONAL ENEMY

Not all fictional trials on film presented such clear-cut examples of cinematic melodrama. Often action or adventure films, satires, and comedies of the late 1920s included a scene of formalized judgment and shifted into melodramatic gear for the purposes of rendering poetic justice. Much like agitsudy, fictional trials in films that fell outside melodrama in its strictest sense still used the genre's clichés of villains and heroes and its dominance of effect over cause to make their message comprehensible to the intended audience. As the decade progressed, the storehouse of melodramatic images, gestures, and intertitles brought by Soviet directors into revolutionary propaganda from pre-revolutionary and American films took on distinctly Soviet significations, which could immediately suggest the ritual of samokritika (self-criticism) and its corollary, *chistka* (purge). Using the melodramatic mode allowed directors to incorporate poetic justice into a variety of film genres and allowed them greater flexibility in depicting fictional trials, which strayed far from the theatrical agitsud's meticulous reproduction of courtroom detail. The diffusion of trials, formal and otherwise, into a variety of cinematic genres resulted in the dissemination of trials outside the fictional court depicted on film and reflected an ever more pressing need to locate the enemy both in fiction and in real life.

T. Lukashevich's 1929 film *Prestuplenie Ivana Karavaeva (The Crime of Ivan Karavaev)* illustrates the power of melodramatic suggestion in movies that combined equal parts of melodrama and heroic adventure. Lukashevich's film addresses the intertwined problems of bureaucratization and *smychka* (worker-peasant solidarity), engaging a host of stereotypical images in the process. Although *The Crime of Ivan Karavaev* lacks *Saba*'s ability to induce tears and *The Parisian Cobbler*'s density of plot, Lukashevich nonetheless relies on the stereotypes of foes and friends familiar in these two films to set the stage for the struggle between bureaucratic Nepmen and the proletarian hero. The opening frames of the film show the luxurious apartment of the president of the local trust, the cozy domain of "The queen of door-curtains, the princess of tea-services . . . the lady of the house Madame Nakomliaeva." The camera suddenly cuts from this petit bourgeois refuge to the local factory, where we meet the proletarian Karavaev among the smiling, perspiring workers, who have just elected him to represent their interests at the trust. In an inversion of the archetypal quest, which normally pushes the hero from the domestic sphere out into the great wide world, Karavaev finds himself taken out of the public collective of the factory and thrust into the private sphere of Nepmen at the trust. The intrusion of the healthy, ruddy, handsome Karavaev into the corrupt circle of bespectacled bureaucrats bodes no good: what will happen when a worker is isolated from the collective in a snug den of counter-revolutionary wolves?

Rather than capitulate to the temptations of bribery and coquettish secretaries, Karavaev holds "to the class line" at his new job. When instructed to give the trust's lone sowing machine to a kulak, Karavaev devises a way to disobey his superiors and to give the sowing machine to peasants at the local collective farm instead. The bureaucrats are outraged at Karavaev's insubordination, and the confused hero returns to his fellow workers at the factory for support. When Karavaev asks if he has done the right thing, his comrades answer, "From the point of view of class, of course, you are right, but you can't act anarchically . . . go back to work." When Karavaev returns to the trust, the bureaucrat-enemies place him under arrest. In a gesture of class solidarity, the factory workers storm into the trust and demand justice in Karavaev's case. They turn to the local Party Secretary Rybakov and ask him to determine who is at fault, Karavaev or his superiors. Rybakov points out that Ivan has been "willful" in his treatment of the situation and announces: "And now . . . there will be a public trial [obshchestvennyi sud] for you." Rather than moving to an official courtroom, Rybakov renders his judgment on the spot and allows the outraged workers to speak in Karavaev's defense: "In our opinion, according to the class line, Karavaev is right." Without any further testimony or deliberation, Rybakov announces that Karavaev is indeed in the right and that "The sowing machine should be given [to the collective farm] on credit." Karavaev smiles in relief and the foiled kulak marches angrily off. The trial ends not simply in Karavaev's vindication, but in a purge instigated by Rybakov and the workers at the local trust. After a final warning to Karavaev not to act so willfully in the future, the film closes with images of happy factory workers sweeping the trust clean, as frightened bureaucrats skulk away.

The spontaneity of Karavaev's trial shows that an actual courtroom was not necessary for the literalization of poetic justice in fictional trials on film. Rather, the use of standard melodramatic images of the downtrodden, proletarian hero and the bribe-taking, effete Nepman made the reversal of their positions inevitable, regardless of the formality of the court judging between them. In addition, the group of workers supporting Karavaev act not only as the defender in Rybakov's makeshift trial but also as the audience of the trial within the film. As in *Saba*, the proletarian chorus shows the audience outside the film the appropriate response to Karavaev's alleged crime, as well as its role in instigating such Soviet *samosudy* and carrying out their sentences. *The Crime of Ivan Karavaev* realizes the Soviet myth of the proletariat's spontaneous collective will, however, with the important addition of Rybakov's fatherly ideological guidance. Like the workers in the film, spectators in the movie house were supposed to volunteer for "the shock brigade" of purges designed to locate the petit bourgeois enemy and to sweep him out of socialist society under Party supervision.

If the melodramatic modeling of characters and situations in *The Crime of Ivan Karavaev* encouraged moviegoers to apply its poetic justice to their own lives, P. Dolina's 1930 film *The Secret of the Rapid* showed them precisely how to do this. The fictional trial at the end of the film is none other than a theatrical agitsud, complete with confession, repentance, and reintegration into the community on the part of both the actor cast in the role of the accused and his real-life counterpart within the film. As propaganda agitating against the old way of life, *The Secret of the Rapid* focuses on a backward, illiterate worker, Lazar' Koboz, who sabotages factory production in his resistance to new, mechanized modes of work. In the rush to fill an important government order, the factory director appeals to Koboz's years of technical expertise in manufacturing a milling instrument for the assembly line. As a remnant "of the old regime," Koboz claims that he alone can fill the order because of a mysterious "secret of the rapid" that he holds. The director suspects that Koboz is "lying and sabotaging!" and he decides finally to work around the drunken, self-pitying Koboz. When other workers at the factory succeed in manufacturing the needed part and discover that "the secret of the rapid" is a figment of Koboz's imagination, they eagerly shout, "We should try him! to trial!"

In the wake of these calls to justice, Koboz drinks himself into a stupor and collapses on his bed. The groggy Koboz is suddenly woken up by the sounds of a parade in the village streets, which he follows to its destination at the local workers' club. Much to his surprise, there he sees a poster announcing "The Trial of Lazar' Koboz." He enters the club, and from the back of the auditorium, Koboz observes an actor dressed to represent him with his head hung in shame. Koboz listens to the passionate denunciations of other workers who state, "We have no place for those like Lazar' among us." The factory director takes the stand to explain compassionately that "Lazar' is not a wrecker [*vreditel'*] or a traitor [*izmennik*] . . . [but] an unhappy ignoramus." The scales fall from Koboz's eyes, he comes to the front of the auditorium, and the bolt that allegedly held "the secret of the rapid" falls from his hands. Koboz instructs the actor playing him to leave the stage; he assumes the penitent pose originally taken by the actor and meekly confesses, "I am guilty." The audience listens quietly to Koboz's repentance and then leaves the auditorium. At the end of the agitsud, Koboz's friends praise him for having done the right thing, and a weak smile begins to flicker on his once hardened, now contrite face. As the film ends, Lazar is reunited with not only his fellow workers but also his wife, who previously had abandoned him as a slacker and a drunk.

The Secret of the Rapid illustrates the almost seamless continuity between fictional trials and real judgment, which had been incorporated into the myth of the functioning Soviet collective by the end of the 1920s. Although, by the end of the decade, actual agitsudy were becoming increasingly rare on theatrical stages, the genre's cinematic depiction continued to

Lazar Koboz, who allegedly holds "the secret of the rapid," reads the poster announcing his own mock trial. From reel 6 of *Sekret rapida (Secret of the Rapid)*, P. Dolina, 1930, Ukrainfil'm.

teach the same lesson of conversion to Bolshevism, using many of the same melodramatic characters and conventions. As was the case in the agitsud, the audience within *The Secret of the Rapid* responded with both the sympathy and the empathy necessary to reform individual spectators such as Koboz within the film. But as was the case in *Saba,* the audience inside the film also provided the script for spectators in the movie house. By moving the agitsud from the actual theater to a theater on film, *The Secret of the Rapid* simultaneously replicated and augmented the threefold paradigm of the agitsud. Such metapropaganda not only expanded the narrative of Koboz's crime and his reintegration into the community but also provided valuable instruction on bringing the mock trial's lesson into the moviegoer's life. The smooth functioning of the cinematic agitsud in *The Secret of the Rapid* indicated the ease with which fictional enemies could be found and suggested that locating the enemy would be no more complicated in real life than it was in the movies.[30]

In spite of the clear path toward justice described in *The Secret of the Rapid,* obstacles often did arise in the search for the fictional enemy, as is illustrated by a subset of films featuring unjust Soviet trials. Such films provided intriguing twists and turns along the road to poetic justice by depicting good citizens who suffered the temporary victimization of an overhasty or overzealous court. A momentary breach of justice, which the moviegoer could usually identify with ease, provided the uncomplaining proletarian hero with yet another opportunity to suffer unfairly and to prove valiantly that he merited the triumph that would inevitably be his. A. Razumnyi's 1925 revolutionary adventure *Tiazhelye gody (The Difficult Years)* provides a good example of this subset of movies, in which the good Bolshevik always respects the revolutionary tribunal's decision, even if it is unfairly made on the basis of purely circumstantial evidence.

The rather complicated plot of Razumnyi's film centers on the return of an exiled Russian revolutionary named Petrov to his family after twelve years in tsarist prisons. Petrov discovers that his family has abandoned his revolutionary fervor during the intervening years for the comfort and depravity of petit bourgeois life. In frustration, Petrov leaves the city for the Russian countryside where his two children, the honest Vera and the wily Sergei, eventually join him. Vera's husband, the proletarian Ageev, is caught with contraband goods in their home and consequently put on trial. As a loyal Bolshevik, the innocent Ageev abides by the revolutionary tribunal's decision that he is guilty of trading with black marketers. Yet Petrov smells a rat in his own home and discovers that Sergei is the one responsible for the stolen goods. Meanwhile, in the court, Ageev dutifully signs the papers for his own arrest and imprisonment. Petrov calls the court at the very last minute and reveals his son's hidden guilt. Ultimately, the judge releases Ageev from custody and declares Sergei "an enemy of the people." The relative ease with which Petrov turns his natural son over to the court in favor of his son-in-law shows that a good citizen's blood is not thicker than water, that a Bolshevik father's loyalties ultimately lie with the Soviet state. Ageev's patience and indestructible belief in the justice of the court's decision mark him as the melodramatic hero of *The Difficult Years* and assure the viewer that he will, by the movie's end, be amply rewarded for his perseverance.

Films such as *The Crime of Ivan Karavaev, The Secret of the Rapid*, and *The Difficult Years* strayed far from the original pattern of legal melodrama; nonetheless, they consistently incorporated melodramatic characters and conventions into their plots as a means of rendering poetic justice on the screen. Whether spontaneous, agitational, or formal, the fictional trial proved crucial to locating the enemy, wherever he might be in Soviet society—in the working collective, the family, or the self. As was true in theatrical agitsudy, the person under accusation might not necessarily be proved guilty, yet the rituals of justice that determined guilt or innocence provided the only means of finding whoever was culpable for the crime in question. The diffusion of poetic justice into genres of early Soviet cinema other than pure melodrama might suggest that legal propaganda on film was slowly losing its power to shape viewers' consciousness. However, the opposite holds true: the ubiquity and flexibility of melodramatic paradigms in these films indicate the ease with which poetic justice could be transported from theater into film and into real life by the end of the 1920s.

ROUTING OUT THE HIDDEN FOE

The diffusion of melodrama's poetic justice into other genres of early Soviet film expanded the narrative of legal mythopoesis first developed in the agitsud, shifting emphasis from confession and repentance to the numerous possibilities for reintegration into society. At the same time, transporting the basic plot of the theatrical mock trial into different genres of film produced variations in the tripartite paradigm that seldom occurred on the stage of the agitsud. For example, unjust trial films such as *The Difficult Years* often excluded the actual criminal from the social order after he was located and had taken the place of the loyal citizen initially put on trial. When this truncation of the threefold pattern appeared in theatrical mock trials, it was usually reserved for *byvshie liudi* (former people) such as the bootlegger Pavlenko in *Trial of Stepan Korolev,* the old quack Fedorovna in *Trial of a Mother,* and the procuress Sviridova in *Trial of a Prostitute and Procuress.* As the decade progressed, this deviation from the agitsud's original plan took on particular importance since it reflected the verdicts of public trials taking place in the country's actual courts. In the first half of the 1920s, the agitsud concentrated on peasant and proletarian defendants, whose conversion to Bolshevism seemed a foregone conclusion if only the error of their ways was brought to their attention. In the second half of the decade, fictional trials on film began to detect new groups of enemies, whose origins lay outside the working class and the USSR and whose fate, as a result, would be expulsion from the social order they undermined.

The danger of trusting "former people" and the need to expel them from the collective are clearly expressed in K. Bolotov's 1929 film *Vreditel' (The Wrecker).* Much as in *The Difficult Years,* the action of *The Wrecker* culminates in an unjust trial, but Bolotov situates his story among a group of young Pioneers, which reproduces the adult melodrama of Razumnyi's film on a child's level. With crime and justice scaled down to appropriately childish dimensions, a typical melodramatic conflict between two friends emerges: the hardworking proletarian Olesko, devoted to his studies, and the chubby hooligan Iurka, interested only in practical jokes. Iurka persuades Olesko to take part in one of his escapades, and the honest Olesko ends up taking the blame for the ensuing scandal. The outraged students convene a Pioneer court that mimics contemporary adult courts in every detail, including a judge, a gavel, and a jury of one's peers. With their teacher giving occasional nods of approval, the children decide to expel the innocent Olesko from their ranks. In spite of his insistence that he is not to blame, the children's court takes Olesko's cherished Pioneer scarf and revokes his membership to the group. Olesko ultimately accepts the unjust verdict of the Pioneer court and hangs his head in shame.

Eventually, Iurka's capers get out of hand, and the other students discover his identity as school prankster. Once the Pioneers realize that Iurka is the actual villain in their midst, they understand their error, give Olesko back his scarf, and readmit him to their ranks. In the film, Olesko's status as friend and Iurka's as foe are clearly depicted as the products of their respective class memberships: Iurka's parents are petit bourgeois shopkeepers, whereas Olesko's widowed mother works as the washerwoman in the courtyard of Iurka's house. Although the parents continue to live in a mi-

The Pioneer court judges Olesko in *The Wrecker*, as the school teacher looks on in approval. From reel 4 of *Vreditel' (The Wrecker)*, K. Bolotov, 1929, VUFKU.

crocosm of pre-revolutionary class relations, the poetic justice established between their sons reenacts the drama of revolution. The naughty, petit bourgeois Iurka, who is no more than ten years old in the film, must have been born after 1917 and spent his entire life under Soviet power. Nonetheless, his biological inheritance of counter-revolutionary mischief-making means that he will never belong in the Pioneer collective and consequently must be excluded from it.

In a comic rendition of the same theme, Ia. Protazanov's 1927 *Don Diego and Pelegaia* uses an unjust trial to mock "former people" who profit from the ignorance of others by tying their hapless victims in the red tape of the Soviet legal system.[31] The Don Diego of the film's title is actually a rural village stationmaster, who passes most of his time reading chivalric romances that inspire delusions of grandeur, much like a Soviet Don Quixote. When disturbed from his daydreaming by the arrival of a train, Don Diego vents his spleen on a local peasant woman who is illegally crossing the train's tracks to trade with the passengers. He confiscates the potatoes of the illiterate and defenseless Pelegaia and imposes a twenty-five-ruble fine on the impoverished woman for her misconduct. As a result of the stationmaster's legal pedantry, Pelegaia is eventually brought forcibly to court. At the trial, Don Diego argues for the old woman's guilt, using the rhetorical polish that characterized pre-revolutionary advocacy. The frightened woman understands neither the accusation against her nor the legal jargon of the trial. When asked about her membership to the Communist Party of the Soviet Union (referred to by its Russian acronym KPSS in the intertitle, which was pronounced "kapes"), she naively answers, "I don't know any kind of kapess." The clearly innocent woman is thrown in jail as a result of Don Diego's polished performance in court, leaving her forlorn husband to fend for himself during the potato harvest in the countryside.

After several appeals to local authorities, Pelegaia's husband enlists the aid of the local Komsomol. With the help of the local Party secretary, the *komsomol'tsy* finally succeed in cutting through the red tape that originally ensnared Pelegaia and securing her release. Much as in *The Crime of Ivan Karavaev,* a purge comes on the heels of Pelegaia's vindication and the local court that imprisoned her is cleansed of its unthinking bureaucrats. The actual villain in the film, the bitter and malicious Don Diego, is lumped together with the former bureaucrats, who suddenly find themselves on the other side of the dock in the Soviet legal system. The happy ending of *Don Diego and Pelegaia* makes light of the suffering caused to the peasant woman and her husband, as they innocently ask their rescuers to let them join the Komsomol, an organization intended for people less than half their age. Nonetheless, Protazanov painted a bleak picture of the country's legal system, whose bureaucrats looked suspiciously similar to their pre-revolutionary predecessors. The moviegoer might have giggled along with the bust of Trotskii that bursts into merry laughter at the film's end, but the poetic justice that returned Pelegaia to her farm also demanded that Don Diego and his ilk be banished from their bureaucratic posts in Soviet society.

Comedies that incorporated the melodramatic modeling of friends and enemies such as *Don Diego and Pelegaia* could deliver a much darker and more direct message by focusing on the hidden foe and his ridiculous attempts to incorporate himself into socialist society. I. Pyr'ev's adventure comedy *The Government Bureaucrat* (1930) did just this and showed that even an unwitting enemy lies beyond all hopes for rehabilitation if he belongs to the vestiges of the petite bourgeoisie. The government bureaucrat of the film's title, an accountant at a train factory by the name of Fokin, epitomizes the self-interested and apolitical philistinism associated with his social class at the end of the decade.

When the film begins, there is still hope that Fokin might remain a functioning part of the train factory where he works. However, after a series of comic chase scenes, shoot-outs, and slapstick misadventures, Fokin finds himself with a suitcase full of money stolen from the train factory, which, on the urging of his greedy wife, he decides to keep. In one of the many twists and turns in the film's plot, Fokin inadvertently hands the suitcase of money over to the Soviet authorities and is hailed a valiant hero instead of the despicable thief he was only a day before. The local Party organization praises him for his heroism and nominates him for their upcoming elections. The once apolitical government bureaucrat now dreams of using Party politics for his personal advancement.

Needless to say, Fokin is never elected by his fellow workers. Instead, he is put on trial with the head of an underground ring of saboteurs that hired the thief who mistakenly gave Fokin the money. During his trial, a series of damning intertitles appears on the movie screen, labeling Fokin a "Member of the Black Hundred . . . Bandit . . . Wrecker . . . Counter-Revolutionary." In another surprisingly long series of intertitles, the judge of the trial indignantly explains: "The growth of socialist construction is meeting the violent opposition of an outmoded class! . . . In these criminals we are judging . . . Wrecking! [*vreditel'stvo*] . . . Apoliticalness! . . . Malicious philistinism! . . . and the chaff of the past. . . . We will mercilessly replace all who dare to stand in our path to socialism." The audience at Fokin's trial within the film condemns the government bureaucrat just as forcefully as the judge: after the court secretary reads Fokin's jail

The three accused of embezzlement hear the court's sentence in *The Government Bureaucrat*. From left to right: the head of the trust, the government bureaucrat Fokin, and the thug. From the last reel of *Gosudarstvennyi chinovnik (The Government Bureaucrat)*, I. Pyr'ev, 1930, Soiuzkino.

sentence, the spectators all rise and point their fingers at the petit bourgeois bureaucrat receiving his just deserts. Politically indifferent bureaucrats like Fokin qualified as neutral fellow travelers only a few years earlier; but by 1930 such people received the label of class enemy, which required their removal by force from the working collectives they sabotaged either purposely or through political apathy. For all its vaudeville antics, *The Government Bureaucrat* delivered the ominous message that some would-be members of the new society not only lay beyond all hope of redemption but also merited ruthless expulsion from society for their passive sabotage.

Depicting expulsion from the socialist collective significantly altered the threefold paradigm originally laid out in the agitsud. The enemy of the people was still expected to confess and to repent before the Soviet court; however, only proletarian and peasant defendants could be trusted to make such statements with the sincerity that merited rehabilitation. As a result, defendants in cinematic trials that relied on melodrama for their construction of legal mythopoesis fell into two distinct categories: peasants and proletarians who strayed unknowingly and momentarily from the correct path, and the "former people" who had caused them to go astray. The formal constraints and historical development of the theatrical agitsud prevented it from ever treating the second group of villains in detail, and the diffusion of melodrama across a variety of cinematic genres proved necessary to give the relatively rigid paradigm of the agitsud the flexibility necessary to prosecute such reprobate defendants. This expansion in the categories of possible enemies of the people also reflected the diversity of actual court cases at the end of the decade, in which foreign spies and hidden saboteurs began to gain new visibility. Cinematic trials no longer delivered the monolithic message of the theatrical mock trial, yet they impressed on their viewing public that fictional trials and actual trials, in all their myriad incarnations, functioned on the same premises and with much the same consequences wherever they appeared.

The majority of the feature films that located and tried the hidden enemy lacked the daring experimentation and ground-breaking innovation for which early Soviet cinema is usually known. Nonetheless, they managed to achieve the alchemical blend of education and enlightenment necessary for effective propaganda. The threefold paradigm of confession, repentance, and reintegration into the community, which the agitsud first formulated for Soviet legal drama in the first half of the 1920s, reappeared in expanded form in feature films from the second half of the decade. Rather than being a direct translation from one medium into another, the introduction of legal mythopoesis into film altered and augmented the originally theatrical pattern. The melodramatic moment of the defendant's confession and unmasking that lay at the heart of the agitsud became full-fledged cinematic melodrama, whose archetypal characters and conventions promised to be easily legible to a mass audience and sufficiently flexible to penetrate a wide variety of films. Expanding the melodramatic nature of Soviet courtroom drama allowed new classes of enemies and new strategies for their elimination to enter the paradigm of the agitsud, stressing the need for Party intervention and the tight scripting of spectator reactions at public trials. No longer was the drama of legal mythopoesis restricted to samokritika, that is, the search for the enemy hidden within the individual. Now this search could be directed outward, at the petite bourgeoisie, bureaucrats, and other likely candidates for purging.

Both the agitsud and the legal propaganda on film had developed during the 1920s as means to complement the didactic messages of actual trials of the day. As such, they provided idealized images of the internal enemy's conversion to Bolshevism, the external enemy's expulsion, and the audience's response to both of these. Courtroom dramas on stage and screen duplicated the actual legal codes and practices of the decade. However, neither agitsudy nor filmed trials were intended to serve as models for the evolving institution of the show trial in nonfictional courts. Yet it was precisely these idealized images that entered the courtroom in the first show trial of the Stalinist era, the so-called Shakhty Affair of 1928. On the other side of the footlights and the movie screen, the melodramatic modeling of friend and foe extended into the country's actual courtrooms, where the real-life justice administered in show trials such as the Shakhty Affair set a melodramatic stage for Stalin's Great Terror.

CHAPTER FOUR

MARBLE COLUMNS AND JUPITER LIGHTS IN THE SHAKHTY AFFAIR

By the late 1920s fictional trials, both on stage and screen, had successfully manufactured the threefold paradigm of confession, repentance, and reintegration into society that had always been lacking in actual trials of the decade. Such famous defendants as Boris Savinkov and the provocateur Okladskii commanded the attention of the Soviet public in the actual courtrooms but consistently refused either to repent of their crimes or to acknowledge the right of the Soviet Union to judge their wrongdoing.[1] The first legal case that returned the theatrical and cinematic model of the public trial to the country's courtrooms was the *Shakhtinskoe delo* or Shakhty Affair of 1928. Commonly called the first show trial of the Stalinist era, the Shakhty Affair followed to its logical end the rather diffuse and sometimes confusing call for realism in the agitsud and filmed trials: if fictional trials were intended to approximate their real-life counterparts to the highest degree possible, actual trials provided the ultimate in legal realism. The incalculably higher stakes of life and death in actual litigation gave the Shakhty Affair a realism greater than any theatrical or cinematic trial. The anticipated agitational impact on spectators seemed immeasurably more than that of a mere play or silent movie with a similar theme. So long as the enemy of the Soviet people could be compelled to identify himself, to confess, and to repent, the real courtrooms of the 1920s promised to be the most potent and, hence, were the preferred venue for legal propaganda.

As we saw in popular films of the 1920s, it was impossible to transfer the paradigm of confession, repentance, and social reintegration into a new venue without altering the paradigm itself. Shifting the mock trial's model of mythopoetic justice onto the screen redistributed the weight of each of the three elements of the paradigm, and the introduction of mythopoetic justice into actual courtroom procedure reapportioned their importance. The absolute realism of the Shakhty Affair compelled the accused, and (just as important) the spectators, to incorporate the trial's verdict, sentencing, and often fatal consequences into their understanding of the legal drama. As a result, the final element of the paradigm—social reintegration—became little more than a ritualized plea on the part of the accused, who, in forty-nine out of fifty-three cases, was expelled from Soviet society at the end of the Shakhty Affair. Regardless of the defendant's ignorance of his crimes or the sincerity of his confession, the mere fact that those occupying the chair of the accused received the label of enemy of the people necessarily led to their imprisonment or execution.

The removal of the third element from the paradigm of mythopoetic justice was neither inevitable nor predicated on the theatrical and cinematic forms of legal propaganda that came before the Shakhty Affair. Rather, the complex and often conflicting economic, political, and social forces that emerged during the New Economic Policy had by 1928 brought the Soviet Union to the brink of yet another revolution. The relative freedom of the NEP had come to an end with the institution of the first five-year plan, and the plethora of independent institutions that characterized the 1920s gave way to monolithic state-sponsored unions modeled on the increasingly totalitarian Soviet government.[2] The need to mobilize all of Soviet society toward the ambitious goals of the first five-year plan, as well as the necessity of finding a scapegoat when these goals were not reached, forced the state to find and institutionalize new rituals that could serve these ends.[3] Show trials such as the Shakhty Affair drew upon theatrical and cinematic forms of legal propaganda to manufacture the necessary enemies of the state, upon which the government and the people could blame the absence of anticipated benefits in the accelerated growth of the country's industrial production.

Before 1928 actual show trials uncovered, defined, and expelled the apparent and self-proclaimed enemy from the Soviet Union's newly formed social order. Starting with the Shakhty Affair, the enemy became invisible and was lurking in the very heart of Soviet industry and society. No longer did he follow the model of the SRs prosecuted in 1922 and proudly state his opposition to the Soviet regime; instead, he was most probably an upstanding member of society who subtly and secretly sabotaged the construction of socialism. A new model of the show trial, provided by the Shakhty Affair, proved necessary to detect these internal saboteurs and to force them to confess publicly their responsibility for any shortfalls in meeting the targets of the planned economy. The Central Committee of the Communist Party under the direction of Stalin himself encouraged this public trial of coal-mining engineers from the Donbass as the new legal model for routing the enemies of Soviet socialism.[4]

CREATING THE ENEMY

An overview of the basic events of the Shakhty Affair shows that this particular court case has much in common with its predecessors, in particular with the trial of the SRs in 1922, as well as with the trials of the Great Terror for which it would provide the model. The public proceedings of the Shakhty Affair opened on May 18, 1928, in the glare of international media. As was the case in the trial of the SRs, preparation for the public portion of the case had begun several months before with the apprehension and imprisonment of the accused, in addition to a coordinated media campaign that began two months prior to the trial's start.[5] By the time the Shakhty Affair officially began in the columned hall of the Moscow House of Soviets, the Soviet public was thoroughly familiar with the group of German and Russian engineers from the highest echelons of the Soviet coal industry, all accused of coordinating a vast network of sabotage whose roots lay outside the Soviet Union and whose branches reached across Soviet heavy industry as a whole.

The inclusion of a few German engineers among the defendants of the Shakhty Affair created understandable tension in German-Soviet relations, and as a result, a remarkably small amount of time and attention was spent on questioning the German engineers about their alleged crimes.[6] Instead, Nikolai Krylenko, who headed the prosecution of the Shakhty Affair just as he had during the trial of the SRs, put most of his effort into extracting confessions from the Russian engineers occupying the witness stand. The presiding judge, Andrei Vyshinskii, allowed Krylenko to dominate the testimony given by the accused and to conduct his interrogations in a free and easy manner.[7] As a result, the prosecution successfully extracted confessions from the majority of the men on trial and, with these confessions, managed to convict forty-nine of the accused Shakhty engineers.

In spite of the overwhelmingly successful outcome of the trial from the prosecution's point of view, the Shakhty Affair did not pass without incident. Foreign press correspondents and their Soviet counterparts were often at a loss to make sense of the murky circumstances of the crimes being examined and the confusing series of confessions, recantations, and repeated confessions that came to light during the course of testimony. Nonetheless, the Soviet media relentlessly demanded the death sentence for the Shakhty engineers, just as it had for the accused SRs in the 1922 trial. After approximately six weeks of public hearings, the Soviet court handed down its verdict on July 5, 1928: three engineers were acquitted, eleven were sentenced to death, thirty-eight were given prison sentences of lengths varying from one and a half to ten years, and a single remaining Russian engineer "fell ill . . . 'with a protective conscious reaction,'" in other words, suffered a mental breakdown during interrogation and was hospitalized. The trial's outcome was taken as proof positive of the existence of sabotage in Russian heavy industry, which initiated a series of wrecking trials that spread in a domino effect ever wider throughout Soviet industry and ever deeper into the Soviet technical intelligentsia.[8]

As this brief synopsis of the Shakhty Affair illustrates, many of the theatrical and cinematic features of the 1928 public trial were borrowed almost directly from the 1922 trial of the SRs, which had provided the reigning model of the Soviet show trial throughout the 1920s. As in the 1922 trial, the backdrop for the Shakhty Affair was the marble columned hall of the former Moscow Nobles club, with its ornate crystal chandeliers, now known as the House of Soviets. This time, however, the organizers of the trial constructed a special elevated platform on which court officials, witnesses, and the accused sat and gave testimony. Foreign press correspondents describe a courtroom modeled on the theatrical stage but ready for the movie camera. One wrote:

> Their presence [of the defending counsel], purely a matter of form, served only to enhance the scenic effects of the specially built and artificially lighted judicial dais, which was large enough to hold the fifty-one defendants, three judges, the prosecutor and his staff, a dozen lawyers, half a dozen stenographers, and a large detachment of GPU guards armed with rifles and fixed bayonets.

Another wrote:

> Sputtering Jupiter lights played on the scene, photographers and cinema cameramen maneuvered their equipment into position. . . . The gleaming white marble columns had sprouted ugly clusters of loud-speakers. Immense crystal chandeliers shimmered in the shifting lights. But the dominant note was a blatant red—red cloths on the tables on the platform, red inscriptions on the walls.[9]

The red backdrop for the Shakhty Affair provided a strong contrast with the opulence of the surrounding hall, much as in the case of the SRs' trial.

The same red banners were draped throughout the room; the same glaring lights of the media illuminated the proceedings; large loudspeakers added to the stage broadcast interrogation and testimony to the audience.

Although the camera-ready sets of the two trials were somewhat similar, the costuming of those who acted on the carefully prepared stage differed significantly. The accused SRs had dressed themselves in the romantic garb of nineteenth-century revolutionaries to gain their audience's sympathy; the engineers on trial in the Shakhty Affair donned typical workers' clothing in the hope of eliciting the sympathy of a court representing the interests of the working class, as the correspondent for *Berliner Tageblatt* noted: "The accused, in jackets, top-boots, and often without collars, look themselves quite proletarian."[10] Given that the engineers on trial all came from the upper ranks of the Soviet technical intelligentsia, their decision to dress down as proletarians shows that a small portion of the theatrical and cinematic means of representation still lay in the hands of the accused.

Comments on the costuming of the defendants were all but drowned out by the particularly strong reaction drawn by head prosecutor Krylenko with his choice of clothes, as *New York Times* correspondent Eugene Lyons noted: "Throughout the six crowded weeks of the trial [Krylenko] wore sports clothes—riding breeches, puttees, a hunting jacket. We called it a hunting outfit and its fitness for his role added to the drama of the proceedings. Krylenko, the man-hunter." As an experienced functionary in the show trials of the 1920s, Krylenko clearly chose his costume for its emblematic significance. Not only Lyons and his fellow reporters from abroad, but also Soviet newsmen, the spectators, and the accused could visually identify the head prosecutor's role as huntsman for the truth and tracker of the class enemy.[11] Since Krylenko played the leading role in the Shakhty Affair, we cannot underestimate the impact of his hunting costume on those watching the trial either live or on newsreels. The defendants changed from day to day; "Krylenko, the man-hunter" remained center stage, interrogating, improvising, and determining the shape and direction of the legal drama.

If we compare the Shakhty Affair to the trial of the SRs in terms of set and costuming, all such comparisons break down once we examine the script and the tight control Krylenko exercised over it in the later case. The SRs had successfully defied the Soviet court and maintained their opposition to the Bolshevik regime—even if they had lost their case in 1922. The mere fact that foreign defenders were allowed to enter Russia and the courtroom of the earlier trial meant that the accused SRs still had a significant amount of control in representing themselves and their case to the

Soviet court. On the contrary, the 1928 Shakhty Affair culminated in the confession of over 90 percent of the accused and took the form of "a modern morality play with Evil personified on the stage. Evil confessing, even insisting on its own evil nature."[12] Even if a small number of the defendants forgot their lines and others willfully improvised out of turn, the Shakhty Affair seldom deviated from its set script of confession and repentance. Under the strict guidance of Krylenko, each defendant methodically revealed first his criminal activities, second his counter-revolutionary sentiments, and third his ultimate goal of overthrowing the Soviet regime. Although the venue had changed and consequently the result of such testimony was imprisonment or death, those who confessed in the Shakhty Affair repeated the threefold formula of mythopoetic justice that had first found its home in the mock trial and later been modified in filmed trials of the 1920s.

The confessions of those accused in the Shakhty Affair were formulaic and rarely changed from defendant to defendant. The conventional nature of such testimony arose not only because confession within the mythopoetic formula of justice was by necessity the articulation of predetermined discourse, but also because each defendant confessed on behalf of the social class he represented, the last vestiges of the pre-revolutionary nobility. This double determination of witnesses' testimony gave the engineers on trial no choice but "to confess and to repent" and tended to undermine the apparent sincerity of their statements. Even Soviet journalists—convinced of the truth of these revelations of personal and class guilt—mockingly described the conventional and repetitious form they took:

> The following routine has been worked out. Each of the accused in the Shakhty Affair starts his testimony with an autobiographical sketch and ends with a "turning point." He wrecked, ruined, wreaked havoc, and then, he thought:
> —I really like Soviet power. I adore it. I won't wreck any more.[13]

In this passage, we observe a subtle yet highly important bifurcation in the inherent theatricality and cinematicality of the Soviet show trial. The Soviet journalist has unmasked the defendants' statements in the Shakhty Affair as melodramas in miniature, as the repetition of the only script that might have given the accused any hope of salvation. According to this view, the accused tried to hide his counter-revolutionary essence behind a theatrical fiction. The Soviet reporter and the prosecution headed by Krylenko successfully unmasked the feigned repentance to reveal the class enemy for the trial's audience. However, while the confessions by rote of the Shakhty defendants provided their only hope of acquittal, such confessions were also the only script offered to the accused by the prosecution.

The journalist's damning description of these confessions neglects to point out that the Shakhty engineers had little choice in what they said on the witness stand, that the means of theatrical and cinematic representation lay almost exclusively in Krylenko's hands, and that these melodramas of samokritika figured as an integral part in the larger drama of unmasking internal saboteurs who supposedly threatened Soviet hegemony. The theatricality of the Shakhty defendants made their statements repetitious, conventional, and hence false. Conversely, Krylenko's equally artificial theatricality affirmed his authority and the seeming authenticity of the trial's reproduction of mythopoetic justice.

Although journalists and prosecution alike questioned the sincerity of the confessions made during the trial, the testimony of the accused nonetheless proved that the good Soviet citizen was loyal above all else to the working class as represented by the Soviet government. The case of the Kolodub brothers—both tried and convicted in the Shakhty Affair—illustrates how loyalty to the state eclipsed even familial bonds. The older brother, Emel'ian, broke under Krylenko's interrogation and implicated himself and his younger sibling, Andrei, in a written confession. When Andrei was called to the defendant's bench, he questioned the elder Kolodub in a moving episode that proved the older brother scarcely grasped the meaning, let alone the consequences, of the word "counter-Revolutionary."[14] If his older brother's denunciation was not sufficiently demoralizing, Andrei Kolodub's son wrote a letter to the newspaper *Krasnyi shakhter (The Red Miner)* decrying his father's crimes and renouncing his family name:

> Knowing my father to be a full-grown enemy and a hater of workers, I add my voice to the demand of all workers to punish cruelly the counter-revolutionaries. Since I have had no familial contact with the Kolodubs for about two years and consider carrying the surname Kolodub disgraceful any longer, I am changing my surname to Shakhtin.

The son's objection to carrying the name Kolodub is understandable considering the surname entered contemporary Soviet vocabulary as a synonym for "industrial sabotage" in the word *kolodubshchina* (Kolodubitis). The thirteen-year-old Kirill created a new surname, Shakhtin, using the same word that provided the appellation for the entire trial, *shakhta* (the Russian word for "mine shaft"). Hence, a full two years before the legendary Pavlik Morozov would allegedly denounce his own father only to perish at the hands of village kulaks, the case of the Kolodub family illustrated that the good Soviet citizen's loyalties belonged not to the family but to the state.[15]

The Shakhty engineers expressed a good portion of such loyalty to the working class and the Soviet state as a desire to return to productive life as a Soviet citizen, to contribute their skills to the industry they had supposedly worked so hard to cripple through acts of sabotage. In the mock trial and feature films from before 1928, such statements indicate the promise of the Soviet state to rehabilitate the former enemy and to allow him to return to the working-class fold. However, in the Shakhty Affair, these pleas to return to the social order fell under the same rubric of false melodrama as the statements of confession and contrition that preceded them. At the end of his book on the Shakhty Affair the court's president, Vyshinskii, offered a sampling of such appeals to rejoin the country's workforce:

> "If you preserve my life and give me the chance to work, I swear to replace a hundredfold the damage I've caused," said one of the defendants.
>
> "If I can still be of use to the Soviet government, I'll make every effort to be of benefit to the maximum degree. You see, now I can overturn mountains," . . . —said another.
>
> "I've committed many mistakes and crimes. I'm not asking for anything. But I do declare—I have been reborn. I've become a new person, and I can prove it," said a third.

The religious flavor of these three statements—as seen in such expressions as "hundredfold," "overturn mountains," and "I have been reborn"—reveals another instance of bifurcated theatricality. While the defendants represented themselves as prodigal sons who should rightfully be welcomed back home by the Soviet father/state, Vyshinskii labeled them a pack of Judases who had sold their savior.[16] The court president did not allow the accused to follow the script of a good Christian's confession and joyous rebirth but, instead, exposed the Shakhty engineers by imposing his own script of Judas's betrayal and inevitable demise. Once again, the court bared the melodramatic device that the accused hoped would lead to their acquittal without threatening the larger drama of the Shakhty Affair. On the contrary, such unmasking of the hidden enemy actually gave greater credence and authenticity to the larger melodrama directed by Vyshinskii and Krylenko.

Any attempt to defend the enemies of the people in the 1928 trial was also condemned as false melodrama by prosecutors and journalists covering the case. As was the case in the many fictional trials that preceded the Shakhty Affair, the lawyers provided by the Soviet court system offered no real defense for crimes to which the accused had already confessed. Although the group of accused engineers included three Germans, the organizers of the trial did not repeat their mistake of allowing foreign defenders (who had seriously interfered with the trial of the SRs) to take part in the 1928 trial. Instead, the counsel for defense in the Shakhty Affair was made up of famous members of the pre-revolutionary Russian bar. In spite of their training in so-called bourgeois law, the defense lawyers "meticulously avoided any suggestion of doubt as to the genuineness of the confessions, or anything which might reflect on the G.P.U. . . . The total effect of their speeches, therefore, was to reinforce the state's case!" Although the counsel for defense of the Shakhty engineers played a role incomprehensible to foreign journalists familiar with the Western legal tradition, Soviet citizens, who had seen the mock trials and filmed trials of the 1920s, expected the counsel for the defense in the 1928 trial to rephrase and repeat the statements of the prosecution.[17]

Finding the correct line of defense for the Shakhty engineers must have been all but impossible for lawyers trained in pre-revolutionary traditions of legal defense, since any attempt to return to so-called bourgeois techniques of legal advocacy revived the persistent accusations of theatricalized behavior on the part of the accused. Soviet journalist Ryklin described what he labeled these "tricks" of self-defense:

> Berezovskii complains of his fate. Kalganov laments his poor education. Babenko snivels and mumbles. Andrei Kolodub poses as an honest lover of dramatic art. Emel'ian Kolodub sweetly smiles and is full of amazement.
>
> All of these are grimaces and gestures carefully thought out, strictly weighed, and possibly checked in front of a piece of mirror.
>
> All of this is a trick for self-defense.

Any engineer who refused to confess immediately earned the damning title of a "skillful actor" who employed "theatrical gestures" to act out his defense. Any defense lawyer who indeed defended his client's interests was accused of using flashy tricks to distract the audience from the truth of the defendant's confession. In short, not only the defendants but also their advocates repeated the script of earlier fictional trials on stage and screen in the testimony they gave during public hearings.[18]

The harsh sentences that followed confession, repentance, and the plea for social reintegration proved for everyone that the chances, if any, of returning from the witness stand to productive life in Soviet society were extremely slim in 1928. This held true for those on trial as well as for those watching the trial. The threefold paradigm of confession, repentance, and social reintegration had successfully been imported from fictional trials of a few years earlier into the actual courtroom of the Shakhty Affair. Nevertheless, in making this shift, the paradigm itself was truncated, its third component being all but eliminated from the paradigm of the Stalinist show trial. The importance of this alteration in the model of mythopoetic justice lay in the Soviet court's ability to command an ever larger portion of the theatrical and cinematic means of representation, not only in the actual courtroom but also in the country as a whole.

Garbage, Vermin, and Germs

A significant factor in eliminating the third element from the paradigm of mythopoetic justice was the grotesquely colorful vocabulary used to describe the accused during the Shakhty Affair. A panoply of terminology relating to disease and filth had always figured prominently in depictions of the enemy of the Soviet people, but it received detailed elaboration in the propaganda surrounding the 1928 case. By labeling the Shakhty engineers wreckers, vermin, insects, germs, human garbage, Soviet journalists effectively dehumanized the men on trial and eliminated the possibility of their rejoining Soviet society on any kind of equal footing. In particular, the conscious development of wrecking or sabotage terminology afforded a unique opportunity in the 1928 trial to combine and conflate the many such negative metaphors that had evolved more or less independently before the Shakhty Affair.

The use of dehumanizing metaphors in descriptions of the class enemy has roots in pre-revolutionary rhetoric and dates back to the earliest days of Bolshevik power. In 1918, in an article devoted to the development of competition in socialist society, Lenin himself described the enemies of Bolshevism as "these survivors of a damned capitalist society, this refuse of humanity, these hopelessly rotten and deadened limbs, this infection, plague, ulcer, inherited by socialism from capitalism." Later in the same article, he spoke of the necessity of ridding the new society "of all the dangerous insects, of the flea-swindlers, of the bedbug-rich, and so on." Four years later, the poet Dem'ian Bednyi replicated Lenin's use of the insect metaphor in one of his verses dedicated to the trial of the SRs, in which he refers to the SR Party as a cloud of "bourgeois mosquitoes of the White Guard." From the very first days after the October Revolution, metaphors of garbage, germs, and insects abounded in descriptions of the enemies of the people.[19]

The trial of the SRs elicited an especially colorful attack from Anatolii Lunacharskii who mixed and matched these tropes in his depiction of the accused. In the closing chapter of his pamphlet *Byvshie liudi (Former People)*, Lunacharskii boldly calls the entire SR Party "a stinking abscess." A few paragraphs later, he explains precisely what he means:

> The sharpest draft, the most abrupt changes from hot to cold, deep wounds are not dangerous for a person, if it were not for the entire world of germs that surrounds us, that uses the insufficient blood flow of this or that part of the organism as a result of catching cold and spreads its putrid activity into the depths of every sore. Such a germ is the SR Party. Having survived a difficult crisis, the heavily wounded country should attend to asepsis, to the complete cauterization by means of severe disinfection, of all of these saboteurs [*vrediteli*] of life.

In Lunacharskii's extended metaphor, the accused SRs are not simply a sore on the body of Soviet society that will heal if cleansed and given the proper care. They figure more perniciously as the germs that invade and infect such sores, that threaten to enter the country's bloodstream and cut short the very life of the new society if means of disinfection are not swiftly and ruthlessly applied. One page later, Lunacharskii suggests that the distribution of propaganda literature by members of the court such as himself can function as the first "means of disinfection." Nonetheless, we can imagine that those without the literary education of Lunacharskii, those incapable of separating the literary trope from that which it describes, would interpret this elaborate metaphor literally as license to exterminate those who received the label of germ.[20]

If the germ and disease metaphors received full elaboration during the trial of the SRs, the rich potential of parasite and vermin metaphors went virtually untouched until the Shakhty Affair. Much like their SR predecessors, the engineers on trial in 1928 were routinely referred to as "Former people! Garbage. Dirt. Slush."[21] Yet more frequently occurred the word *vreditel'* (wrecker, saboteur). Although the term had appeared in this context previously (as the passage from Lunacharskii illustrates), *vreditel'* acquired a new meaning in 1928 and figured with remarkable frequency and prominence in nearly every book, article, and quotation concerning the Shakhty Affair. The word *vreditel'* comes from the verb *vredit'* (to injure, harm, hurt) and originally referred to agricultural pests or vermin.[22] In an article in *Pravda* bearing the blunt title "Vrediteli," one journalist describes the origin of this omnipresent appellation:

Wrecker, this is a new word in Soviet vocabulary. Before this word, such a term didn't exist. Rather, this term was used only for insects and birds who damaged crops and destroyed wooden buildings. Wrecker, this was some kind of little beetle or grasshopper undermining young stems. Wrecker, this is some kind of worm eating away the beams of buildings, an aphid damaging vineyards. Until this time, there hasn't been such a profession among people. Those people who brought harm were not necessarily wreckers. In any case, there was not massive and professional wrecking.

Later, the author laments that "this breed of human insects" has become an all too painful reality in Soviet industry, and he describes the need to find "immunity against the infection of wrecking" to combat the capitalist West, which is "ready to send down a dark cloud of insect-like people, wreckers."[23] By mixing the metaphor of germs and disease with that of insects and wrecking, the author removes all semblance of humanity from the engineers on trial: no longer are the Shakhty defendants people with the rights and privileges of any member of society. Instead, they are harmful, infection-spreading locusts that must be exterminated and eliminated before they descend on the Soviet Union in a malignant cloud. The accused SRs suffered only sporadic and partial dehumanization through the use of such metaphors in 1922, but the defendants of the Shakhty Affair were systematically reduced to the level of unintelligent and despised life-forms by the term *vreditel'* and the associative clusters appended to it.

The vocabulary of wrecking appeared throughout Soviet press coverage of the trial and was consequently adopted by the trial's audience across the country. When polled, workers in a number of industries reproduced the calls to "clean out all the specialists with a sandblaster" and to "purge the USSR of this trash."[24] The terminology of germs and insects also had the secondary effect of expanding the net of suspicion and guilt cast by the Shakhty Affair to encompass an ever larger group of people.

Vyshinskii, in his book *Itogi i uroki shakhtinskogo dela (Outcomes and Lessons of the Shakhty Affair)*, provides an interesting example of this by-product of the mixed germ/wrecker metaphor in an explanation of the internal enemy uncovered by the Shakhty Affair. He calls the coal industry the "energetic heart of all of our economic organism" and asserts that this organism has fallen ill with the grave illnesses of "over-confidence [and] over-love of specialists." According to his analysis, the 1928 trial correctly diagnosed these illnesses, stopped their progress, and instituted necessary healing measures. Yet, long before Vyshinskii provides such a happy prognosis for the Soviet body politic, he states in the opening pages of his book that the sabotage uncovered by the Shakhty Affair was "epidemic and infectious." Given the significance of these two terms in 1928 (the year penicillin had only just been discovered), it seems doubtful that the healing measures instituted by the trial would be sufficient to halt for long the progress of the illness of wrecking.[25]

Some joyously celebrated the victory of the working class at the close of the Shakhty Affair by proclaiming, "the enemy is broken, the enemy is vanquished, the enemy is lain prostrate on the ground." Others feared that such joy was premature: "The Shakhty case is not the last trial of wreckers. We should acknowledge this bitter truth and not conceal it." Stalin himself added his voice to the chorus confirming this grim conclusion:

> We cannot consider the so-called Shakhty Affair an accident. The "Shakhty-ites" are now sitting in every branch of industry. Many of them have been caught, but far from all have been caught. . . . Bourgeois wrecking is an indubitable indicator of the fact that capitalist elements are far from putting down their weapons, that they are amassing their forces for new attacks against Soviet power.

Stalin made the connection between internal sabotage and hostile capitalist forces outside the Soviet Union seem logical and inevitable by depicting industrial wrecking as an inescapable extension of open warfare.[26]

Indeed, the trials that followed on the heels of the Shakhty Affair proved that powers abroad caused the infectious disease of wrecking to spread into other branches of Soviet industry and into the very heart of the Soviet leadership itself by the end of the 1930s. Nonetheless, the expanding web of guilt and trials in the 1930s, as historians have amply proved, was not the result of industrial espionage conducted by enemy forces.[27] Rather, the tendency of the Stalinist show trial toward infinite expansion resulted from the introduction of the rhetorical devices discussed above into the paradigm of mythopoetic justice.

CREATING THE AUDIENCE

Given the intensity and scope of the metaphors stripping the Shakhty engineers of human dignity, we have difficulty imagining that those watching the 1928 trial would identify with the accused, as spectators of fictional trials from a few years earlier apparently had. However, the paradigm of mythopoetic justice had initially evolved—in the agitsud and filmed trials—to precisely these ends. When this particular model of legal drama entered the actual courtroom, it necessarily brought with it audience identification with the accused, a feature that had been absent from actual show trials of the 1920s. No self-respecting Soviet citizen watching the SRs was expected either to identify with them or to contemplate the possibility of having committed the same counter-revolutionary crimes. Yet, those watching the Shakhty Affair were compelled to empathize with the accused engineers, even if the constructed spectacle of the trial denied the smallest amount of sympathy for those under indictment. In the Shakhty Affair the tie between the defendants in the witness stand and the spectators in the audience was just as carefully manufactured and scrupulously maintained as was the script for confession.

One of the primary means of manufacturing such empathy devoid of sympathy was the careful control over who attended the six weeks of public hearings. As was true with the SRs, the general public could gain entrance to the 1928 trial by pass only. The secret police distributed these tickets to construct an audience that would function as "an accusing chorus, mocking the pitiful attempts of some of the prisoners to defend themselves." The most important feature of this blaming chorus chosen by the GPU was not its composition but its nearly incalculable size. Each day the four thousand people who attended live hearings of the Shakhty Affair changed almost entirely, as one foreign correspondent noted: "deserving factory workers, school children, out-of-town delegations, visiting peasant groups. . . . More than 100,000, it was estimated, in this way saw a tiny segment of the proceedings." Vyshinskii placed this estimate even higher, at a grand total of over 150,000 members of the Soviet working class in attendance at the trial.

By bringing the greatest number of Soviet citizens possible into direct contact with the testimony of the Shakhty Affair, organizers of the trial hoped not only to change each individual spectator via the legal drama but also to turn these spectators into living conduits of trial propaganda who would carry the lessons they had absorbed from the courtroom into their homes and workplaces. Walter Duranty pointed out:

> The picked "audiences" at these trials automatically became channels for spreading, at a given moment determined by the authorities (i.e. Stalin), certain views and opinions which the said authorities wished to have impressed upon the nation. This "eyewitness" reporting by word of mouth and vivid personal description proved much more effective than newspaper or radio propaganda.[28]

Although Duranty's irony betrays his own anti-Soviet (and more specifically, anti-Stalinist) sentiments years after the trial transpired, his analysis nonetheless describes accurately the effect trial organizers expected the mass audience of the Shakhty Affair to have. When we add the vast print, radio, and newsreel campaigns to these living channels of Shakhty propaganda, we realize that although the trial's initial audience within the Soviet Union numbered approximately one hundred thousand, its effective audience was countless, encompassing the entire Soviet nation. If we choose to include foreign audiences who learned of the Shakhty Affair in the news coverage of international press correspondents in attendance at the public hearings, then the audience for the 1928 trial extends even farther to span the entire globe.

Sheer numbers were not the only salient feature of the trial's audience within the Soviet Union. True to the paradigm of mythopoetic justice, participation in the events of the trial also figured as a defining feature of the audience. Propaganda surrounding the trial described the involvement of the working class in all phases of the Shakhty Affair, particularly in raising and lowering the curtain on the intricately constructed legal melodrama. Common workers had allegedly uncovered the original sabotage that resulted in litigation, demanding that the wreckers be called to account in court. As in mock trials of only a few years before, four engineers seated on the court's raised dais visually represented the participation of proletarian spectators in judging the defendants.[29] These four representatives of the trial's immense audience assured the actual instigators and judges of the trial, the Soviet proletariat, that the court protected their class interests and ultimately would carry out their will. Although the true nature of spectators' interest and willingness to participate in the Shakhty Affair is impossible to determine, the myth of proletarian involvement in the trial produced some of its most passionate propaganda and functioned as a rallying cry for Soviet reporters:

> The millions of proletarians who groaned for centuries under the yoke of the tsars, nobles, factory owners and mine owners.
> The millions who fought for a better life, bathed in blood.
> The millions who rose up and utterly crushed the capitalist order in our country.
> The millions building socialism.
> They are passing judgment.

Just like the audience of the agitsud and in filmed trials, spectators of the Shakhty Affair simultaneously occupied a multiplicity of roles as they watched the legal drama unfold. They acted as police, judge, and jury both in the courtroom and beyond its confines. Similar to the angry mob at the June 20, 1922, demonstration during the SR trial, the audience of the Shakhty Affair broke through the fourth wall, entered the courtroom, and demanded the death sentence for the accused engineers.[30]

The righteous indignation of the Soviet proletariat, whether spontaneous, manufactured, or some combination of the two, does little to explain how the condemning chorus of the trial's spectators could actually empathize with the Shakhty engineers whose death they so noisily demanded. Certainly, the element of audience identification seems in the Shakhty Affair to have receded from its prominent position in mock trials, whose fictional plaintiffs ceaselessly repeated that they were no different from those who watched and judged them. This reduction in the visibility of audience empathy arises in part because the discourse of samokritika had been fully articulated in Soviet propaganda in 1928.[31] It proved sufficient merely to invoke this ritual of simultaneous self-objectification and self-correction in the Shakhty Affair for audience members to occupy, at the same time, the seemingly contradictory positions of the subject and object of such harsh judgment during the trial. As a result, although propaganda around the 1928 case seemed to be devoted exclusively to removing all sympathy for the Shakhty engineers from the viewing public, the rhetoric of samokritika, which the defendants themselves used and the trial propaganda repeated, constructed the empathy necessary to induce spectators to reproduce this ritualized self-judgment in themselves. Hence, the repertoire of roles reproduced by the audience on the other side of the raised stage of the Shakhty Affair included not only those of police, judge, and jury, but also that of the accused enemy of the people himself.

Lest the audience, scattered across the entire expanse of the Soviet Union, fail to understand these multiple roles, the propaganda campaign of 1928 included a number of short documentary films and newsreels that took the legal drama of the Shakhty Affair into any village or club, no matter how distant from Moscow, that was lucky enough to have a movie projector.[32] At first glance, these brief works seem to hold little interest since they sometimes lack the theatrical and even the cinematic polish of the Shakhty Affair itself, as well as the narrative unity of later trial documentaries from the sound era. In particular, the *Sovkino-Zhurnal* newsreels of the trial offer a predictable series of shots of the prosecution ardently and convincingly making its case, followed by shots of the defendants hanging their heads in shame and interspersed with placard-like intertitles denouncing the "Destroyers of the Soviet economy."[33] The short feature *Delo ob ekonomicheskom kontrrevoliutsii v Donbasse (An Affair of Counter-revolution in the Donbass)* followed this conventional trial footage with an equally conventional depiction of Soviet industry striding ahead now that it had been taken out of the hands of saboteurs.

Yet if we compare these 1928 newsreels to Dziga Vertov's 1922 coverage of the trial of the SRs in *Kinopravda,* a startling new message appears in these seemingly average newsclips.

First, the *Sovkino-Zhurnal* newsreels show the rigidly hierarchical organization of the Shakhty Affair as opposed to the more egalitarian staging of the earlier trial. Vertov's 1922 newsreels depicted the almost intimate atmosphere of the earlier trial, in which audience and court members occupied the same space and shared similar behavior. In striking contrast, the raised platform of the later trial supported an unbroken line of massive wooden tables, standing before equally massive wooden chairs, whose backs rose approximately a foot above the heads of court officials. The movie cameras looked up at ordered stacks of legal briefs on these tables, stacks so tall as to obscure occasionally the imposing figures of authority seated behind them. Those watching the newsreels replicated the gaze of spectators who attended the trial's public hearings: the defendants were approximately on the same level as the viewer, but one had actually to look up through the hierarchy to see the judge, president, and people's representatives at the trial. Although the proletarian spectator had been told that he acted as police, judge, and jury, the physical separation of the audience from the court visually represented his true place—at the bottom of the hierarchical legal drama taking place. The spectacle maintained the rhetoric of audience participation, compelling its viewers to reproduce internally the roles of police, judge, and jury; but the hierarchical organization of the court, as seen in these newsreels, made it unequivocally clear to the spectator that his actual role in court was closer to that of the accused, whose position in the courtroom approximated the spectator's own.

Second, the *Sovkino-Zhurnal* reports served to homogenize and discipline the audience, that is, to reduce the many individual viewers—with their own personal reactions in Vertov's newsreels from 1922—to a single, obedient, spectating mass. In *Kinopravda,* Vertov focused on viewers at the SR trial (who, oddly enough, seemed more interested in their cigarettes and the other people around them than in the testimony of the trial). In the radically different, rigidly hierarchical depiction of *Sovkino-Zhurnal,* the audience occupied orderly, parallel rows of chairs with all eyes fixed on the raised dais at the front of the room. The personal features of individual audience members disappeared, and in their place an anonymous but well-organized viewing mass emerged. Those who watched the close-ups of the attentive, disciplined audience in these newsreels could have no doubts as to what their own response to this spectacle should be. No degree of distraction, dissent, or humor was allowed. The rhetoric of the Shakhty Affair repeated stock phrases brought from the avant-garde theater into legal propaganda by the mock trial, such as the need for audience participation, improvisation, and spontaneity. Whereas the theatrical and cinematic spectacle that grew out of this rhetoric mandated that spectators take an active, creative part in the melodrama, it utterly eliminated any possibility to improvise or react spontaneously. Instead, newsreels of the 1928 trial dictated a script to the trial's audience that was just as inflexible as the script imposed on the accused Shakhty engineers.[34]

That both audience and accused performed entirely predetermined scripts in the Shakhty Affair reinforces the proximity of these two within the emerging paradigm of the Stalinist show trial. The simultaneous condemnation of but identification with the enemies of the people occupying the witness stand compelled the trial's spectators to undergo the ritual of samokritika, so that they might detect and correct any counter-revolutionary tendencies lurking within themselves. In essence, this was no more than a translation of the mythopoetic justice of earlier agitsudy and filmed trials to the actual courtroom at the end of the 1920s. However, the translation itself changed the very model it implemented by separating sympathy from empathy, two elements that

The audience of the Shakhty Affair in the great columned hall of the Moscow House of Soviets. From *Sovkinozhurnal* no. 14, 1928.

previously had gone hand in hand in the earlier fictional trials. In light of the significantly more destructive nature of the crimes for which the Shakhty engineers were indicted and the increasingly lethal consequences such crimes entailed, the elimination of sympathy from the viewer's script guaranteed the protection not only of Soviet industry but also of the viewer himself.

MISSED CUES AND FUMBLED PROPS

The emerging paradigm of the Stalinist show trial makes evident the theatrical and cinematic modeling of the Shakhty Affair as a whole, something which Soviet propaganda of the time did not so much downplay as ignore altogether. Contrary to their Soviet counterparts, foreign newspapermen who attended the public hearings from May through July 1928 commented on the spectacular nature of the Shakhty Affair—in particular, on the missed cues and fumbled props that showed how Krylenko and Vyshinskii's control over the trial was not as tight as court officials might have wished. The coverage of foreign correspondents afforded a rare opportunity to uncover the show trial's theatrical and cinematic devices, which would be hidden entirely from view by the time of the Great Terror eight years later. The initial transferral of mythopoetic justice from the stage and screen of five years before into the actual courtroom required rehearsal and refinements from actors and directors alike. In the words of Eugene Lyons, "When half a hundred men are corralled for an ordeal of death in the sight of the entire world, the best-planned melodrama may go askew."[35]

Foreign reporters identified the largest crack in the trial's facade as the accused engineers' lack of credibility. Soviet propagandists blamed the defendants themselves for the formulaic, melodramatic, and hence less than convincing nature of their testimony. The foreigners in attendance such as Lyons looked elsewhere for an explanation of such clearly scripted confessions:

> I doubt in half a hundred men from the same social layers in any other race could have done so well as these Russians. Certainly no other race would have offered so much natural histrionics. Those who confessed and willingly played Krylenko's game tended to overplay their roles. With an artist's instinct for emphasis they built themselves into arch-traitors, into personifications of the bourgeois intellectual and everything communists despise. The Slavic talent for hyperbole was among the things most fully demonstrated in this demonstration trial.[36]

Lyons's sarcasm toward Slavic histrionics aside, this passage points to the many problems that would arise because of differences between Krylenko's script for the trial and the defendants' understanding of that script. Poor casting and shoddy rehearsal proved problematic and often combined to render defendants' statements close to absurd.

Some defendants simply refused to produce anything at all resembling a confession while sitting in the witness box. A certain Rabinovich, who figured as a prominent functionary in the Soviet mining bureaucracy and had allegedly worked as the head of the "Moscow Center" of sabotage, calmly asserted his innocence throughout questioning. In the face of direct accusations of wrecking, Rabinovich had the courage to confront his accuser:

> Mukhin declared under oath that he handed Rabinovitch a bribe for himself and further bribes for distribution among other defendants.
>
> Rabinovitch walked over to within two feet of Mukhin and, peering straight into his eyes, said, "Tell me, please, about whom are you speaking, about me or somebody else?"
>
> "I am talking about you," Mukhin replied.
>
> "Why do you lie, eh?" Rabinovitch exclaimed. "Who told you to lie? You know you gave me no money."
>
> Mukhin, pastier and paler than before, repeated his story like a tutored automaton.[37]

Since Rabinovich's testimony came late in the trial, his confrontation of the informer Mukhin and his refusal to confess created a serious rupture in the mounting melodrama. Krylenko ultimately proved incapable of forcing Rabinovich to follow the script. Such recalcitrant witnesses simply did not testify in later trials of the Great Terror characterized by total confession.

If Rabinovich was either too stubborn or too intelligent to play a part that would prove his guilt, other defendants confessed so willingly and in such evident ignorance of the meaning of their own words that Soviet and foreign reporters alike had to laugh at their statements. The engineer Eliadze confessed with such zeal that he implicated the entire Russian technical intelligentsia in wrecking: "I'm not the only guilty one. All engineers are the same. We are all created in the same image . . . the entire technical staff educated in the spirit of the old order, with a very small exception, are of the same ilk and are equally unreliable for the Soviet order." Later, still on the witness bench, Eliadze described his own "turning point," which brought him to confess. During a visit to Moscow, he saw the public trolleys running to and fro in the streets and realized that Soviet power was not as bad as he first imagined.[38] Krylenko had made a serious mistake in casting Eliadze as an informer in the Shakhty Affair since he lacked all credibility as a witness in the case.

Although we have no incontrovertible evidence, it is likely that grueling interrogations and torture first arose as techniques for rehearsing defendants during the Shakhty Affair.[39] According to some historians, the prosecution had just begun to learn coercive techniques of extracting and scripting confession: "These were [Krylenko's] first steps towards staging a trial, for the first time the 'repentance' of the accused was extracted." Vyshinskii also took part in directing the trial during public hearings, and he often called for recesses that allowed Krylenko to remind witnesses of their proper role. In the words of Reswick: "the memories of the accused began to snap, causing wide cracks in the rising structure of the frame-up. In moments of embarrassment Vyshinskii would get out from under by declaring a recess. In due time these intermissions came to be known as 'rehearsal.'" In spite of whatever torture or coercion took place behind the scenes of the Shakhty Affair, only thirty of the fifty-three accused engineers, that is, slightly over 50 percent, confessed.[40] This percentage certainly outstrips that of the SR trial, in which only two defector/informers from the SR Party pleaded guilty. Nonetheless, later trials would end with the confessions of each and every one of the accused, which shows that trial organizers learned much from their casting and rehearsal mistakes in 1928.

The ineffectiveness of the prosecution's rehearsal techniques came to light in the most vivid example of a botched performance in the Shakhty Affair. The engineer Skorutto, who supposedly took part in the Moscow circle of saboteurs with Rabinovich, originally refused to confess in public. After sufficient rehearsal of an unknown kind behind the scenes, Skorutto capitulated and admitted to wrecking. As it happened, his wife attended that day's session, and upon hearing her husband's confession, she cried out, "It's a lie! Kolia, why are you doing this!"[41] Skorutto immediately retracted his initial statement and Krylenko asked for a court recess. After several days away from the witness stand, Skorutto returned to uphold his original confession, predictably expressing his desire to return to the Soviet workforce.[42] Although we can only imagine what prompted Skorutto to confess either the first or the second time, the statement of another defendant named Babenko gives us a good indication. When Babenko recanted his confession as Skorutto did, he alluded to coercive interrogation techniques that prompted such self-denunciation: "I scarcely knew what I signed . . . I was driven to distraction by threats, threats, so I signed . . . I tried to withdraw it before the trial, but . . . but. . . ."[43] In the cases of Babenko and Skorutto, Krylenko had chosen to put on the stage of the Shakhty Affair men who were either not yet prepared or altogether unable to play the role of the contrite penitent. Such deviations from the melodramatic script of the trial proved to Soviet reporters that the accused engineers were indeed culpable; to foreign correspondents, they suggested the opposite.

Those who represented the international media also expressed skepticism at the physical evidence or props that were introduced into the trial's public hearings. In his account, Lyons tells how "A raincoat, sent from Germany as a 'signal' for sabotage" was clumsily introduced into the courtroom. By the standards of Western correspondents, such physical evidence held little power to convince: "We waited in vain for a genuine piece of impersonal and unimpeachable testimony—an intercepted letter perhaps, a statement or document that did not carry the suspicion of G.P.U. extortion. The 'far-reaching international intrigue' never did emerge."[44] Rather than strengthen the state's case against the alleged saboteurs, such feeble efforts to substantiate the indictments had the opposite effect on foreign newspapermen. Although some observers upheld the validity of the charges and confessions during the trial, a larger portion of the international media looked incredulously upon the drama of justice being staged for them.[45]

The commentary of the foreign press emphasized the staging mistakes made during the Shakhty Affair and pointed to the explicitly theatrical and cinematic model of fictional trials that was first brought into the actual courtroom in 1928. To their credit, Soviet journalists neither ignored nor diminished the missed cues and fumbled props pointed out by their Western counterparts. However, Soviet reporters took the very same incidents that the outside world had discredited and used them as yet another means of confirming the trial's authority for spectators within the country. By 1928 the theatrical and cinematic means of representation lay almost entirely in the hands of the Soviet state, and any attempt to deviate from the totalizing script of the Shakhty Affair was automatically corrected and transformed into conformity to the paradigm of mythopoetic justice. Much of the success of the Shakhty Affair in first articulating the discourse of the Stalinist show trial lay precisely in the script's ability to take any testimony, no matter how good, bad, or irrelevant, and still convict the engineers on trial.

The totalizing and ever expanding discourse of the Shakhty Affair made it what one historian has called the dress rehearsal for later show trials of the 1930s.[46] During the decade following 1928, each successive show trial would build upon the foundation of accusations and confessions of the trial preceding it, honing the theatrical and cinematic techniques of the Stalinist show trial to virtual perfection. What started with an obscure group of mining engineers in the Donbass coal region eventually reached such revolutionary leaders as Rykov, Tomskii, and Bukharin in the purge trials of 1936–1938. Only when the hostility of the capitalist West resulted in open gunfire at the start of the Second World War did the ever widening circle of sabotage, espionage, and suspicion cease to find its stage in the columned hall of the House of Soviets.

Although later cases would hide the fundamentally theatrical and cinematic nature of the Stalinist show trial, the Shakhty Affair still betrayed the fact that the paradigm of mythopoetic justice that was first developed in the mock trial and later augmented in filmed trials provided the model for the legal drama of 1928. In contrast to the 1922 trial of the SRs, which set the standard for Soviet show trials of the NEP, the means of representation lay almost exclusively in the hands of the Soviet state as represented by court officials and the prosecution during the Shakhty Affair. As a result, the alterations that took place in the paradigm of mythopoetic justice during translation into the actual courtroom served to strengthen the state's case against the enemy of the people and to guarantee the outcome of the trial in the courtroom and beyond. By labeling the Shakhty engineers germs, vermin, and human garbage, by showing their confessions to be falsely melodramatic, and by forcing spectators to empathize with an enemy that commanded no sympathy whatsoever, the court of the Shakhty Affair compelled the entire country to rout out the enemy wherever he might be hidden. The intense realism of the Shakhty Affair also forced spectators to acknowledge that anyone who should so much as fall under suspicion of wrecking risked expulsion from the social order, if not death. If we choose to doubt the effectiveness of bringing this theatrical and cinematic paradigm into the Shakhty Affair, we need only to think of the startling successes of the collectivization and the industrialism in the Soviet economy that accompanied the show trials of the next decade.

The connection between the Stalinist show trial and avant-garde Russian theater from the first two decades of the twentieth century might seem far-fetched at first glance. On closer examination, however, the Shakhty Affair proves the ability of the Stalinist show trial to fulfill the extremely ambitious if not utopian goals of avant-garde theatrical theorists. Plans for a Dionysian, creative, or proletarian theater that would spill into everyday life, that would embrace ever larger groups of people, that would transform social life into an aesthetic endeavor never achieved these goals within the theater proper. Yet the Stalinist show trial invaded all of Soviet reality, engulfed an ever larger part of the population, and changed society into a vast arena for fabricated indictment, confession, and contrition. Much as the theatrical experiments of the 1920s ended in the dictatorship of the director in the Russian theater, the political experiments of the same time ended in Stalin's dictatorship of the Soviet state. By the 1930s, Soviet statecraft had become Soviet stagecraft: those who wrote, directed, and staged the script controlled the actors as well as the audience.

CHAPTER FIVE

THE REDOUNDING RHETORIC
OF LEGAL SATIRE

Modernist artistic theory played a vital role in helping to articulate the patterns of mythopoetic justice that appeared in propaganda theaters, popular movie houses, and actual courtrooms during the 1920s. Yet the innovative artistic practice, usually associated with modernism after the revolution, was all but absent from the legal spectacles that appeared in all three venues. Contemporary censors recognized that many agitsudy and agitfilms had forgone formal innovation and artistic polish for the sake of a clearly comprehensible, politically correct message. In spite of the aesthetic crudeness of these works, the censors of Glavrepertkom regularly approved them for consumption by the Soviet Union's broad viewing masses. As a result, the melodramatic plays and films that provided models of legal drama for the Shakhty Affair rarely fell under the rubric of avant-garde art.

Nonetheless, as the breadth and diversity of the materials attest, the ideas of lawful judgment, revolutionary justice, samokritika (self-criticism), and chistka (purging) proliferated in all areas of Soviet society and culture during the 1920s, including the artistic avant-garde. On one hand, literary and dramatic trials occurred frequently throughout the decade and helped to define the ever changing cultural institutions of the 1920s. On the other hand, the work of some of the decade's most visible playwrights and film directors incorporated these legal concepts and reflected another aspect of the developing legal consciousness of post-revolutionary Russia. For example, Lev Kuleshov's two cinematic masterpieces from the 1920s—*Neobychainye prikliucheniia Mistera Vesta v strane bol'shevikov (The Extraordinary Adventures of Mr. West in the Land of the Bolsheviks)* of 1924 and *Po zakonu (By the Law)* of 1926—both climax in sensational and shocking trial scenes. Likewise, all three of Vladimir Maiakovskii's plays composed after the revolution, *Misteriia-*

buff (Mystery-Bouffe) (1918, 1921), *Klop (Bedbug)* (1927), and *Bania (Bathhouse)* (1930), incorporate the metaphors of vermin and germs that played a central role in judging between friends and enemies during the decade. In addition, Nikolai Erdman's two plays, *Mandat (Mandate)* of 1925 and *Samoubiitsa (Suicide)* of 1932, explore the appropriation of the vocabulary of legal mythopoesis by those against whom it was employed. An examination of these influential yet ambiguous works will help us to discern the relationship between the legal mythopoesis discussed in preceding chapters and the artistic avant-garde on stage and screen that originally fostered its development.

The present study has until now been devoted to instances of lowbrow culture, but discussing highbrow culture in the context of the emerging institution of the show trial serves two important functions. First, examining works by Kuleshov, Maiakovskii, and Erdman allows us to see that the ideas, images, and terminology of legal mythopoesis did not necessarily lead to show trials such as the Shakhty Affair. On the contrary, unmasking the hidden enemy or forcing him into samokritika could take on a number of different forms and serve a variety of ends much less clear than those previously discussed. Second, exploring the work of these authors in light of legal mythopoesis adds a new dimension to our understanding of the demise of the Russian avant-garde at the end of the 1920s. In the first half of the decade, modernist films and plays unmasking the hidden enemy or compelling his samokritika were positively received and became part of the era's dramatic and cinematic canons. As the 1920s came to an end, however, works that dared to construct their own trials and to render their own judgments met increasingly hostile reviews from critics and censors, who pushed all three of these artists to the margins of Soviet high culture (and, in Maiakovskii's case, beyond). Although the modernist agenda laid the foundation for the institution of the show trial, legal mythopoesis in the wake of the Shakhty Affair wanted nothing to do with modernism.

The most visible difference between legal melodrama on stage and screen and the avant-garde experimentation of Kuleshov, Maiakovskii, and Erdman—beyond their relative positions within the artistic canon—was one of genre. In the venues of high culture, legal judgment and unmasking the country's enemies tended to take the form of satire, which like melodrama stimulated heated debate among those in search of appropriate genres for revolutionary art. Notwithstanding the long tradition of satire on Russia's professional stage and the genre's success in professional theaters after 1917, the viability of satire in Soviet theater and literature had fallen into question by the end of the 1920s.[1] Soviet critics' discomfort with the defiantly chaotic and hybrid nature of satire was entirely understandable in the context of dramatic art devoted to revolutionary propaganda. By its very definition, satire resists the clear ideology, teleology, and closure that is found in melodrama and that is required by mythopoetic justice. In place of melodrama's stock characters and formulaic poetic justice, satire offers carnivalization of both content and form. The satirical play borrows characters from the reality beyond the footlights and appropriates a mélange of literary and scenic forms for their depiction. This dual parody of form and content produces friction between stage and life, which gives theatrical satire its didactic edge.[2]

In a 1929 debate that appeared on the pages of *Literaturnaia gazeta,* proponents of satire described the genre's educational function using the same tropes of personal and social hygiene that had developed in conjunction with samokritika and chistka. The ongoing discussion of satire's usefulness in Soviet culture focused on its ability "to cleanse [*raschishchat'*] the consciousness in order to prepare it for a reconstruction unexampled in the whole world."[3] Artists such as Kuleshov, Maiakovskii, and Erdman pushed early Soviet legal images and rhetoric toward ever greater satiric carnivalization in an effort to aid in the cleansing process. However, artistic strictures and political demands tugged in the opposite direction, and by the early 1930s satire and satirists alike were purged from Soviet drama and film.

Satirists who borrowed the concepts and jargon of mythopoetic justice for plays and films at the end of the 1920s committed the dangerous act of toying with an already fixed formula. The ambivalent reviews of *By the Law* and the banning of *Bathhouse* and *Suicide* illustrate the displeasure that such satirical experimentation aroused. The demise of the Russian avant-garde at the end of the 1920s, the institution of the monolithic Writer's Union in 1932, and the implementation of socialist realism as the country's reigning aesthetic in 1934 are well-documented moments in the story of Stalin's cultural revolution. The fate of the avant-garde experimentation of Kuleshov, Maiakovskii, and Erdman repeats the story told by historians and literary scholars about Stalin's consolidation of cultural hegemony. At the same time, the disappearance of such explorations into the legal concepts associated with show trials demonstrates that the very venues responsible for the creation of mythopoetic justice were excluded from refining and elaborating its threefold paradigm by 1930. Instead, artists who dared to tamper with the set formula for detecting the hidden enemy and compelling his confession, as in the Shakhty Affair, were themselves forced to confess the error of their ways and were denied all hope of contributing to the legal sphere, of which their works had once been an integral part.

The Cleansing Flood of Mystery-Bouffe

All three of Maiakovskii's major plays from the 1920s literalize the metaphors of germs, vermin, and parasites, which provided the tropes necessary not only for rendering mythopoetic justice but also for debating satire's utility during the decade. Maiakovskii embraced this associative cluster with unusual enthusiasm, most probably because of his own obsession with personal hygiene. According to one contemporary, the playwright "was a maniac for cleanliness and felt an almost pathological fear of infection. He washed his hands an unusual number of times a day, and whenever he was away from home, he used the soap he carried in his [own] soap holder." It comes as no surprise that someone who displayed what psychologists now label obsessive-compulsive behavior would adopt and expand the metaphors of social hygiene in his writing. For example, in a 1923 article entitled "Mozhno li stat' satirikom?" ("Is it possible to become a satirist?") Maiakovskii answered this question in the affirmative and encouraged aspiring satirical writers to realize "the possibility to clean [pochistit'] the Soviet 'interior' more seriously" in their writing.[4] In Mystery-Bouffe Maiakovskii took this advice to heart and actualized the implications of the hygiene metaphor that promised to clean the dirt from Soviet society.

As the playwright's first drama written in service of the revolution, Mystery-Bouffe: A Heroic, Epic, and Satiric Representation of Our Epoch enjoyed success on the stage of the Meyerhold Theater primarily because of Maiakovskii's skillful use of the satirist's traditional tools. The playwright mixed the genres of medieval mystery and opera-bouffe, as the play's title indicates; he incorporated topical material that would, according to his own instructions, be changed in subsequent productions; and he lampooned the bourgeois and imperialist West in figures such as French premier Georges Clemenceau and British prime minister David Lloyd George.[5] However, a large part of the play's success as satire was because Maiakovskii not only conceived of Mystery-Bouffe as a satirical cleansing of post-revolutionary society but also portrayed this cleansing in the action of the play. The plot is extremely simple: a flood, symbolic of worldwide revolution, swallows up the earth, and all that remains of humankind are seven pairs of the bourgeois Clean and seven pairs of the proletariat Unclean. Maiakovskii places the hygiene metaphor at the very heart of his drama by reworking the biblical story of the flood into a modern-day mystery of Every Proletariat.[6] As an elemental force beyond the control of all the characters in the play, Unclean or Clean, revolution surges from country to country, east and west, north and south, in a planetary tidal wave. The deluge washes away the bourgeoisie and all its evils, leaving a world cleansed of capitalism and purified for the building of communism. In order to survive the flash flood, the Unclean build an ark and overthrow the oppressive rule of the Clean on their way to the promised land.

At first glance, Maiakovskii seems to confuse his labels for the two choruses in the play and to contradict the expected aftermath of a revolutionary flood. If the deluge cleanses the world and purifies humanity, why do only those labeled dirty, impure, and Unclean ultimately survive its bath? Maiakovskii uses this contradiction to contrast the two meanings of *chistyi* (physically clean and spiritually pure). The chorus of the Unclean has the grimy fingernails and thick calluses of the working class: it is unwashed in the literal sense of the word. Despite the actual dirt that covers the Unclean, their hearts and minds are immaculate. Conversely, the chorus of the Clean is comprised of well-groomed, fashionably dressed, delicately perfumed ladies and gentlemen, with souls fouled and dirtied by capitalism. The external cleanliness of the Clean superficially covers their spiritual filth. Maiakovskii has chosen the labels for the play's two choruses not solely out of a love of irony but also to unmask the inverse relationship between the characters' external and internal purity.

Although the Unclean are actually far cleaner than their bourgeois oppressors, they nonetheless undertake a journey to purify themselves further. The Unclean pass from hell, into heaven, and through *chistilishche* (purgatory), which they themselves must tidy up in order to become the masters of earth and builders of a worldly paradise. The dénouement takes place as the Unclean collectively labor to restore order in *Razrukha* (the Land of Ruin) and to construct the new, socialist Eden by the sweat of their own brows. Coincidentally, Maiakovskii includes a laundress and chimney sweep among the Unclean to illustrate their role as the janitors of the planet. When the Unclean enter the Land of Ruin, one of their number explains their custodial duty: "What should we do? We need to clean up [*raschistit*]." Although the flood of revolution swept uncontrollably over the Unclean at the play's beginning, they now make a conscious decision to sanitize the planet and make "The path even, smooth, and clean [*chist*]." Maiakovskii underscores the agency of the Unclean in constructing the earthly paradise, contrasting them with their lazy, freeloading, Clean counterparts.[7]

Maiakovskii's use of terminology for personal and domestic hygiene in *Mystery-Bouffe* suggests the closely related metaphor of parasites sucking the lifeblood of the working class. In an article previewing the 1918 production of the play, Lunacharskii provides this designation for the Unclean to which Maiakovskii only alludes by describing *Mystery-Bouffe* as "a cheerful, symbolic voyage of the working class which gradually frees itself from its parasites after the Revolutionary flood."[8] As the experience of the Shakhty Affair would attest almost ten years later, parasites became increasingly difficult to exterminate and germs ever harder to disinfect as the 1920s progressed. Nonetheless, during the era of *Mystery-Bouffe*, eliminating the enemies of the revolution seemed as simple, inevitable, and permanent as the flood imagery in the play implied. By realizing the very metaphor for satire in the action of *Mystery-Bouffe,* Maiakovskii created a play that denounced the old way of life and pointed the way to revolutionary consciousness, much like an agitsud.

During the period of revolution and civil war in which *Mystery-Bouffe* was produced, Maiakovskii's creative interpretation of the terminology for describing the friends and enemies of Soviet power elicited enthusiastic praise. One critic boldly claimed that *Mystery-Bouffe* created "the style of new theatrical writing, the rhythm of the new theatrical Revolution."[9] The clear line separating the play's dramatis personae into good and bad characters reflected the belief that the friends and foes of the new country were easily discernible, as well as the conviction that each citizen of the Soviet Union displayed outward signs that corresponded accurately to his political demeanor, be it benevolent or hostile. Although Maiakovskii's play included a few revolutionary turncoats, they plainly belonged to the enemy camp and would be swept away in the flood of revolution along with their supposedly Clean colleagues. The Uncleans' spontaneous judgment of their oppressors functioned in the play as a revolutionary samosud and reflected the elemental and spontaneous notion of proletarian justice popular at the time. Because of its formal innovation and allegorical cleverness, the literalization of metaphors for social cleanliness in Maiakovskii's first play coincided with and contributed to the formation of revolutionary justice in the first years after October 1917.

MR. WEST AND THE MOCK TRIAL

Mystery-Bouffe's simple division of friends from enemies became considerably more complicated at the beginning of the NEP. By 1924, the year in which Kuleshov's feature film *The Extraordinary Adventures of Mr. West in the Land of the Bolsheviks* appeared, the number and variety of enemies of the Soviet state had increased, as had their wile and secretiveness. The climactic trial scene in *Mr. West* uses these ever more complex ideas of proletarian legality in a somewhat convoluted way. The film's courtroom drama differs markedly from those in *Saba, The Parisian*

Cobbler, or *The Government Bureaucrat,* since *Mr. West* does not pretend to depict a legitimate Soviet tribunal. Instead, the trial at the end of *Mr. West* parodies the legitimate organs of Soviet justice in order to arouse the simultaneous laughter and indignation of the film's audience. *Mr. West* takes the imagery and legal ritual of a revolutionary tribunal out of their original context and places them where the viewer expects them least. The resulting juxtaposition serves above all to critique those who would use proletarian justice to their own, bourgeois advantage. However, as was true of parodic trials in general, the film's critique ultimately redounds upon the images and rituals of Soviet justice themselves.

In the fascination with Hollywood that gripped the silent movie industry in the Soviet Union, Kuleshov introduced an American-style adventure story and American cinematic techniques into *Mr. West,* which provided a working laboratory for the director's ground-breaking experiments in film editing and acting.[10] Ironically, Kuleshov's Americanization in *Mr. West* served to ridicule the film's American title character and to mock the naive opinions held by such Americans about Soviet Russia. Because of such ludicrous stereotypes, John West, the president of the YMCA on vacation in Bolshevik Moscow, falls prey to a band of supposedly communist bandits.[11] After a series of hilarious Hollywood-style chase scenes and high-wire stunts, this gang of nefarious Nepmen stage a mock trial to frighten West into handing over ever increasing amounts of money. As the designation of mock trial suggests, Kuleshov preserved the forms of a revolutionary tribunal from the early 1920s, which would be easily recognizable to the film's original audience.[12] The kangaroo court in the film is composed of three people—a president, a secretary, and a public prosecutor—who organize their papers, pens, and ink behind a large rectangular table, just as in real-life trials or agitsudy of the era. In addition to the setting the ritual of the court also follows a Soviet model: first the court's secretary reads the trumped-up accusation against West; then the public prosecutor provides eloquent, arm-waving testimony as to West's guilt; and finally the highest measure of punishment, the "Death sentence," is handed down to the cowering defendant.

In spite of its revolutionary form, *Mr. West*'s mock court is peopled by decidedly counter-revolutionary specimens. Instead of true Bolshevik judges (represented in the film by the leather-jacketed Chekist who ultimately rescues West from his kidnappers), the court is populated by a sly pack of former people, costumed to represent West's stereotype of a Bolshevik. They include the déclassé "Count" Zhban (who directs the action of the mock court from atop a staircase), a prostitute named "the Countess" (who clings to West and cues his terror), and several petty thieves and pickpockets. By the end of the mock trial, poor John West seems a hapless victim whose ignorance and naiveté have left him vulnerable to Zhban's gang. The parodic trial reveals the greed of these criminals, who costume themselves as stereotypical Russian outlaws, threaten execution by the ax, and appropriate the forms of the Soviet court for their own financial gain.

If *Mr. West* were simply another legal melodrama, the viewer would expect John West to be yet one more of the genre's long-suffering heroes, who must endure valiantly until the tables turn in his favor. Indeed, poetic justice is served by the end of the film, but John West follows neither the pattern of the defiant revolutionary nor that of the obedient Soviet citizen temporarily victimized by an unjust trial. Instead, Kuleshov's satire shows John West as a bespectacled, gullible coward, who shakes in his shoes, hides his face from the exaggerated gestures of his accusers, submits to the farcical court without a fight, and pays whatever bribe is necessary to secure his freedom. The camera is positioned behind West's back during most of the trial scene, allowing the moviegoer to approximate the defendant's view of the court. When West first sees the shirtless executioner wielding his oversized ax, he hides his head in the Countess's bosom, and the camera shows the costumed criminals laughing at the lily-livered West. This shift in the camera's perspective undercuts any sympathy for the accused American by allowing the viewer to see behind the scenes of the film's mock trial as John West never manages to do. His inability to recognize the clearly staged nature of the trial shows that John West misunderstands the forms of justice used by his accusers. By buckling under the threats of such a ludicrously constructed trial and submitting to Zhban's blackmail, West shows "the true face of the American philistine and his hypocrisy."[13] Although Zhban and his gang commit an undoubtedly greater crime, West is partly to blame for the mock trial's farcical misappropriation of Soviet justice.

A *deus ex machina* in the person of the leather-jacketed Chekist proves necessary to rescue John West from his captors. This contrived escape, as well as the use of documentary film footage to simulate West's viewing of Soviet troops from atop the walls of the Kremlin, forces the satire beyond the mock trial and into initially nonparodic characters and situations in the film.[14] Without a complementary, nonparodic judgment of Zhban and his gang to recuperate the justice parodied in the bogus trial, the viewer is left to interpret the rigid adherence to the forms of the Soviet tribunal not only as a means of showing the counter-revolutionary motives of Zhban's gang but also as a possible critique of the very legal system that the criminals use against West. The viewer immersed in early Soviet legal discourse can read against the grain of Kuleshov's film and draw a comparison between the avaricious bandits orchestrating West's trial—in which he has lost the right to express himself freely, to deny accusations, and even to know the nature of the crime of which he stands accused—and the countless trials, both real and fictional, that did the same in the name of proletarian justice. The parodic trial in *Mr. West* might initially serve to critique those opposed to Soviet power, be they simple-minded Americans or opportunistic Nepmen; but in the end, Kuleshov's parody of Bolshevik justice could be read as a denunciation of the very institutions the director claimed his film supported. This potentially subversive reading of the parodic trial in *Mr. West* received no commentary from the director or critics at the time; nonetheless, it illustrates the inherently multivalent nature of parodies of Bolshevik justice in contrast to the univalent legal melodramas of the same era.

ERDMAN'S *MANDATE*

As a film like *Mr. West* demonstrates, multivalent parodic trials proved acceptable during the mid-1920s in popular Soviet culture. Feature films, comic agitsudy, and vaudeville vignettes shone a farcical light on the usually serious rituals and rhetoric of proletarian justice, as a number of Erdman's circus sketches written for the well-known clown Vitaly Lazarenko illustrate.[15] These short skits filled the forms of Soviet justice with slapstick comedy and replaced the sober testimony of defendants and witnesses with ribald jokes. In "The Comradely Court Case at Housing Cooperate No. 1519," "The People vs. Vitaly Lazarenko," and "The Divorce" (all 1927), Erdman created vaudeville versions of the Soviet tribunal of his day. The judge in each circus trial played the role of a gullible straight man, while the clown-defendant Lazarenko misappropriated the verbal expressions of trial testimony and confession in his hilarious attempts to get himself off the hook. As a seemingly simpleminded trickster, Lazarenko could mock and distort the forms of Soviet justice, pouring buckets of water over the judge's head and even swearing that the plaintiff was "a daughter-of-a-bitch."[16] The carnivalization of legal forms and rhetoric was entirely permissible before mythopoetic justice crystallized in the 1928 Shakhty Affair.

Erdman's first full-length play, *Mandate,* did not venture into a direct parody of legal forms like the circus sketches written for Lazarenko.[17] Nonetheless, the playwright depicted, in the eccentric characters peopling his 1925 play, the independent and often perverted life that the rituals and rhetoric of Soviet justice could acquire. Strikingly similar in this regard to both Gogol's *Inspector General* and Sukhovo-Kobylin's *Trilogy, Mandate* deformed the official language of friends and foes, severing its connection to actual phenomena and creating preposterous notions of the enemy's identity and location in the world on stage.[18] As a result of this distortion of early Soviet legal language, critics reacted to Erdman's work by sorting its cast of characters into friends and foes, in essence subjecting *Mandate* to the real-life corollary of the rhetoric enacted and parodied by the characters in the play. Although the specific objects of Erdman's satire in *Mandate* are far from clear, the criticism surrounding this play evinces a compelling need to locate the enemy precisely, to draw parallels between the enemies on stage and those in real life, and to subject Erdman's imaginary characters to the real-life rituals of confession and repentance. *Mandate* survived the ideological court of the critics in 1925 largely because of its cast of characters from the bygone, pre-revolutionary era, which allowed critics to read the play much like an agitsud.

The records of *Mandate*'s premiere in the Meyerhold Theater show that Erdman's comedy was not only praised by critics but was also extremely popular with audiences who laughed out loud at the absurd antics of the déclassé Guliachkin family.[19] Erdman's free-for-all farce focuses on an unlikely assemblage of *byvshie liudi* who inhabit the once elegant apartment of the former merchant Pavel Guliachkin. The play's plot revolves around Pavel's scheme to join the Communist Party so that he can offer himself, a card-carrying Party man, as the dowry for his old maid sister. Pavel's alleged membership in the Party arises spontaneously from his unpremeditated exclamation to a group of surly tenants: "Silence! I am a Party man."[20] The threads of the play's plot become increasingly tangled, and Pavel's words spoken initially to silence an antagonistic boarder take on a curious life of their own. His verbal threat materializes on a piece of awe-inspiring paper, which he waves as a much feared mandate to keep the neighbors at bay.

Pavel is not alone in allowing disembodied words to take on flesh and dictate behavior in *Mandate*. All the characters in the play display an unusual, unconscious tendency toward "social mimicry and parroting" that make them not only fearful of Pavel's mandate but also prone to misinterpret the statements of others in a similar manner (311). When his ruse is finally exposed after a series of hilarious misadventures, a disgruntled tenant threatens to call the police to expose Pavel's mandate for the flimsy piece of paper it truly is. The police curiously refuse to come to the Guliachkin apartment, let alone arrest its petit bourgeois inhabitants. Rather than express relief that he escaped the powers that be, Pavel questions his family's very existence in the final line of the play: "Momma, if they don't even want to arrest us, then how can we live, Momma? How can we live?" (80). All of Pavel's verbal constructs collapse around him, and Erdman's comic search for a suitor ends in existential crisis.

In the tradition of the Gogolian grotesque, *Mandate* develops out of confusion and ends in utter chaos. The play's dialog and action mimic the logical progression of cause and effect but nonetheless lack any actual coherence. By the end of *Mandate,* the plot has escalated in a chain reaction of characters' absurd and exaggerated responses to random words and objects on the stage. The truly disturbing lack of correspondence between words and what they signify leads one of the play's characters to question, "Does anything really happen for any reason these days?" (32). Yet the problem of semiotic disjunction that this question betrays escaped the vast majority of critics who preferred to focus their attention on the play's depiction of "parasitic elements" in Soviet society (67). Not unlike reviewers of the premiere of Gogol's *Inspector General* approximately a century before, those writing about *Mandate* struggled to determine and describe the relationship between real-life enemies of the Soviet state and Erdman's imaginary den of former people caught in an illogical brouhaha on stage. Because of the characters' clearly pre-revolutionary class affiliations, Soviet critics interpreted *Mandate* as an agitsud and stated that the play "creates an indictment against Russia of the past and warns contemporary Russia. . . . The show forces you to think. It cautions against premises, it leads to conclusions."[21]

The show's leading actor, Erast Garin, confirmed this moralizing interpretation by describing Meyerhold's production of *Mandate* as "a 'judgment day' of the Blagushin petite bourgeoisie," as "the inspired fury against the petite bourgeoisie of an artist worked out in algebra."[22] Although the venues were entirely different, critics and actors analyzed Erdman's play using the ideological categories articulated in the agitsud and strove to condemn Erdman's characters for social parasitism, as if they stood trial in a mock court. Two critics writing for *Zhizn' iskusstvo* stated:

> The characters of *Mandate* are wretched and sunken creatures, moral foxes, the lumpen-bourgeoisie. They are a bourgeoisie declassed by the Revolution, degenerating and dying out—a terrifying and disgusting phenomenon on the background of Soviet society.[23]

Pavel Markov concurred with this opinion:

> Guliachkins can appear in our present-day Russia. . . . Erdman's comedy is about these people, their distorted lives and the enthusiastic petite bourgeoisie reviving itself. . . . Erdman exposes the miserable emptiness of the

formulae and ideas by which some representatives of the intelligentsia lived in the years after the Revolution, who are now capable of taking the comedy as an agonizing accusation.[24]

Rather than reading Erdman's verbal artistry as an indictment of the legal rhetoric used by the characters on stage as they accuse each other of monarchism, revolution, and counter-revolution, critics preferred to interpret the disjunction of signifier and signified as the playwright's judgment against people like Guliachkin. In a process surprisingly similar to Pavel's entry into the Communist Party, critics took the words and characters of *Mandate* and granted them lives of their own beyond the footlights, performing an act of reverse theatricality that forced the play's absurd, fictional characters into categories designed for the Soviet Union's real-life enemies.

According to one American reporter who attended a performance of *Mandate*, Soviet audiences watching Erdman's play also identified it as an indictment, however, of an entirely different group of criminals. Spectators drew a parallel between Guliachkin and "Stalin's underworld gangsters and racketeers," expressing their approval of the play by shouting, "Stalinist crooks! Hypocrites!" at various points throughout the performance.[25] Although theater critics described *Mandate* as if it contained the straightforward moral message of an agitsud, audience reactions betrayed the subversive potential of Erdman's play and the dangerous multivalence of the categories of friends and enemies in a satirical context. The timing of *Mandate*'s premiere in the middle of the NEP allowed the play to prosper for several years in the Meyerhold theater. However, the play's subversive undertones would lead to its removal from the country's theatrical repertoire in the early 1930s, when satirical representations of former people and their failed attempts to become members of the socialist state were replaced by the solemn ceremony of real-life show trials.

TRIAL BY THE LAW?

As the 1920s progressed, the risk inherent in placing Bolshevik justice in a satirical context became ever greater. Kuleshov's second major film of the decade, *Po zakonu (By the law)*, repeated *Mr. West*'s use of a parodic trial but was greeted with more ambivalent criticism in 1926 than its predecessor two years previously. Once again, Kuleshov adapted an American plot for the screenplay, basing his new film on Jack London's short story "The Unexpected," set at the turn of the nineteenth century in the far reaches of the Alaskan Yukon. London wrote "The Unexpected" as an exploration of the psychic and moral implications of vigilante justice in a lawless and unsettled land, and Kuleshov's reworking exposed the religious and class biases of such justice carried out in the name of church and state. The director himself explained that *By the Law* was intended to provide a vivid depiction of "The inhumanity of people that religion sincerely conceals, [and] the cruelty that it allows."[26]

London's story takes place among a group of Alaskan gold prospectors and focuses on the consequences of a double murder committed in an isolated cabin. Rather than praise the perseverance of those who survive, as London does in his story, Kuleshov shows that the film's two heroes, Edith and Hans Hanson, have done no more than remain true to their class interests by trying and executing the film's murderer and villain, Michael Dennin. Kuleshov presents life at the prospecting site as a microcosm of capitalist society on the brink of revolution, casting the Hansons in the role of bourgeois oppressors and Dennin in that of the downtrodden proletariat. From the opening frames of *By the Law,* Dennin is shown as subject to the Hansons' will and alienated from the fruits of his labor at the prospecting camp. His cold-blooded murder of the two other members of the gold-mining team constitutes a shocking attempt to overturn the unjust economic and social system at the prospecting cabin.

As a result of the characters' clearly depicted class affiliations, the viewer of *By the Law* is predisposed to believe that any court the Hansons might construct in the secluded cabin would do no more than reconstitute the oppressive forms of capitalist justice, which in fact it does. Their minimalist reconstruction of British jurisprudence is so reduced in its members and procedures as to expose the seeming objectivity of bourgeois law as fetishistic ritual posturing. The trial begins as Hans pulls a rectangular wooden table into place and hangs a picture of Queen Victoria on the wall of the cabin. Edith joins in the preparations by clutching her Bible, gazing on the portrait of the Queen, and standing with Hans behind the table. Throughout the trial, the camera returns to these two images—Edith's hands wrapped around the Bible and the portrait of Queen Victoria—which simultaneously constitute the legitimacy of the court for the Hansons and its illegitimacy for the Soviet viewer.

As in *Mr. West,* the court in *By the Law* looks and functions much like a Soviet tribunal, in spite of its clearly non-Soviet judges. The rectangular table covered with a fresh, checkered tablecloth, on which paper, pen, and a candle have been carefully arranged, suggests a Soviet courtroom more than the English bar. The rituals of rising as the court is called to order, of reading the charges against the defendant, and of allowing him to speak once the trial reaches its end, all copy Soviet courtroom practice of the time.

However, as a series of intertitles points out, Edith and Hans occupy every role in their makeshift court (except that of defendant), acting as judge, jury, prosecutor, defender, witness, and even plaintiff. Although the film's trial mimics the officially sanctioned Soviet court, Edith and Hans have in fact created a samosud, in which "a chance crowd, often instigated by the actual criminals, assumes the rights of investigator, judge, and bailiff." Much like legal experts who tried to suppress samosudy in the Russian countryside at the end of the 1920s, Kuleshov portrays such a spontaneous and unsanctioned method of combating crime as a crime itself.[27]

The verdict that Dennin shall be hanged by the neck until dead hardly comes as a surprise to the film's viewer, who finds that the Hansons' fetishes expose rather than disguise their predetermined outcome for the trial. Yet Dennin is an unusually compliant defendant, who confesses with apparent regret and submissively marches to his death. Much like John West, Dennin hangs his head when he testifies, but in shame and resignation rather than in fear. His acquiescence to the Hansons' samosud casts Dennin in the role of the long-suffering melodramatic hero and suggests that he will triumph in due time when poetic justice is served. In fact, Kuleshov pardons the condemned and executed Dennin in the film's most significant departure from London's original story line. Unlike the ending of "The Unexpected," the closing shots of By the Law show the hanged criminal returning to the Hansons' cabin with a broken rope around his neck. Dennin threatens his terrified judges and, in the film's final frame, boldly stalks off into the dark rainy Alaskan night. Within the religious universe that Edith and Hans occupy, the broken rope dangling from Dennin's neck attests to God's reversal of their verdict and the illegitimacy of their court. Dennin's indestructibility also proves the strength of the proletariat, which can be neither contained nor destroyed by bourgeois law. Dennin's resurrection at the film's end proves the injustice of the Hansons' samosud and unmasks their alleged objectivity as bourgeois self-interest.

Several elements of the reconstruction of justice in the Hansons' cabin militate against such an orthodox reading of the film. No one who has seen By the Law can condemn the Hansons or sympathize with Dennin as completely as does the reading offered here. First, Alexandra Khokhlova's performance in the role of Edith constantly draws the viewer's attention away from Dennin, who spends most of the film bound and immobile, literally in the background. Khokhlova's portrayal of Edith's mounting psychological tension—in which naturalistic gestures are slowly replaced by close-ups of the actress's grimacing face—diminishes Dennin's presence in the film. Second, the conflict between the Hansons and Dennin is cast not simply in terms of class warfare but also in terms of the stock Hollywood narrative of an endangered woman. As a member of the weaker sex, Edith risks not only murder but also rape if Dennin should escape and carry out his destructive plans. In spite of Hans's protection, Edith gains the viewer's sympathy because she figures as the potential female victim in the struggle with the outlaw Dennin.

In addition, the viewer must remember that the Hansons' is not the only samosud in the film: Dennin's brutal murder is his attempt to take the law into his own hands and to rectify social injustice at the prospecting site. If the viewer compares these two instances of vigilante justice, the Hansons' court of two people and a rope seems more compassionate and just than Dennin's act with a loaded rifle. Although Kuleshov gave Dennin the last word in *By the Law,* the demonic representation of this ghost that does return—invading the Hansons' cabin during a terrifying thunderstorm and disappearing into the pitch black of the Alaskan night much like a ghoulish specter from *The Cabinet of Dr. Caligari* or *Nosferatu*—severely undermines any sympathy the viewer might have for him. The Hansons' appeal to the allegedly higher powers of God and queen notwithstanding, their reconstruction of bourgeois justice strives toward a moral and compassionate ideal of which Dennin is entirely ignorant.

The ambiguity of friend and foe in *By the Law* leads to a corresponding ambiguity of real-life counterparts for the Hansons' improvised trial. Despite the suggestion that the Hansons' court mimics bourgeois justice, the spectator is urged to identify Dennin's trial and execution with those he knows in his own home in Soviet Russia: after the trial has ended, Edith reassures Hans that they have acted "Just like in a court at home [*u nas*]."[28] In addition, the portrait of a young Queen Victoria, to which the camera returns throughout the trial scene, suggests a parodic inversion of the iconographic representations of Lenin in Soviet courts of the time. The fundamental resemblance of the Hansons' samosud to Soviet tribunals encourages spectators to read the trial in *By the Law* as a somber rendition of the farcical trial Kuleshov filmed in *Mr. West,* and, just as in the earlier film, Kuleshov provides no recuperation of justice to prevent the viewer from drawing such a parallel. Instead, the closing scene of *By the Law* suggests that such a recuperation of justice would do no more than allow the vengeful, resurrected Dennin to improvise justice in his own samosud. The orthodox Soviet reading of the film that Kuleshov himself sanctions gives way to a harshly critical vision of a country in which monstrously indestructible murderers condemn their hapless enemies by their own law.

The press surrounding the premiere of *By the Law* did not fully explore the problematic gaps and possibilities for interpretive slippage created by the film's parodic trial. Critics nonetheless alluded to the inherent danger of importing American stories and editing techniques into Soviet film. The critic Khrisanf Khersonskii was so offended by the American tendencies of *By the Law* that he thought it better to lock the film in a safe than allow for its public distribution.[29] After the release and failure of Kuleshov's next American adaptation of an O. Henry short story, the 1933 film *Velikii uteshitel' (The Great Consoler)*, the director himself acknowledged that, in his "blind acceptance of American film culture" in the 1920s, he had unwittingly introduced "bourgeois consolation" into his work and "diverted the masses from the class struggle."[30] The satiric inversion of friends and enemies by means of the parodic trial created disturbing shades of gray in the coalescing system of mythopoetic justice, which increasingly demanded representation exclusively in black and white. The gradual marginalization of Kuleshov from film production into film pedagogy during the next decade arose out of complex aesthetic and institutional factors; yet, the director's innovative appropriation of the forms of Soviet justice created films that could never fulfill the edict to entertain and enlighten with the clarity that official Soviet organs ever more insistently required.

TRIAL OF A BEDBUG

Like Kuleshov's second film, Maiakovskii's second play of the 1920s was intended to support the Soviet worldview but contained the seeds of its own satirical undoing. *Bedbug* premiered in early 1929, less than a year after the Shakhty Affair, and it was one of the last works of Soviet drama or film to use legal rhetoric successfully in a satirical context. Meyerhold's production of *Bedbug* offered a plainly negative portrayal of one species of the enemies of Soviet power, the Nepman; and the play opened to the enthusiastic reviews of critics and spectators alike. Maiakovskii's creative use of tropes for social hygiene in *Bedbug* increased the irony and ambiguity of the play's pro-Soviet message, in effect challenging the official renditions of the germ and parasite metaphors articulated in the Shakhty Affair. In particular, Maiakovskii's fanciful literalization of the vermin metaphor in *Bedbug* created a questionable sympathy for the play's title character and offered a dangerous alternative to the rapidly crystallizing language of mythopoetic justice.

Critics and spectators immediately recognized the hero of *Bedbug*, Ivan Prisypkin, as the quintessence of the petit bourgeois, as "a character who has been petit-embourgeoisified to the point of complete bestiality." More rightfully called the play's antihero, Prisypkin appears in the cast of characters as "a former worker, a former party member, currently a fiancé."

Not unlike Guliachkin in *Mandate*, Prisypkin plans to capitalize on his impeccable proletarian lineage and his newly acquired membership in the Communist Party to arrange a marriage with the curvaceous and alluring beautician Elzevira Davidovna Renaissance, the daughter of a prosperous Nepman. Prisypkin's willingness to sell his birthright presents a damning portrait of workers enlisted in the Communist Party as part of the *leninskii prizyv* (Lenin enrollment), which was designed to increase proletarian membership in the Party immediately after Lenin's death. Although some critics attacked Maiakovskii for depicting such a happy-go-lucky enemy of socialism, the playwright firmly believed that Prisypkin's alienation from the working class proved that "political philistinism follows from social philistinism." Worse than any other variety of *byvshie liudi,* Prisypkin has betrayed his class, his country, and his recently raised revolutionary consciousness. As a Soviet-style Judas, Prisypkin is an ideal candidate for samokritika and chitska.[31]

Much as in *Mystery-Bouffe,* Prisypkin's enemy status develops in the first half of *Bedbug* (set in 1929) through a correlation between superficial personal hygiene and deeply embedded moral filth. As his name indicates, Prisypkin is a *syp'* (rash or eruption) on the skin of Soviet society that requires *prisypka* (dusting powder) to alleviate the itch. Just like the Clean in *Mystery-Bouffe,* Prisypkin's personal hygiene is only skin deep, as his former buddies from the working class point out. Prisypkin dresses and carries himself like a gentleman, but "He's got sideburns like a dog's tail, and he doesn't even wash—he's afraid to muss them."[32] His impending marriage to the Renaissance family intensifies this message of superficial cleanliness. Prisypkin has thrown aside his working-class fiancée to wed the daughter of a stereotypically avaricious family of Jewish Nepmen, every member of which works in the family barbershop and beauty salon, in the personal hygiene trade. Prisypkin has abandoned his proletarian heritage of dirty calluses earned by manual labor to join a family with carefully filed fingernails and intricately coifed hair. The orgiastic wedding of "unknown but great labor with prostrate but charming capital" turns (predictably) into a drunken brawl that literally ignites the wedding party, which is then consumed in the ensuing flames (238).

In the second half of *Bedbug* (set in 1979), Maiakovskii passes judgment on the philistine Prisypkin by literalizing the vermin metaphor referred to in the play's title. Prisypkin has carried a tiny insect-passenger on his person into the world of the future, which resurrects both him and his bedbug after fifty years of frozen sleep in the burned-out basement of the wedding party. Prisypkin's thin layer of grooming no longer hides his petit bourgeois filth from the world of 1979, whose standards of cleanliness are much higher than those of fifty years ago. The scientists of the future begin to worry about "the danger of spreading the bacteria of brown-nosing and conceit . . . about the possibility of introducing an epidemic of brown-nosing!" (247, 249). In actual fact, as soon as Prisypkin comes back to life, the diseases of love, profanity, smoking, and drinking appear in society for the first time in fifty years. Prisypkin's "unsanitary customs" prove dangerously contagious in the sterile environment of the future (255). The present world in the first half of the play merely criticized Prisypkin's betrayal of class, country, and revolution, but the world of the future correctly judges him as the true parasite in the play: Prisypkin is a leech sucking the blood of socialist society, a virtual Typhoid Mary spreading a host of social ills.

The scientists of the future show more interest in the rare insect Prisypkin has brought into their midst than they do in its smelly and infectious host. Only by offering himself as a source of food for the bedbug and as a rare specimen of wildlife in his own right does Prisypkin find a home for himself in the zoo of the future. The zoo's director explains the complex relationship between the human parasite Prisypkin and the insect he feeds:

> I have just become convinced, by means of interrogation and comparative beastiology, that we are dealing with a terrifying, anthropomorphic impostor, and that it is the most startling and parasitic of parasites. . . . They are two, differing in size but the same in essence: they are the famous *Bedbugus normalis* and . . . and the *Philistinus vulgaris*. Both are found in the musty mattresses of time. *Bedbugus normalis,* when it has grown fat and drunk on the body of a single human, falls under the bed. *Philistinus vulgaris,* when it has grown fat and drunk on the body of all humankind, falls on top of the bed. That's the only difference! (271–72)

With great curiosity, the future world labels Prisypkin a parasite and ultimately determines that he is less than human. Maiakovskii uses the same quasi-scientific, quasi-medical, and ultra-hygienic terminology as coalesced in the Shakhty Affair to dehumanize Prisypkin in *Bedbug*. As the play comes to its close, Prisypkin is more and more frequently compared to vermin, to bacteria, and even once to a mastodon. Finally, through the use of the neuter pronoun *ono* (it), the zoo director demotes Prisypkin permanently to the status of animal. In spite of countless attempts to raise Prisypkin "up to human level," he remains a dangerous source of what one critic calls "the bacilli of love and drunkenness" (263).[33] As a social parasite, Prisypkin must be quarantined and kept behind a series of filters that eliminate the threat of an epidemic of petit bourgeois backsliding—called *tarakanovshchina* (cockroachitis)—among the citizens of the future.[34]

In spite of the play's politically attuned message, as a piece of satirical propaganda *Bedbug* displayed several shortcomings quickly noticed and questioned by critics. Prisypkin never realizes the superficiality of his personal hygiene, never grooms his soul as he does his body, never joins the sterile society that cages him in the zoo. The proletarian traitor longs for the small creature comforts and discomforts that gave his life meaning fifty years in the past and that keep him in a state of primitive filth in the future. Prisypkin never finds sufficient reason to join the society of 1979, consequently he never cleans up his act so he can become part of it. Maiakovskii portrays Prisypkin as the quintessential class foe, whose enemy status is a secret to no one except himself. However, *Bedbug* shows that proletarian backsliders like Prisypkin are not only incapable of rejoining socialist society but also entirely unwilling to confess their crimes and repent of any wrongdoing.

Furthermore, Prisypkin elicits the spectator's sympathy with his sentimental poeticizing, his earthy *joie de vivre,* and his final appeal to his contemporaries in the audience at the play's end. Prisypkin's dislike of the sterile world of the future diminishes its appeal for spectators of *Bedbug,* and the curious response of the citizens of the future to the infectious Prisypkin forces the spectator to question how joyous an entirely antiseptic future would be. Most of the inhabitants of the future run in fear from Prisypkin, but a small portion find themselves inexorably drawn toward the symptoms of the diseases he carries, so much so they even volunteer as candidates for infection. Much like the germs of wrecking and counterrevolution, the microbes of petit bourgeois degeneracy are highly virulent. Even momentary contact with a carrier of such microbes results in infection in the form of fox-trotting, beer drinking, and lovemaking, as the scientifically designed air-conditioner separating Prisypkin from visitors in the zoo shows. The sterile society of the future cannot control the spread of Prisypkin's diseases and discovers that "The epidemic is spreading. . . . The epidemic is becoming an ocean" (258–59). The social ills Prisypkin brings with him from the past find a surprisingly firm foothold in the future, and as a result Prisypkin's dislike of the new society acquires a dangerous veracity.

As was the case with the metaphors of germs, vermin, and garbage used in the Shakhty Affair, the very possibility of eliminating the diseases carried by Prisypkin comes into question by the end of *Bedbug.* When taken together with the attraction of these ills and the almost palpable fondness for the lost past that emerges in the second half of the play, the need for such a disinfected future devoid of dirt, feeling, and romance becomes equivocal. The critic Boris Alpers sensed this equivocation in the play and criticized *Bedbug* for not taking its satire far enough. According to Alpers, Maiakovskii's play focuses on an insignificant part of the petite bourgeoisie and, as a result, paints the object of its satire in only the most general of contours.[35]

In fact, the opposite holds true: the playwright accurately reveals a dangerous element lurking in Soviet society and depicts Prisypkin's crimes in living colors. However, by maintaining Prisypkin's amiability throughout his extension of the vermin metaphor, Maiakovskii resists the trope's foregone conclusion that parasites must be eradicated. In *Bedbug*, Maiakovskii shows that the ease of locating the enemy and compelling him to confess is offset by the utter impossibility of eliminating the social forces from which he arose and of integrating him into the society of the future. Maiakovskii's satire no longer contains the simple propaganda message that the theater of 1929 demanded. Instead, *Bedbug* subverts the legal discourse used to condemn Prisypkin and questions the very vision of the future it intended to defend.

SCRUBBING THE BATHHOUSE CLEAN

If the subversive undertones of *Bedbug* went virtually unnoticed by censors and critics in 1929, the redounding satire of Maiakovskii's last major play, written only one year later, did not. The primary object of the playwright's lampoon in *Bathhouse* was the Soviet Union's leviathan bureaucracy. Maiakovskii also included a play within his play that chastised the contemporary theater for uninspired and incomprehensible revolutionary propaganda. The metatheatrical third act of *Bathhouse* created understandable tension between the playwright and his critics. In spite of this, *Bathhouse* as a whole provided what seemed to be clearer and less problematic satire than *Bedbug*. In place of Prisypkin, who received the audience's simultaneous scorn and sympathy, Maiakovskii placed an undeniably anti-Soviet enemy who bears the full brunt of spectators' condemnation. Despite the playwright's clearly pro-Soviet message, Maiakovskii's last major play failed to satisfy Soviet censors because of the unacceptability of satire at the end of the 1920s as a means of labeling and condemning the enemies of Soviet socialism.[36]

Maiakovskii all but eliminated the vermin and germ metaphors from the dramatic action of *Bathhouse*. By 1930 the terminology of wreckers, purging, and self-criticism had been fully articulated, and instead of embellishing the hygiene metaphor in the action of *Bathhouse*, Maiakovskii reserved it for his title. In jest, the playwright claimed that he named his play *Bathhouse* "Because it's the one thing that isn't there."[37] All jesting aside, Maiakovskii's title referred to no action within the play itself but to its didactic function as a work of satire that strove "to make/organize a bathhouse [*ustroit' baniu*]," that is, to carry out a purge.[38] In an article introducing a published excerpt from the play's sixth act, Maiakovskii explained, "What is the *Bathhouse*? Whom does it wash? The *Bathhouse* is a 'drama in six acts with a circus and fireworks.' The *Bathhouse* washes (it simply launders) bureaucrats."[39] Maiakovskii also incorporated the cleansing metaphor into the slogans he composed for the walls of Meyerhold's theater during performances of the play. For example, "We can't clean the swarm of bureaucrats right away/And there are neither enough bathhouses nor enough soap for us."[40] In his title and commentary on the satiric function of *Bathhouse,* Maiakovskii repeated the cleansing and social hygiene tropes that appeared in the action of his two earlier works.

These rather oblique references to social hygiene were intended to legitimate the purging of a new species of renegade Bolshevik, the bureaucratic boss. The play's antihero and villain, "The superbureaucrat and superidiot Pobedonosikov," exemplifies the problem of Party degeneracy to an even greater degree than had Prisypkin in *Bedbug.*[41] A dubious political past, extreme self-absorption, and pedantic adherence to administrative procedure, all mark Pobedinosikov clearly as a foe in *Bathhouse* and lead predictably to his exclusion from the time machine driven by the Phosphorescent Woman to bring model workers to the society of the future. Critics readily recognized Pobedonosikov's enemy status within the play and even coined the term *pobedonosikoshchina* (Pobedonosikovitis), which described not only what plagued the world of *Bathhouse* but also the real-life red tape on which the play was based.[42]

Given that Pobedonosikov is destined for elimination from the society of the future, it is quite surprising that he uses the terminology of *samokritika* and *chistka* more often than any other character in the play. Only with extreme irony does Maiakovskii place accusations of being a member of "the petite bourgeoisie . . . a remnant of the past, chains of the old way of life" in Pobedonosikov's mouth, since he himself is their clearest illustration. The soon-to-be-purged Pobedonosikov uses contemporary political phraseology to rid himself of those who place obstacles in his hedonistic path (including his own wife, whom he encourages to commit suicide), and he presents the most conspicuous example of what the Phosphorescent Woman calls the "parasites and enslavers" infesting Soviet society.[43] Only the supernatural appearance of the Phosphorescent Woman stops his misappropriation of the jargon of mythopoetic justice and compels Pobedonosikov's own self-criticism and purging when the curtain falls in the last act. Although *Bathhouse* depicts the necessity of cleansing the Soviet state of bureaucracy, the play also demonstrates that Pobedonosikov and his ilk freely abuse the terminology of social hygiene to conceal and protect their enemy status. As a result, Maiakovskii's unmasking of the internal bureaucratic enemy calls into question the political orthodoxy of all bureaucrats, particularly those bandying about such words as "wrecker" and "parasite."

The satire of Soviet bureaucrats in *Bathhouse* proved so extensive that it was, in effect, a critique of all Soviet bureaucracy if not the entire Soviet state. As a result, the censors of Glavrepertkom did not allow the play's production, and Maiakovskii's attempt to cleanse Soviet bureaucracy of its stagnation proved instead the impossibility of theatrical satire of this type. Rather than serving the playwright's stated aims, *Bathhouse* made Maiakovskii himself suspect and susceptible to the cleansing and purging described in all three of his major plays. The banning of *Bathhouse* proved that the satirical techniques Maiakovskii had developed in *Mystery-Bouffe* and *Bedbug* were distressingly out of place and time in 1930, leaving the playwright mired in accusations of ideological as well as artistic counter-revolution.[44] Ironically, Maiakovskii had helped to elaborate the very metaphors of cleansing that would purge him, his theatrical works, and theatrical satire as a whole from the Soviet stage of the next decade. By employing "satire's parasitic appropriation of other forms," Maiakovskii's three major plays effectively exterminated themselves from the Soviet Union's active theatrical repertoire at the end of the 1920s.[45]

SCRIPTED SUICIDE

Erdman's artistic fate at the end of the 1920s resembled Maiakovskii's in several respects. After the startling success of *Mandate,* Erdman found that the same dramatic techniques and grotesquely comic characters, which had made this play a hit in 1925, rendered *Suicide* unstageable in 1932. The predominantly good reviews of *Mandate,* which had hailed Erdman as the new Gogol, gave way to vicious denunciations of *Suicide* as a counter-revolutionary instance of "white guardism" in the theater.[46] Even though three of the era's most prominent directors expressed interest in mounting productions of *Suicide,* Glavrepertkom refused to approve the play for public performance, acting on the direct recommendations of Stalin and Lazar' Kaganovich. Yet unlike Maiakovskii, who silenced critics with his shocking suicide only months after the premiere of *Bathhouse* and was subsequently canonized as the revolution's greatest poet, Erdman endured the painful long-term consequences of artistic transgression. After exile to Siberia in 1933, Erdman never wrote another full-length play, confining his work to safe venues such as popular screenplays and dramatic sketches until his death in 1970.

Much like *Mandate, Suicide* explores the relationship between word and deed through the linguistic deformation of peculiarly Soviet concepts. The action is set in the bosom of the Soviet family, in a communal apartment with its petit bourgeois habitués. The action revolves around a displaced worker, Semen Podsekal'nikov, whose futile attempts to give his life meaning lead to thoughts of suicide. The exhausted lament of Podsekal'nikov's wife at the play's beginning—"we can't go on living like this"—plants the seeds of suicide in his head, which friends and neighbors begin inadvertently to nurture.[47] When news of Podsekal'nikov's impending death goes public, representatives from a host of marginalized social groups—including Russia's dying intelligentsia, the merchant class, art, romantic love, and even the church—try to commandeer his suicide for their own publicity campaigns. In a repetition of the bizarre illogic of *Mandate,* Semen's self-destruction becomes a hot commodity since "that which the living can think, only the dead can say" (108).

As in the earlier play, the farcical plot of *Suicide* leads to existential crisis when Podsekal'nikov questions what he will find beyond the grave, if he manages to follow the advice of his newfound allies and kill himself. Podsekal'nikov discovers the meaning of life only when faced with death, and in an act of cowardly courage, he decides to play the role of a suicide without actually taking his own life. The motley crew of Podsekal'nikov's supporters are pronouncing a moving eulogy over his coffin when unexpectedly he rises from the grave to the amazement of all assembled. Rather than rejoicing that Podsekal'nikov is still among the living, those who wished to launch their causes via his suicide accuse him of counterrevolutionary sabotage. Podsekal'nikov's newfound friends turn vicious as they rise up in an angry samosud. Luckily, Podsekal'nikov is saved from the wrath of his former backers by the announcement of another, successful suicide, that of Fedia Petunin, who explains his decision to end his life in a farewell note that states, "Podsekal'nikov is right. It's really not worth living" (164). Someone has finally taken the leap from word to deed but with fateful and truly fatal consequences.

The escalating chaos of *Mandate* reappears in *Suicide,* as does the deformation of contemporary legal rhetoric that labeled friends and enemies. However, the fictional characters in *Suicide* lack one essential feature that allowed those in *Mandate* to survive the judgment of critics seven years before. As the last vestiges of tsarist decadence, the Guliachkins presented critics with clear examples of former people, who would allegedly disappear from Soviet society as the revolution receded into the past. In contrast, the characters in *Suicide* illustrate the tenacity of such former people by their use and abuse of language connected to the Soviet present. As a result, censors interpreted Erdman's satire as a mocking exaggeration of contemporary society, labeling it "extremely reactionary.... The play is politically false."[48] When reviewers connected the action on stage in *Suicide* to real life beyond the footlights, they decided that Erdman's play leveled accusations so broad, so strongly reiterated and vividly painted, that by the play's end they constituted a condemnation of the entire Soviet system.

Rather than examining the dangerously autonomous life of words in Erdman's play, critics read the fanciful speeches of various characters as counter-revolutionary pronouncements, assuming that the play's dramatis personae spoke on behalf of the author. The character of Aristarkh Grand-Skubik, in particular, incited the wrath of reviewers with his flowery, pedantic speechifying on behalf of the remains of the Russian intelligentsia. When Grand-Skubik describes the intelligentsia's untenable position in Soviet society as that of an old chicken who has hatched a nest full of ducks, critics did not question the fantastic conglomeration of animals and allegory:

> Who do you think that chicken is? It's our intelligentsia. Who do you think those eggs are? Those eggs are the proletariat. . . . [The intelligentsia] sat and sat, and finally hatched them. Proletarians hatched out of the eggs. They grabbed the intelligentsia and dragged it to the river. "I'm your mom," exclaimed the intelligentsia. "I sat on you. What are you doing?" "Swim," roared the ducks. "I don't swim." "Well, fly." "Is a chicken even a bird?" said the intelligentsia. "Well, sit." And they really sat us down. Here my brother-in-law has been sitting in prison for five years. Do you understand the allegory? (130)

Instead of laughing at Grand-Skubik's ludicrous parable and its equally preposterous presentation, critics took this speech as evidence of the playwright's counter-revolutionary sentiments. When Erdman's censors looked for positive characters who might offset Grand-Skubik's allegories in *Suicide,* they were disappointed and distressed by the shallow philosophizing of Egorushka, the lone Marxist in the play. Egorushka's mixture of registers as he describes cruising young women—"from a Marxist point of view . . . you end up with such filth that I can't tell you" (114)—stunned and confused the play's critics. The overwhelming conclusion of those who heard preliminary readings of *Suicide* was that the language of the play "cannot be called anything other than reactionary" and that "such phrases will definitely mobilize the spectator. Naturally, not the working spectator, but the philistine spectator."[49]

The debates surrounding *Suicide* found a few hesitant supporters of Erdman's adaptation of the Gogolian grotesque to the Soviet scene. However, the majority of those who previewed the play decided that Erdman's latest work fell dangerously close to theatrical sabotage. They subjected the characters of *Suicide* to the same scrutiny as the defendants in actual show trials and found them a dangerous cluster of counter-revolutionary conspirators:

> What does this play consist of? What is its goal, its purpose? What does it give the spectator? It's nothing but a bouquet for the bourgeoisie. . . . Who is presented here as central figures? There isn't any intelligentsia. What we have is a bouquet, a complex, a combination of a priest, a kulak, a merchant, and a petit bourgeois. They have to be differentiated. We have to understand that they are class enemies. Do you really think that class enemies are waging their battle by assuring the public that as they say, "we are dying"? No. They find other methods for their struggle—elements of arson and sabotage.

This particular critic granted Erdman's fictional characters the extraordinary ability to commit actual crimes and indicted them and the play as a whole for supporting the "very segments of society, against whom an all-out attack of the class war has been declared." Those judging the play even stated that their detection and eradication of ideological sabotage in plays such as *Suicide* ultimately carried more importance than the GPU's dealings with real people accused of actual sabotage at the time.[50]

Although the critics' desire to connect the fictional world of *Suicide* with reality outside the theater resulted in gross misreadings of Erdman's play, there remains a grain of truth in the accusations of petit bourgeois ideology in the play. The character of Podsekal'nikov indeed epitomizes boorishness and philistinism, much like Guliachkin and Prisypkin had before him. The highly ambivalent heroes of *Mandate* and *Bedbug* successfully walked the boards in 1925 and 1929 because their sad fates were understood as just deserts. In contrast, Podsekal'nikov undergoes a petit bourgeois epiphany at the end of *Suicide* that goes unpunished and, hence, questions fundamental premises of Soviet society at the time. When Podsekal'nikov looks his own death in the face, he discovers that life has value in and of itself, that the everyday pleasures of a good meal justify existence. Although Fedia Petunin's successful suicide literally steals the final words of the play from the other's lips, Petunin has taken his life because "Podsekalnikov is right." Critics recognized that Podsekal'nikov's discovery of the value of individual experience contradicts "the very essence of all of society . . . that the collective is higher than the individual" (161). Podsekal'nikov's awakening challenges the most important lesson of mythopoetic justice, as he renounces any attempt to work for a higher cause and upholds the deeply personal values that mock trials and show trials alike repudiated.

Ironically enough, Podsekal'nikov's thoroughly petit bourgeois philosophy proves his salvation in the play. As long as fuzzy notions of participating in socialist society stimulate his actions, Podsekal'nikov finds himself on the brink of suicide, but as soon as he places his own life above any cause he might represent, he finds ample reason to live in merely satisfying his stomach. He asks Soviet society for a single privilege: "allow us to say that it's difficult for us to live. Even if it's just like this, in a whisper, 'It's difficult for us to live.' . . . give us the right to whisper" (163). Critics vociferously objected to Podsekal'nikov's whisper and likened it to "the rustling of cockroaches." Those who objected to the play assumed that Podsekal'nikov's whisper was the same as the playwright's: "Podsekal'nikov wants to give [the white guard] the right to whisper. But Erdman wants to give it a trumpet of Jericho, so that it can bellow out from the stage."[51] The whisper of dissent for which Podsekal'nikov pleads is precisely what show trials in the theater, on the movie screen, and in the courtroom sought to silence. Like the single microbe that can infect and cause an epidemic, Podsekal'nikov's isolated whisper could echo, evoke replies, and be amplified to resound throughout the Soviet Union. Podsekal'nikov does not commit physical suicide in the play, but his plea for the right to whisper constitutes ideological suicide for his character and proved close to artistic suicide for the playwright.

Podsekal'nikov barely scrapes by with his life in *Suicide*, and outside the play he died a quick death at the hands of the theatrical censors. The director of the Vakhtangov Theater detected the essentially superficial reading of Erdman's critics and pointed out that no one had managed to condemn the play through "an exhaustive Marxist analysis." However, such exhaustive analysis proved unnecessary: *Suicide* had already condemned itself through its misappropriation of concepts associated with mythopoetic justice and prompted Stalin to declare that the play was "somewhat empty and even harmful."[52] By 1932 the Soviet state exerted complete control over the production and application of such notions as "friend," "enemy," "legality," and "justice." Erdman's attempt to explore these ideas in *Suicide* and to manipulate their meanings through satire was, in essence, the playwright's own dissenting whisper, which critics and censors silenced with their denunciations of the play.

As the failures of both *Bathhouse* and *Suicide* vividly illustrate, the images, tropes, and language of legal mythopoesis lost their ability to generate black-and-white enemies of Soviet power when placed in the context of satire. The inherent ambiguity and heteroglossia of these avant-garde satires meant that they did not assist in the process of legal devolution taking place in popular Soviet culture and the real-life Soviet court. Trials that adhered to the melodramatic paradigm of mythopoetic justice reunited morality and the law under the almost religious banner of Marxism-Leninism. On the contrary, Kuleshov's parodic trials, Maiakovskii's parasites, and Erdman's samosudy strained against this devolutionary shift in Soviet law and expressed a growing anxiety with the official organs and rituals of Soviet justice. In western Europe, artworks that express similar moments of cultural crisis, such as Aeschylus' *Eumenides,* Shakespeare's *Merchant of Venice,* or Kafka's *Trial,* pushed the evolutionary process of the law forward, questioning current notions of justice and urging their revision.[53] In the Soviet Union at the end of the 1920s, avant-garde artworks expressing the legal crisis of Stalin's cultural revolution were ruthlessly expurgated and their authors marginalized in a process that repeated the very patterns they once helped to create.

The account of these authors' success during the 1920s and their subsequent marginalization in the 1930s repeats the well-known story of the death of the Russian avant-garde. At the same time, it tells us that the rhetoric and forms of justice that converged in the Stalinist show trial did not dictate the final script that would be repeated in each of the great Moscow trials of 1936–1938. The subtlety of *By the Law* and the nuances of *Bedbug* prove that the developing legal consciousness of early Soviet society contained a number of different aspects, many of which were suppressed in the construction of mythopoetic justice. Successfully locating and exterminating the internal foes of Soviet power required not only creating a specifically melodramatic enemy but also eliminating all competing versions, which allowed spectators to question the truth of defendants' confessions and the ultimate outcome of legal mythopoesis. That Kuleshov, Maiakovksii, and Erdman all intended to aid the construction of socialism in the works discussed in this chapter indicates the increasingly compressed possibilities for employing such ideas as proletarian justice or the enemy of the people, as well as the ever expanding control of the Soviet state in all areas of cultural production.

CHAPTER SIX

FOR EACH ENEMY, ANOTHER TRIAL

The elimination of avant-garde plays and films from the previously broad spectrum of legal propaganda did not mean that courtroom drama left the Soviet stage and screen. During the cultural revolution of the early 1930s, those like Kuleshov, Maiakovskii, and Erdman who rashly altered the patterns of legal mythopoesis found their works banned in spite of the orthodox messages they intended to teach. However, those who did not tamper with the prescribed formula for confession, contrition, and reintegration into society met little opposition to indicting the enemies of the people in fictional trials. Suspending the rich tradition of dramatic satire at the end of the 1920s abolished the most problematic venue for mythopoetic justice, and the increasingly strict censorship of scripts and screenplays ensured that courtroom dramas would render the unitary message of agitsudy without risking transgression. The Shakhty Affair reoriented the hierarchy of media and genres appropriate for Soviet legal propaganda, signaling the ouster of the avant-garde and a newfound preference for cinema over the theater. The 1928 trial taught legal specialists not only the value of complementing the theatrical modeling of the show trial with cinematic finishes but also the efficacy of presenting the trial's mass audience with the last word in legal realism. The paradigm of legal mythopoesis inherited from the agitsud remained mostly intact during and after the Shakhty Affair. Yet the agitsud itself disappeared, along with the parodic trial, giving way to new types of trials that stressed the cinematic reproduction of a fictional reality.

Without a doubt, the most important genre of legal propaganda in the 1930s was the actual show trial, which located and condemned enemies of all stripes with increasing frequency and efficiency. These actual trials received the direct approval of Stalin, who encouraged the melodramatic shaping of defendants' testimony. In a 1930 letter to Molotov, he wrote:

An explanation of Kondratiev's "case" in the press would be appropriate *only in the event* that we intend to put this "case" on trial. Are we ready for this? Do we consider it necessary to take this "case" to trial? Perhaps it will be difficult to dispense with a trial.

By the way, how about Messrs. Defendants admitting their *mistakes* and disgracing themselves politically, while simultaneously acknowledging the strength of the Soviet government and the correctness of the method of collectivization? It wouldn't be a bad thing if they did.[1]

The master plot sketched by Stalin comes directly from the agitsudy, trials on film, and show trials of a few years before. This melodramatic story reappears in the 1930 trial of the Industrial Party and the Metro-Vickers trial of 1933, which unmasked more of the spies and wreckers whose existence the Shakhty Affair had proved. As if in a chain reaction, successive branches of the Soviet economy were subjected to the samokritika and chistka that this master plot implied; and the enemies of the Soviet people methodically "admitted their *mistakes*" in the same columned hall in Moscow that provided the stage for the 1922 SR trial and the Shakhty Affair. The show trials of the 1930s repeated the theatrical and cinematic modeling of their 1928 progenitor—perfecting the techniques of mythopoetic justice and preparing them for the country's leadership.

As legal mythopoesis spread horizontally through industry and vertically to the highest ranks of the Party and the military, the institution of the show trial also traveled to the Soviet provinces. Trials that took place outside the country's center, it is interesting to note, implemented the lessons of the Shakhty Affair with greater flexibility and variation. If the internationally publicized show trials of the 1930s can be likened to professional theater, their provincial counterparts were amateur productions. Show trials in the provinces imitated the courts of Moscow and Leningrad in many respects but were several years behind the times in their staging techniques. Distance from the center gave those who organized provincial show trials greater freedom, which sometimes resulted in accusations reading like works of nineteenth-century Russian satire instead of like a legal indictment. In addition, the primarily peasant audience of provincial show trials appears to have participated with genuine enthusiasm in these legal spectacles, making them into "participatory political theater" not unlike an agitsud.[2] In spite of these departures, the provincial version of the *pokazatel'nyi protsess* proves that legal mythopoesis in the institution of the show trial reached almost every region, industry, and class of the Soviet Union by the early 1930s.

The marked increase in actual trials was accompanied by the appearance of a new genre of legal propaganda: the feature-length trial documentary film. The major show trials of the previous decade regularly provided the subject for newsreels and short features, as was the case with Vertov's reportage on the SR trial in *Kinopravda* and *Sovkino-Zhurnal*'s coverage of the Shakhty Affair. Trial documentaries of the 1920s reached and disciplined an audience spread across the vast reaches of the Soviet Union; yet none of these newsreels pretended to tell the whole story of bringing the country's adversaries to justice. The first full-length documentary to depict an entire show trial was produced in conjunction with the case of the Industrial Party, and the cinematic shaping of the trial's narrative substantially intensified the message of earlier newsreels and shorts. Moreover, the selective editing of the many hours of actual courtroom testimony in *Protsess Prompartii (13 dnei) (The Trial of the Industrial Party [13 Days])* by Ia. Posel'skii (1931) brought the story of an actual show trial into conformity with that of filmed legal melodramas from the decade before. The combination of documentary film's heightened realism and the melodramatic unmasking of the hidden enemy made the feature-length trial documentary the second most important genre of legal propaganda in the 1930s and the decade's answer to the agitsud.

The success of the feature-length trial documentary lay in its obvious dependence on the actual courtroom and real-life rituals of justice for the depiction of legal mythopoesis. Rather than turning to the theater or cinema for mythopoetic authority, as show trials of the 1920s had originally done, legal propaganda of the 1930s did just the opposite. Similar to trial documentaries, plays and feature films incorporating fictional trials were compelled to reproduce the actual legal procedures of their day and could no longer improvise on the theme of justice as Kuleshov, Maiakovskii, and Erdman had done. The banning of Mikhail Kalatozov's 1931 agitfilm *Gvozd' v sapoge (A Nail in the Boot)* illustrates the inherent danger of tampering with the fixed rules of legal mythopoesis and of deviating in any way from the master plot described above. Works that avoided this pitfall, such as Aleksandr Afinogenov's 1931 play *Strakh (Fear)* and Ivan Pyr'ev's 1936 film *Partiinyi bilet (The Party Card)*, culminated in trials that looked and functioned like their real-life counterparts. In both works, the final courtroom scene identifies the enemy lurking in Soviet society and compels him to confess his unwitting participation in counter-revolutionary wrecking. The only departure of such plays and films from the pattern articulated in actual trials of the time was the ongoing myth of the enemy's rehabilitation. In real-life trials of the 1930s, the defendant was convicted and universally condemned, but in fictional works such as *Fear* and *The Party Card*, the court displays an almost anachronistic compassion toward those found guilty of hindering the construction of socialism. Even in this romantic inversion of the outcome of actual show trials, the media and genres that created legal mythopoesis in the 1920s returned to the courtroom for authoritative images and language in the 1930s.

A NAIL IN THE BOOT

The movement away from fictional genres of legal propaganda was clearly expressed in Glavrepertkom's decision in 1931 to ban Kalatozov's silent film *A Nail in the Boot*. Even though Kalatozov's film represented a creative addition to the state's campaign against defective goods (known as *brak*), the director's use of earlier paradigms for fictional trials failed as an instance of mythopoetic justice in the early 1930s. The film copies the threefold pattern of confession, repentance, and reintegration into the community that originated in the agitsud and informed melodramatic films such as *Saba* and *The Parisian Cobbler*. At the same time, *A Nail in the Boot* fell into the subset of movies featuring unjust Soviet trials, which included *The Crime of Ivan Karavaev* and *The Difficult Years*. Kalatozov's creative recycling of a variety of fictional trials would seem to assure the success of *A Nail in the Boot*. Nonetheless, the movie was attacked in the film industry press and prohibited from public screening by Glavrepertkom.[3] Even though Kalatozov followed in the footsteps of numerous film directors who successfully brought the agitsud to the screen, his recombination of earlier paradigms of mythopoetic justice in effect challenged the images and rhetoric of the actual Soviet court in 1931.

When examined as legal propaganda from before the Shakhty Affair, *A Nail in the Boot* presents a relatively orthodox rendition of both the theatrical mock trial and the real-life show trial.[4] The film tells the story of a well-intended Red Army soldier who tries to save his comrades on an armored train during a simulated enemy attack. The soldier is clandestinely sent from the stranded train with a dispatch requesting additional "arms" and troops. He reaches the back lines too late, because of a nail in his boot, which prevents him from crossing a barbed-wire barricade separating him from his support. For the offense of not delivering the dispatch, the soldier's "crime was judged by a court of proletarians," which reproduces the stock images and vocabulary of agitsudy from the end of the 1920s. As the trial scene begins, the camera pans across the mock courtroom, showing the standard raised dais and attentive audience seen in feature films and documentaries from the 1920s. The active involvement of those attending the soldier's trial, including a brigade of politically aware children, makes the opening moments of the trial scene seem the consummate example of an agitsud.

Like most courtroom scenes in silent features, the soldier's trial contains extensive intertitles, to help the film's viewer interpret the images on screen. Initially, these intertitles define the soldier's crime, reiterate its gravity, and describe its dire consequences. In a series of pointed questions, the state's prosecutor explains that the soldier's behavior during mock military maneuvers constitutes an actual betrayal of his army comrades, his class, and the revolution:

> Does the accused know that maneuvers are just like war? . . .
> Does he understand the full importance of delivering the dispatch? . . .
> Does he understand the oath of a soldier to the Revolution? . . .
> You're taken prisoner. The enemy orders—shoot your own men! . . .
> You shoot! The undelivered dispatch is just such a bullet! . . .
> Knowing the duty and honor of a proletarian. . . .
> He pitied his own feet and the armored train perished. . . .
> He betrayed.

After each question, the soldier's eyes meet those of his accuser and his head sinks ever lower, signaling the defendant's confession and contrition for his crime. At the end of the prosecutor's diatribe, the soldier slumps crestfallen in his chair, and the angry audience at the trial shouts, "Kill him, the vermin [*gad*]." The children's brigade enters the court with toy guns in hand, waving a large banner that proclaims, "We don't want fathers like this." If the soldier's trial were to end at this moment, *A Nail in the Boot* would reproduce exactly the action and desired effect of agitsudy of only a few years before. Kalatozov clearly depicts the soldier's coming to consciousness and the audience's active role in judging his crime.

The soldier's trial continues, however, with a sudden reversal in the labels of accuser and accused. Throughout the prosecutor's speech, the audience in the movie theater, unlike that in the film, knows that the soldier did his best to deliver the dispatch, that he risked his well-being and seriously injured his bare feet to deliver the message while on maneuvers.[5] As a result, the film's spectator recognizes that the court's indictment of the soldier is unjust, expecting that the denunciation of the court will be revoked and that the long-suffering soldier will finally triumph through the rendering of poetic justice. The tension between the crowd's growing wrath and the soldier's thinning patience becomes palpable as the camera cuts from angry spectators shouting their condemnation to the silent—but enraged—defendant. The intertitles that flash on the screen accurately describe the crowd's fury at the traitor: "There are moments—the impassioned heart is full of anger . . . and longer than the longest speeches, a single word is uttered." Yet these ominous words apply equally to the soldier's rising indignation with the mock court that refuses to acknowledge the extenuating circumstances of his crime. When the court gives the soldier the right to speak in his own defense, he neither reiterates his confession nor submits to the unjust verdict of the court. Instead, he rises to his feet and defiantly proclaims,

> I'm not the only guilty one. . . .
> If a brick is poorly baked [cut to a falling smokestack] . . .
> and steel is not hardened [cut to a train running off the tracks]. . . .
> A nail. . . .
> A nail in the boot . . .
> you perished on the armored train . . .
> you sewed defective boots. . . .
> You are traitors of defense. . . .
> What? am I alone guilty? . . .
> Confess that you yourselves are guilty!

The soldier takes off the boot that prevented him from completing his mission and points an accusing finger at the trial's spectators, who now are the ones to hang their heads in shame. With this sudden turning of the tables, the mock trial in the film is instantaneously transformed into the actual judgment of those who produced the defective boot. The indictment and condemnation of the trial's audience, which was always implicit in the agitsud, becomes explicit in the soldier's menacing gaze and accurately placed accusations.

By the end of *A Nail in the Boot,* not only the guilty bootmakers but also the entire audience at the trial confess to having produced defective goods that sabotaged the soldier's mission. The band of children ready to condemn him now redirects its wrath to "Defective goods—our enemy," and the bootmaker promises to sew boots without any nails at all. The closing frames of *A Nail in the Boot* apply the message of confession, repentance, and social reintegration to the film's audience. A final pair of intertitles asks if those watching the movie are not guilty of the same crime: "Among you sitting in the movie theater. . . . Are there many such shoemakers?"[6] As had been the case in earlier feature films and newsreels, the audience on the screen provides a model of behavior for the audience watching the screen, prompting the moviegoer to eradicate defective goods that hinder the construction of socialism.

Notwithstanding Kalatozov's inventive reworking of a variety of fic-

The accused soldier of *A Nail in the Boot* waves the faulty footwear that caused him to fail on his mission and accuses those seated in the courtroom of producing defective goods. From reel 6 of *Gvozd' v sapoge (A Nail in the Boot)*, M. Kalatozov, 1931, Goskinoprom Gruzii.

tional trials, *A Nail in the Boot* was condemned for its "incorrect depiction of the Red Army" and was never shown to its intended audience in the Soviet Union.[7] The alleged falseness of Kalatozov's depiction of the Red Army might well have been the result of including saboteurs in the cadre of soldiers who first accuse and then confess in the film's mock trial. Behind this rather vague criticism lies the fact that the soldier on trial in the film does not follow the pattern of the submissive, obedient citizen. Unlike other defendants in feature films with unjust trials, the soldier neither waits for the Soviet court to rectify its unjust decision nor seeks the approval of an appropriate authority figure once he has decided to act willfully. The soldier defiantly disobeys the mock court and uses the same theatrical gestures and potent metaphorical language in his own defense as the prosecution uses initially in its accusation. In addition, Kalatozov has made the soldier's fate itself the transposition of the children's rhyme "For the want of a nail the shoe was lost" and has embellished the soldier's denunciation of the accusing crowd of saboteurs with powerful images that complete the other aphorisms he brings to his defense.[8] By 1931 the defendant's role was one of submission in actual Soviet courts. The ability of Kalatozov's fictional defendant to wield the theatrical means of persuasion and to correct the court's faulty evaluation is more reminiscent of the 1922 trial of the SRs than of later trials, in which the accused was deprived access to the theatrical means of representation or was exposed as falsely theatrical in his defense. Kalatozov's depiction of the Red Army is arguably incorrect, but his headstrong hero in A Nail in the Boot falls decidedly outside the paradigm of mythopoetic justice put into place after the Shakhty Affair.

Furthermore, the elemental wrath and spontaneous participation of the film's proletarian spectators is shown to have been terribly misplaced by the end of the film. The crowd and the court display as much enthusiasm for routing out defective goods as they once did for punishing the well-intended, sabotaged, and ultimately innocent soldier. A Nail in the Boot was indeed overly successful in showing the ever widening web of sabotage in the Soviet Union.[9] As the soldier's damning accusation shows, the guilt he initially took on his own shoulders ultimately belonged to the fictional court that allowed defective boots to be manufactured and tried to cover its tracks by putting him on trial. Although A Nail in the Boot addresses the distressing problem of defective goods (a topic of undeniable importance as Soviet society industrialized), the film nevertheless uses a legal paradigm that is already out-of-date, one that contradicts the image of the Stalinist show trial's omnipotent and infallible court. Although Kalatozov's subject matter in the film must have met with Glavrepertkom's approval, his conflation of theatrical and cinematic variations on the fictional trial could not have done so in 1931.

THE TRIAL OF THE INDUSTRIAL PARTY

In the same year as the prohibition of A Nail in the Boot, a documentary film of the 1930 trial of the Industrial Party appeared on Soviet movie screens, linking for the first time cinematic images of the enemies of the people with the actual sounds of confession. Since 1918 cinema had helped to propagate the messages of show trials and to shape their narrative along melodramatic lines. Trial documentaries of the 1930s looked back for both ideological and stylistic guidance to the newsreels and short features of the earlier decade, and in particular to Vertov's skillful treatment of the SR trial.[10] Nevertheless, trial documentaries of the 1920s never exceeded three or four reels of film and, hence, provided ideologically correct news coverage instead of a feature-length story (usually six to eight reels). In this regard, Posel'skii's 1931 film provided the turning point: cinematic editing gave coverage of the trial of the Industrial Party a newfound narrative continuity, which the sounds of courtroom testimony enhanced.[11]

The Trial of the Industrial Party figures as the primogenitor of the feature-length, documentary trial film, as well as one of the first sound movies ever produced in the Soviet Union. That the struggling Soviet film industry devoted scarce resources to a trial film as one of its first experiments in talking cinema indicates the importance not only of transmitting the lessons of show trials on film but also of linking their visual and oral aspects in the trial's cinematic record. Over four times the length of any preceding trial documentary, this film (comprised of eight reels) duplicates and expands the master narrative of earlier newsreels and demonstrates that by 1930 the theatrical paradigm of the Stalinist show trial was being staged for a movie audience.

In the print media that accompanied the case of the Industrial Party, journalists, court officials, and Stalin himself described the 1930 trial as the logical consequence of the Shakhty Affair. As the state's prosecutor Nikolai Krylenko stated in his closing argument, the trial of the Industrial Party was "a reproduction of the Shakhty trial on a broadened base."[12] The 1928 case had proved the existence of sabotage and espionage in Soviet industry, and thus the Shakhty Affair provided the model of questioning and testimony in 1930.[13] The eight defendants allegedly belonging to the Industrial Party came from the highest levels of Soviet economic planning and were accused of having counter-revolutionary contact with hostile foreign powers. The most prominent prisoner on the bench, Professor Ramzin, confessed to the charges against him and even testified to his connection with Rabinovich, one of the convicted defendants from the Shakhty case. Like the earlier trial, the accusations in the trial of the Industrial Party addressed actual problems in the uneven development of the Soviet economy but diverted attention from the Soviet state, which otherwise would bear responsibility for economic shortfalls. Likewise, a media campaign outside the courtroom anticipated and accompanied the 1930 trial, which once again fell under the direction of court president Vyshinskii and prosecutor Krylenko. For all these similarities, from the state's point of view the trial of the Industrial Party proved more successful than the Shakhty Affair: all eight of the defendants confessed to wrecking and espionage and expressed a profound desire to return to productive life in the Soviet economy.[14]

The compliant confessions of Ramzin and his cohorts gave Posel'skii more suitable material than any director of earlier trial films had ever had.

Stalin's guidance in formulating the trial's script, as shown in a letter to the head of the secret police Menzhinskii, helped to produce testimony suitable for preservation on film.[15] Cinematic editing of the trial's raw material created a narrative that eliminated the type of theatrical blunders that had proved problematic in the Shakhty Affair. Luckily, the outtakes from *The Trial of the Industrial Party* have been preserved in Russian film archives under the title of *Zagovov interventov (A Conspiracy of Interventionists)*, described in the archive catalog as a sound chronicle of the 1930 case. *A Conspiracy of Interventionists* contains numerous contradictions in the defendants' scripted testimony and verbal sparring between the accused and the court, that is, moments less than flattering to prosecutor Krylenko and president Vyshinskii. For example, the camera in *A Conspiracy of Interventionists* is sometimes entirely out of focus or jiggles sloppily as it pans across the court. At times, Krylenko's face is poorly framed and Vyshinskii's is obscured by table lamps or microphones. Although such shots suited defendants in Posel'skii's film, they proved altogether unworthy of the trial's heroes and were consequently cut from the final version of *The Trial of the Industrial Party*. In addition, *A Conspiracy of Interventionists* includes smiling or laughing defendants and court members smoking cigarettes, both examples of behavior that appeared in newsreels from the 1920s but disappeared from Posel'skii's finished product.

Not only did editing make the narrative of *The Trial of the Industrial Party* highly selective, but it is also quite probable that many of the sequences in Posel'skii's film were not shot while court was in session but during rehearsals that anticipated the trial's public performance. The consciousness of the trial's filmability, as well as the live audience in the Moscow House of Soviets, prompted court officials to rehearse witnesses and defendants and might have impelled those making a documentary film to incorporate ideologically appropriate images even if they were not part of the actual event being chronicled.[16] While Kuleshov and Chiaureli imported documentary footage into *Mr. West* and *Saba* to buttress the fictional world on film, Posel'skii conceivably imported fictional passages into *The Trial of the Industrial Party* to enhance the reality he portrayed.

Despite its carefully filmed and edited material, *The Trial of the Industrial Party* does not tell a complicated story: Posel'skii's film is very long (running well over two hours), remarkably monotonous, and presents little more than a series of simple juxtapositions between the enemies of the people and the judges and spectators at the trial. The elegantly decorated, columned courtroom in which Soviet legal officials occupy heavy, tall-backed chairs provides a striking contrast to the disheveled clothing and frightened expressions of the accused. The disparity between individual

Filming the trial of the Industrial Party. From reel 2 of a special edition of *Soiuzkino-Khronika* titled *Protsess "Promyshlennoi partii," (Trial of the "Industrial Party"),* no. 1, 1930.

defendants, sweating under the glare of movie lights and obscured by large microphones, and the orderly rows of hundreds of audience members reiterates the defendants' isolation. To strengthen this opposition, the film uses different camera angles to depict judges, audience, and accused. Generally, the camera looks up at the raised dais of the court or is situated on the same level as the judges. From this perspective, the camera must look down on the mass of spectators, whose individual faces rarely appear in the film. Regardless of camera angle, both judges and spectators are usually shown full face. On the contrary, defendants are shot primarily from above and behind for medium-range shots and predominantly in profile for close-ups. Such polarized use of camera angles communicates the vast gulf separating the enemies on trial from their judges and audience.

The use of close-ups in profile might merely have provided a way for cameramen to shoot around the many microphones that screened the faces of the accused as they testified at the trial. However, the unusual number and frequency of such shots in profile constitute the visual definition or cinematic mug shot of the accused men. Like abnormal biological specimens, Ramzin and his codefendants are depicted not as individuals but as illustrations of a single enemy type, which the camera reveals through its repeated angles and close-ups in profile. This deliberate visual monotony is reinforced by the almost identical scripts repeated by all eight defendants in the witness stand. Even more uniformly than the Shakhty engineers, the professors on trial in the Industrial Party case confess their crimes, repent their wrongdoing, and beg to be let back into the Soviet workforce. The repetition of the nearly identical images and words of Ramzin, Charnovskii, Kalinnikov, and so on renders the many depictions of individual enemies into a single portrait of the protoenemy.[17]

As part of this definition of the enemy type, the majority of the accused men are shown poorly dressed, with dog-eared scripts for confession in their hands. Although the sincerity of confession is of paramount importance, *The Trial of the Industrial Party* depicts the defendants as falsely theatrical and melodramatic, while their accusers maintain a cinematic illusion of spontaneity and control over the trial. The camera work and editing of *The Trial of the Industrial Party* show the theatrical devices that defendants try to use to exculpate themselves. At the same time, Posel'skii's film keeps the Soviet court's use of theatrical and cinematic convention hidden from view. To underscore this contrast, the film's soundtrack juxtaposes the firm, accusing voices of Krylenko and Vyshinskii with the unsure, often broken confessions of the men on trial.[18] With the addition of sound and the substantial expansion of the trial's narrative, the feature-length trial documentary became the new agitsud, unmasking internal, hidden enemies for the Soviet Union's moviegoing public.

Despite its narrative simplicity and repetition, *The Trial of the Industrial Party* reshapes actual trial testimony along melodramatic lines and brings the story of the Stalinist show trial closer to that of fictional trials on film.[19] The individual statements of each defendant replicate the enemy's melodramatic unmasking, much as in *Saba* or *The Secret of the Rapid*. Unlike either of these feature films, *The Trial of the Industrial Party* depicts the possibility of leniency from the real-life court and that of rehabilitation as slim to nonexistent.[20] Nonetheless, Posel'skii's film depicts the sentence handed down in the actual courtroom as the fulfillment of the poetic justice required by the defendants' stories of sabotage, betrayal, and treason. The almost complete elimination of scenes outside the great hall means that those watching *The Trial of the Industrial Party* relied entirely on the drama inside the courtroom for their understanding of the stereotypical villains and heroes of melodrama.

The combined visual and auditory typecasting of Ramzin and his codefendants defines the melodramatic villain for moviegoers, but where is the downtrodden, long-suffering, melodramatic hero? Vyshinskii and

Krylenko represent one possibility for heroes, since they deal the decisive blows in the legal battle on film. Yet neither Vyshinskii nor Krylenko falls under the rubric of a victim of the defendants' crimes; rather, as members of the court, they are tools indispensable to rendering poetic justice. The actual victim of the economic wrecking described here is none other than the audience of the trial within the film, along with its counterpart seated in the movie theater. In the place of the often lachrymose victims of fictional trials on film, those watching Posel'skii's film see avidly interested spectators, who listen in rapt attention to the testimony of witnesses, much like their predecessors in newsreels of the Shakhty Affair. In addition, like their precursors in Vertov's films of the SR trial, the audience inside *The Trial of the Industrial Party* expresses its enthusiastic involvement in a mass demonstration, replete with parading soldiers, tanks, burning torches, and enormous banners carried through the dark snowy streets of Moscow. *The Trial of the Industrial Party* casts the entire Soviet citizenry in the role of the melodramatic victim, who now exults as the villainous wreckers receive their just deserts.

The defendants in the trial of the Industrial Party hear their sentences. The key defendant and witness, Professor Ramzin, looks down in shame in the middle of the frame. From reel 8 of *Protsess Prompartii (13 dnei)* (*The Trial of the Industrial Party [13 Days]*), Ia. Posel'skii, 1930, Soiuzkinokhronika.

The importance of melodramatic unmasking in this film becomes clear in its most climactic episode. After the majority of the defendants have initially testified, the engineer Osadchii is called as a witness to German involvement in industrial sabotage. Before Osadchii has a chance to speak, president Vyshinskii reminds the defendant of his oath to tell the truth. After hearing these words, Osadchii breaks off his testimony and confesses his own participation in economic wrecking. The completely unanticipated unmasking of the enemy breathes new life into the formula for confession and repentance repeated by all the defendants in the film. In addition, Osadchii's sudden turnaround in front of microphones and movie cameras shows the moment of conversion, which for other defendants has already taken place off camera. As Osadchii elaborates the details of his crimes, a series of cuts underscores the melodrama: the movie camera moves from above the defendant's head to show a journalist with camera in hand recording Osadchii's confession for posterity. Then the film cuts to the audience listening to his confession, showing it first as a unified spectating mass, next in close-ups of individual viewers, and lastly in its totality. The movement of the camera and this relatively rapid cutting make Osadchii's testimony stand out from the rest of the film, which consists primarily of long sustained shots maintaining the same camera angle and focus for minutes at a time. This high drama reveals the underlying melodrama of all the confessions as well as the fundamentally melodramatic nature of the film's narrative as a whole.

The brief, silent newsreels released as part of the propaganda campaign surrounding the case of the Industrial Party duplicate the melodramatic story told in Posel'skii's film. In particular, the technique of the cinematic mug shot reappears in these news shorts and other trial films produced in the first half of the 1930s.[21] Although these short subjects lack sound, in many ways they resemble Posel'skii's talking picture more than the trial films of ten years before. Posel'skii's work served to codify the cinematic representation of friends and enemies, eliminating all ambiguity from the master narrative. As a result, silent newsreels that follow in the wake of *The Trial of the Industrial Party* had no need for the ample intertitles of 1920s to make their meaning clear.

Proof of this point lies in three silent films produced as part of the so-called Menshevik trial in 1931, all of which repeat and condense the technique of the cinematic mug shot. These three films—*Internatsional interventov (The International of Interventionists)*, *Sud idet (Order in the Court)*, and *Blok interventov (The Blok of Interventionists)*, all from 1931—contain long sequences, in which some five to ten of the men on trial are named in an intertitle and then shown (often in profile) for five to ten seconds while giving testimony in the witness stand. The rapid cutting from defendant to defendant, as well as the repetition of the same camera angle for each, intensifies the impression of their similarity, effectively reducing them to caricatures of the protoenemy. *The Blok of Interventionists* follows these cinematic mug shots with a series of newspaper cartoons depicting several of the men on trial. By using the visual cues established in Posel'skii's film, directors of silent trial newsreels in the early 1930s could evoke the complete master narrative of the Stalinist show trial without quoting it in its entirety—and also without sound.

As the Menshevik trial illustrates, most of the show trials that came in the wake of the case of the Industrial Party became the subject of feature-length documentary films. Like *The Trial of the Industrial Party,* these trial films placed defendants' testimony in a melodramatic mold, which consequently shaped the audience within the film into the downtrodden—but ultimately victorious—victim. In each film, the camera told the same story of poetic justice, using the same set, the columned hall of the Moscow House of Soviets, and the same cast of characters, Krylenko, Vyshinskii, the enemy, and the audience.[22] The anti-NEP rhetoric that characterized show trials up to and including the Shakhty Affair gave way to accusations against Trotskiite spies, whom documentary film could define visually and verbally as a single enemy type. The remarkable consistency of setting, characters, cinematic style, and the interlacing crimes and accusations in all of these films create the metanarrative of mythopoetic justice in the 1930s. This cinematic story of confession, contrition, and an utterly futile appeal for reintegration into the community was the 1930s' version of the 1920s' agitsud.

PROPAGATING AND DISPELLING FEAR

The death sentences handed down in the trial of the Industrial Party sent a harsh message to the Soviet technical intelligentsia, which the dramatists Maksim Gor'kii and Aleksandr Afinogenov reproduced in plays written the following year. Gor'kii composed *Somov i drugie (Somov and Others)* in 1931 (first published 1941) as a fictional prologue to the trial of the Industrial Party. The drama describes life among a group of wreckers, who are apprehended by an agent from the People's Commissariat of Internal Affairs, or NKVD, in the final moments of the play. However, Gor'kii was never satisfied with the script of *Somov and Others,* which he declined both to publish and to stage during his lifetime.[23] Afinogenov's *Fear,* which provided a subtext for the confessions of the 1930 trial, premiered simultaneously in Moscow and Leningrad, where the play met enthusiastic responses from spectators and critics alike.[24] Afinogenov took the struggle to purge and politicize the Soviet sciences as his subject matter in the play, building a cast of characters around a fictional group of professor-enemies that bears a striking resemblance to the defendants in the trial of the Industrial Party.[25]

Afinogenov's dramatization of the fall of men such as Professor Ramzin created a psychological portrait of the enemy, which had much greater depth and complexity than those in real-life trials or on documentary film. In the character of Professor Borodin, the playwright revealed not only the social struggle but also the inner conflict of specialists resistant to the new sciences. As if in confirmation of the testimony provided in the trial of the Industrial Party, *Fear* showed that even the most well-intended member of the old intelligentsia would stumble into the hands of wreckers and spies if he did not embrace the political basis of scientific research. Despite the playwright's schematic approach to scientific method and a tendency to stereotype secondary characters, the premiere of *Fear* in both Moscow and Leningrad was hailed as a stride forward in proletarian dramaturgy.[26]

In fact, the critics' few lingering complaints of schematic character development show that Afinogenov patterned his dramatis personae on the melodramatic stereotypes of friends and enemies that had percolated through *agitki* of the 1920s into actual trials of the 1930s. *Fear*'s cast of characters is clearly divided into two camps: the friends of class-based methods of analysis in the Soviet social sciences and (as one would imagine) their foes. Easily identifiable as the play's positive characters, the camp of friends is peopled by Soviet renditions of the melodramatic underdog. The old Bolshevik Klara Spasova acts as their ideological mother figure, nurturing these positive characters with a kind of political tough love. Spasova's speech denouncing Borodin's dangerous ideology in the third act of *Fear* provides the play's climax and marks her as a mouthpiece of political orthodoxy.[27] Her youthful double, Elena Makarova, also belongs in the camp of friends because of her proletarian background, membership in the Communist Party, and sincere desire to work for the advancement of Soviet science. Since her plans to analyze human behavior according to social class are initially thwarted, the viewer accordingly identifies Makarova as the hardworking, long-suffering female heroine, who will eventually triumph through the rendering of poetic justice. Also in the camp of the friends are Makarova's young pioneer step-daughter and Khusain Kimbaev, a stereotypical central Asian described as a young man "with high cheek bones" and round glasses.[28] The truly proletarian origins and unqualified love of labor of all four of these characters mark them as a positive force in the play and alert the viewer of their eventual victory.

In contrast to the relatively small camp of friends, that of foes is quite large and contains a wide variety of enemies of socialism. Unlike real-life trials, in which adversaries of all kinds were reduced to a single enemy type, *Fear* depicts the nuances that distinguish intellectual sabotage from deliberate wrecking and undercover espionage. The most insidious enemy of progress in the Institute for Physiological Stimuli does not even appear on stage. The archenemy Professor Kotomin has already been arrested when the play begins, and his name is invoked at key moments during the action, suggesting his similarity to the real-life Professor Ramzin. Kotomin figures as the head of an unnamed group of scientific conspirators, which prompts the viewer to draw a parallel with the Industrial Party case. If understanding the archenemy of *Fear* requires real-life trials of the era as a subtext, then Afinogenov's play creates yet another subtext for actual show trials by describing what happens in the archenemy's wake.

The saboteurs and wreckers under Kotomin's sway predictably conceal their truly despicable colors at the play's beginning. Among them appear a number of mid-level bureaucrats from the institute's administration: a professor of ancient eastern religions named Zakharov, the institute's secretary Vargasov, and the perpetual graduate student Kastal'skii. Zakharov and Vargasov plan to send Kastal'skii on business to Germany, where he will "carry a certain message abroad" (68).

In addition to these three followers of Kotomin, a host of accessory enemies appear in *Fear* as the unintentional aides to the plans of this wrecking troika. The institute's director falls under their influence; the retrograde party member and Makarova's estranged husband, Tsekhovoi, succumbs to their blackmail; Tsekhovoi's impoverished mother provides them with the material necessary to blackmail her son. The losing combination of bad class background, political ignorance, and extreme selfishness makes other characters vulnerable to the troika's overtures and provocation. Taken in its entirety, this variegated cluster of enemies constitutes the camp of "rats," the most colorful insult hurled between positive and negative characters in the play.[29]

The two most interesting and important members of the camp of rats prove to be Borodin and his son-in-law Bobrov, both of whom manage to escape the evil influence of the saboteurs and join the camp of friends. For Bobrov, casting off his vain, lazy, artsy wife proves decisive in his battle to discover the true connection between science and political ideology. Bobrov successfully denies his former ties with the convicted Kotomin and forges friendships with Makarova and Kimbaev, as the first step on his path toward rebirth. Because of his youth and proximity to the working class, Bobrov's reawakening takes place relatively smoothly and rapidly in the play. However, the same changes prove significantly more problematic for the older Borodin, whose story of conversion to the new way of life fuels the central conflict and plot of *Fear*.

The struggle between the bourgeois Borodin and his proletarian graduate students not only figures as a conflict between two politically opposed generations but also encompasses the revolutionary struggle between social classes, genders, and even nationalities. With the support of Spasova and Kimbaev, Makarova tries to modify Borodin's research plans in an attempt to move them out of the realm of pure theory. At first Borodin agrees to Makarova's proposed alterations, but only so that he can sabotage the new methods of research recommended by her. In his passion for abstract science and his deeply embedded, pre-revolutionary ways of thought, Borodin remains ignorant that Kastal'skii, Zakharov, and ultimately Kotomin have a vested interest in his sabotage. In spite of his high ideals and genuine love of science, Borodin has fallen into the hands of the enemy and abetted the scheme to sabotage the institute. The actor playing the role in *Fear*'s Moscow premiere recognized that Borodin is the fictional counterpart of convicted men such as Ramzin: "He's just a typical counter-revolutionary. . . . Such people should be thrown in jail."[30]

As the actor's response to his role suggests, the judgment of Borodin is foretold at the play's beginning, long before he actually falls under police investigation. To strengthen the foreshadowing of Borodin's trial, Afinogenov places a number of subtle markers earlier in the play (13, 82). For example, when Borodin discovers the unrequited love of his pre-revolutionary past, he is reminded of his lost youth in which he recited poetry under "the lights of the columned hall" in a student recital (106). Although this memory initially pulls Borodin back to a gentler time and place, it ultimately pushes him forward to his own indictment in the same columned hall. Borodin recognizes that the intervening twenty years have changed the spectacles taking place in this particular venue and have transformed people such as himself from aspiring lovers into candidates for purging: "Kirghizes with high cheek bones are driving out the scientists, professors are being put in jail" (19). When Borodin contemplates the disappointing betrayal of Kotomin, he also describes his own fate: "There's no one you can trust. Even friends will betray you. Kotomin is on trial. He joined a wrecking party. . . . Such a nice person, and now a scoundrel!" (70). Borodin's remarks not only foreshadow his police investigation but also prompt the recognition of his own guilt: "I've fallen in with the class enemies. Thank you. Look at me, guys: a living class enemy!" (72–73).

Long before Borodin confesses his enemy status, he and his proletarian adversaries enter a makeshift courtroom during an official meeting of the institute's presidium. At the beginning of the third act of *Fear*, the governing body of the institute upholds Borodin's scientific leadership in an unjust trial. Borodin triumphs temporarily in the struggle against Makarova because two minions of Kotomin—Vargasov and Zakharov—are seated in the judges' chairs. Although these judges adhere to the rules and rituals of Soviet justice, they wield them to counter-revolutionary ends and reinforce the cult of Borodin's personality at the institute. The officials sitting beside Vargasov and Zakharov at the hearing do nothing more than sip tea, nibble sandwiches, and talk on the phone. Makarova, Bobrov, and Kimbaev defend themselves forcefully before these bogus judges. In spite of their outrage at the kangaroo court's decision, the proletarian graduate students abide by the directive that they support Borodin's research, which contends that "only love, hunger, anger, and fear" stimulate human behavior (4). Makarova, Bobrov, and Kimbaev fall into the pattern of good Soviet citizens subjected to an unjust trial: although they suspect foul play is afoot, none of them disobeys the presidium's ruling, and they redirect their struggle into new channels.

The presidium's perversion of justice is overruled in the beginning of the fourth and final act of *Fear* when Borodin finally falls under investigation. This recuperation of justice focuses on Borodin's counter-revolutionary research at the institute and uncovers the ring of saboteurs taking orders from Kotomin. One by one, Borodin's former allies accuse him of crimes they actually committed. Zakharov heaves an almost audible sigh of relief when he learns most of his misdeeds have gone undetected. Nonetheless, he points an accusing finger at Borodin, as does Vargasov, who calls Borodin the originator of "the program of our scientific party" (93). Kastal'skii performs the quintessential act of betrayal when he states, "Professor Borodin is guilty of all of my crimes" (95). As a consequence of these dovetailing confessions, the demoralized Borodin is removed from the directorship of the institute and confronted with the harsh truth that he is the unwitting tool of scientific saboteurs and spies. The once proud and defiant Borodin realizes the truth of his opponents' point of view and renounces his counter-revolutionary belief in fear as the prime catalyst of human behavior.

Although Borodin now believes he is of no use to Soviet science, his former adversary Makarova urges him to confess his error publicly and to rejoin the cadre of reformed scientific workers. The play ends with Borodin's humble confession and his appeal to be reeducated so that he can return to work at the institute, not in the director's office but in the laboratory: "I want to work. . . . I was afraid of Makarova, I closed the door of my office from her, I led her down the wrong path. . . . And I opened the door to [Kastal'skii]. . . . I will tell this to everyone" (111). Makarova welcomes Borodin back into the institute with open arms, showing the compassion and charity of Soviet justice, which allows old specialists to help in the construction of the new science.

Unlike Kalatozov's recuperation of justice in *A Nail in the Boot*, Afinogenov's ordering of an unjust trial followed by a just trial reinforces the paradigm of mythopoetic justice found in real-life show trials of the early 1930s. On one hand, Kalatozov's film allows the accusations of wrecking to expand in a seemingly infinite manner, to encompass the court, the audience, and eventually the film's viewers. On the other hand, Afinogenov concentrates the guilt in *Fear* in the character of Borodin de-spite the presence of other enemies in the play. Borodin's confession and rehabilitation reveal the psychological drama behind the sworn statements methodically offered by defendants in actual trials. While the accused in the Shakhty Affair and the trial of the Industrial Party were never seen in their private studies debating the orthodoxy of their views, the audience of *Fear* could watch Borodin gradually realize his personal guilt and could observe the profound samokritika that precedes confession. The difficulty of Borodin's conversion underscores the psychological implications of joining the new order: "The rebirth of a person is not like fixing a tractor. . . . A member of the gentry standing in the assembly line is still not a pro-letarian" (23). Borodin's conversion to Soviet methods of science in *Fear* fills in the psychological gap in the testimony of actual trial defendants and, in doing so, maintains the legal mythopoesis constructed in the Stal-inist show trial.[31]

Nevertheless, in contrast to the actual trials and their documentary record on film, *Fear* portrays the possibility of returning to the scientific community once the enemy has repented. The final component of the agit-sud's tripartite paradigm had been reduced to ritualized pleas on the part of defendants in real-life trials of the early 1930s. Actual defendants such as Ramzin begged for clemency and a second chance rarely if ever given by the Soviet court. On the contrary, Borodin receives the opportunity to renew himself without asking and returns to productive life in the insti-tute's laboratory. Borodin's unforced acceptance of his judges' offer shows his worth to the new regime and allows the audience to imagine his enthu-siastic participation in the institute's research after the curtain falls in *Fear*. In actual trials of the time, the absolute guilt of the accused and the im-possibility of his rehabilitation were predetermined by his indictment; in the fictional world of *Fear*, the scales of justice still weigh the evidence and take mitigating circumstances into account. The fiction of forgiving and benevolent judgment maintained in *Fear* provides a counterbalance to the vengeful sentences handed down in actual show trials of the day. If a fictional character such as Borodin could be exonerated and participate in the building of socialism, real-life defendants such as Ramzin and his cohorts only had their deeply ingrained enemy nature to blame for the Soviet court's condemnation.

Fear relies on the mythopoetic justice of real-life trials for the construction of a fictional world, which in its turn supports the institutions of justice portrayed in the play. Not only does Afinogenov's play provide a glimpse behind the scenes of defendants' confessions in actual trials, it also describes the ever widening web of guilt that emerged from the trials and simultaneously fueled them. While the police investigation censures Borodin and purges the institute, the most pernicious wreckers in *Fear* have been unmasked only for the play's spectator and have not been put on trial in the play itself. The destructive Kotomin has indeed been judged and condemned, but his lackeys Kastal'skii, Vargasov, and Zakharov mysteriously disappear at the end of the play. Although it seems most likely that they too have gone the way of Kotomin, the possibility still exists that the troika of wreckers in the institute continue their sabotage in a new place and by new methods. Afinogenov's play shows that "feelings once considered innate are dying away . . . envy, jealousy, anger, and fear are disappearing . . . collectivity, enthusiasm, joie de vivre are growing" (22) for those who are friends of Soviet progress. Nevertheless, the anxiety remains that Kotomin and his ilk will coerce new, unsuspecting victims to join their association and continue their sabotage only temporarily impeded. Afinogenov's play effectively does what Lunacharskii would recommend for socialist realist drama in a 1933 speech: the playwright sings the glory of those victimized by the enemies of Soviet power and unmasks the hidden enemy in his drama, which constitutes "an act of self-knowledge, self-judging, [and] self-organization."[32]

THE PARTY CARD

Plays such as *Fear* put fictional enemies on the Soviet stage to corroborate and illustrate the confessions of defendants in actual trials of the early 1930s. Feature films offered additional proof of the reality of the crimes of wrecking, sabotage, and espionage, proving that cinema was a more powerful medium for substantiating the false charges leveled in the era's show trials. Stalin's avid interest and personal involvement in the Soviet film industry confirmed Lenin's statement from approximately ten years before that cinema was the most important and most powerful of the Soviet arts.

In spite of Stalin's apparent inability to grasp the aesthetic principles of film, he acted as the country's supreme movie censor for almost twenty years, monitoring and correcting the fictional reality presented on film for consumption by the Soviet masses. Not only the watchfulness of Stalin, but also that of Glavrepertkom, the Party, and various amateur organizations that claimed a right to inspect cinematic releases, all increased the difficulty of bringing films to their intended audience during the decade and underscored the importance of the fictional reality portrayed in feature films.[33]

A startling percentage of the movies that survived these multiple levels of censorship depict the melodramatic unmasking of the enemy of the people. Approximately one-sixth of the over three hundred (308) films released in the Soviet Union between 1933 and 1940 deals with the battle against spies and saboteurs, as Peter Kenez describes in his history of film under Stalin:

> The scenarios closely resembled the tales of the most vicious story-teller of them all, Andrei Vyshinsky, the Chief Prosecutor at the purge trials. In the films, as in the confessions at the trials, the enemy perpetrated the most dastardly acts out of an unreasoned hatred for decent socialist society. In fifty-two out of the eighty-five films dealing with contemporary life (i.e. more than half) the hero (for it was usually a man) unmasked hidden enemies who had committed criminal acts. The hero could never be too vigilant. The enemy turned out sometimes to be the hero's best friend, sometimes his wife, and sometimes his father.[34]

As the decade's reworking of the agitsud, trial documentaries created a unified portrait of a single enemy type. Feature films from the same era took the protoenemy from documentaries such as *The Trial of the Industrial Party* and explained his multifarious origins and variegated work. Most films devoted to exposing wreckers and saboteurs from the 1930s, such as *Putevka v zhizn' (The Road to Life)* by N. Ekk (1931), *Krestiane (Peasants)* by F. Ermler (1935), and *Bol'shaia zhizn' (A Great Life)* by L. Lukov (1939), did not contain formal trial scenes and instead relied on the decade's ubiquitous notions of samokritika and chistka to render poetic justice. Yet the movie labeled by Kenez as "the most morally reprehensible Soviet film of the 1930s"—I. Pyr'ev's *The Party Card* (1936)—included an unjust trial scene in its unmasking of the hidden enemy and exposed the devices of mythopoetic justice, which provided the subtext of all movies dedicated to routing enemies of the people. In addition, Py'rev's film has the dubious distinction of having been approved for distribution by Stalin himself, after the Mosfilm studios rejected it as "unsuccessful, false, and distorting Soviet reality."[35]

Like many other Soviet films that culminate in a trial scene, *The Party Card* employs legal mythopoesis to preach a message tailor-made for one of the era's many propaganda campaigns. As part of the effort to purge the Communist Party's ranks through document verification in the mid-1930s, Pyr'ev's film taught that the ordinary paper cards issued to Party members were no less sacred than membership itself.[36] To instill this lesson of the card's almost holy significance, *The Party Card* employs the mythic characters and situations that socialist realism brought into the movies in the early 1930s. For example, the action of *The Party Card* revolves around the ubiquitous triad of "party leader, simple person, and wrecker," which appears in all genres of Soviet film of the time.[37] Regardless of the type of film—drama, adventure, comedy, even musical—each member of the triad follows predetermined parameters for character development and, consequently, articulates a foregone set of spectator expectations. In *The Party Card,* the simple girl Anka suffers in the hands of the wrecker Pasha (who happens to be her husband), while the valiant party leader Iasha uncovers Pasha's crime and rescues Anka from the enemy's clutches. As a further articulation of viewer expectations, *The Party Card* places this triad of characters in an inversion of the decade's most successful and long-lived cinematic genre, the Soviet legend film.[38] Rather than depicting a famous leader in the revolutionary struggle such as Lenin, Chapaev, or Suvorov, *The Party Card* focuses on an enemy who masquerades as a leader and who rises ever higher through the ranks of peasants and workers until his inescapable undoing. By placing a villain in the legendary hero's position for the majority of the film, *The Party Card* magnifies the villain's crimes and creates suspenseful anticipation of his inevitable downfall.

If spectator expectations were not sufficiently formed by the film's mythic characters and inverted genre, *The Party Card* cast both its people and its plot in the mold of traditional melodrama, which entails presuppositions of its own. The hidden enemy (Pasha) and the needlessly suffering victim (Anka) prepare the viewer for the rendering of poetic justice, which naturally happens at the end of the film. To intensify the struggle that presages poetic justice, the classic love triangle is superimposed on the triad of party leader, simple person, and class enemy. The wrecker (Pasha) and the honest party leader (Iasha) struggle both in the 1930s version of class warfare and in melodramatic rivalry for Anka's love. Although Iasha is absent from the middle third of the film's action, his return initiates the rendering of poetic justice and signals the film's highly melodramatic climax. Like nineteenth-century theatrical melodramas, whose curtains typically fell on a stage littered with weapons and corpses, *The Party Card* culminates as Anka points a loaded pistol at her enemy-husband, who falls to his knees, begs for her mercy, and knocks the pistol from Anka's hand at the very moment the NKVD and Iasha appear in the doorway.

The original title of Pyr'ev's film, *Anka,* would suggest that *The Party Card* tells the story of the oppressed heroine. However, the portrait of the wrecker Pasha is more fully developed than that of the heroes in the film, who never go beyond the clichés of the innocent childlike woman and the jilted, hardworking lover. On the contrary, Pasha Kuganov breaks out of the abnormal, biological stereotype of the enemy that appears in *The Trial of the Industrial Party.* Pasha is handsome, virile, intelligent; he plays the part of the good Soviet worker so convincingly that everyone around him is deceived in the first half of *The Party Card,* including the film's viewer. When the movie begins, Pasha shows up in Moscow with a small wooden suitcase, the typical young man from the provinces with little more than his own ambition to make it big in the country's capital. Through a stroke of luck, Pasha meets Anka and Iasha who help him get a job at the factory where they work. Anka's cheerful working-class family provides the ideal home for the enterprising Pasha, and he begins to court Anka and to climb the social ladder. Like Anka, the film's spectator is seduced by Pasha's square jaw and rugged good looks, his Soviet-style ambition, and his ability to work. In the first half of the film, the swarthy and determined Pasha is a welcome replacement for the fair, timid, politically preoccupied Iasha as the champion of Anka's heart. But Anka's (and the viewer's) suspicions are aroused when one of Pasha's ex-girlfriends, the similarly dark-skinned Marusia, tells Anka that her fiancé's father was purged as a kulak.

From this point onward, the audience's understanding of Pasha Kuganov takes a turn for the worse, while the trusting Anka continues to love and to live with an enemy of the people. When she learns of Pasha's less than pristine class origins, the honest Anka proposes telling the Party leadership at the factory where they work. The wily Pasha diverts her plans by starting a fire at the factory, which he subsequently extinguishes, making himself into a hero. Instead of being exposed as a wrecker, Pasha earns membership in the Communist Party and moves one rung higher up the ladder of Soviet success. The audience of the film now understands his deceitfulness and begins to suspect he is none other than the evil kulak Dziubin, whom Iasha has uncovered as the murderer of the Komsomol secretary in the town where he now lives. Yet Anka still trusts the snake that has slithered into her heart and home. When her precious Party card is stolen and used by a foreign spy for three days, Anka and her coworkers are entirely dumbfounded, but the film's audience knows Pasha is to blame. The split between the audience's and characters' understanding creates the suspense that propels the plot forward.

The sharp contrast between Anka's continuing love for Pasha and the audience's utter condemnation of him shows the danger of the hidden enemy, who can use even the most loyal and vigilant Soviet citizen in his counter-revolutionary plans.[39] Despite all his criminality, Pasha is not put on trial. Like many of the films discussed above, the courtroom drama in Pyr'ev's film revolves around the innocent victim, Anka, who has unknowingly harbored an enemy of the people and unwittingly provided him access to invaluable Party documents. Anka's trial takes place before several judges from the local Party leadership and a jury of her peers, following the model of the unjust trial before which the obedient Soviet citizen humbly confesses. Initially, Anka denies her guilt in the theft of her Party card, and the rank-and-file Party members at her trial cannot decide whether she is responsible or not. Pasha provides the decisive testimony at the trial when he states categorically that his wife is to blame, and finally the contrite Anka admits "I am guilty" and is summarily expelled from the Party. Although the judges at her trial clearly suspect Pasha's involvement, Anka still does not realize that her husband's condemnation is an attempt to cover his own tracks. Anka's confession indicates her realization that the negligence that led to the theft of her Party card is no less a crime than the enemy agent's misuse of her documents. Ironically, the Party requires Anka's confession of guilt as proof of her innocence, as evidence of both her loyalty and her ignorance of Pasha's wrecking activities. Anka's willingness to subordinate herself entirely to the needs of the Party proves she is blameless and shows her value as a Party member, even if the verdict of her trial seems to state the opposite.

While covering his tracks, Pasha makes the mistake that leads to his unmasking. Rather than testifying that Anka's documents were missing for only three days, Pasha betrays his personal knowledge of the crime by mentioning that the Party card was gone for five entire days. After this blunder, one by one, the true facts concerning Pasha Kuganov come to light: Iasha returns from Siberia with information that proves Pasha is the murderer Dziubin; and Marusia finally exposes the extent of Pasha's crimes to the devastated Anka. Initially duped by Pasha's good looks, the film's viewer now understands the real arrangement of friends and enemies in the film: Anka and Iasha are the fair-haired heroes, whereas Marusia and Pasha are the swarthy villains. In the film's final scene, Anka proves her innocence and Party loyalty once again by aiming the loaded

Anka points a pistol at her husband, the wrecker Pasha who stole her membership card to the Communist Party, and turns him over to the secret police. From reel 10 of *Partiinyi bilet (The Party Card),* I. Pyr'ev, 1936, Mosfil'm.

gun at Pasha Kuganov, calling him by the enemy's real name Dziubin for the first time. When the NKVD rescue Anka from the clutches of her evil husband, she has proved that her loyalty to the Party is stronger than any marriage vow.

Anka's confession and contrition at her trial preach a clear message of Party allegiance in *The Party Card,* one that is reinforced by her apparent willingness to execute her spouse. After she passes through the harrowing episodes of the trial and the confrontation with her villain-husband, Anka can rejoin the Party, be reunited with Iasha, and return to the working collective at the factory from which she was temporarily alienated. Much like *Fear,* Pyr'ev's film reproduces the confession, repentance, and reintegration into the community found in mock trials from a decade before, even though actual show trials of the time eliminated the final element from this threefold paradigm. Although the class enemy was ruthlessly exterminated in real-life trials and in films like *The Party Card,* the myth of rehabilitation continued unabated, appearing in other movies of the decade such as *The Road to Life* and *Zakliuchennye (Prisoners)* (Cherviakov,

1936). In all these films, the use of legal mythopoesis maintains the fiction of the Soviet court's compassion and absolute justice, even in the face of a seemingly unjust verdict. In addition, that the enemy Pasha goes undetected by his friends, family, and wife for some six years justifies the ever increasing vigilance demanded by real-life trials.

The remarkable path taken by Pyr'ev's film, from the dustbin at Mosfilm to the country's movie screens, shows the appeal of *The Party Card* to Stalin himself and the movie's centrality in the canon of socialist realism on film. While the studio deemed Pyr'ev's work a failure because of its exaggeration of everyday life, Stalin evidently found the distortions of *The Party Card* a convincing portrayal of the reality under construction in institutions such as the Stalinist show trial. In fact, the supreme censor was responsible for changing the title of K. Vinogradskaia's original screenplay from *Anka* to *The Party Card,* underlining the film's utility for the Communist Party's purges of its ranks in the middle of the decade.[40] Like *The Party Card, Peasants,* and *A Great Life,* many feature films of the 1930s confirmed the lessons of legal mythopoesis, providing a vital means of justifying and propagating Stalin's Great Terror.

As the ever increasing importance of cinema during the 1930s shows, the Shakhty Affair created a watershed in the production of mythopoetic justice. Before 1928 the Soviet courts turned to the stage and screen to learn the techniques of theatrical and cinematic representation that gave the institution of the show trial its mythopoetic authority. After 1928, however, the opposite was true. Once the Soviet court mastered the theatrical and cinematic techniques of legal mythopoesis, it effectively took up Plato's recommendation to censor the performing arts and to exclude them from the law. The overly creative or anachronistic use of fictional trials doomed to failure not only avant-garde experiments by Kuleshov, Maiakovskii, and Erdman, but also seemingly orthodox works of propaganda, as Kalatozov discovered with the banning of *A Nail in the Boot.* Beginning in the early 1930s, the recipe for success in legal propaganda required stricter adherence to the facts of real-life trials, signaling a shift from fictional to documentary genres such as the feature-length trial documentary film. The cinematic shaping of the sights and sounds of an actual courtroom allowed this genre to define a single enemy type, which authors of works of fiction elaborated in plays and movies that provided the subtext for confessions in actual trials. The 1928 Shakhty Affair initiated a movement away from theater toward the cinema, which provided the most important means for documenting, propagating, and substantiating the crimes of Stalin's Great Terror and their necessary punishment.

Although the preferred genres and media of legal propaganda changed in the wake of the Shakhty Affair, the documentary and feature films responsible for buttressing the lessons of actual trials in the 1930s bore a striking resemblance to their precursors from a decade before. Despite the greater proximity to the reality of the show trials, legal propaganda of the 1930s continued to rely heavily on melodrama, which infused courtroom drama of all varieties with suspense and excitement. The literalization of poetic justice in real and fictional courtrooms of the decade taught essentially the same lessons as the agitsud, even if opportunities for audience participation had already been reduced to the passive consumption of images and sounds. Defendants on stage, screen, and the witness bench continued to repeat the tripartite formula for confession, repentance, and social reintegration initially articulated in the agitsud, even though rehabilitation took place exclusively in the realm of fiction. The ongoing myth of the Soviet court's compassion provided a happy ending for the era's legal melodramas, as well as a stark contrast to the harsh sentences handed down in real-life trials. The interlacing and complementary stories told by legal propaganda on stage, on screen, and in actual courts received the direct approval of Stalin himself, pointing to the overwhelming importance of the show trial's constructed reality in the collective consciousness of Stalin's Russia.

CONCLUSION

The emergence of mythopoetic justice out of the utopian aspirations of Russia's avant-garde theater and cinema corroborates a story told by other scholars of Soviet culture. As was true in literature and the representational arts, a sizable gap separated revolutionary experiments on the Soviet stage and screen during the 1920s from the conventionalized kitsch that dominated the artistic marketplace during the 1930s. Nonetheless, courtroom dramas of both decades shared a common goal that defied periodization, distinctions of medium, and generic categorization. In all venues, trials of the enemies of Soviet power strove for the revolutionary transformation of the viewer's consciousness and the creation of socialist society out of the new, collective man.[1] The diverse theatrical and cinematic currents, which flowed out of Viacheslav Ivanov's vision of a Dionysian theater in the first two decades of the twentieth century, led neither directly nor inexorably to orchestrated displays of samokritika during Stalin's Great Terror. However, theories of a revitalized theater capable of shaping the human spirit connected the poet-philosopher's modernist ambitions to the disturbing reality of the Stalinist show trial.

Theater proved instrumental in codifying the ritualized confession, repentance, and pleas for social reintegration that became the backbone of the Stalinist show trial beginning with the 1928 Shakhty Affair. The unassuming agitsud united seemingly alien strains of social, legal, and religious ritual from pre-revolutionary Russia, creating an entirely new hybrid in the Soviet ritual of samokritika. Cinematic counterparts of theatrical mock trials took the miniature melodrama of confession at the heart of the agitsud and translated it into full-blown melodrama on film. The literalization of poetic justice in movies such as *Saba* and *The Secret of the Rapid* preached the lesson of the internal enemy's conversion to the new way of life and proved easier to control and to distribute than its theatrical predecessor had ever been. In addition, the shift from theater to film altered the model of spectatorship for all trials of the era, laying to rest the nagging question of audience participation.

Together, theater and cinema of the 1920s created a fictional world in which hidden saboteurs secretly labored to undermine the construction of socialism. The Shakhty Affair brought this fictional world into actual existence by placing the melodramatic characters and situations of earlier mock trials in a real Soviet court. Undoubtedly, acts of sabotage and espionage in fact took place during industrialization and collectivization in the Soviet Union. However, the historical record has proved that those crimes actually committed were less frequent, less organized, and less malicious than the Soviet public was led to believe by their depictions in the Shakhty Affair and in feature films of the era. Fictional trials on stage and screen did not originate in the 1920s with an eye to their transposition into the actual court; yet they produced the theatrical and cinematic shaping of the Stalinist show trial, as well as a necessary fictional world in which real-life trials were justifiable and necessary. By the time the paradigm of confession, repentance, and reintegration into society came into the actual courtroom, those organizing the Shakhty Affair had learned to wield complete control over the theatrical and cinematic means of representation in the 1928 trial.

After these two currents converged in the columned hall of the Moscow House of Soviets, the possibilities for legal propaganda shifted noticeably in the early 1930s. Although the Stalinist show trial originally relied on theater and cinema for the construction of mythopoetic justice, it now obscured its spectacular origins once the effectiveness of this formula was confirmed before an international audience. In the wake of the 1928 case, the preferred media and genres of legal propaganda changed entirely, preparing the way for the ever escalating propaganda campaign that would culminate in Stalin's Great Terror. Long before the most famous trial of the Terror—that of Bukharin and Rykov in 1938—the coalescing forces of mythopoetic justice had been fixed and codified for the country's viewing public. Already in the 1931 trial of the Industrial Party, the ultrarealist documentary trial film dominated the many types of legal propaganda, while fictional renditions of the enemy's unmasking provided a background and subtext for real-life courtroom drama.

The publicity surrounding the so-called Great Trial of Bukharin and Rykov illustrates that the theatrical and cinematic techniques of the Stalinist show trial remained essentially unchanged during the seven years separating this case from that of the Industrial Party. Although testimony during the Great Trial still deviated at times from the set script for defendants' confession, media reports in newspapers, on the radio, and on film edited the proceedings so they reiterated the story of wrecking and espionage that the Soviet public had heard for approximately ten years.[2] In particular, I. Kopalin's 1938 documentary film *Prigovor suda—prigovor naroda (The Sentence of the Court Is the Sentence of the People)* transformed the lengthy and tedious testimony of the Great Trial into a seamless and efficient narrative of the enemy's unmasking. Kopalin's movie is the most infamous trial film of the 1930s and has provided documentary filmmakers of later decades with invaluable footage of the Bukharin and Rykov case.

The Sentence of the Court contains very few shots of the accused enemies of Soviet power. Although Kopalin relied on techniques established in the earlier part of the decade for documenting a show trial, Bukharin, Rykov, and their codefendants have been virtually eliminated from the film's story. This disappearance constitutes a reweighting of the trial narrative's constituent parts and indicates the degree to which spectators already understood the images and rituals on screen. Over 80 percent of *The Sentence of the Court* is devoted to the closing speech of state prosecutor Vyshinskii, who describes the crimes of the accused in ruthlessly clear words and gestures. Throughout Vyshinskii's escalating tirade, the camera cuts from close-ups of the state prosecutor to similar shots of the court and of individual audience members, many of whom bear an uncanny resemblance to the prosecutor himself. Although the viewer sees other types of people (women and soldiers, for example) seated in the columned hall in medium and long-range shots, the camera singles out young to middle-aged men wearing suits or eyeglasses similar to Vyshinskii's. Earlier trial films such as Posel'skii's *The Trial of the Industrial Party* suggested that the moviegoer's position was most similar to that of the accused, but Kopalin's film encourages spectators to identify with prosecutor Vyshinskii.

The elimination of the accused from *The Sentence of the Court* shows the remarkable efficacy of earlier cinematic mug shots, which had already determined the archetype of the enemy long before 1938. At the same time, this disappearance communicates a new and disturbing message to the Soviet viewing public. The absence of Bukharin and Rykov from the movie screen not only confirms their absolute malignancy but also implies an inherent danger in showing the face of the enemy on film. The accused appear only three times during the movie, for a total of no more than a single minute. The first two times, the camera focuses on the backs of the defendants seated in the dock, their heads hung in an appropriately shameful posture. The third time, Vyshinskii describes the criminals under indictment. He shouts, "There they are, wreckers, spies, enemy agents" and the camera immediately cuts to show the faces of the men who merit such alarming labels. The camera pauses for no more than five seconds on the faces of the accused; and, contrary to expectations, the viewer sees neither vermin nor monsters. Instead, the film shows a group of plainly dressed middle-aged men, who resemble prosecutor Vyshinskii and those seated in the audience. The brevity of this shot, as well as its anticlimactic nature, draws attention to this particular episode in the film and makes it the climax of *The Sentence of the Court*. Unlike earlier cinematic mug shots, which depicted the accused as abnormal biological specimens, this brief glance of seemingly ordinary and inoffensive faces shows that the enemy of the people, for all his moral atrocity, looks just like the average man on the street.

In spite of this shift in the use of the cinematic mug shot, Kopalin's film repeats other messages and techniques typical of the documentary trial film. The last of the four reels that comprise the movie is devoted exclusively to showing the participation of the Soviet people in the Great Trial. The fourth reel begins with the court president pronouncing the death sentence and then cuts to a series of three intertitles: "The country met the just sentence of the supreme court with unanimous approval . . . DESTROY . . . the Trotskiite-Bukharinist gang of spies and murderers." From this point on, the film does no more than demonstrate its title by depicting two rallies, in which proletarian and peasant speakers imitate Vyshinskii in their vehement denunciations of Bukharin and Rykov. The film comes to an end as iconographic images of Ezhov and Stalin appear on the screen and those attending the mass meeting in the film loudly applaud. This final reel of the film most probably contains lengthy fictional sequences, which help to create a smooth narrative of the Soviet masses' endorsement of the death sentence; Kopalin was even better known than Posel'skii for incorporating acted segments into his documentary films.[3] *The Sentence of the Court* illustrates the completely scripted nature of the Soviet masses' participation in show trials of the 1930s, as well as the disturbing absence of any clear line between acted and authentic behavior. This last and greatest trial film of the 1930s provides a highly condensed version of perhaps the most important metanarrative of the Stalinist era, the unmasking of the hidden enemy and his subsequent exposure to the wrath of the Soviet masses.

Although documentary films like Kopalin's dominated the propaganda campaign surrounding the Great Trial, feature films and plays continued to construct a context in which the vengeance of the country's court and populace was warranted. Several movies of the late 1930s that corroborated the message of actual show trials received the attention and encouragement of Stalin himself, much like *The Party Card.* For example, the first and second series of *Velikii grazhdanin (A Great Citizen)* by F. Ermler (1937, 1939) provide a fictionalized account of the 1934 murder of Sergei Kirov, an event that most historians use to mark the beginning of the Great Terror. The second of these two movies culminates in the trial of those who assassinated Comrade Shakhov (Kirov's counterpart in the film) and ends with an unsettling shot of spies mingling with mourners at Shakhov's funeral. Stalin's direct intervention helped to shape Ermler's screenplay for the second series of *A Great Citizen,* whose errors the supreme censor corrected so that the film would accurately reflect the political fiction on which the Great Terror was premised.[4] Like trial documentaries, fictional legal dramas of the late 1930s gained their legitimacy by elaborating the story of real-life trials, in effect substantiating crimes that had never taken place and paving the way for further *samokritika* and *chistka.*

Particularly interesting in this regard is the work of Lev Sheinin, not only a popular journalist and playwright during the 1930s but also a member of Vyshinskii's "friendly team" in charge of organizing and directing all the great Moscow trials beginning with the Metro-Vickers case in 1933.[5] Sheinin surely used his experience as an investigator in the procurator's office of the RSFSR while cowriting the 1938 play *Ochnaia stavka (The Confrontation)* with the dramatists "the Tur Brothers."[6] *The Confrontation* tells the typical story of foreign operatives (this time from Germany) destroying the lives and work of hardworking Soviet citizens. The archenemy in the play bears the most common of Russian names, Ivan Ivanovich Ivanov, which points to the alleged ubiquity of saboteurs in the Soviet Union.

The most remarkable aspect of this already well-worn story is the enthusiastic reaction the play received from audiences in 1938. As John Scott describes in his memoirs, the production of *The Confrontation* in Magnitogorsk created a palpable anxiety among its spectators: "The tension in the theater was contagious. A young peasant-faced boy of eighteen sitting next to me clutched the handle of the seat with his big rough hands, and closed his mouth for a moment to swallow." During intermission, "the audience relaxed as though each of them had been undergoing electric treatments and the switch had just been thrown off. Then everyone burst into conversation, discussing the play and the acting."[7] Sheinin's play elicited precisely the response that the organizers of *agitsudy* had sought to achieve some ten years previously, in spite of the complete absence of a court or trial in the play.

Sheinin's story in *The Confrontation* proved so powerful that it was adapted to the screen one year later in the film *Oshibka Inzhenera Kochina (Engineer Kochin's Mistake)* by A. Macheret (1939). A Stalinist version of the detective movie, Macheret's film focuses on the efforts of a state investigator to uncover a ring of spies operating in Moscow.[8] The movie has two climactic moments that reinforce the importance of confession before the Soviet authorities. The first is the death of the film's love interest, Kseniia, played by the Soviet Union's greatest movie star, Liubov' Orlova, who played the role af Anka in *The Party Card* and also sang and danced her way to fame in musicals during the 1930s. Kseniia is murdered by the enemy only moments after she has confessed her own betrayal of the Soviet Union to her beloved Kochin, but before she has the chance to repeat her confession in the presence of the state's investigator. The film's second climax happens as a result of Kseniia's death, when the NKVD detectives expose the spy ring that destroyed her and force its members into a confrontation that leads to their own confessions. The importance of these two crises lies in the contrast they provide to Engineer Kochin's own confession, which not only allows investigators to find Kseniia's murderer but also lets Kochin keep his life. The closing scene of *Engineer Kochin's Mistake,* in which Kochin and the investigators meet while hunting wildfowl, paints an oddly intimate yet violent picture of the Soviet citizen's relationship to investigating authorities. Like Sheinin's play, its adaptation to the screen transformed the script for a real-life show trial into a fictional scenario that propped up the fabricated indictments of the Bukharin and Rykov trial.

Sheinin played an exceptional role in creating both the show trials of the Great Terror and the fictional reality needed to back up their charges. We can scarcely marvel at the willingness of this member of Vyshinskii's "friendly team" to construct the fictional reality of the Stalinist show trial; however, we must remember that Sheinin was not alone. Many of those more lucky than Kuleshov, Maiakovskii, and Erdman survived the cultural revolution of the early 1930s by expressing a remarkable complicity with the authorities who designed the legal spectacles of the decade. For the most part, the multileveled censorship that brought the works of Sheinin, Afinogenov, and Pyr'ev to the Soviet viewing public did not need to suppress counter-revolutionary scripts or screenplays, because works declaring open opposition to Soviet power were almost nonexistent. As the failure of *A Nail in the Boot* and the success of *The Party Card* illustrate, the banning or passing of an individual film did not occur on the basis of the author's subversive tendencies or message but, rather, because of the work's ability to substantiate and buttress the fictional reality of the era.[9]

Although the Soviet state struggled with expressions of popular dissent throughout the 1930s, the official conduits for artistic expression and propaganda were rarely confronted with open opposition and instead had the task of evaluating competing renditions of this fictional reality.[10] Apparently, the very myths manufactured to shape the inchoate masses ten years before exerted an inescapable power over their creators during the 1930s.

The Stalinist show trial continued its life as a theatrical spectacle played for a movie audience until a new type of enemy replaced the hidden saboteurs of the 1930s. After the Soviet Union's entrance into the Second World War, the very real and dangerous enemies of Hitler and Fascism supplanted the fictional internal enemy constructed by the show trials. Not only did public trials cease to take place in the columned hall, but the plays and movies providing their justification and corroboration also disappeared. Beginning in the 1940s, the fictional enemy on the movie screen was usually a hostile outsider whose sole aim was the invasion and devastation of Soviet territory, as seen in the films *Ona zashchishchaet rodinu (She Defends the Motherland)* by F. Ermler (1943) and *Padenie Berlina (The Fall of Berlin)* by M. Chiaureli (1949).[11] The restoration of peace after the war allowed the rituals of samokritika and chitska to return to discussions of Party politics and Soviet science in the succeeding decades, but the full panoply of mythopoetic justice was never completely resurrected. A more micromanaged approach to maintaining ideological orthodoxy replaced the melodramatic literalization of poetic justice in highly visible public trials.[12]

The utopian experiment of mythopoetic justice permeated almost every avenue of existence during the early Soviet period, including economics, politics, culture, science, the arts, and personal life. While the retreat from large public spectacles of justice after the war suggests that legal mythopoesis disappeared from Soviet and Russian society, the ubiquitous courts, trials, and confessions of the 1920s and 1930s have left an indelible impression on the country's collective consciousness. The call for public discussion of the crimes of Stalinism often took the form of a dramatized "court of conscience" or "court of history" during the 1980s, evincing the Russian public's desire to inflict similarly harsh judgment on those deemed responsible for the Great Terror.[13]

In the post-Soviet era, the highly publicized trial of the Communist Party in 1992 displayed this same desire to turn the legal tables on those who once ruled the country in the name of the proletarian and peasant masses. Held before Russia's newly created Constitutional Court only months after the putsch of August 1991, the Communist Party case was widely hailed as "Russia's Nuremberg" and was initiated by President

Boris Yeltsin in the hopes of declaring the country's former ruling class both unconstitutional and criminal.[14] In an unusual parallel with early Bolshevik tribunals, this yearlong judicial spectacle was charged with the task of changing the individual consciousness of the country's ex-rulers and rewriting Soviet history as an essentially criminal act. Yet the movement away from totalitarian legality toward Western-style advocacy and objectivity in the Russian legal system prevented an easy verdict and kept the Constitutional Court from merely ruling as Yeltsin might have wished. The split decision handed down in the 1992 case shows the tremendous distance between the Constitutional Court and its Stalinist predecessors.[15] In contrast to the show trials of the 1920s and 1930s, the Russian court afforded equal access to the theatrical and televised means of representation to prosecution and defense alike. In an attempt to resume the process of legal reform begun in 1864 but interrupted by seventy years of Soviet power, the dovetailing of theatrical and legal agon in post-Soviet Russia has reversed the devolution of legal mythopoesis in the hopes of pushing Russian society and culture forward into a new era.

NOTES

INTRODUCTION

1. The tendency of historians of and commentators on the Great Terror to use a theatrical metaphor to damn the purges is so widespread it occurs in virtually every document on the topic that I have had the opportunity to examine. Interesting examples include G. S. Agabekov, *Ch. K. za rabotoi* (Berlin: Izd. Strela, 1931), 79–86; Anton Antonov-Ovseenko, "Teatr Iosifa Stalina," *Teatr* 8 (August 1988): 118–39; N. P. Antsiferov, *Iz dum o bylom. Vospominaniia* (Moscow: Feniks, Kul'turnaia initsiativa, 1992), 354; A. Avtorkhanov, *Tekhnologiia vlasti* (Frankfurt am Main: Posev, 1976), 112; V. A. Kovalev, *Raspiatie dukha. Sudebnye protsessy stalinskoi epokhi* (Moscow: Izd. NORMA, 1997); Roi Medvedev, *O Staline i stalinizme* (Moscow: Progress, 1990), 247; Aleksandr I. Solzhenitsyn, *The Gulag Archipelago, 1918–1956: An Experiment in Literary Investigation*, vols. 1–2, trans. Thomas Whitney (New York: Harper and Row, 1973), 362–411; H. Hessell Tiltman, *The Terror in Europe* (New York: Frederick A. Stokes, 1931), 92; Robert C. Tucker, *Stalin in Power: The Revolution from Above, 1928–1941* (New York: W. W. Norton, 1990), 6, 77, 171; Dmitrii Volkogonov, *Triumf i tragediia. Politichesii portret I. V. Stalina v 2-kh knigakh* (Moscow: Izd. Agentstva pechati Novosti, 1989); and Bertram D. Wolfe, "Dress Rehearsals for the Great Terror," reprinted from *Studies in Comparative Communism* 3, no. 2 (April 1970). For a notable exception to this trend, see Sheila Fitzpatrick's entertaining and insightful examination of rural purges using a theatrical metaphor in "How the Mice Buried the Cat: Scenes from the Great Purges of 1937 in the Russian Provinces," *Russian Review* 52 (July 1993): 299–320.

2. Erika Fischer-Lichte, "Theatricality: A Key Concept in Theatre and Cultural Studies," *Theatre Research International* 20, no. 2 (1995): 85.

3. Ibid., 87. Marvin Carlson also points to the danger of using such an ahistorical and acultural model of the theater as a heuristic device, in "Theatre History, Methodology and Distinctive Features," *Theatre Research International* 20, no. 2 (1995): 95.

4. René Fülöp-Miller, *The Mind and Face of Bolshevism: An Examination of Cultural Life in Soviet Russia*, trans. F. S. Flint and D. F. Tait (London: G. P. Putnam's Sons, 1927); René Fülöp-Miller and Joseph Gregor, *The Russian*

Theatre: Its Character and History with Especial Reference to the Revolutionary Period, trans. Paul England (Philadelphia: J. B. Lippincott, 1929); Richard Stites, *Revolutionary Dreams: Utopian Vision and Experimental Life in the Russian Revolution* (New York: Oxford University Press, 1989).

5. Iu. M. Lotman, "Teatr i teatral'nost' v stroe kul'tury nachala XIX veka," in *Izbrannye stat'i v trekh tomakh* (Tallinn: Aleksandra, 1992), 1:269–86. Several American scholars have continued Lotman's study of theatricality in Russian society. For prominent examples, see Priscilla R. Roosevelt, *Life on the Russian Country Estate: A Social and Cultural History* (New Haven: Yale University Press, 1995); Richard Wortman, *Scenarios of Power: Myth and Ceremony in Russian Monarchy* (Princeton: Princeton University Press, 1995); Edith W. Clowes, "Merchants on Stage and in Life: Theatricality and Public Consciousness," in *Merchant Moscow: Images of Russia's Vanished Bourgeoisie,* ed. James L. West and Iurii A. Petrov (Princeton: Princeton University Press, 1998), 147–59.

6. Erika Fischer-Lichte, "From Theatre to Theatricality: How to Construct Reality," *Theatre Research International* 20, no. 2 (1995): 98–103.

7. Arthur Koestler, *Darkness at Noon,* trans. Daphne Hardy (New York: Macmillan, 1952).

8. Aristotle first made the comparison between oratorical delivery and acting in *The Art of Rhetoric,* trans. H. C. Lawson-Tancred (London and New York: Penguin Books, 1991), 217. Cicero expanded the comparison to suggest that actors provide the model for effective delivery, in *De Oratore,* trans. E. W. Sutton (Cambridge: Harvard University Press, 1942), 107. Tacitus also compared the court to a theater in his "Dialogue on Orators," in *Tacitus' Agricola, Germany and Dialogue on Orators,* trans. Herbert W. Benario (Norman: University of Oklahoma Press, 1991), 128. For one of the almost countless examples of contemporary descriptions of trial lawyers as actors, see Sam Schrager's Chapter 1, "Drama," in *The Trial Lawyer's Art* (Philadelphia: Temple University Press, 1999), 17–37.

9. For discussions of popular legal culture in America, see "Symposium: Popular Legal Culture," *Yale Law Journal* 98, no. 8 (June 1989): 1545–709; Lloyd Chiasson, ed., *The Press on Trial: Crimes and Trials as Media Events* (Westport, Conn.: Greenwood Press, 1997); Ronald L. Goldfarb, *TV or Not TV: Television, Justice and the Courts* (New York: New York University Press, 1998); and Robert Hariman, ed., *Popular Trials: Rhetoric, Mass Media, and the Law* (Tuscaloosa: University of Alabama Press, 1990). Most scholars date the emergence of law and literature as an academic discipline from James Boyd White's 1973 publication of *The Legal Imagination: Studies in the Nature of Legal Thought and Expression* (Boston: Little, Brown, 1973). Since this time, a number of seminal works have appeared that address both law in literature and law as literature, including James Boyd White, *Heracles' Bow: Essays on the Rhetoric and Poetics of the Law* (Madison: University of Wisconsin Press, 1985); Richard A. Posner, *Law and Literature: A Misunderstood Relation* (Cambridge: Harvard University Press, 1988); and Stanley Fish, *Doing What Comes Naturally: Change, Rhetoric, and the Prac-*

tice of Theory in Literary and Legal Studies (Durham, N.C.: Duke University Press, 1989). For recent commentary and synopses of the development of law and literature as a discipline, see Lenora Ledwon, ed., *Law and Literature: Text and Theory* (New York: Garland Publishing, 1996); Ian Ward, *Law and Literature: Possibilities and Perspectives* (Cambridge: Cambridge University Press, 1995); Bruce L. Rockwood, ed., *Law and Literature Perspectives* (New York: Peter Lang, 1996); Theodore Ziolkowski, *The Mirror of Justice: Literary Reflections of Legal Crisis* (Princeton, N.J.: Princeton University Press, 1997). The study of law and literature has only recently been introduced into the study of Russian culture, as seen in Harriet Murav, *Russia's Legal Fictions* (Ann Arbor: University of Michigan Press, 1998).

10. For example, see White's discussion of Sophocles' *Philoctetes* and the *Oresteia* in *Heracles' Bow*, 3–27, 168–91; Daniel J. Kornstein's treatment of Shakespeare's oeuvre in *Kill All the Lawyers? Shakespeare's Legal Appeal* (Princeton: Princeton University Press, 1994); Ward's overview of Shakespeare in *Law and Literature*, 59–89; and Ervene Gulley, "'Dressed in a Little Brief Authority': Law as Theater in *Measure for Measure*," in Rockwood, *Law and Literature*, 53–80. In Russian literary studies, I. T. Goliakov uses this approach to prove the bourgeois nature of prerevolutionary literature in his two studies, *Sud i zakonnost' v russkoi khudozhestvennoi literature XIX veka* (Moscow: Izd. Moskovskogo universiteta, 1956) and *Sud i zakonnost' v khudozhestvennoi literature* (Moscow: Gos. izd. Iuridicheskoi lit., 1959).

11. For examples, see Milner S. Ball, "The Play's the Thing: An Unscientific Reflection on Courts under the Rubric of Theater," *Stanford Law Review* 28, no. 1 (November 1975): 81–115; and John E. Simonett, "The Trial as One of the Performing Arts," *American Bar Association Journal* 52 (December 1966): 1145–47.

12. For examples, see Paula R. Backscheider, *Spectacular Politics: Theatrical Power and Mass Culture in Early Modern England* (Baltimore: Johns Hopkins University Press, 1993); Gary Boire, "Theatres of Law: Canadian Legal Drama," *Canadian Literature* 152, no. 3 (1997): 124–44; Sue-Ellen Case and Janelle Reinelt, eds., *The Performance of Power: Theatrical Discourse and Politics* (Iowa City: University of Iowa Press, 1991); Terry Castle, *Masquerade and Civilization: The Carnivalesque in Eighteenth-Century English Culture and Fiction* (London: Methuen, 1986); Jody Enders, *The Medieval Theater of Cruelty: Rhetoric, Memory, Violence* (Ithaca: Cornell University Press, 1999) and *Rhetoric and the Origins of Medieval Drama* (Ithaca: Cornell University Press, 1992); Stephen Greenblatt, *Renaissance Self-Fashioning: From More to Shakespeare* (Chicago: University of Chicago Press, 1980); Karen Hermassi, *Polity and Theater in Historical Perspective* (Berkeley and Los Angeles: University of California Press, 1977); Loren Kruger, *The National Stage: Theatre and Cultural Legitimation in England, France, and America* (Chicago: University of Chicago Press, 1992); Mona Ozouf, *Festivals and the French Revolution*, trans. Alan Sheridan (Cambridge: Harvard University Press, 1988); John J. Winkler and Froma Zeitlin, eds., *Nothing to Do with Dionysus? Athenian Drama and Its*

Social Context (Princeton: Princeton University Press, 1990).

13. For a detailed description of these many similarities, see Richard Garner, *Law and Society in Classical Athens* (New York: St. Martin's Press, 1987), 95–109; and Jennifer Wise, *Dionysus Writes: The Invention of Theatre in Ancient Greece* (Ithaca: Cornell University Press, 1998), 129–41.

14. Johan Huizinga, *Homo Ludens: A Study of the Play Element in Culture* (New York: Harper and Row, 1970), 97 (quotation); Jacob Burckhardt, "Der koloniale und agonale Mensch," *Griechische Kulturgeschichte* (Leipzig: Alfred Kröner Verlag, 1929), 3:46–108; and Walter Benjamin, *The Origin of German Tragic Drama*, trans. John Osborne (Frankfurt am Main: Suhrkamp Verlag, 1963), 115–18.

15. Michael Lloyd, *The Agon in Euripides* (Oxford: Clarendon Press, 1992), 1, 19 (quotation); Jacqueline Duchemin, *L'ΑΓΩΝ dans la tragédie grecque* (Paris: Société d'Edition les Belles Lettres, 1945); and Garner, *Law and Society in Classical Athens*, 95–125.

16. Jacob Burckhardt, *History of Greek Culture*, trans. Palmer Hilty (New York: Frederick Ungar, 1963), 227–54; Huizinga, *Homo Ludens*, 168. Kenneth Burke describes the tie between law and tragedy in ancient Greece as a proliferation of the forensic. Burke, *Attitudes toward History*, 3rd ed. (Berkeley and Los Angeles: University of California Press, 1984), 38–39.

17. Garner, *Law and Society in Classical Athens*, 97–99; Wise, *Dionysus Writes*, 134–35.

18. A variety of scholars share this fundamental axiom of legal development, including Durkheim, Weber, and a number of legal anthropologists. See Steven Lukes and Andrew Scull, *Durkheim and the Law* (New York: St. Martin's Press, 1983); Max Weber, "The Formal Qualities of Modern Law," in *Sociological Writings*, ed. Wolf Heydebrand (New York: Continuum, 1994), 211–27; A. S. Diamond, *Primitive Law Past and Present* (London: Methuen, 1971); Alan Watson, *The Evolution of Law* (Baltimore: Johns Hopkins University Press, 1985).

19. Ziolkowski, *Mirror of Justice*, 242–56 (243). Ziolkowski cites the interesting example of Roland Freisler, who had so effectively learned the techniques of the Soviet show trial that he became known as the "Nazi Vyshinskii" (245).

20. For a comparative study of film propaganda in early Soviet Russia and Nazi Germany, see Richard Taylor, *Film Propaganda: Soviet Russia and Nazi Germany* (London: Croom Helm, 1979).

21. Fischer-Lichte, "Theatricality," 86–87.

22. Richard Wagner, "Art and Revolution," in *Richard Wagner's Prose Works*, vol. 1, *The Art-Work of the Future, &c.*, trans. William Ashton Ellis (London: Kegan Paul, Trench, Trübner, 1895), 21–65. Friedrich Nietzsche, *The Birth of Tragedy from the Spirit of Music and The Genealogy of Morals*, trans. Francis Golffing (New York: Anchor Books Doubleday, 1956).

23. Prominent examples of such collections of articles include *Teatr: Kniga o novom teatre. Sbornik statei* (St. Petersburg: Izd. Shipovnik, 1908); *Krizis teatra. Sbornik statei* (Moscow: Knigoizdatel'stvo Problemy iskusstva, 1908); *V sporakh*

o teatre. Sbornik statei (Moscow: Knigoizdatel'stvo pisatelei v Moskve, 1914).

24. Romain Rolland, *Le théâtre du peuple* (Paris: Cahiers de la Quinzaine, 1903); Edward Gordon Craig, *The Art of the Theatre* (Edinburgh: T. N. Foulis, 1905); Georg Fuchs, *Die Revolution des Theaters: Ergebuisse aus dem Münchener Kunstler-Theater* (Munich: G. Muller, 1909). For a discussion of the impact of these three men on Russian theater at the turn of the century, see Evg. A. Znosko-Borovskii, *Russkii teatr nachala XX veka* (Prague: Plamia, 1925), 246–52, 411.

25. Michael Green, "Viacheslav Ivanov," in *The Russian Symbolist Theatre: An Anthology of Plays and Critical Texts* (Ann Arbor: Ardis, 1986), 109–11. For the significance of Ivanov's theory within symbolist poetry, see "Zavety simvolizma," in Viacheslav Ivanov, *Sobranie sochinenii* (Brussels: Foyer Oriental Chrétien, 1974), 2:588–603.

26. Viacheslav Ivanov, "Predchuvstviia i predvestiia. Novaia organicheskaia epokha i teatr budushchego," in *Po zvezdam. Stat'i i aforizmy* (St. Petersburg: Izd. Ory, 1909), reprint, Bradda Books, Letchworth, Herts., England), 202, 195. References to this work will henceforth be given parenthetically in the text. Unless otherwise noted, all foreign language translations are my own.

27. Andrei Belyi, "Teatr i sovremennaia drama," in *Kniga o novom teatre,* 273. For the views of other symbolists who did not support Ivanov's theories, see Valerii Briusov, "Realizm i uslovnost' na stsene," in ibid., 243–59; Fyodor Sologub, "Teatr odnoi voli," in ibid., 177–98; and Aleksandr Blok, "O teatre," *Sobranie sochinenii v shesti tomakh,* vol. 4, *Ocherki, stat'i, rechi, 1905–1921* (Leningrad: Khudozhestvennaia Literatura, 1982), 58–91.

28. James von Geldern notes the common language used by both symbolists and Bolsheviks in discussions of the new theater in "Nietzschean Leaders and Followers in Soviet Mass Theater, 1917–1927," in *Nietzsche and Soviet Culture: Ally and Adversary,* ed. Bernice Glatzer Rosenthal (Cambridge: Cambridge University Press, 1994), 129. Irina Gutkin also treats the overlapping terminology and ideology of socialist realism and symbolism in *The Novel of Socialist Realism as a Phenomenon of Literary Evolution* (Ph.D. dissertation, University of California at Berkeley, 1989).

29. N. N. Evreinov, *Teatr kak takovoi (Obosnovanie teatral'nosti v smysle polozhitel'nogo nachala stsenicheskogo iskusstva i zhizni)* (St. Petersburg: Sklad Izd. Sovremennoe Iskusstvo, 1912), 20–23.

30. For monograph-length studies of Evreinov's life and work in the theater, including his unusual position in the theatrical politics of his day, see Spencer Golub, *Evreinov: The Theatre of Paradox and Transformation* (Ann Arbor: UMI Research Press, 1984) and Sharon Marie Carnicke, *The Theatrical Instinct: Nikolai Evreinov and the Russian Theater of the Early Twentieth Century* (New York: Peter Lang, 1989).

31. Evreinov, *Teatr kak takovoi,* 9. References to this work will henceforth be given parenthetically in the text.

32. For a history of the Ancient Theater, see Eduard Stark, *Starinnyi teatr* (St. Petersburg: Izk. N. I. Butkovskoi, 1911). For more information on the idea of

monodrama, see Nikolai Evreinov, "Introduction to Monodrama," in *Russian Dramatic Theory from Pushkin to the Symbolists: An Anthology,* trans. and ed. Laurence Senelick (Austin: University of Texas Press, 1981), 183–99.

33. See also Nicholas Evreinoff, "To My God—Theatrarch," in *The Theatre in Life,* ed. and trans. Alexander I. Nazaroff (New York: Brentano's, 1927), 128–31.

34. Nikolai Evreinov, "Teatroterapiia," *Zhizn' iskusstva* 578–79, October 9–10, 1920, 1. Nikolai Evreinov, *Samoe glavnoe. Dlia kogo komediia, a dlia kogo i drama, v 4 deistviiakh* (St. Petersburg: Gos. Izd., 1921).

35. For descriptions of this mass spectacle, see Nikolai Evreinov, "Vziatie zimnego dvortsa," *Krasnyi militsioner* 14, November 15, 1920, 4–5; James von Geldern, *Bolshevik Festivals, 1917–1920* (Berkeley and Los Angeles: University of California Press, 1993), 1–3, 199–207; Stites, *Revolutionary Dreams,* 93–97; and Füllöp-Miller, *Mind and Face of Bolshevism,* 147–49.

36. Nikolai Evreinov, *Istoriia telesnykh nakazanii v Rossii* (Kharkov: Progress, 1994), 64; Evreinov, "Teatral'noe iskusstvo na sluzhbe u obshchestvennoi bezopastnosti," *Zhizn' iskusstva* 792–97, August 2–7, 1921, 4.

37. Nikolai Evreinov, *Shagi Nemezidy. Dramaticheskaia khronika v 6-ti kartinakh iz partiinoi zhizni v SSSR (1936–1938)* (Paris: Vozrozhdenie, 1956).

38. Ia. B. Brukzon, *Problema teatral'nosti. (Estestvennost' pered sudom marksizma)* (Petrograd: Izd. Tret'ia strazha, 1923).

39. Christopher Read, *Culture and Power in Revolutionary Russia: The Intelligentsia and the Transition from Tsarism to Communism* (New York: St. Martin's Press, 1990), 111–33; Stites, *Revolutionary Dreams,* 70–72; and G. V. Titova, *Tvorcheskii teatr i teatral'nyi konstruktivizm* (St. Petersburg: SLAPTI, 1995), 13–35. For a history of the Proletkul't movement as a whole, see Lynn Mally, *Culture of the Future: The Proletkult Movement in Revolutionary Russia* (Berkeley and Los Angeles: University of California Press, 1990).

40. I was able to review the first (Petrograd: Izd. Kniga, 1918), fourth (Petrograd: Gos. Izd., 1920), and fifth (Moscow-Petrograd: Gos. Izd., 1923) editions of this work (the second and third editions would seem to be reprints of the first edition, if the preface to the fourth is accurate). Unless otherwise noted, all references to *Tvorcheskii teatr* are to the fourth edition, which contains material from Kerzhentsev's brochure *Revoliutsiia i teatr* (Moscow: Izd. Dennitsa, 1918) and significant additions based on theatrical developments that took place between 1918 and 1920.

41. For Lunacharskii's description of a socialist theater, see Anatolii Lunacharskii, "Sotsializm i iskusstvo," in *Kniga o novom teatre,* 7–40. Titova also discusses Kerzhentsev's debt to his theoretical predecessors, including Lunacharskii, Rolland, Wagner, Ivanov, and Belyi. Titova, *Tvorcheskii teatr i teatral'nyi konstruktivizm,* 44–48.

42. P. M. Kerzhentsev, *Tvorcheskii teatr. Puti sotsialisticheskogo teatra* (Petrograd: Izd. Kniga, 1918), 45–47 (quotation from p. 45).

43. Rolland, *Théâtre du peuple,* 14–15. Kerzhentsev, *Tvorcheskii teatr,* 38.

References to this work will henceforth be given in the text.

44. This opinion is stated most forcefully in the first edition of *Tvorcheskii teatr*. By the fifth edition, Kerzhentsev softens somewhat: in 1923 he admits the usefulness of full-time theatrical professionals in transmitting "the necessary alphabet of the theatrical trade" (91).

45. P. M. Kerzhentsev, *Sredi plameni. Teatral'noe predstavlenie v 3-kh deistviiakh s intermediiami* (Petrograd: Gos. Izd., 1921), 43.

46. For a discussion of the impact of Kerzhentsev's work on professional theaters of the early 1920s, see Titova, *Tvorcheskii teatr i teatral'nyi konstruktivizm*, 58–77. An examination of Kerzhentsev's obsession with organization and efficiency, and of his desire to find a means of controlling every aspect of proletarian life, is beyond the scope of this work but would prove interesting. As an advocate and founding member of Nauchnaia Organizatsiia Truda (NOT, or the Scientific Organization of Labor), he authored several books and brochures that indicate the lengths to which he took this interest. For examples, see P. M. Kerzhentsev, *Kak vesti sobranie* (Leningrad: Izd. Priboi, 1925) and *Kak chitat' knigu?* (Khar'kov: Izd. Molodoi rabochii, 1924).

47. Lenin allegedly made this statement in conversation with Anatolii Lunacharskii. Anatoli Lunacharsky, "Conversation with Lenin. I. Of All the Arts," in *The Film Factory: Russian and Soviet Cinema in Documents*, ed. and trans. Richard Taylor (Cambridge: Harvard University Press, 1988), 56–57. See also G. Boltianskii, *Lenin i kino* (Moscow-Leningrad: Gos. Izd., 1925), 19; A. M. Gak, ed., *Samoe vazhnoe iz vsekh iskusstv. Lenin o kino. Sbornik dokumentov i materialov*, 2nd ed. (Moscow: Izd. Iskusstvo, 1973), 164, 167.

48. Denise J. Youngblood, *Movies for the Masses: Popular Cinema and Soviet Society in the 1920s* (Cambridge: Cambridge University Press, 1992), 13–28.

49. For a discussion of the debate between education and enlightenment as the cinema's primary goal, see ibid., 35–49.

50. S. Eisenstein, "Montazh attraktsionov," *Lef* 3 (June–July 1923): 70–75. For commentary on Meyerhold's use of cinematic techniques, see Ia. Brukzon, *Tvorchestvo kino* (Leningrad: Kolos, 1926), 25–35; Pavel Poluianov, *Gibel' teatra i torzhestvo kino. [Pamflet.]* (N. Novgorod: Tip. Nizhpoligraf, 1925), 38; and O. M. Brik, "Kino v teatre Meierkhol'da," *Sovetskii ekran* 20, May 18, 1926, 19–20.

51. *Kinematograf. Sbornik statei* (Moscow: Gos. Izd., 1919), 3. For a similar description of cinema as propaganda, see *Kino v rabochem klube. Sbornik statei i ofitsial'nikh materialov* (Moscow: Izd. VTsSPS, 1926), 37; and V. Miuntsenberg, *Kino i revoliutsiia* (Moscow: Izd. Mezhrabpom, 1925), 7.

52. For good examples of theoretical writings by Kuleshov and Eisenstein, which established the independent, artistic sphere of cinema without such reference to the theater, see Lev Kuleshov, "The Art of Cinema," in *Kuleshov on Film: Writings by Lev Kuleshov*, trans. Ronald Levaco (Berkeley and Los Angeles: University of California Press, 1974), 41–123; and Sergei Eisenstein, *Film Form: The Film Sense*, trans. Jay Leyda (New York: Meridian Books, 1968).

53. Viktor Shklovskii, "Drama i massovye predstavleniia," in *Khod konia.*

Sbornik statei (Moscow/Berlin: Knigoizd. Gelikon, 1923), 59.

54. For example, the journal *Maski* sponsored a series of articles under the general heading "Who Will Win, Cinema or Theater?" during 1912–1913. Maiakovskii's contributions to the ongoing debate appeared in the journal *Kine-zhurnal* in 1913 and are reprinted in V. V. Maiakovskii, "Teatr, kinematograf, futurizm," "Unichtozhenie kinematografom 'teatra' kak priznak vozrozhdeniia teatral'nogo iskusstva," and "Otnoshenie segodniashnego teatra i kinematografa k uskusstvu cho neset nam zavtrashnii den? (Polezna i dlia kritikov)," in *Polnoe sobranie sochinenii* (Moscow: Gos. Izd. Khudozhestvennoi Literatury, 1955), 1:275–85. Maiakovskii's fellow futurist B. Shaposhnikov also stated that the theater needed to learn from cinema if it hoped to survive in the modern age. See his theatrical manifesto of futurism, "Futurizm i teatr," *Maski* 7–8 (1912–1913): 30.

55. E. Samuilenko, *Kinematograf i ego prosvetitel'naia rol'* (St. Petersburg: Tip. Slovo, 1912), 4. This work was also republished in 1919 under the same title. B. Kerzhentsev, "Sotsial'naia bor'ba i ekran," in *Kinematograf,* 86. For historical accounts of the early Soviet cinema as a means of propaganda, see Richard Taylor's two monographs, *The Politics of the Soviet Cinema, 1917–1929* (Cambridge: Cambridge University Press, 1979), 26–42; and *Film Propaganda,* 44–80.

56. Denise J. Youngblood, *Soviet Cinema in the Silent Era, 1918–1935* (Ann Arbor, Michigan: UMI Research Press, 1985), 4.

57. F. Shipulinskii, "Dusha kino. (Psikhologiia kinematografa)," in *Kinematograf,* 18; B. Kerzhentsev, "Sotsial'naia bor'ba i ekran," in *Kinematograf,* 87; Brukzon, *Tvorchestvo kino,* 20–21. Shipulinskii, "Dusha kino," 18 (quotation).

58. For examples of Vertov's extreme advocacy of the nonfiction film, see Dziga Vertov, "We: A Version of a Manifesto," in Taylor, *Film Factory,* 69–72, and "The Cine-Eyes: A Revolution," in ibid., 89–94.

59. Brukzon, *Tvorchestvo kino,* 8; Shipulinskii, "Dusha kino," 20; Brukzon, *Tvorchestvo kino,* 22; A. Toporkov, "Kinematograf i mif," in *Kinematograf,* 47.

60. A. Katsigras, "Opyt fiksatsii zritel'skikh interesov," in I. N. Bursak, ed., *Kino* (Moscow: Proletkino, 1925), 51.

61. Samuilenko, *Kinematograf i ego prosvetitel'naia rol',* 5; P. I. Liublinskii, *Kinematograf i deti* (Moscow: Knigoizd. Pravo i zhizn', 1925), 81.

62. "ARK," in *Kinematograf,* 99.

63. Liublinskii, *Kinematograf i deti,* 12.

64. Toporkov, "Kinematograf i mif," 51–52 (quotation); Poluianov, *Gibel' teatra i torzhestvo kino,* 42.

65. Brukzon, *Tvorchestvo kino,* 33–35; Toporkov, "Kinematograf i mif," 48; Poluianov, *Gibel' teatra i torzhestvo kino,* 35; S. Krolov, *Kino vmesto vodki* (Moscow-Leningrad: Moskovskii rabochii, 1928), 30–31. Toporkov, "Kinematograf i mif," 52.

66. *Kino v rabochem klube,* 33–35; *Kino v derevniu* (Moscow: Izd. Krasnaia nov', 1924).

67. Youngblood, *Movies for the Masses,* 3–5, 20, 51.

1: IMPERIAL PRECEDENTS AND THE FIRST BOLSHEVIK SHOW TRIALS

1. For a discussion of the systematic repression of political radicals by the tsarist courts, see Samuel Kucherov, *Courts, Lawyers and Trials under the Last Three Tsars* (Westport: Greenwood Press, 1974), 197–212; N. A. Troitskii, *Tsarskie sudy protiv revoliutsionnoi Rossii. Politicheskie protsessy, 1871–1880 gg.* (Saratov: Izd. Saratovskogo universiteta, 1976).

2. Joan Neuberger, "Popular Legal Cultures: The St. Petersburg Mirovoi Sud," in *Russia's Great Reforms, 1855–1881*, ed. Ben Eklof et al. (Bloomington: Indiana University Press, 1994), 231. For overviews of the legal reforms of 1864, see Kucherov, *Courts, Lawyers and Trials*, 21–106; and W. Bruce Lincoln, *The Great Reforms: Autocracy, Bureaucracy, and the Politics of Change in Imperial Russia* (DeKalb: Northern Illinois University Press, 1990), 105–17.

3. Laura Engelstein, "Revolution and Theater of Public Life in Imperial Russia," in *Revolution and the Meanings of Freedom in the Nineteenth Century*, ed. Isser Woloch (Stanford: Stanford University Press, 1996), 327, 337.

4. Lincoln, *Great Reforms*, 113; Richard S. Wortman, *The Development of a Russian Legal Consciousness* (Chicago: University of Chicago Press, 1976), 279.

5. Alexander K. Afanas'ev, "Jurors and Jury Trials in Imperial Russia, 1866–1885," in *Russia's Great Reforms*, ed. Ben Eklof et al. (Bloomington: Indiana University Press, 1994), 217. Neuberger, "Popular Legal Cultures," 231 (quotation).

6. Afanas'ev, "Jurors and Jury Trials in Imperial Russia," 223–28. Afanas'ev asserts the predominantly peasant composition of prerevolutionary juries, in spite of the property requirement that effectively excluded the majority of Russia's lower classes from being included in jury lists (215).

7. Neuberger, "Popular Legal Cultures," 231–33; Peter Czap Jr., "Peasant-Class Courts and Peasant Customary Justice in Russia, 1861–1912," *Journal of Social History* 1, no. 2 (winter 1967): 175, 164–68, 173. Czap uses these terms as indicators of the application of customary law (165).

8. Stephen P. Frank, "Popular Justice, Community and Culture among the Russian Peasantry, 1870–1900," *Russian Review* 46, no. 3 (July 1987): 240–42. Although Frank asserts that the samosud was prevalent through the end of the nineteenth century, the Soviet state's interest in eradicating this popular legal practice at the end of the 1920s indicates that it still flourished in the Russian countryside as late as 1927. See N. Lagovier, *O samosudakh* (Moscow-Leningrad: Gos. Izd., 1927).

9. Frank, "Popular Justice," 244. For an elaboration of the many circumstances in peasant life that might result in a samosud and the form any given samosud would take, see I. Shrag, "Krest'ianskie sudy vladimirskoi i moskovskoi gubernii," *Iuridicheskii vestnik* 7–8 (June–August 1877): 58–86; Kniaz' V. V. Tenishev, "Samosud i vidy ego," in *Pravosudie v russkom krest'ianskom bytu* (Briansk: Tip. L. I. Utina, 1907), 33–54.

10. Engelstein, "Revolution and Theater," 336–37.

11. For comprehensive discussions of the trials of political radicals during this period, see Troitskii's two monographs: *Tsarizm pod sudom progressivnoi obshchestvennosti, 1866–1895 gg.* (Moscow: Mysl', 1979) and *Tsarskie sudy protiv revoliutsionnoi Rossii.* For speeches from the most visible of these trials, see S. M. Kazantsev, *Sud prisiazhnykh v Rossii. Gromkie ugolovnye protsessy, 1864–1917 gg.* (Leningrad: Lenizdat, 1991).

12. Engelstein, "Revolution and Theater," 338 (quotation); Neuberger, "Popular Legal Cultures," 236. For examples of law court reporting from the early 1880s, see "Moscow Court Reporting," *Entertaining Tsarist Russia: Tales, Songs, Plays, Movies, Jokes, Ads, and Images from Russian Urban Life, 1779–1917,* ed. James von Geldern and Louise McReynolds (Bloomington: Indiana University Press, 1998), 212–17. For descriptions of the prominent postreform trials that preceded the Zasulich case, see Murav, *Legal Fictions,* 55–91; Franco Venturi, *Roots of Revolution: A History of the Populist and Socialist Movements in Nineteenth-Century Russia,* trans. Francis Haskell (New York: Alfred A. Knopf, 1960), 585–96; V. Soukhomline, *Les procès célèbres de la Russie* (Paris: Payot, 1937); and Wortman, *Russian Legal Consciousness,* 279–82.

13. Wortman, *Russian Legal Consciousness,* 280–82.

14. "Predislovie," in A. F. Koni, *Vospominaniia o dele Very Zasulich,* vol. 2 of *Sobranie sochinenii v vos'mi tomakh* (Moscow: Izd. Iuridicheskaia literatura, 1966), 11. These memoirs of the trial's president, A. F. Koni, provide the most lengthy and complete account of the Zasulich case, including transcripts of the trial as they appeared in newspaper reports of the time and a series of official letters and documents associated with the case. The following account of the trial refers frequently to these memoirs, and page references will be given parenthetically in the text. See also Jay Bergman, "The Trepov Shooting," in *Vera Zasulich: A Biography* (Stanford: Stanford University Press, 1983), 19–62; G. A. Gallanin, ed. *Protsess Very Zasulich (Sud i posle suda)* (St. Petersburg: Tipo-Litografiia S. M. Muller, n.d.); and Samuel Kucherov, "The Case of Vera Zasulich," *Russian Review* 11, no. 2 (April 1952): 86–96, reproduced in his monograph *Courts, Lawyers and Trials,* 214–25.

15. Quoted in Bergman, *Vera Zasulich,* 39.

16. "Predislovie," in Koni, *Very Zasulich,* 12 (quotation); Bergman, *Vera Zasulich,* 42.

17. Engelstein, "Revolution and Theater," 342. "Predislovie," in Koni, *Very Zasulich,* 12; Troitskii, *Tsarizm pod sudom progressivnoi,* 221. Koni provides a complete list of the members of the jury in *Very Zasulich,* 92–93.

18. Koni, *Very Zasulich,* 63. Koni lists the recipients of the tickets he distributed (89–90). Bergman, *Vera Zasulich,* 45; Kucherov, "Vera Zasulich," 92–93.

19. Bergman, *Vera Zasulich,* 49.

20. G. K. Gradovskii, quoted in "Predislovie," in Koni, *Very Zasulich,* 14. Koni also remembers this famous article and its role in the publicity that followed the trial (180–81).

21. See also Bergman, *Vera Zasulich,* 43; Kucherov, "Vera Zasulich," 94;

Venturi, *Roots of Revolution*, 606. Bergman mentions that Aleksandrov was compared to Camille Desmoulins, the famous Dantonist orator (54).

22. Irina Paperno, *Chernyshevsky and the Age of Realism: A Study in the Semiotics of Behavior* (Stanford: Stanford University Press, 1988), 17–20.

23. Bergman, *Vera Zasulich*, 42–43; Paperno, *Chernyshevsky*, 18.

24. Koni repeats the phrase *krovavyi samosud* or some variant of it in several places in his memoirs. *Very Zasulich*, 71, 74, 75, 170.

25. For an analysis of the reversal of judgment in the Zasulich trial and the ensuing enthusiasm of the crowd as an instance of carnival, see Murav, *Legal Fictions*, 68.

26. Quoted in Wortman, *Russian Legal Consciousness*, 283.

27. Gallanin includes newspaper coverage from *Severnyi Vestnik* describing the public demonstration after the Zasulich trial. Gallanin, *Protsess Very Zasulich*, 109–11. See also Bergman, *Vera Zasulich*, 54; Venturi, *Roots of Revolution*, 606. Koni remembers hearing reports that a theater company in Naples staged a play based on the Zasulich trial. Koni, *Very Zasulich*, 229.

28. Engelstein, "Revolution and Theater," 333–43.

29. L. N. Tolstoi, *Polnoe sobranie sochinenii* (Moscow: Gos. Izd. Khudozhestvennoi Literatury, 1958), 62:411; Maksim Gor'kii, *Mat'*, vol. 4 of *Sobranie sochinenii v vosemnadtsati tomakh* (Moscow: Gos. Izd. Khudozhestvennoi Literatury, 1960), 371–88. For descriptions of other highly visible political cases that passed through the tsarist courts before 1917, see Kucherov, *Courts, Lawyers and Trials*, 225–68.

30. V. I. Lenin, "O zadachakh Narkomiusta v usloviiakh Novoi ekonomicheskoi politiki," in *Polnoe sobranie sochinenii* (Moscow: Gos. Izd. Politicheskoi Literatury, 1964), 44:397. Trotskii also believed in the "educational significance" of public trials, as a telegram discussing the organization of the 1919 trial of Mironov attests. Kovalev, *Raspiatie dukha*, 23. For a discussion of Soviet law as parent and teacher, see Harold J. Berman, *Justice in the USSR: An Interpretation of Soviet Law* (Cambridge: Harvard University Press, 1963), 282–84, 299–311.

31. Peter H. Solomon Jr., *Soviet Criminal Justice under Stalin* (Cambridge: Cambridge University Press, 1996), 44–46. For a comprehensive history of early Soviet legal institutions, see John N. Hazard, *Settling Disputes in Soviet Society: The Formative Years of Legal Institutions* (New York: Columbia University Press, 1960).

32. Svetlana Boym, *Common Places: Mythologies of Everyday Life in Russia* (Cambridge: Harvard University Press, 1994), 95–102. Boym supports her analysis of such antitheatrical theatricality by analyzing F. M. Dostoevskii's reaction to trials by jury in *Dnevnik pisatelia, 1877 sentiabr'–dekabr', 1880 avgust. Polnoe sobranie sochinenii v tridtsati tomakh* (Leningrad: Izd. Nauka, 1984), 26:51–54. Murav also analyzes Dostoevskii's reactions to these trials in "Dostoevsky's *Diary*: A Child Is Being Beaten," in *Legal Fictions*, 125–55.

33. Sergei Kobiakov, "Krasnyi sud. Vpechateleniia zashchitnika v revoliutsionnykh tribunalakh," in *Arkhiv russkoi revoliutii* (Berlin: I. V. Gessen, 1922; reprint, Moscow: Terra-Politizdat, 1991), 7:247, 251.

34. Ibid., 246. Kobiakov continues the comparison of early Bolshevik courts to their counterparts from the French Revolution throughout this article. For a discussion of Lenin and Trotskii's appropriation of terror from the French revolutionary model, see John Keep, "1917: The Tyranny of Paris over Petrograd," *Soviet Studies* 20, no. 1 (July 1968): 31–32; and Dmitry Shlapentokh, *The French Revolution and the Russian Anti-Democratic Tradition: A Case of False Consciousness* (New Brunswick: Transaction, 1997), 263–82. For a general discussion of the parallels drawn between the revolution of 1917 and the French Revolution, see Tamara Kondrat'eva, *Bol'shevik—iakobintsy i prizrak termidora* (Moscow: Izd. Ipol, 1993), and Dmitry Shlapentokh, *The Counter-Revolution in Revolution: Images of Thermidor and Napoleon at the Time of the Russian Revolution and Civil War* (New York: St. Martin's Press, 1999).

35. For histories of theater and spectacle during the French Revolution, see Marvin Carlson, *The Theatre of the French Revolution* (Ithaca: Cornell University Press, 1966); Ozouf, *Festivals and the French Revolution;* and Noel Parker, "Theatre and Festivals: Performing the Revolution," in *Portrayals of Revolution: Images, Debate and Patterns of Thought on the French Revolution* (Carbondale: Southern Illinois University Press, 1990), 38–74.

36. Bessie Beatty, "In Place of the Guillotine," in *The Red Heart of Russia* (New York: Century, 1919), 292–311. References to this work will henceforth be given parenthetically in the text. Albert Rhys Williams attended the first revolutionary tribunal with Beatty and describes his experience in *Journey into Revolution: Petrograd, 1917–1918* (Chicago: Quadrangle Books, 1969), 163–66.

37. Williams, *Journey into Revolution*, 164.

38. Kobiakov, "Krasnyi sud," 265 (another observer). Kobiakov also comments on the participation of spectators in both prosecution and defense at early Soviet trials (249).

39. A. V. Peshekhonov, *Pochemu ia ne emigriroval?* (Berlin: Obelisk, 1923), 53. Baroness Sophie Buxhoeveden echoed Peshekhonov's sarcasm in her observation that trials held in Siberia during the first months after October 1917 were "a farce." See *Left Behind: Fourteen Months in Siberia during the Revolution, December 1917–February 1919* (London: Longmans, Green, 1929), 100.

40. Lenin, *Polnoe sobranie sochinenii,* 44:397; Kobiakov, "Krasnyi sud," 251–52.

41. Dziga Vertov, *Kino-Nedelia,* nos. 1, 3, 14, 35 (1918–1919). For descriptions of these early newsreels, see Iu. A. Poliakov and S. V. Drobashenko, eds., *Sovetskaia kinokhronika, 1918–1925. Annotirovannyi katalog,* vol. 1, *Kinozhurnaly* (Moscow: Tsentral'nyi Gos. Arkhiv Kinofotofonodokumentov SSSR, 1965) 9, 11, 18, 33.

42. Vertov's coverage of the Mironov trial originally appeared in *Kino-Nedelia* 35, February 14, 1919. The footage has unfortunately been lost from archival copies of *Kino-Nedelia,* but it appears in reel 3 of the feature-length documentary *Istoriia grazhdanskoi voiny,* 1921.

43. "The Trial of Nicholas Romanov," quoted in Mark D. Steinberg and

Vladimir M. Khrustalëv, *The Fall of the Romanovs: Political Dreams and Personal Struggles in a Time of Revolution* (New Haven: Yale University Press, 1995), 233. For more documentation of plans for a trial of Nicholas II, see 224–25, 287–88. In his memoirs of the revolution, Kerenskii states it was evident that the leaders of the Soviet Union "wanted to throw [Nicholas II] into the Peter and Paul Fortress and then reenact the drama of the French Revolution by having the tyrant publicly executed." Alexander Kerensky, *Russia and History's Turning Point* (New York: Duell, Sloan and Pearce, 1965), 238.

44. Leon Trotsky, *My Life: An Attempt at an Autobiography* (New York: Charles Scribner's Sons, 1931), 190; Leon Trotsky, *Trotsky's Diary in Exile: 1935*, trans. Elena Zarudnaya (Cambridge: Harvard University Press, 1958), 80 (quotation), 82. Lisa A. Kirschenbaum, "Scripting Revolution: Regicide in Russia," unpublished paper presented at 1997 conference "Inventing the Soviet Union," at Indiana University.

45. Trotsky, *Trotsky's Diary in Exile*, 81; Kirschenbaum, "Scripting Revolution," 25.

46. For descriptions of show trials preceding that of the SRs, see Solzhenitsyn, *The Gulag Archipelago*, 310–54; Kovalev, *Raspiatie dukha*, 6–57. For an insider's account of the staging of a regional show trial during the 1920s, see Agabekov's description of a trial he helped organize and on whose panel of judges he sat. G. S. Agabekov, *Ch. K. za rabotoi* (Berlin: Izd. Strela, 1931), 79–88.

47. N. V. Krylenko, *Za piat' let, 1918–1922 gg. Obvinitel'nye rechi po naibolee krupnym protsessam, zaslushannym v moskovskom i verkhovnom revoliutsionnykh tribunalakh* (Moscow-Petrograd: Gos. Izd., 1923), 8.

48. Leonard Schapiro, *The Origin of the Communist Autocracy: Political Opposition in the Soviet State, First Phase, 1917–1922* (Cambridge: Harvard University Press, 1955), 140–52.

49. My analysis of the SR trial relies largely on Marc Jansen's monograph *A Show Trial under Lenin: The Trial of the Socialist Revolutionaries, Moscow, 1922* (The Hague: Martinus Nyhoff, 1982). Jansen provides the most complete account of the SR trial; however, David Shub briefly recounts the trial's event in "The Trial of the SRs," *Russian Review* 23, no. 4 (October 1964): 362–69. Solzhenitsyn's description of the 1922 trial is heavily skewed and relies on a limited number of sources and accounts. Solzhenitsyn, *Gulag Archipelago*, 354–67.

50. Semenov published his accusations before the trial in G. Ssemjonow (Wassiljew), *Die Partei der Sozial-revolutionäre in den Jahren 1917–1918 (Ihre Kampftätigkeit und militärischen Aktionen)* (Hamburg: Kleine Bibliothek der Russischen Korrespondenz, 1922). For February 1919, see Jansen, *Show Trial*, 6–9.

51. "Rech' tov. Bukharina," *Trud* 259, November 13, 1927, 3.

52. F. A. Mackenzie, *Russia before Dawn* (London: T. Fisher Unwin, 1923), 232.

53. Paxton Hibben, "Moscow's Treason Trial," *Nation* 65, no. 2986, September 27, 1922, 300. Mackenzie also describes the setting for the trial in detail, in *Russia before Dawn*, 234; and Walter Duranty gives a description in his report

"Defy Soviet Court in Treason Trial," *New York Times,* June 10, 1922, 1.

54. Hibben, "Treason Trial," 300.

55. Mackenzie, *Russia before Dawn,* 238; E. Olitskaia, *Moi vospominaniia* (Frankfurt am Main: Posev, 1971), vol. 1, pts. 1–6, 154. *Dvenadtsat' smertnikov. Sud nad sotsialistami-revoliutsionarami v Moskve* (Berlin: Izd. zagranichnoi delegatsii PSR, 1922), 54; Mackenzie, *Russia before Dawn,* 234; Emile Vandervelde and Arthur Wauters, *Le procès des socialistes révolutionnaires à Moscou* (Brussels: Librairie du Peuple, 1922), 129.

56. Mackenzie, *Russia before Dawn,* 248. Walter Duranty describes an audience that listened in rapt attention ("Defy Soviet Court in Treason Trial," 1), and one that threatened to tear the accused to pieces at points during the trial ("Goad Communists to Fury in Moscow," *New York Times,* June 12, 1922, 3). Mackenzie wrote that the trial ran "Day after day, six days a week, all through June, right up to August . . . from midday till close on midnight. . . . Long before the end everybody was wearied" (*Russia before Dawn,* 238, 243). S. P. Mel'gunov states that the public grew tired of the trial long before its end; see *Vospominaniia i dnevniki. Vypusk II (Chast' tret'a)* (Paris: Les Editeurs Réunis, 1964), 79. Hibben describes public indifference to the trial ("Treason Trial," 300).

57. For the first estimate, see V. M. Zlobina, *Bor'ba partii bol'shevikov protiv melkoburzhuaznogo vliianiia na rabochii klass v pervye gody NEPa (1921–1925 gg.)* (Moscow: Izd. Moskovskogo universiteta, 1975), 102; for the second, see Mackenzie, *Russia before Dawn,* 240–41, and Nurmin, "Protsess eserov. (Zamechaniia i vpechatleniia.)," *Krasnaia nov'* no. 4 (July–August 1922): 272. Pitirim A. Sorokin places the head count at a mere fifty thousand in *Leaves from a Russian Diary—and Thirty Years After* (Boston: Beacon Press, 1950), 297.

58. For example, in his account of the demonstration, Walter Duranty states, "The Communists throughout Russia are watching the reaction of the peasant masses." He continues that the vast majority of demonstrators were "just interested in the show, pleased with the extra holiday, gratified by the rolling music, whose choruses it sang under the warm June sun" ("Soviet Chiefs Stage Anti-Treason Show," *New York Times,* June 22, 1922, 3). According to an obviously biased source, a large number of the participants were actually paid as Cheka agents and Party members to participate in the June 20, 1922, demonstration (*Dvenadtsat' smertnikov,* 75). Boris Dvinov echoes this opinion in his assertion that the masses participated in the demonstrations from a fear of starvation; *Ot legal'nosti k podpol'iu (1921–1922)* (Stanford: Hoover Institution on War, Revolution and Peace, 1968), 137. Tiltman also asserts that the demonstrators' wrath was entirely staged (*Terror in Europe,* 80), as does G. P. Maximoff, in *The Guillotine at Work: Twenty Years of Terror in Russia (Data and Documents)* (Chicago: Chicago Section of the Alexander Berkman Fund, 1940), 215. P. E. Mel'gunova-Stepanova claims that the demonstration was acted out by large numbers of schoolchildren in *Gde ne slyshno smekha. . . . Tipy, nravy i byt' Ch.K. Otryvki iz vospominanii (1917–1922 gg.)* (Paris: Rapid-Imprimerie, 1928), 189–91. Mackenzie also mentions that there was an unusual number of young

children taking part in the demonstration (*Russia before Dawn*, 241).

59. *Dvenadtsat' smertnikov*, 79 (quotation); Mackenzie, *Russia before Dawn*, 239; Olitskaia, *Moi vospominaniia*, 155.

60. Dziga Vertov, *Kinopravda*, nos. 1–4, 7–8 (1922). For descriptions of these newsreels, see Poliakov and Drobashenko, *Kinozhurnaly*, 41–47. This material was reedited to make a three-reel documentary film entitled *Protsess pravykh Es-erov s 8-go iiuliia po 7-oe avgusta 1922 g.* (1923). For a brief discussion of Vertov's coverage of the SR trial as a precedent for future trial documentaries, see Liliana Mal'kova, "Litso vraga," in *Kino. Politika i liudi (30-e gody)* (Moscow: Materik, 1995), 85.

61. Some of the more bizarre and fascinating instances of propaganda were Petrushka puppet plays, which traveled the country depicting the lessons of the trial, political poems by such luminaries as Dem'ian Bednyi and Vladimir Maiakovskii, and popular songs that preached the lessons of the trial. *Dvenadtsat' smertnikov*, 41–42; V. Maiakovskii, "Ballada o doblestnom Emile," *Izvestiia* 117, no. 1556, May 28, 1922, 2; Dem'ian Bednyi, "Dlia esera—ego zhe mera," *Pravda* 135, June 20, 1922, 3, and "Gnetuchka: Polushutia, poluvser'ez," *Pravda*, July 20, 1922, 2.

62. Drobashenko notes that Vertov frequently used fictional sequences in his early documentaries, especially to reenact historical events. S. V. Drobashenko, *Istoriia sovetskogo dokumental'nogo kino. Uchebno-metodicheskoe posobie* (Moscow: Izd. Moskovskogo universiteta, 1980), 9.

63. The newsreel coverage of these trials in the mid-1920s resembles that of the SR trial. For the Savinkov trial, see Vertov, *Lenigradskii Goskino-kalendar'* 6 (Leningrad, 1924), or *Goskino kalendar'* 28 (Leningrad, 1924), which has essentially the same footage. For Okladskii's trial, see *Sud nad provokatorom Okladskim* (Moscow, 1925), and a reworking of this same footage in *Goskino kalendar'* 46 (Moscow, 1925).

2: THE MOCK TRIAL

1. Harriet Murav similarly describes prerevolutionary political trials as instances of carnival in *Legal Fictions*, 55–91.

2. For a description of the genesis of melodrama in revolutionary France, and its subsequent history on the popular stages of France, England, and the United States, see Frank Rahill, *The World of Melodrama* (University Park: Pennsylvania State University Press, 1967).

3. Wylie Sypher, "Aesthetic of Revolution: The Marxist Melodrama," in *Tragedy: Vision and Form*, ed. Robert W. Corrigan (New York: Harper and Row, 1981), 216–24.

4. For a brief discussion of enantiodromia within melodrama, see Robertson Davies, *The Mirror of Nature: The Alexander Lectures, 1982* (Toronto: University of Toronto Press, 1983), 26–27.

5. Mikhail Iampolskii, "Vina—pokaianie—donos," in *Russian Culture in*

Transition: Selected Papers of the Working Group for the Study of Contemporary Russian Culture, 1990–1991, ed. Gregory Freidin (Stanford: Department of Slavic Languages and Literatures, 1993), 218.

6. Numerous authors document the development of propaganda theater in early Soviet Russia, including Fülöp-Miller, *Mind and Face of Bolshevism;* Fülöp-Miller and Gregor, *Russian Theatre;* N. A. Gorchakov, *Istoriia sovetskogo teatra* (New York: Izd. im. Chekhova, 1956); P. A. Markov, *The Soviet Theatre* (London: Victor Gollancz, 1934); Konstantin Rudnitsky, *Russian and Soviet Theatre: Tradition and the Avant-Garde,* trans. Roxane Permar, ed. Dr. Lesley Milne (London: Thames and Hudson, 1988); Marc Slonim, *Russian Theater: From the Empire to the Soviets* (New York: Collier Books, 1961); and von Geldern, *Bolshevik Festivals.*

7. Gorchakov, *Istoriia sovetskogo teatra,* 89–90. For a discussion of the Red Petrushka, see Catriona Kelly, *Petrushka: The Russian Carnival Puppet Theatre* (Cambridge: Cambridge University Press, 1990), 179–211.

8. I. V. Rebel'skii, *Instsenirovannye sudy (Kak ikh organizovyvat' i provodit')* (Moscow: Izd. MGSPS Trud i kniga, 1926), 10–11. At the end of the nineteenth century, a popular debate over Pushkin's morality and his status as a poet took the form of a *sud chesti* (court of honor). B. V. Nikol'skii, *Sud nad Pushkinym. Pis'mo k V. P. Bureninu* (St. Petersburg: Tip. A. S. Suvorina, 1897).

9. For a fictional account of a post-revolutionary literary trial of Pushkin's *Evgenii Onegin,* see V. Kaverin, *Dva kapitana* (Moscow: Khudozhestvennaia Literatura, 1979), pt. 3, ch. 2, pp. 135–39. For an account of a moot court used for pedagogical purposes, see the description of *Sud nad duel'iu* held in 1922 in the Institut Zhivogo Slova. B. M. Fillipov, *Zapiski "Domovogo"* (Moscow: Izd. Sovetskaia Rossiia, 1978), 111–12.

10. Von Geldern, *Bolshevik Festivals,* 109; V. Golovachev and B. Lashchilin, *Narodnyi teatr na Donu* (Rostov na Donu: Rostovskoe oblastnoe knigoizd., 1947), 55–58; V. A. Zakrutkin, "O russkom narodom teatre v sviazi s donskimi zapisiami," in Golovachev and Lashchilin, *Narodnyi teatr na Donu,* 28.

11. Rebel'skii, *Instsenirovannye sudy,* 13–14.

12. L. Tamashin, *Sovetskaia dramaturgiia v gody grazhdanskoi voiny* (Moscow: Gos. Izd. Iskusstvo, 1961), 57–60. For general studies of mass festivals, see von Geldern, *Bolshevik Festivals;* Alexander Zakharov, "Mass Celebrations in a Totalitarian System," in *Tekstura: Russian Essays on Visual Culture,* ed. and trans. Alla Efimova and Lev Manovich (Chicago: University of Chicago Press, 1993), 201–18; and Katerina Clark, *Petersburg, Crucible of Cultural Revolution* (Cambridge: Harvard University Press, 1995), 122–34.

13. Von Geldern, *Bolshevik Festivals,* 108–10.

14. Rebel'skii, *Instsenirovannye sudy,* 14. For additional titles and descriptions of mass mock trials, see Gorchakov, *Istoriia sovetskogo teatra,* 88, and Tamashin, *Sovetskaia dramaturgiia,* 57–60. Richard Taylor also describes agitfilms that contained similar trials during the civil war period. Taylor, "A Medium for the Masses: Agitation in the Soviet Civil War," *Soviet Studies* 22, no. 4 (April 1971): 569.

15. For brief accounts of the agitsud by theater historians, see Gorchakov, *Istoriia sovetskogo teatra*, 89; Markov, *The Soviet Theatre*, 140; Tamashin, *Sovetskaia dramaturgiia*, 57–60; and *Le théâtre d'agit-prop de 1917 à 1932*, vol. 1, *L'URSS-recherches* (Lausanne: La Cité–L'Age d'Homme, 1977), 52–54. Elizabeth A. Wood also describes the generic features of the agitsud and provides a taxonomy of the genre in her forthcoming monograph, *Performing Justice: Agitation Trails in Revolutionary Russia.*

16. Fülöp-Miller, *Mind and Face of Bolshevism*, 141.

17. Kerzhentsev, *Tvorcheskii teatr*, 130.

18. Markov, *The Soviet Theatre*, 140 (quotation), 142.

19. "Sud nad Leninym," *Pravda* 83, April 22, 1920, 2.

20. "Sud nad Vrangelem," *Vestnik teatra* 72–73, November 7, 1920, 16–17. A nearly identical account of this mock trial can be found in "Obzor agitatsionnogo materiala: Instsenirovka agitatsionnykh sudov," *Vestnik agitatsii i propagandy* 3, November 25, 1920, 25–27. When discussing these agitsudy, I have chosen to cite the Russian title at first instance with the English translation given in parentheses. Further citations are to the English title for clarity. This is not to imply that there are actual English versions.

21. "Sud nad Vrangelem," 16.

22. Boris Fillipov, *Muzy na fronte. Ocherki, dnevniki, pis'ma* (Moscow: Izd. Sovetskaia Rossia, 1975), 31; Vsevolod Vishnevskii, "Dvadtsatiletie sovetskoi dramaturgii," in *Sovetskie dramaturgi o svoem tvorchestve. Sbornik statei* (Moscow: Izd. Iskusstvo, 1967), 150 (quotation).

23. "Sud nad Vrangelem," 16.

24. Rebel'skii, *Instsenirovannye sudy*, 7.

25. An exception to this pattern is L. M. Vasilevskii who figured as a minor poet before the revolution. Nonetheless, his claim to fame as the coauthor of several agitsudy with his wife comes from his status as a medical doctor qualified to comment on the social and medical consequences of illegal abortions and white lightening. See L. M. Vasilevskii and L. A. Vasilevskaia, *Sud nad akusherkoi Lopukhinoi sovershivshei operatsiiu aborta, sledstviem chego iavilas' smert' zhenshchiny* (Tver': Izd. Oktiabr', 1923), and *Sud nad samogonshchikami. Delo Karpova Tikhona i ego zheny Agaf'i po obvineniiu v izgotovlenii i tainoi torgovle samogonkoi* (Petrograd: Izd. Oktiabr', 1923).

26. Semenov, "Agit-sud," *Derevenskii teatr* 2 (September 1925): 14–15. A brief overview of the typical agitsud can also be found in B. Vetrov and L. Petrov, *Agitsud i zhivaia gazeta v derevne* (Moscow-Leningrad: Gos. Izd., 1926), 24–28.

27. Archives of TsGALI, fond 656, o. 1, d. 2636. Otzyv No. 1203 of B. S. Sigal, *Sud nad Ivanom Lobachevym.*

28. Ibid., Otzyv No. 1367 of B. S. Sigal, *Sud nad mater'iu, vinovnoi v plokhom ukhode za det'mi.*

29. B. S. Sigal, *Sud nad Stepanom Korolevym (Posledstviia p'ianstva). Instsenirovka suda v 2-kh aktakh* (Moscow: Kooperativnoe Izd. Zhizn' i znanie, 1924, 1926); and *Sud nad mater'iu, vinovnoi v plokhom ukhode za det'mi,*

povlekshem za soboi smert' rebenka (Sanitarno-prosvetitel'naia instsenirovka v 2 aktakh) (Leningrad: Biblioteka zhurnala Gigena i zdorov'e rabochei i krest'ianskoi sem'i, 1926) and (Leningrad: Izd. Leningradskaia Pravda, 1928 and 1929).

30. Sigal, *Sud nad Stepanom Korolevym,* 13.

31. Steve Neale, "Melodrama and Tears," *Screen* 27, no. 6 (November–December 1986): 6–7.

32. Sigal, *Sud nad Stepanom Korolevym,* 4, 34, 48.

33. Ibid., 56.

34. Sigal, *Sud nad mater'iu, vinovnoi v plokhom,* 8.

35. Ibid., 20.

36. Ibid., 28.

37. Sigal, *Sud nad Stepanom Korolevym,* 7, and *Sud nad mater'iu, vinovnoi v plokhom,* 5. In the preface to *Sud nad Stepanom Korolevym,* Sigal writes that "The staging should be kept strictly within the framework of a real trial" (1).

38. Sigal, *Sud nad Stepanom Korolevym,* 9. For the general guidelines of swearing in witnesses, see Vetrov and Petrov, *Agitsud,* 26. For other vivid examples of this practice, see N. Glebova, *Sud nad delegatkoi. Delo po obvineniiu delegatki Tikhonovoi, ne vypolnivshei svoego proletarskogo dolga* (Moscow-Leningrad: Gos. Izd., 1924), 5; A. I. Akkerman, *Sud nad prostitutkoi. Delo gr. Zaborovoi po obvineniiu ee v zaniatii prostitutsiei i zarazhenii sifilisom kr-tsa Krest'ianova* (Moscow-Leningrad: Gos. Izd., 1923), 9.

39. For example, the judge in one agitsud states that "the current case is only a small episode in an enormous epic—the battle of two principles—of the old way of life, which is dying away, and of the new, which is coming to take its place." Boris Andreev, *Sud nad starym bytom. Stsenarii dlia rabochikh klubov ko dniu rabotnitsy 8-go marta (s metodicheskimi ukazaniiami)* (Moscow-Leningrad: Izd. Doloi Negramotnost', 1926), 26.

40. A. Vilenkin, *Kak postavit' agitsud v izbe-chital'ne* (Leningrad; Gos. Izd., 1926), 5.

41. Rebel'skii, *Instsenirovannye sudy,* 7–9; S. Dolinskii and S. Bergman, *Massovaia rabota v klube. Metodika, illiustrativnyi material, uchet opyta* (Moscow: Izd. Rabotnik prosveshcheniia, 1924), 51, 55.

42. L. Reinberg, *Instsenirovannye proizvodstvennye sudy* (Moscow: Izd. MGSPS Trud i Kniga, 1926), 8; Rebel'skii, *Instsenirovannye sudy,* 3.

43. For several examples, see Vilenkin, *Kak postavit',* 7; Vetrov and Petrov, *Agitsud,* 47; N. Leonov, "Agro-sudy," *Derevenskii teatr* 2 (September 1925): 25; Semenov, "Agit-sud," 15; and Dolinskii and Bergman, *Massovaia rabota v klube,* 52.

44. For examples, see Vilenkin, *Kak postavit',* 9; Rebel'skii, *Instsenirovannye sudy,* 27, 37; Vetrov and Petrov, *Agitsud,* 23, 32; Semenov, "Agit-sud," 15; and Reinberg, *Instsenirovannye,* 39. For a discussion of spectator participation in actual trials of the era, see Solomon, *Soviet Criminal Justice,* 46.

45. B. S. Sigal, *I. Sud nad pionerom-kuril'shchikom. II. Sud nad neriashlivym pionerom (Dve instsenirovki),* (Moscow: Kooperativenoe Izd. Zhizn' i znanie, 1927), 3.

46. Rebel'skii, *Instsenirovannye sudy,* 45.

47. E. B. Demidovich, *Sud nad polovoi raspushchennost'iu* (Moscow-Leningrad: Doloi Negramotnost', 1927), 6.

48. Sigal, *Sud nad mater'iu, vinovnoi v plokhom,* 24.

49. For examples, see Rebel'skii, *Instsenirovannye sudy,* 31, 46, 50; Vetrov and Petrov, *Agitsud,* 25, 33; Dolinskii and Bergman, *Massovaia rabota v klube,* 55; and L. Indenbom, *Agrosudy. Sud nad vrediteliami, sud nad sorniakami, sud nad beskormitsei, sud nad kolkhozom, sud nad dezerterom pokhoda za urozhai i drugie; Dlia provedeniia v periody podgotovki vesennei i osennei posevnykh kampanii i na prazdnike urozhaia* (Moscow: Izd. Krest'ianskaia gazeta, 1929), 15.

50. R. D., *Sud nad domashnei khoziaikoi* (Moscow-Leningrad: Gos. Izd., 1927), 22 (audience members). See the testimony of Patakeev in Vasilevskii and Vasilevskaia, *Sud nad samogonshchikami,* 22–23 (planted witnesses); also D. N. Deev, *Sud nad zarazivshim sifilisom zhenu (Sanitarnaia p'esa)* (Ekaterinoslav: Izd. Otdela Zdravookhraneniia i Dorkul'trana Ekaterininskoi zheleznoi dorogi, 1924), 5; Sigal, *I. Sud nad pionerom-kuril'shchikom,* 9, 36; Sigal, *Sud nad grazhdaninom Fedorom Sharovym po obvineniiu v zarazhenii tripperom. (Instsenirovka suda v 2-kh aktakh)* (Leningrad: Izd. Zhizn' i znanie, 1925), 34; B. Starko, *Sud nad Fordom* (Moscow-Leningrad: Gos. Izd., 1928), 12; Demidovich, *Sud nad polovoi raspushchennost'iu,* 26.

51. Rebel'skii, *Instsenirovannye sudy,* 10, 40–42. This also proved to be a common practice in casting actors for the cinema during the 1920s, especially for Lev Kuleshov, and was appropriately called typage.

52. Vilenkin, *Kak postavit',* 12; Dolinskii and Bergman, *Massovaia rabota v klube,* 53; Akkerman, *Sud nad prostitutkoi . . . Zaborovoi.* For another example of a mock trial received as a real trial, see the report of Kl. Gul'binskaia, "Sud nad sifilitkom," *Rabochii zritel'* 19, September 14–21, 1924, 17. Walter Duranty also reported that a 1929 mock trial of twelve textile workers received the same press coverage as a real trial. *Duranty Reports Russia,* ed. Gustavus Tuckerman Jr. (New York: Viking Press, 1934), 364. "Vorova s prostitutsiei," *Pravda* 179, August 14, 1921, 4; "Popravka," *Pravda* 183, August 19, 1921, 2.

53. E. K., review of "Agrosud" by B. Shapiro and N. Gol'dshtein, in *Repertuarnyi biullenten' Glaviskusstva RSFSR* 2 (February 1929): 16.

54. Quoted in Dolinskii and Bergman, *Massovaia rabota v klube,* 98.

55. Vasilevskii and Vasilevskaia, *Sud nad samogonshchikami,* 34.

56. Dolinskii and Bergman, *Massovaia rabota v klube,* 57; Indenbom, *Agrosudy,* 23–24.

57. *Sud nad negramotnym* (Tashkent: Izd. Turkglavpolitprosveta, 1923). See also Andreev, *Sud nad starym bytom;* Boris Andreev, *Sud nad chitatelem* (Leningrad: Izd. Knizhnogo Sektora GUBONO, 1924), 3; and Demidovich, *Sud nad polovoi raspushchennost'iu,* 3.

58. These characters appear respectively in A. Nikolaev, *Avio-agitsud* (Moscow: Izd. ODVF RSFSR, 1925); Sigal, *I. Sud nad pionerom-kuril'shchikom;* Leonid Subbotin, *Sud nad korovoi. Krest'ianskaia p'esa* (Moscow: Izd. Novaia

Derevnia, 1928); and N. M. Naumov, *Kto vinovat? (Sanitarnyi sud)* (Moscow: Biuro sanitarnogo prosveshchenia Mosgorzdravotdela, 1939).

59. Akkerman, *Sud nad prostitutkoi . . . Zaborovoi,* 7.

60. Also highly unrealistic were the personifications of animals or ideological abstractions that appeared in some agitsudy, such as N. Goncharova-Viktorova, *Korovii sud. Agro-komediia v 3-kh kartinakh* (Moscow-Leningrad: Izd. MODPiK, 1927), in which the entire court is composed of actors costumed as various farm animals.

61. Rebel'skii, *Instsenirovannye sudy,* 42–43. Viktor Ardov, "Alimenty" and "Poltinnik pogubil (Rastratnoe)," *Sovetskii vodelvil' (dlia klubnykh, komsomol'skikh i rabochikh teatrov)* 3 (1927): 3–9 and 20–26; Viktor Ardov, "Delo o prokhodnoi komnate," *Sovetskii vodevil' dlia rabochego, kres'ianskogo i komsomol'skogo teatra* 4 (1929): 12–21.

62. Vetrov and Petrov, *Agitsud,* 27, 29, 11 (quotation). See also Indenbom, *Agrosudy,* 6, 16.

63. Reinberg, *Instsenirovannye,* 40.

64. Demidovich, *Sud nad polovoi raspushchennost'iu,* 38–39.

65. Dolinskii and Bergman, *Massovaia rabota v klube,* 53.

66. Glebova, *Sud nad delegatkoi,* 16.

67. According to Solomon, the sentences in demonstration trials conducted by actual courts were usually harsher than was normal for the crime on trial (*Soviet Criminal Justice,* 45).

68. Walter Benjamin, *Moscow Diary,* trans. Richard Sieburth, ed. Gary Smith (Cambridge: Harvard University Press, 1986), 49–50 (49).

69. Deev, *Sud nad zarazivshim,* 31.

70. A. E. Frolov, *Sud nad svin'ei. P'esa v 3-kh deistviiakh dlia postanovki v narodnykh domakh, domakh krest'ianina i izbakh-chital'niakh* (Pokrovsk: Glavlit no. 1060, 1928), 40, 47 (quotation).

71. Andreev, *Sud nad starym bytom,* 11–12.

72. Sigal, *I. Sud nad pionerom-kuril'shchikom,* 22 (quote); Goncharova-Viktorova, *Korovii sud,* 25 (quote); Vasilevskii and Vasilevskaia, *Sud nad akusherkoi Lopukhinoi,* 63.

73. A. I. Akkerman, *Sud nad prostitutkoi i svodnitsei. Delo grazhd. Evdokimovoi, po obvineniiu v soznatel'nom zarazhenii sifilisom i grazhd. Sviridovoi v svodnichestve i soobshchnichestve* (Moscow: Izd. Narkomzdrava, 1924, 1925), 50, 61.

74. Leonov, "Agro-sudy," 25.

75. Zakharov describes a similar movement away from unscripted, spontaneous participation in mass festivals of the 1920s to the rigidly choreographed mass parades of the 1930s and 1940s ("Mass Celebrations," 210, 214–18).

76. For a discussion of the impact of the aesthetic aims of the avant-garde upon the art of socialist realism, see Boris Groys, *The Total Art of Stalinism: Avant-Garde, Aesthetic Dictatorship, and Beyond,* trans. Charles Rougle (Princeton: Princeton University Press, 1992); Irina Gutkin, *The Novel of Socialist Real-*

ism as a Phenomenon of Literary Evolution (Ph.D. dissertation, University of California at Berkeley, 1989).

77. For an interesting discussion of the manner in which the form and function of the agitsud penetrated institutions of higher learning in the 1920s, see Michael David-Fox, *Revolution of the Mind: Higher Learning among the Bolsheviks, 1918–1929* (Ithaca: Cornell University Press, 1997), 171–78.

78. Andrei Sinyavsky, *Soviet Civilization: A Cultural History,* trans. Joanne Turnbull and Nikolai Formozov (New York: Little, Brown, 1990), 180. In the mid-1920s, a Moscow theatrical club staged a *Trial of Dramatists Who Don't Write Roles for Women,* in which the most famous actors, directors, and playwrights of the time participated. A. K. Gladkov, *Pozdnye vechera. Vospominaniia, stat'i, zapiski* (Moscow: Sovetskii pisatel', 1986), 180–81, and *Aktery bez grima* (Moscow: Sovetskaia Rossiia, 1971), 197–98. In 1924, debate of the play *Prazdnik Iorgena* also took the form of a mock trial. "Sudy nad p'esami," *Rabochii zritel'* 27, November 18–25, 1924, 9; "Sud nad 'Prazdnikom Iorgena'," *Rabochii zritel'* 29, December 3–9, 1924, 11–12; "Po povodu suda," *Rabochii zritel'* 30, December 10–16, 1924, 9. General literary issues were also often discussed using a trial format—for example, *Sud nad pornografiei v literature. (Diskussia, ustroennaia mestkomom pisatelei 17 noiabria 1925 goda v Dome Pechati nad proizvedeniem A. Volzhskogo—"Druz'ia po Volge")* (Moscow: Vserossiiskii soiuz Krest'ianskikh pisatelei, 1926). Discussion of films in the 1920s was encouraged in the form of mock trials; *Kino v rabochem klube,* 52. Prominent cinema trials included "Sud nad Garri Pilem," *Pravda* 138, no. 3970, June 16, 1928, 6, and "Obshchestvennyi sud nad tipazhem," *Kino* 31 (1928): 4.

79. Mikhail Shatrov, *Diktatura sovesti. Spory i razmyshleniia vosem'desiat shestogo goda v dvukh chastiakh, Teatr* 6 (June 1986): 3–37. For a description of the "trials of history" conducted by the student study group for the History of Antiquity and the Middle Ages, see *Zerkalo istorii. Dvadtsat' let kruzhku istorii drevnosti i srednevekov'ia: Sbornik statei* (Moscow: RGGY, 1992), 7–9, 15–38.

3: TRIALS ON FILM

1. For brief descriptions of these films, neither of which survives in its entirety in the archives, see Bursak, *Kino,* 11, 39; and *Istoriia sovetskogo kino, 1917–1931* (Moscow: Izd. Iskusstvo, 1969), 1:530–31. For mock trials that provide the theatrical counterparts of these two agitfilms, see Vasilevskii and Vasilevskaia, *Sud nad akusherkoi Lopukhinoi;* and Mikhail Grokhovskii, *Delo konovala Leshchetkina. P'esa v 1 deistvii* (Tver': Izd. Tverskogo Gubzempravleniia, 1926).

2. Quoted in Davies, *Mirror of Nature,* 25–26.

3. Sheila Fitzpatrick, *The Commissariat of Enlightenment: Soviet Organization of Education and the Arts under Lunacharsky, October 1917–1921* (Cambridge: Cambridge University Press, 1970), 153. For discussions of Lunacharskii's call "Back to Ostrovskii!" see Robert Leach, *Revolutionary Theatre* (London:

Routledge, 1994), 142–50; and Rudnitsky, *Russian and Soviet Theatre,* 116–19.

4. In his contribution to the influential collection of essays on the new theater, Lunacharskii had already mentioned melodrama as the most desirable genre. A. Lunacharskii, "Sotsializm i iskusstvo," *Teatr: Kniga o novom teatre. Sbornik statei,* 34. He also discussed the utility of melodrama for the mass spectator in "Voskresshaia melodrama," *Teatr i iskusstvo* 18, May 3, 1915, 304–6. In addition, Lunacharskii wrote in 1922 that "for already twenty years, I have pointed out, in speeches and the press, the enormous significance of melodrama." A. V. Lunacharskii, "Pravel'nyi put'," *Sobranie sochinenii v vos'mi tomakh* (Moscow: Izd. Khudozhestvennaia Literatura, 1964), 3:112. Maksim Gor'kii also advocated melodrama for a revitalized theater as early as 1914. K. D. Muratova, "M. Gor'kii i sovetskii teatr," *Iz istorii russkikh literaturnykh otnoshenii, 18–20 vekov* (Moscow-Leningrad: Izd. Akademii nauk SSSR, 1959), 292.

5. Romain Rolland, "Quelques genres de théâtre populaire: Le mélodrame," in *Théâtre du peuple,* 130–36. For the Russian translation, see Romain Rolland, "Melodrama," in *Narodnyi teatr,* trans. I. Gol'denberg (St. Petersburg: Izd. Tovarishchestva Znanie, 1910), 94–99.

6. Rolland, *Narodnyi teatr,* 98.

7. Linda Williams discusses the similar merger of tragedy and melodrama in American culture, which results in the fact that "Americans read Greek tragedy melodramatically." Linda Williams, "Melodrama Revisited," in *Refiguring American Film Genres: History and Theory,* ed. Nick Browne (Berkeley and Los Angeles: University of California Press, 1998), 53–54.

8. Rolland, *Narodnyi teatr,* 97–98, 95.

9. Lunacharskii, "Kakaia nam nuzhna melodrama?" *Sobranie sochinenii,* 2:212, and "Pravel'nyi put'," ibid., 3:112. Lunacharskii asserted in his 1918 article "Voskresshaia melodrama," that "the tragedies of Shakespeare are the essence of melodrama" (305).

10. Lunacharskii, "Kakaia nam nuzhna melodrama?" *Sobranie sochinenii,* 2:213–15 (213).

11. Lunacharskii, "Pravel'nyi put'," ibid., 3:113–14.

12. Von Geldern, *Bolshevik Festivals,* 110.

13. M. Gor'kii, "O geroicheskom teatre," *Arkhiv A. M. Gor'kogo,* (Moscow: Gos. Izd. Khudozhestvennoi Literatury, 1951), 3:221 (quote); P. A. Markov, "'Dve sirotki.' Vol'nyi teatr," *O teatre v cheyrekh tomakh* (Moscow: Iskusstvo, 1976), 3:7–8 (quote); V. E. Meierkhol'd, "'Uchitel' Bubus' i problema spektaklia na muzyke (Doklad, prochitannyi 1 ianvaria 1925 g.)," in *Stat'i, pis'ma, rechi, besedy* (Moscow: Izd. Iskusstvo, 1968), 2:76; Alisa Koonen, *Stranitsy zhizni* (Moscow: Iskusstvo, 1985), 304.

14. For a chronology of the melodrama debate and productions of melodramas in Soviet theaters of the 1920s, see Daniel Gerould and Julia Przybos, "Melodrama in the Soviet Theater, 1917–1920: An Annotated Chronology," in Daniel Gerould, ed., *Melodrama* (New York: New York Literary Forum, 1980), 75–92. For a description of one of the era's most popular new melodramas, Aleksei

Faiko's *Chelovek s portfelem (The Man With a Briefcase)* of 1929, see Harold B. Segel, *Twentieth-Century Russian Drama: From Gorky to the Present,* updated ed. (Baltimore: Johns Hopkins University Press, 1993), 213–21.

15. Robert Russell, *Russian Drama of the Revolutionary Period* (Basingstoke, England: Macmillan, 1988), 34–36; Muratova, "M. Gor'kii i sovetskii teatr," 298–300; and Gerould, *Melodrama,* 79. For a reprint of the newspaper advertisement soliciting contributions to this playwriting competition and the article announcing the decision of the jury, see N. S. Pliatskovskaia, ed., "Dramaturgicheskie konkursy," in A. Z. Iufit, ed. *Russkii sovetskii teatr, 1917–1921* (Leningrad: Iskusstvo, 1968), 359–60.

16. Anatolii Lunacharskii, "Revolutionary Ideology and Cinema—Theses," in Taylor, *Film Factory,* 109, 110. For the original Russian version of Lunacharskii's theses, see A. V. Lunacharskii, "Revoliutsionnaia ideologiia i kino: Tezisy," *Lunacharskii o kino. Stat'i, vyskazyvaniia, stsenarii, dokumenty* (Moscow: Izd. Iskusstvo, 1965), 35–39.

17. The screenplay of this movie was published as A. Lunacharskii, *Medvezh'ia svad'ba. Melodrama na siuzhet Merime v 9 kartinakh* (Moscow: Gos. Izd., 1924).

18. Adrian Piotrovskii, "Melodrama ili tragediia?" in *Teatr, kino, zhizn'* (Leningrad: Izd. Iskusstvo, 1969), 63–65; and "Khudozhestvennye techeniia v sovetskom kino," in ibid., 234–40.

19. Youngblood, *Movies for the Masses,* 72–73.

20. For a discussion of the reception of *The Bear's Wedding,* see Youngblood, *Movies for the Masses,* 85. For a discussion of the stylistic peculiarities of prerevolutionary Russian cinema, see Yuri Tsivian, "Some Preparatory Remarks on Russian Cinema," in Paolo Cherchi Usai, ed., *Silent Witnesses: Russian Films, 1908–1919* (British Film Institute and Edizioni Biblioteca dell'Immagine, 1989), 24–43.

21. Mary Ann Doane, "Melodrama, Temporality, Recognition: American and Russian Silent Cinema," *East-West Film Journal* 4, no. 2 (June 1990): 69–89.

22. Courtroom scenes were a recurrent feature of melodrama on the French, English, and American stages, as Rahill notes in *World of Melodrama,* 53–60. For a discussion of the role of tears in the reception of cinematic melodrama, see Neale, "Melodrama and Tears," 6–22.

23. For brief descriptions of the temperance play as a genre of melodrama, see Rahill, *World of Melodrama,* 240–46; Michael R. Booth, "The Drunkard's Progress: Nineteenth-Century Temperance Drama," *Dalhousie Review* 44, no. 2 (summer 1964): 205–12, and "Introduction," in *Hiss the Villain: Six English and American Melodramas* (New York: Benjamin Blom, 1964), 28–29; and Jeffery D. Mason, "*The Drunkard* (1844) and the Temperance Movement," in *Melodrama and the Myth of America* (Bloomington: Indiana University Press, 1993), 61–87.

24. Lunacharsky, "Revolutionary Ideology and Cinema—Theses," 109.

25. Tsivian, "Some Preparatory Remarks," 34–38.

26. For the treatment of this theme in an agitsud, see I. Bozhinskaia,

Prestuplenie Ivana Kuznetsova (Svobodnaia liubov') (Moscow: Molodaia gvardiia, 1927); Demidovich, *Sud nad polovoi raspushchennost'iu*. For a comic rendition of this theme, see Viktor Ardov, "Alimenty," 3–9. For a general discussion of Ermler's work in the Soviet cinema, see Youngblood, *Movies for the Masses*, 139–52.

27. Youngblood, *Movies for the Masses*, 145–47.

28. Eric Naiman, *Sex in Public: The Incarnation of Early Soviet Ideology* (Princeton: Princeton University Press, 1997), 257–63; Anne E. Gorsuch, "'A Woman Is Not a Man': The Culture of Gender and Generation in Soviet Russia, 1921–1928," *Slavic Review* 55, no. 3 (fall 1996): 641–42; Sheila Fitzpatrick, *The Cultural Front: Power and Culture in Revolutionary Russia* (Ithaca: Cornell University Press, 1992), 83–84.

29. Youngblood, *Movies for the Masses*, 144–45, 161.

30. S. Iutkevich uses metapropaganda in a similar manner in his 1928 film *Kruzheva (Lace)*. Set among *komsomol'tsy* at a lace factory, the film depicts the positive effects of wall-newspapers as a means of propaganda.

31. For information on Protazanov's long and productive career in pre- and post-revolutionary Russian film, see Youngblood, *Movies for the Masses*, 105–21.

4: MARBLE COLUMNS AND JUPITER LIGHTS IN THE SHAKHTY AFFAIR

1. For a brief description of Savinkov's 1924 trial that describes the trial as "the greatest theatrical performance I ever attended" and the defendant's closing speech as "the greatest piece of oratory I have ever heard," see Walter Duranty, *I Write as I Please* (New York: Simon and Schuster, 1935), 243–46. Duranty had a complex relationship with Stalinism and Stalin, whose apologist he was for many of the years he was on assignment in the Soviet Union for the *New York Times*. For an account of his career as an American journalist chronicling Stalin's Russia, see S. J. Taylor, *Stalin's Apologist: Walter Duranty, the New York Times's Man in Moscow* (New York: Oxford University Press, 1990).

2. The creation of the Union of Soviet Writers in 1932 provides a good example of this phenomenon. For an explanation of its development out of competing literary associations in the 1920s, see Robert A. Maguire, *Red Virgin Soil: Soviet Literature in the 1920's* (Ithaca: Cornell University Press, 1987).

3. Medvedev, *O Staline i stalinizme*, 226, 230; William Reswick, *I Dreamt Revolution* (Chicago: Henry Regnery, 1952), 246; Michal Reiman, *The Birth of Stalinism: The USSR on the Eve of the "Second Revolution,"* trans. George Saunders (Bloomington: Indiana University Press, 1987), 58.

4. Medvedev, *O Staline i stalinizme*, 229; Reiman, *Birth of Stalinism*, 59; Kovalev, *Raspiatie dukha*, 92–93.

5. Reiman, *Birth of Stalinism*, 60; Eugene Lyons, *Assignment in Utopia* (New York: Harcourt, Brace, 1937), 114.

6. Kurt Rosenbaum, "The German Involvement in the Shakhty Trial," *Russian Review* 21, no. 3 (July 1962): 238–60; Louis Fischer, *The Soviets in World Af-*

fairs: A History of Relations between the Soviet Union and the Rest of the World (London: Jonathan Cape, 1930), 2:772–74; Reiman, *Birth of Stalinism,* 123–52.

7. Reswick, *I Dreamt Revolution,* 247. Vyshinskii would play this role throughout the trials of the 1930s and would eventually prove instrumental in purging Krylenko in 1938. For discussions of Vyshinskii's life and activity in the Soviet legal system, see Arkady Vaksberg, *The Prosecutor and the Prey: Vyshinsky and the 1930s' Moscow Show Trials,* trans. Jan Butler (London: Weidenfeld and Nicolson, 1990), and Robert Sharlet and Piers Beirne, "In Search of Vyshinsky: The Paradox of Law and Terror," in *Revolution in Law: Contributions to the Development of Soviet Legal Theory, 1917–1938,* ed. Piers Beirne (Armonk, N.Y.: M. E. Sharpe, 1990), 136–56.

8. A. Agranovskii, "'Perturkaksis'," in A. Agranovskii, Iu. Alevich, and G. Ryklin, *Liudi-vrediteli. Shakhtinskoe delo* (Moscow-Leningrad: Gos. Izd., 1928), 17 (quotation). For a description of the defendant who suffered a mental breakdown, named Nekrasov, see Lyons, *Assignment in Utopia,* 116–17. Industrial sabotage seems to have indeed existed in the Soviet Union at this time, as witnessed by John Scott, *Behind the Urals: An American Worker in Russia's City of Steel* (Bloomington: Indiana University Press, 1973), 174, 182–85. John Littlepage repeats the assertion in his own account of work and life in the Soviet gold industry, in "Red Wreckers in Russia," *Saturday Evening Post* 210, no. 27, January 1, 1935, 10–11, 53–55.

9. The first quotation is from Reswick, *I Dreamt Revolution,* 247. I am at a loss to explain Reswick's numbering of the trial's defendants at fifty-one since the official count was fifty-three. The second quotation is from Lyons, *Assignment in Utopia,* 114.

10. Paul Scheffer, "Das Klassengericht," *Berliner Tageblatt* 251, May 30, 1928, 1.

11. Lyons, *Assignment in Utopia,* 116 (quotation). Louis Fischer also refers to Krylenko's "hunting costume," in *Men and Politics: An Autobiography* (New York: Duell, Sloan and Pearce, 1941), 503. Scheffer describes Krylenko's line of questioning as a net cast to catch all fish ("Das Klassengericht," 1).

12. Wolfe, "Dress Rehearsals," 8 (quotation). Lyons notes this change between the two trials (*Assignment in Utopia,* 131).

13. Lyons, *Assignment in Utopia,* 122; Ryklin, "Uporstvuiushchie dvoriane," in *Liudi-vrediteli,* 20–28; Agranovskii, "Polpravdy—ne v schet," in *Liudi-vrediteli,* 38 (quotation); Ryklin, "Pod vliianiem tramvaia," in *Liudi-vrediteli,* 77 (quotation).

14. Lyons, *Assignment in Utopia,* 126–27; *Liudi-vrediteli,* 159.

15. *Liudi-vrediteli,* 155 (quotation), 159–60; Wolfe, "Dress Rehearsals," 15. For an interesting discussion of the construction and significance of the myth of Pavlik Morozov, see Iurii Druzhnikov, *Informer 001: The Myth of Pavlik Morozov* (New Brunswick, N.J.: Transaction, 1997). In the trial of the Industrial Party in 1931 another son, Ksenofont Sitnin, denounced his father and demanded his death. Vaksberg, *Prosecutor and the Prey,* 52.

16. A. Vyshinskii, *Itogi i uroki shakhtinskogo dela* (Moscow-Leningrad: Gos. Izd., 1928), 99–100 (quotation), 24.

17. Lyons, *Assignment in Utopia,* 130 (quotation); Agranovskii, "Polpravdy—ne v schet," in *Liudi-vrediteli,* 34.

18. Agranovskii, "Chtoby—ne byt' banal'nym," in *Liudi-vrediteli,* 117; Ryklin, "Nelegkaia rabota," in ibid., 59 (quotation); Agranovskii, "Klevetniki," in ibid., 62 ("actor"), 64 ("gestures"); Agranovskii, "Chtoby—ne byt' banal'nym," in ibid., 114.

19. Lenin, "Kak organizovat' sorevnovanie?" in *Polnoe sobranie sochinenii,* vol. 35, *Oktiabr' 1917–mart 1918* (Moscow: Gos. Izd. Politicheskoi Literatury, 1962), 200, 204; Dem'ian Bednyi, "Gnetuchka: Polushutia, poluvser'ez," *Pravda,* July 20, 1922, 2.

20. A. V. Lunacharskii, *Byvshie liudi. Ocherk istorii partii es-erov* (Moscow: Gos. Izd., 1922), 79, 80, 81.

21. Agranovskii, "'Vziatka'," in *Liudi-vrediteli,* 105. Nurmin also refers to the accused SRs as *musor* (garbage) in "Protsess es-erov," 271.

22. L. Zaslavskii, "Vrediteli," *Pravda,* no. 115, May 19, 1928, 3; Marcus Wheeler, *The Oxford Russian-English Dictionary* (Oxford: Clarendon Press, 1984), 92.

23. Zaslavskii, "Vrediteli," 3.

24. Matt Lenoe, *Stalinist Mass Journalism and the Transformation of Soviet Newspapers, 1926–1932* (Ph.D. dissertation, University of Chicago, 1997), 312. For similar descriptions of popular reactions to the trials of 1935–1938, see Sarah Davies, *Popular Opinion in Stalin's Russia: Terror, Propaganda and Dissent, 1934–1941* (Cambridge: Cambridge University Press, 1997), 118–21, 130–31; and Sheila Fitzpatrick, *Everyday Stalinism, Ordinary Life in Extraordinary Times: Soviet Russia in the 1930s* (New York: Oxford University Press, 1999), 190–217.

25. Vyshinskii, *Itogi i uroki shakhtinskogo dela,* 3, 90, 13.

26. Ibid., 100; S. D. Shein, *Sud nad ekonomicheskoi kontr-revoliutsiei v Donbasse. Zametki obshchestvennogo obvinitelia* (Moscow-Leningrad: Gos. Izd., 1928), 11; I. V. Stalin, "O pravom uklone v VKP(b)," in *Sochineniia,* vol. 12, *Aprel' 1929–iiun' 1930* (Moscow: Gos. Izd. Politicheskoi Literatury, 1953), 14, 12.

27. For three influential works that argue this point, albeit from different standpoints, see Robert Conquest, *The Great Terror: A Reassessment* (New York: Oxford University Press, 1990); J. Arch Getty, *Origins of the Great Purges: The Soviet Communist Party Reconsidered, 1933–1938* (New York: Cambridge University Press, 1987); and Robert W. Thurston, *Life and Terror in Stalin's Russia, 1934–1941* (New Haven: Yale University Press, 1996).

28. Wolfe, "Dress Rehearsals," 10; Lyons, *Assignment in Utopia,* 122; Vyshinskii, *Itogi i uroki shakhtinskogo dela,* 84; Walter Duranty, *USSR: The Story of Soviet Russia* (Philadelphia: J. B. Lippincott, 1944), 155.

29. Agranovskii, "Ob instinkte," in *Liudi-vrediteli,* 57; Scheffer, "Das Klassengericht," 1.

30. G. Ryklin, "Uporstvuiushchie dvoriane," in *Liudi-vrediteli*, 21 (quotation); Lyons, *Assignment in Utopia*, 130.

31. For a discussion of the first official samokritika campaign in the Party in 1928, see David-Fox, *Revolution of the Mind*, 127–32. By 1935, the ritual of samokritika had changed to *kritika i samokritika* (criticism and self-criticism). Alexei Kojevnikov, "Rituals of Stalinist Culture at Work: Science and the Games of Intraparty Democracy circa 1948," *Russian Review* 57 (January 1998): 33–34. By 1948 *kritika i samokritika* was labeled the single defining feature of the Marxist-Leninist worldview. M. A. Leonov, *Kritika i samokritika—Dialekticheskaia zakonomernost' razvitiia sovetskogo obshchestva. Stenogramma publichnoi lektsii, prochitannoi 24 fevralia 1948 goda v Tsentral'nom lektorii Obshchestva v Moskve* (Moscow: Pravda, 1948), 6.

32. These include *Delo ob ekonomicheskoi kontrrevoliutsii v Donbasse* (1928); *Shakhtinskii protsess* (Eshurin, 1928); and four issues of *Sovkino-Zhurnal* 14, 23, 27 (1928), and no. 1 (1931). For a brief description of the documentary film coverage of the Shakhty Affair, see Mal'kova, "Litso vraga," in *Kino. Politika i liudi (30-e gody)*, 80–82.

33. *Sovkino-Zhurnal* 23 (1928).

34. Several newsreels devoted to other trials from this period replicate the messages of the *Sovkino-Zhurnal* newsreels of the Shakhty Affair. For comparison, see *Sovkino-Zhurnal* 26 (1929); *Sovkinokhronika* 18 (1930); *Sovkino-khronika/zhurnal* 16 (1930); and *Sovkinokhronika/zhurnal* 10 (1930). For similar coverage of two trials taking place in the countryside, see *Soiuzkinozhurnal* 43 (1928) and *Sovkinokhronika/zhurnal* 74 (1929). For comparable depictions of two trials taking place in Muslim regions of the Soviet Union, see *Sud nad ubiitsei v Uzbekistane* (1930) and *Sovkinokhronika/zhurnal* 21 (1930).

35. Lyons, *Assignment in Utopia*, 115.

36. Ibid., 119.

37. Louis Fischer, *The God That Failed*, ed. Richard Crossman (New York: Harper, 1949), 209–10; and *Men and Politics*, 503 (quotation).

38. Ryklin, "Ogovor," in *Liudi-vrediteli*, 11 (quotation); *Liudi-vrediteli*, 171.

39. Medvedev asserts that, already during this trial, methods such as sleep deprivation and isolation cells with chilled or heated floors were used to extract the necessary confessions from the accused (*O Staline i stalinizme*, 229). He also describes the rehearsal of another trial in which all the accused were brought together to coordinate their fabricated confessions (247).

40. Ksenia Leont'eva, "Zabytye zhertvy," *Novoe russkoe slovo*, December 8, 1954, n.p.; Wolfe, "Dress Rehearsals," 11 (quotation); Reswick, *I Dreamt Revolution*, 248 (quotation); Wolfe, "Dress Rehearsals," 11.

41. *Liudi-vrediteli*, 301 (quotation); Lyons, *Assignment in Utopia*, 124–25.

42. *Liudi-vrediteli*, 306.

43. Lyons, *Assignment in Utopia*, 123.

44. Ibid., 118 (both quotations). See also Wolfe, "Dress Rehearsals," 14.

45. Lion Feuchtwanger was convinced of the validity of the trials of

1936–1937, as he describes in *Moscow, 1937: My Visit Described for My Friends,* trans. Irene Josephy (New York: Viking Press, 1937), 112–40; Upton Sinclair also upheld the validity of the show trials of the 1930s whereas Lyons was entirely convinced of their falsehood. Sinclair and Lyons, *Terror in Russia? Two Views* (New York: Richard R. Smith, 1938); Eugene Lyons, *Stalin: Czar of all the Russias* (Philadelphia: J. B. Lippincott, 1940), 244–53. Walter Duranty and Louis Fischer walked a middle path, as seen in the former's *The Kremlin and the People* (New York: Reynal and Hitchcock, 1941), 7, and the latter's contribution to *The God That Failed,* 209.

46. Wolfe's entire article is devoted to proving this thesis.

5: THE REDOUNDING RHETORIC OF LEGAL SATIRE

1. J. A. E. Curtis, "Down with the Foxtrot! Concepts of Satire in the Soviet Theatre of the 1920s," in *Russian Theatre in the Age of Modernism,* ed. Robert Russell and Andrew Barratt (New York: St. Martin's Press, 1990), 225–28; Rudnitsky, *Russian and Soviet Theatre,* 205–7.

2. Brian A. Connery and Kirk Combe, "Theorizing Satire: A Retrospective and Introduction," in *Theorizing Satire: Essays in Literary Criticism,* ed. Brian A. Connery and Kirk Combe (New York: St. Martin's Press, 1995), 5.

3. "O putiakh sovetskoi satiry," *Literaturnaia gazeta* 13, July 15, 1929, 1. Other articles in this debate include A. Lezhnev, "Na put' k vozrozhdeniiu satiry," *Literaturnaia gazeta* 1, April 22, 1929, 2; V. Blium, "Vozrodit'sia li satira?" *Literaturnaia gazeta* 6, May 27, 1929, 2; G. Iakubovskii, "O satire nashikh dnei," *Literaturnaia gazeta* 11, July 8, 1929, 3; and M. Rogi, "Puti sovetskoi satiry oshibko tov. Bliuma," *Literaturnaia gazeta* 14, July 22, 1929, 3.

4. Wiktor Woroszylski, *The Life of Mayakovsky,* trans. Boleslaw Taborski (New York: Orion Press, 1970), 331; Maiakovskii, "Mozhno li stat' satirikom?" in *Polnoe sobranie sochinenii* 12:30.

5. Maiakovskii, *Misteriia-buff,* in *Polnoe sobranie sochinenii,* 2:43–46.

6. For a discussion of the significance of water and flood symbolism in Maiakovskii's poetry, see Edward J. Brown, *Mayakovsky: A Poet in Revolution* (Princeton: Princeton University Press, 1973), 200.

7. *Misteriia-buff,* in *Polnoe sobranie sochinenii,* 2:331, 340.

8. Lunacharskii, "Kommunisticheskii spektakl'," in *Sobranie sochinenii* 3:40.

9. Samuil Margolin, "Vesna teatral'noi chrezmernosti," *Vestnik rabotnikov* 10–11 (1921): 122. For a discussion of *Mystery-Bouffe* as an example of festival theater immediately after the revolution, see von Geldern, *Bolshevik Festivals,* 66–71.

10. For Kuleshov's theories on montage and acting, see Lev Kuleshov, *Iskusstvo kino,* vol. 1 of *Sobranie sochinenii v trekh tomakh* (Moscow: Iskusstvo, 1987), 163–225; as well as his articles from the period, such as "Nash byt i amerikanizm," in *Sobranie sochinenii v trekh tomakh,* 1:93–94, and "Pochemu ia ne rabotaiu," in ibid., 107–9.

11. The name of the film's protagonist is taken from an American utopian novel of the late nineteenth century, Edward Bellamy's *Looking Backward* (New York: Dover Publications, 1996). However, any resemblance between the two works ends here, since in place of the novel's leap into the future, Kuleshov makes his Mr. West leap into Bolshevik Russia.

12. Vlada Petric notes this similarity in her discussion of *Mr. West*'s subtext in "A Subtextual Reading of Kuleshov's Satire *The Extraordinary Adventures of Mr. West in the Land of the Bolsheviks* (1924)," in *Inside Soviet Film Satire: Laughter with a Lash,* ed. Andrew Horton (Cambridge: Cambridge University Press, 1993), 70.

13. Kuleshov, "50 let v kino," in *Sobranie sochinenii v trekh tomakh,* 2:78.

14. Petric, "A Subtextual Reading," 70–71.

15. "The Comradely Court Case at Housing Cooperative No. 1519," "The People vs. Vitaly Lazarenko," and "The Divorce," in Nikolai Erdman, *A Meeting about Laughter: Sketches, Interludes and Theatrical Parodies by Nikolai Erdman with Vladimir Mass and Others,* trans. John Freedman (Luxembourg: Harwood Academic, 1995), 63–78.

16. Erdman, "The Divorce," in ibid., 74.

17. For a general treatment of Erdman's activity in the theater including the plays *Mandate* and *The Suicide,* see John Freedman's various works, including "Nikolai Erdman: An Overview," *Slavic and East European Journal* 28, no. 4 (1984): 462–76; "Introduction," *The Major Plays of Nikolai Erdman: The Warrant and The Suicide* (Luxembourg: Harwood Academic, 1995), ix–xix; and *Silence's Roar: The Life and Drama of Nikolai Erdman* (Oakville, Canada: Mosaic Press, 1992).

18. Freedman, "Introduction," in *Major Plays,* xv.

19. *Mandate*'s leading actor stated that a single performance of the play elicited over three hundred instances of laughter from the audience. Erast Garin, "O *Mandate* i o drugom," in *Vstrechi s Meierkhol'dom. Sbornik vospominanii* (Moscow: Vserossiiskoe Teatral'noe Obshchestvo, 1967), 326.

20. Nikolai Erdman, *Mandat,* in *P'esy, intermedii, pis'ma, dokumenty, vospominaniia sovremennikov* (Moscow: Iskusstvo, 1990), 27. References to this work will henceforth be given parenthetically in the text.

21. P. A. Markov, "Tretii front. Posle 'Mandata'," in *O teatre,* 285, 291. For a synopsis of the reviews of *Mandate,* see Garin, *Vstrechi s Meierkhol'dom,* 324.

22. Garin, *Vstrechi s Meierkhol'dom,* 326, 324.

23. G. Gauzner and E. Gabrilovich, "'Mandat' u Meierkhol'da," *Zhizn' iskusstva* 19, May 12, 1925, 6.

24. Markov, "Tretii front," 287.

25. Reswick, *I Dreamt Revolution,* 110.

26. Jack London, "The Unexpected," *Blackwood's Magazine* 180, no. 1090 (August 1906): 163–80; Kuleshov, "'Vest'—'Luch'—'Po zakonu'," in *Sobranie sochinenii v trekh tomakh,* 1:115.

27. Lagovier, *O samosudakh,* 17 (quotation), 28.

28. In his story London includes a small group of Native Americans as witnesses to Dennin's trial, thereby expanding the audience of the trial to some six or more people. Nonetheless, London is careful to state that these Native American witnesses understood neither why they attended the trial nor what the trial was intended to achieve ("The Unexpected," 176–78).

29. Kuleshov describes Khersonskii's violent reaction in the public debate surrounding *By the Law* in "50 let v kino," in *Sobranie sochinenii v trekh tomakh*, 2:87.

30. Kuleshov, "The Principles of Montage (From 'The Practice of Film Direction')," in *Kuleshov on Film: Writings by Lev Kuleshov*, trans. Ronald Levaco (Berkeley and Los Angeles: University of California Press, 1974), 190–91.

31. Quotations are from "'Klop.' Novaia p'esa Vl. Maiakovskogo," *Vecherniaia Moskva* no. 1, January 2, 1929, 3; Maiakovskii, *Klop*, in *Polnoe sobranie sochinenii*, 11:220; A. Fevral'skii, "Kak sozdavalsia 'Klop'," *Literaturnaia gazeta* 68, no. 559, December 9, 1935, 2.

32. Maiakovskii, *Klop*, in *Polnoe sobranie sochinenii*, 11:229. References to this work will henceforth be given parenthetically in the text.

33. See also B. Alpers, "'Klop' v Teatre imeni Vs. Meierkhol'da," in B. Alpers, *Teatral'nye ocherki v dvukh tomakh* (Moscow: Izd. Iskusstvo, 1977), 2:130.

34. D. Tal'nikov, "Novye postanovki: 1. Klop," *Zhizn' iskusstva* 11, March 10, 1929, 10.

35. Alpers, "'Klop' v Teatre," in *Teatral'nye ocherki v dvukh tomakh* 130–32.

36. During the rehearsal of *Bathhouse*, Maiakovskii wrote additional material that was performed in Meyerhold's theater. Unfortunately, these additions have not been preserved. My discussion of the play is therefore based on the surviving script as published in Maiakovskii's complete collected works. See Maiakovskii, *Polnoe sobranie sochinenii*, 11:674.

37. Maiakovskii, "Vystupleniia na zasedanii khudozhestvenno-politicheskogo soveta Gos. teatra imeni Vs. Meierkhol'da (Na chtenii i obsuzhdenii 'Bania'), 23 sentiabria 1929 goda," in *Polnoe sobranie sochinenii*, 12:379.

38. Professor Gregory Freidin of Stanford University provided this popular metaphor of the period for purging.

39. Maiakovskii, "Chto takoe 'Bania'? Kogo ona moet?" in *Polnoe sobranie sochinenii*, 12:200.

40. Maiakovskii, "(Lozungi dlia spektaklia 'Bania')," in ibid., 11:350. On another poster, the playwright wrote, "Clean and purge [*vypar' i prochist'*] every bureaucrat—/with the worker's broom and art's brush" (ibid., 11:351).

41. N. Goncharova, "'Bania' V. Maiakovskogo," *Rabochaia gazeta* 65, no. 2414, March 21, 1930, 7. The critic V. Ermilov identified Pobedonosikov's crime as Party degeneracy in "O trekh oshibkakh Meierkhol'da," *Vecherniaia Moskva* 63, no. 1876, March 17, 1930, 3.

42. V. Ermilov, "O nastroeniiakh melkoburzhuaznoi 'levizny' v khudozh-

estvennoi literatury," *Pravda* 67, no. 4512, March 9, 1930, 4.

43. Maiakovskii, *Bania*, in *Polnoe sobranie sochinenii*, 11:318–19, 325.

44. The critic S. Mokul'skii accused Maiakovskii of describing the world of the future in *Bathhouse* with an anti-Soviet tinge, in "Eshche o 'Klope'," *Zhizn' iskusstva* 13, January 24, 1929, 10. Other critics of *Bathhouse* also pointed out Maiakovskii's insulting portrayal of Soviet reality and his apparent lack of faith in the very regime he claimed to support in the play. For an example, see Goncharova, "'Bania' V. Maiakovskogo," 7.

45. Connery and Combe, *Theorizing Satire*, 5.

46. Garin, *Vstrechi s Meierkhol'dom*, 326; "The Suicide at the Vakhtangov Theater: A Document," in Erdman, *A Meeting*, 202. For Meyerhold's famous proclamation of Erdman as the continuation of the Gogolian tradition on the Russian stage, see V. E. Meierkhol'd, "Iz otveta na anketu gazety 'Vecherniaia Moskva' (1925 g.)," in *Stat'i, pis'ma, rechi, besedy*, 2:95, 97.

47. Erdman, *Samoubiitsa*, in *P'esy, intermedii*, 85. References to this work will henceforth be given parenthetically in the text.

48. O. Litovskii, *Tak i bylo. Ocherki, vospominaniia, vstrechi* (Moscow: Sovetskii pisatel', 1958), 129–30.

49. "The Suicide," in Erdman, *A Meeting*, 194, 195. Quotations are from ibid., 193, 200.

50. Ibid., 191–92 (quote), 193 (quote), 198.

51. Ibid., 199, 202.

52. Ibid., 203. See also "'Samoubiitsa' Iz stenogramm repetitsii," *Teatr* 1 (January 1990): 128. For a brief description of the truly confusing events that led to the ban on *Suicide*, see Freedman, "Nikolai Erdman: An Overview," 467–69.

53. Ziolkowski, *Mirror of Justice*.

6: For Each Enemy, Another Trial

1. Letter 63, in *Stalin's Letters to Molotov*, ed. Lars T. Lih, Oleg V. Naumov, and Oleg V. Khlevniuk, trans. Catherine A. Fitzpatrick (New Haven: Yale University Press, 1995), 210.

2. Fitzpatrick, "How the Mice Buried the Cat," 300–301.

3. For information on the production and subsequent nonrelease of *A Nail in the Boot*, see Evgenii Margolit and Viacheslav Shmyrov, *(iz"iatoe kino)* (Moscow: Gosfil'mofond Rossii, 1995), 18–19; Evgenii Margolit, "Budem schitat', chto takogo fil'ma nikogda ne bylo," in *Kino. Politika i liudi (30-e gody)*, 148. For discussions of the increased difficulty of producing films in the 1930s because of stricter censorship, see Ekaterina Khokhlova, "Forbidden Films of the 1930s," in *Stalinism and Soviet Cinema*, ed. Richard Taylor and Derek Spring (London: Routledge, 1993), 90–96, and "Neosushchestvelennye zamysly," in *Kino. Politika i liudi, 30-e gody*, 123–31; Peter Kenez, "Soviet Cinema in the Age of Stalin," in Taylor and Spring, *Stalinism and Soviet Cinema*, 58–59.

4. Iu. Bogomolov writes, "*A Nail in the Boot* is a movie made in the 1930s

but belongs to the 1920s due to its form and ideological themes," in *Mikhail Kalatozov (Stranitsy tvorcheskoi biografii)* (Moscow: Iskusstvo, 1989), 63–64.

5. G. Kremlev, *Mikhail Kalatozov* (Moscow: Izd. Iskusstvo, 1964), 53.

6. E. Dzigan successfully used the technique of pushing a film's fictional judgment out onto the real-life spectators in his 1931 movie *Sud dolzhen prodolzhat'sia (The Trial Must Continue)*. Dzigan's film ends with the confession of several men opposed to women in their factory and an iteration of the film's title, which urges viewers to condemn sexism in their own behavior and attitudes.

7. Quoted in Kremlev, *Mikhail Kalatozov*, 57. For a description of the controversy surrounding Kalatozov's film in the contemporary press, see ibid., 54–57.

8. For the original English nursery rhyme, see "Nail," in *The Oxford Dictionary of Nursery Rhymes,* ed. Iona Opie and Peter Opie (Oxford: Oxford University Press, 1997), 383. This nursery rhyme was rendered into Russian by Samuil Marshak, whose translation first appeared in a 1929 issue of the journal *Ezh.* "Gvozd' i podkova," *Sobranie sochinenii v vos'mi tomakh* (Moscow: Izd. Khudozhestvennaia literatura, 1968), 2:95. Marshak's translation adds an enemy *(vrag),* who takes advantage of the blacksmith's oversight in the final stanza of the poem.

9. Margolit, "Budem schitat', chto takogo fil'ma nikogda ne bylo," in *Kino. Politika i liudi (30-e gody),* 148.

10. Mal'kova, "Litso vraga," in ibid., 85. Although Mal'kova identifies the trial documentary as an important genre of Soviet documentary film during the 1920s and 1930s, a widely used textbook on the history of documentary film neglects to mention any of these films or the existence of the genre; Drobashenko, *Istoriia sovetskogo.*

11. *Sovkino-Zhurnal* 1 (1931), entitled *Sud idet (Order in the Court),* also provided documentary coverage of the trial of the Industrial Party.

12. *Protsess "Prompartii" (25 noiabria–7 dekabria 1930 g.). Stenogramma sudebnogo protsessa i materialy priobshchennye k delu* (Moscow: OGIZ–Sovetskoe zakonodatel'stvo, 1931), 438 (quotation); *Udar po interventam. Obvinitel'noe zakliuchenie* (Moscow-Leningrad: Gos. Izd., 1930), 3–6.

13. Medvedev, *O Staline i stalinizme,* 234. Vyshinskii would also refer to the Shakhty Affair in a statement he made at the Metro-Vickers trial in 1933. *The Case of N. P. Vitvitsky et al. charged with Wrecking Activities at Power Stations in the Soviet Union heard before the Special Session of the Supreme Court of the USSR in Moscow, April 12–19, 1993* (Moscow: State Law Publishing House, 1933), 3:34.

14. For a brief description of the events of the trial, see Kovalev, *Raspiatie dukha,* 103–16. For a fascinating but entirely fictional reconstruction of the crimes allegedly committed by Ramzin and his cohorts, see Michael Sayers and Albert E. Kahn, *The Great Conspiracy: The Secret War against Soviet Russia* (Boston: Little, Brown, 1946), 158–68. Additional materials on the trial of the Industrial Party in Russian include K. Levin, *Partiia predatelei* (Moscow: Molodaia gvardiia, 1931); N. Bliskavitskii, ed., *Shpiony i vrediteli pered proletarskim sudom. Pokazaniia*

Ramzina (Moscow-Leningrad: OGIZ–Moskovskii rabochii, 1930); and Karl Radek, *Portrety vreditelei* (Moscow: OGIZ–Moskovskii rabochii, 1931). For materials on the trial in English, see W. M. Holmes, *The Wreckers Exposed in the Trial of the Counter-Revolutionary Industrial Party* (New York: Worker's Library Publishers, 1931); and Andrew Rothstein, ed., *Wreckers on Trial: A Record of the Trial of the Industrial Party Held in Moscow, Nov.–Dec. 1930* (New York: Workers' Library Publishers, 1931).

15. Quoted in *Stalin's Letters to Molotov*, 195–96.

16. Valeriya Selunskaya and Maria Zezina, "Documentary Film: A Soviet Source for Soviet Historians," in Taylor and Spring, *Stalinism and Soviet Cinema*, 179. Drobashenko describes Posel'skii's use of acted scenes in a 1932 edition of *Soiuzkinozhurnal*, and another documentary from the same year titled *Liudi (People)*, stating that this was a common technique for the director and the era (*Istoriia sovetskogo*, 48).

17. For a Jungian analysis of the portrait of the enemy, see Mal'kova, "Litso vraga," in *Kino. Politika i liudi (30-e gody)*, 81–82.

18. In one particularly unflattering moment, the camera closes in on the defendant Kalinnikov as he blows his nose during his confession.

19. Drobashenko notes that many Soviet documentaries of the 1930s closely resembled feature films of the era (*Istoriia sovetskogo*, 50).

20. Apparently, Ramzin did experience the court's leniency and was rehabilitated in 1936, returning to the world of Soviet science where he would receive both an Order of Lenin and the Stalin prize. According to one of Kovalev's informants, this unusual fate was due to Ramzin's role as a NKVD provocateur in the trial of the Industrial Party, in which the testimony he provided was "the scenario of the Lubianka." Kovalev, *Raspiatie dukha*, 116.

21. Newsreels covering the Industrial Party trial include *Za sotsialisticheskuiu derevniu* 17 (1930) and two special editions of *Soiuzkinokhronika* titled *Protsess "Promyshlennoi partii,"* no. 1, November 27, 1930, and no. 2, December 1, 1930. For comparison, see the coverage of the case of a murdered pioneer in *Pioneriia* 2 (1935).

22. Mal'kova, "Litso vraga," in *Kino. Politika i liudi (30-e gody)*, 80.

23. M. Gor'kii, *Somov i drugie (Somov and Others)*, in *Sobranie sochinenii v vosemnadtsati tomakh* (Moscow: Gos. Izd. Khudozhestvennoi Literatury, 1963), 17:269–326. For a discussion of the play's composition, its relationship to the trial of the Industrial Party, and Gor'kii's dissatisfaction with *Somov and Others*, see B. Bialik, *M. Gor'kii. Dramaturg* (Moscow: Sovetskii pisatel', 1962), 376–403.

24. A. Afinogenov, *Strakh*, 2-oe izd. (Leningrad: GIKhL, 1932). For descriptions of the play's premiere in Moscow and Leningrad, see "Strakh," in Aleksandr Afinogenov, *Izbrannoe v dvukh tomakh* (Moscow: Iskusstvo, 1977), 1:547–49. For a brief analysis of the play's plot, see Segel, *Russian Drama*, 240–46.

25. One critic writes that *Fear* was written as a response to the Shakhty Affair. Given the play's timing, however, it seems more likely it was the trial of the Industrial Party (in conjunction with the Shakhty Affair) that influenced

Afinogenov. A. Karaganov, "Dramaturgiia sotsialisticheskogo sozidaniia," in Afinogenov, *Izbrannoe v dvukh tomakh,* 1:15.

26. For examples of these positive reviews, see the discussion of *Fear*'s premiere in Leningrad in the journal *Rabochii i teatr;* V. Rafalovich, "Zametki o 'Strakhe'," *Rabochii i teatr* 15 (1931): 6–7; and S. Mokul'skii et al., "'Strakh' v Gosteatre dramy," *Rabochii i teatr* 16 (1931): 4–7. For reviews that point to the schematism of Afinogenov's play, see Mokul'skii, "'Strakh' v Gosteatre dramy," 5; B. Alpers, "Put' khronikal'noi dramy" and "Obraz v problemnoi drame," in *Teatral'nye ocherki v dvukh tomakh,* 2:223–24, 236–37.

27. Afinogenov's script portrays Spasova as the clear victor in this verbal duel with Borodin, yet the play's ultimate effect rested in the ability of the actress playing Spasova actually to win the rhetorical battle on stage—as Nikolai Petrov, the director of the play's Leningrad premiere points out in his memoirs. The weak acting of the actress cast in the role of Spasova in an early rehearsal almost led to Kirov's ban of the play in Leningrad. In several provincial theaters, the play was in fact deemed too controversial for performance. Nikolai Petrov, *50 i 500* (Moscow: Vserossiiskoe teatral'noe obshchestvo, 1960), 312–21.

28. Afinogenov, *Strakh,* 11. References to this play will henceforth be given in the text.

29. For references to *krysy,* see ibid., 9, 69, 97–98.

30. M. O. Knebel', *Leonid Mironovich Leonidov. Vospominaniia, stat'i, perepiska, zapisnye knizhki, stat'i i vospominaniia o L. M. Leonidove* (Moscow: Gos. Izd. Iskusstvo, 1960), 594. Later, in an interview with the critic Pavel Markov, Leonidov revised his interpretation of the role of Borodin, stating, "I do not see a class enemy in him." Leonidov, "Stenogramma besedy s P.A. Markovym," in ibid., 155.

31. According to Pavel Markov, *Fear* stimulated the debate about old versus new not only within the scientific community but also within the creative collective at the Moscow Art Theater when it premiered. P. A. Markov, "Iz vospominanii: Vstrechi s dramaturgami," in *V khudozhestvennom teatre. Kniga zaliva* (Moscow: Vserossiiskoe teatral'noe obshchestvo, 1976), 271–72.

32. Anatolii Lunacharskii, "Sotsialisticheskii realizm," in *Sovetskie dramaturgi o svoem tvorchestve. Sbornik statei,* ed. Vl. Pimenov (Moscow: Izd. Iskusstvo, 1967), 32.

33. G. Mar'iamov, *Kremlevskii tsenzor. Stalin smotrit kino* (Moscow: Kinotsentr, 1992); Khokhlova, "Forbidden Films of the 1930s," in Taylor and Spring, *Stalinism and Soviet Cinema,* 93.

34. Kenez, "Soviet Cinema," 57. Kenez describes the same phenomenon in his monograph *Cinema and Soviet Society, 1917–1953* (Cambridge: Cambridge University Press, 1992), 164.

35. Quoted in Kenez, "Soviet Cinema," 63.

36. For a description of this technique for purging Party ranks and its results, see "Results of the Review of Party Documents, 25 December 1935," in *Resolutions and Decisions of the Communist Party of the Soviet Union,* ed. Robert H.

McNeal (Toronto: University of Toronto Press, 1974), 3:160–67.

37. Liliia Mamatova, "Model' kinomifov 30-kh godov," in *Kino. Politika i liudi, 30-e gody,* 61.

38. Maya Turovskaya, "The Tastes of Soviet Moviegoers during the 1930s," *Late Soviet Culture: From Perestroika to Novostroika,* ed. Thomas Lahusen and Gene Kuperman (Durham: Duke University Press, 1993), 100; Maya Turovskaya, "The 1930s and 1940s: Cinema in Context," in Taylor and Spring, *Stalinism and Soviet Cinema,* 46–47.

39. The film *Zhena predrevkoma* (Wife of the president of the Revolutionary Committee) by Ivanov-Gai (1925) provides an interesting precursor for *The Party Card.* In this 1925 movie, a loyal Bolshevik activist must sign the death warrant for his own wife, who turns out to be a long-standing member of the White Guard.

40. Kenez, "Soviet Cinema," 63.

CONCLUSION

1. For scholarship that traces the avant-garde roots of socialist realism, see Clark, *Petersburg;* Boris Grois, *The Total Art of Stalinism: Avant-Garde, Aesthetic Dictatorship, and Beyond,* trans. Charles Rougle (Princeton: Princeton University Press, 1992); and Régine Robin, *Socialist Realism: An Impossible Aesthetic,* trans. Catherine Porter (Stanford: Stanford University Press, 1992).

2. For descriptions of the 1938 trial, see Conquest, *Great Terror,* 341–98; and Vaksberg, *Prosecutor and the Prey,* 73–125.

3. Drobashenko, *Istoriia sovetskogo,* 48.

4. For a translation of Stalin's comments on and suggestions for Ermler's screenplay for the second series of *A Great Citizen,* see Kenez, "Soviet Cinema," 65.

5. For a description of Sheinin's role in the show trials of the 1930s, see Vaksberg, *Prosecutor and the Prey,* 66, 74–75. For information on Sheinin's work as a dramatist, see Segel, *Russian Drama,* 305–8; Fitzpatrick, *Everyday Stalinism,* 203.

6. Lev Sheinin and the Tur Brothers, *Ochnaia stavka. P'esa v chetyrekh deistviiakh s prologom* (Moscow-Leningrad: Gos. Izd. Iskusstvo, 1938).

7. Scott, *Behind the Urals,* 198–99, 202.

8. For a brief description of *Oshibka Inzhenera Kochina* see *Istoriia sovetskogo kino,* vol. 2, *1931–1941* (Moscow: Iskusstvo, 1973), 195–96.

9. Kenez discusses this complicity briefly at the end of "Soviet Cinema," 67–68.

10. For more on the expression of dissent during the 1930s, see Davies, *Popular Opinion in Stalin's Russia;* Sheila Fitzpatrick, *Stalin's Peasants: Resistance and Survival in the Russian Village after Collectivization* (Oxford: Oxford University Press, 1994); and Lynne Viola, *Peasant Rebels under Stalin: Collectivization and the Culture of Peasant Resistance* (Oxford: Oxford University Press, 1996).

11. Kenez, *Cinema and Soviet Society,* 235–39, and "Soviet Cinema," 57.

12. For example, see Alexei Kovejnikov's treatment of *diskussiia* and *kritika*

i samokritika as important rituals in the Soviet sciences of the late 1940s. "Rituals of Stalinist Culture at Work: Science and the Games of Intraparty Democracy circa 1948," *Russian Review* 57 (January 1998): 25–52.

13. For examples, see I. Beliaev's 1988 documentary film *Protsess. Chast' vtoraia (The Trial. Part Two),* which styles itself a response to the show trials of the 1930s, and Shatrov's 1986 play *Diktatura sovesti (The Dictatorship of Conscience).*

14. For information on the Communist Party case, see Yuri Feofanov and Donald D. Barry, *Politics and Justice in Russia: Major Trials of the Post-Stalin Era* (Armonk, N.Y.: M. E. Sharpe, 1996), 289–308.

15. For several interesting articles that discuss the various currents in the judicial reform taking place in Russia during the 1990s, see Todd Foglesong, Eugene Huskey, Gordon B. Smith, and Sarah J. Reynolds's contributions under the rubric of "Justice and the Russian Transition," in *Reforming Justice in Russia, 1864–1996: Power, Culture, and the Limits of Legal Order,* ed. Peter H. Solomon Jr. (Armonk, N.Y.: M. E. Sharpe, 1997), 282–396.

SELECTED BIBLIOGRAPHY

ARTICLES AND BOOKS

Afanas'ev, Alexander K. "Jurors and Jury Trials in Imperial Russia, 1866–1885." In *Russia's Great Reforms,* edited by Ben Eklof et al. Bloomington: Indiana University Press, 1994.

Afinogenov, Aleksandr. *Izbrannoe v dvukh tomakh.* 2 vols. Moscow: Iskusstvo, 1977.

———. *Strakh, 2-oe izd.* Leningrad: GIKhL, 1932.

Agranovskii, A., Iu. Alevich, and G. Ryklin. *Liudi-vrediteli. Shakhtinskoe delo.* Moscow-Leningrad: Gos. Izd., 1928.

Alpers, B. *Teatral'nye ocherki v dvukh tomakh.* 2 vols. Moscow: Iskusstvo, 1977.

Aristotle. *The Art of Rhetoric.* Translated by H. C. Lawson-Tancred. London and New York: Penguin Books, 1991.

Beatty, Bessie. *The Red Heart of Russia.* New York: Century, 1919.

Beirne, Piers, ed. *Revolution in Law: Contributions to the Development of Soviet Legal Theory, 1917–1938.* Armonk, N.Y.: M. E. Sharpe, 1990.

Benjamin, Walter. *Moscow Diary.* Translated by Richard Sieburth, edited by Gary Smith. Cambridge: Harvard University Press, 1986.

———. *The Origin of German Tragic Drama.* Translated by John Osborne. Frankfurt am Main: Suhrkamp Verlag, 1963.

Bergman, Jay. *Vera Zasulich: A Biography.* Stanford: Stanford University Press, 1983.

Berman, Harold J. *Justice in the USSR: An Interpretation of Soviet Law.* Cambridge: Harvard University Press, 1963.

Bliskavitskii, N., ed. *Shpiony i vrediteli pered proletarskim sudom. Pokazaniia Ramzina.* Moscow-Leningrad: OGIZ–Moskovskii rabochii, 1930.

Blium, V. "Vozrodit'sia li satira?" *Literaturnaia gazeta* 6, May 27, 1929, 2.

Bogomolov, Iu. *Mikhail Kalatozov (Stranitsy tvorcheskoi biografii).* Moscow: Iskusstvo, 1989.

Boltianskii, G. *Lenin i kino.* Moscow-Leningrad: Gos. Izd., 1925.

Booth, Michael R. "The Drunkard's Progress: Nineteenth-Century Temperance Drama." *Dalhousie Review* 44, no. 2 (summer 1964): 205–12.

———. *Hiss the Villain: Six English and American Melodramas.* New York: Benjamin Blom, 1964.

Boym, Svetlana. *Common Places: Mythologies of Everyday Life in Russia.* Cambridge: Harvard University Press, 1994.

Brooks, Peter. *The Melodramatic Imagination: Balzac, Henry James, Melodrama and the Mode of Excess.* New Haven: Yale University Press, 1976.

Brown, Edward J. *Mayakovsky: A Poet in Revolution.* Princeton: Princeton University Press, 1973.

Brukzon, Ia. *Problema teatral'nosti. (Estestvennost' pered sudom marksizma).* Petrograd: Izd. Tret'ia strazha, 1923.

———. *Tvorchestvo kino.* Leningrad: Kolos, 1926.

Burckhardt, Jacob. *Griechische Kulturgeschichte.* Leipzig: Alfred Kröner Verlag, 1929.

———. *History of Greek Culture.* Translated by Palmer Hilty. New York: Frederick Ungar, 1963.

Burke, Kenneth. *Attitudes toward History.* 3rd ed. Berkeley and Los Angeles: University of California Press, 1984.

Bursak, I. N., ed. *Kino.* Moscow: Proletkino, 1925.

Buxhoeveden, Baroness Sophie. *Left Behind: Fourteen Months in Siberia during the Revolution, December 1917–February 1919.* London: Longmans, Green, 1929.

Carlson, Marvin. "Theatre History, Methodology and Distinctive Features." *Theatre Research International* 20, no. 2 (1995): 90–96.

———. *The Theatre of the French Revolution.* Ithaca: Cornell University Press, 1966.

Carnicke, Sharon Marie. *The Theatrical Instinct: Nikolai Evreinov and the Russian Theatre of the Early Twentieth Century.* New York: Peter Lang, 1989.

The Case of N. P. Vitvitsky et al. charged with Wrecking Activities at Power Stations in the Soviet Union heard before the Special Session of the Supreme Court of the USSR in Moscow, April 12–19, 1933. Moscow: State Law Publishing House, 1933.

Cassiday, Julie A. "Flash Floods, Bedbugs and Saunas: Social Hygiene in Maiakovskii's Theatrical Satires of the 1920s." *Slavonic and East European Review* 76, no. 4 (October 1998): 643–57.

———. "Marble Columns and Jupiter Lights: Theatrical and Cinematic Modeling of Soviet Show Trials in the 1920s." *Slavic and East European Journal* 42, no. 4 (winter 1998): 640–60.

———. *The Theater of the World and the Theater of State: Drama and the Show Trial in Early Soviet Russia.* Ph.D. dissertation, Stanford University, 1995.

Cassiday, Julie A., and Leyla Rouhi. "From Nevskii Prospect to Zoia's Apartment: Trials of the Russian Procuress." *Russian Review* 58, no. 3 (July 1999): 413–31.

Cicero. *De Oratore.* Translated by E. W. Sutton. Cambridge: Harvard University Press, 1942.

Clark, Katerina. *Petersburg, Crucible of Cultural Revolution.* Cambridge: Harvard University Press, 1995.

————. *The Soviet Novel: History as Ritual.* Chicago: University of Chicago Press, 1981.

Connery, Brian A., and Kirk Combe, eds. *Theorizing Satire: Essays in Literary Criticism.* New York: St. Martin's Press, 1995.

Conquest, Robert. *The Great Terror: A Reassessment.* New York: Oxford University Press, 1990.

Corrigan, Robert W., ed. *Tragedy: Vision and Form.* 2nd ed. New York: Harper and Row, 1981.

Czap, Peter, Jr. "Peasant-Class Courts and Peasant Customary Justice in Russia, 1861–1912." *Journal of Social History* 1, no. 2 (winter 1967): 149–78.

David-Fox, Michael. *Revolution of the Mind: Higher Learning among the Bolsheviks, 1918–1929.* Ithaca: Cornell University Press, 1997.

Davies, Robertson. *The Mirror of Nature: The Alexander Lectures, 1982.* Toronto: University of Toronto Press, 1983.

Davies, Sarah. *Popular Opinion in Stalin's Russia: Terror, Propaganda and Dissent, 1934–1941.* Cambridge: Cambridge University Press, 1997.

Doane, Mary Ann. "Melodrama, Temporality, Recognition: American and Russian Silent Cinema." *East-West Film Journal* 4, no. 2 (June 1990): 69–98.

Dolinskii, S., and S. Bergman. *Massovaia rabota v klube. Metodika, illiustrativnyi material, uchet opyta.* Moscow: Izd. Rabotnik prosveshcheniia, 1924.

Drobashenko, S. V. *Istoriia sovetskogo dokumental'nogo kino. Uchebno-metodicheskoe posobie.* Moscow: Izd. Moskovskogo Universiteta, 1980.

Duranty, Walter. "Defy Soviet Court in Treason Trial." *New York Times,* June 10, 1922, 1.

————. *Duranty Reports Russia.* Edited by Gustavus Tuckerman Jr. New York: Viking Press, 1934.

————. *I Write as I Please.* New York: Simon and Schuster, 1935.

————. *The Kremlin and the People.* New York: Reynal and Hitchcock, 1941.

————. *USSR: The Story of Soviet Russia.* Philadelphia: J. B. Lippincott, 1944.

Dvenadtsat' smertnikov. Sud nad sotsialistami-revoliutsionerami v Moskve. Berlin: Izd. zagranichnoi delegatsii PSR, 1922.

Eizenshtein, Sergei. "Montazh attraktsionov. (K postanovke 'Na vsiakogo mudretsa dovol'no prostoty' A. N. Ostrovskogo v Moskovskom Proletkul'te)." *Zhurnal levogo fronta iskussty* 3 (June–July 1923): 70–75.

Eklof, Ben, et al., eds. *Russia's Great Reforms, 1855–1881.* Bloomington: Indiana University Press, 1994.

Enders, Jody. *The Medieval Theater of Cruelty: Rhetoric, Memory, Violence.* Ithaca: Cornell University Press, 1999.

————. *Rhetoric and the Origins of Medieval Drama.* Ithaca: Cornell University Press, 1992.

Engelstein, Laura. "Revolution and Theater of Public Life in Imperial Russia." In *Revolution and the Meanings of Freedom in the Nineteenth Century,* edited by Isser Woloch. Stanford: Stanford University Press, 1996.

Erdman, Nikolai. *The Major Plays of Nikolai Erdman: The Warrant and The*

Suicide. Translated by John Freedman. Luxembourg: Harwood Academic, 1995.

———. *A Meeting about Laughter: Sketches, Interludes and Theatrical Parodies by Nikolai Erdman with Vladimir Mass and Others.* Translated by John Freedman. Luxembourg: Harwood Academic, 1995.

———. *P'esy, intermedii, pis'ma, dokumenty, vospominaniia sovremennikov.* Moscow: Iskusstvo, 1990.

Evreinov, Nikolai. *Istoriia telesnykh nakazanii v Rossii.* Kharkov: Progress, 1994.

———. *Samoe glavnoe. Dlia kogo komediia, a dlia kogo i drama, v 4 deistviiakh.* St. Petersburg: Gos. Izd., 1921.

———. *Shagi Nemezidy. Dramaticheskaia khronika v 6-ti kartinakh iz partiinoi zhizni v SSSR (1936–1938).* Paris: Vozrozhdenie, 1956.

———. "Teatral'noe iskusstvo na sluzhbe u obshchestvennoi bezopasnosti." *Zhizn' iskusstva* 792–97, August 2–7, 1921, 4.

———. *Teatr kak takovoi (Obosnovanie teatral'nosti v smysle polozhitel'nogo nachala stsenicheskogo iskusstva i zhizni).* St. Petersburg: Sklad Izd. Sovremennoe Iskusstvo, 1912.

———. "Teatroterapiia." *Zhizn' iskusstva,* 578–79, October 9–10, 1920, 1.

———. *The Theatre in Life.* Edited and translated by Alexander I. Nazaroff. New York: Brentano's, 1927.

———. "Vziatie zimnego dvortsa." *Krasnyi militsioner* 14, November 15, 1920, 4–5.

Feofanov, Yuri, and Donald D. Barry. *Politics and Justice in Russia: Major Trials of the Post-Stalin Era.* Armonk, N.Y.: M. E. Sharpe, 1996.

Fischer, Louis. *Men and Politics: An Autobiography.* New York: Duell, Sloan and Pearce, 1941.

———. *The Soviets in World Affairs: A History of Relations between the Soviet Union and the Rest of the World.* London: Jonathan Cape, 1930.

Fischer-Lichte, Erika. "From Theatre to Theatricality: How to Construct Reality." *Theatre Research International* 20, no. 2 (1995): 98–105.

———. "Theatricality: A Key Concept in Theatre and Cultural Studies." *Theatre Research International* 20, no. 2 (1995): 85–89.

Fitzpatrick, Sheila. *The Commissariat of Enlightenment: Soviet Organization of Education and the Arts under Lunacharsky, October 1917–1921.* Cambridge: Cambridge University Press, 1970.

———. *The Cultural Front: Power and Culture in Revolutionary Russia.* Ithaca: Cornell University Press, 1992.

———. *Everyday Stalinism, Ordinary Life in Extraordinary Times: Soviet Russia in the 1930s.* New York: Oxford University Press, 1999.

———. "How the Mice Buried the Cat: Scenes from the Great Purges of 1937 in the Russian Provinces." *Russian Review* 52 (July 1993): 299–320.

———. *Stalin's Peasants: Resistance and Survival in the Russian Village after Collectivization.* Oxford: Oxford University Press, 1994.

Frank, Stephen P. "Popular Justice, Community and Culture among the Russian

Peasantry, 1870–1900." *Russian Review* 46, no. 3 (July 1987): 239–65.

Freedman, John. "Nikolai Erdman: An Overview." *Slavic and East European Journal* 28, no. 4 (1984): 462–76.

———. *Silence's Roar: The Life and Drama of Nikolai Erdman.* Oakville, Canada: Mosaic Press, 1992.

Fülöp-Miller, René. *The Mind and Face of Bolshevism: An Examination of Cultural Life in Soviet Russia.* Translated by F. S. Flint and D. F. Tait. London: G. P. Putnam's Sons, 1927.

Fülöp-Miller, René, and Joseph Gregor. *The Russian Theatre: Its Character and History with Especial Reference to the Revolutionary Period.* Translated by Paul England. Philadelphia: J. B. Lippincott, 1929.

Gak, A. M., ed. *Samoe vazhnoe iz vsekh iskusstv: Lenin o kino. Sbornik dokumentov i materialov.* 2nd ed. Moscow: Izd. Iskusstvo, 1973.

Gallanin, G. A., ed. *Protsess Very Zasulich (Sud i posle suda).* St. Petersburg: Tipo-Litografiia S. M. Muller, n.d.

Garin, Erast. "O *Mandate* u o drugom." In *Vstrechi s Meierkhol'dom. Sbornik vospominanii.* Moscow: Vserossiiskoe Teatral'noe Obshchestvo, 1967.

Garner, Richard. *Law and Society in Classical Athens.* New York: St. Martin's Press, 1987.

Gerould, Daniel. "Lunacharsky and Melodrama." *Slavic and East European Performance: Drama, Theatre, Film* 14, no. 3 (fall 1994): 57–59.

Gerould, Daniel, ed. *Melodrama.* New York: New York Literary Forum, 1980.

Getty, J. Arch. *Origins of the Great Purges: The Soviet Communist Party Reconsidered, 1933–1938.* New York: Cambridge University Press, 1987.

Goliakov, I. T. *Sud i zakonnost' v khudozhestvennoi literature.* Moscow: Gos. Izd. Iuridicheskoi lit., 1959.

———. *Sud i zakonnost' v russkoi khudozhestvennoi literature XIX veka.* Moscow: Izd. Moskovskogo universiteta, 1956.

Golovachev, V., and B. Lashchilin. *Narodnyi teatr na Donu.* Rostov na Donu: Rostovskoe oblastnoe knigoizd., 1947.

Golub, Spencer. *Evreinov: The Theatre of Paradox and Transformation.* Ann Arbor: UMI Research Press, 1984.

Goncharova, N. "'Bania' V. Maiakovskogo." *Rabochaia gazeta* 65, no. 2414, March 21, 1930, 7.

Gorchakov, N. A. *Istoriia sovetskogo teatra.* New York: Izd. im. Chekhova, 1956.

Gor'kii, Maksim. *Sobranie sochinenii v vosemnadtsati tomakh.* 18 vols. Moscow: Gos. Izd. Khudozhestvennoi Literatury, 1960.

Grois, Boris. *The Total Art of Stalinism: Avant-Garde, Aesthetic Dictatorship, and Beyond.* Translated by Charles Rougle. Princeton: Princeton University Press, 1992.

Hazard, John N. *Settling Disputes in Soviet Society: The Formative Years of Legal Institutions.* New York: Columbia University Press, 1960.

Hibben, Paxton. "Moscow's Treason Trial." *Nation* 115, no. 2986 (27 September 1922): 299–300.

Holmes, W. M. *The Wreckers Exposed in the Trial of the Counter-Revolutionary Industrial Party.* New York: Worker's Library Publishers, 1931.

Huizinga, Johan. *Homo Ludens: A Study of the Play Element in Culture.* New York: Harper & Row, 1970.

Iakubovskii, G. "O satire nashikh dnei." *Literaturnaia gazeta* 11, July 8, 1929, 3.

Iampolskii, Mikhail. "Vina—pokaianie—donos." In *Russian Culture in Transition: Selected Papers of the Working Group for the Study of Contemporary Russian Culture, 1990–1991,* edited by Gregory Freidin. Stanford: Department of Slavic Languages and Literatures, 1993.

Istoriia sovetskogo kino, 1917–1967. 4 vols. Moscow: Izd. Iskusstvo, 1969.

Iufit, A. Z., ed. *Russkii sovetskii teatr, 1917–1921.* Leningrad: Iskusstvo, 1968.

Ivanov, Viacheslav. *Po zvezdam. Stat'i i aforizmy.* St. Petersburg: Izd. Ory, 1909. Reprint, Bradda Books, Letchworth, Hertfordshire, England.

———. *Sobranie sochinenii.* 3 vols. Brussels: Foyer Oriental Chrétien, 1974.

Jansen, Marc. *A Show Trial under Lenin: The Trial of the Socialist Revolutionaries, Moscow, 1922.* The Hague: Marinus Nyhoff, 1982.

"Kakoi dolzhna byt' sovetskaia satira?" *Rabochii i teatr* 8–9, April 1, 1931, 15.

Kazantsev, S. M. *Sud prisiazhnykh v Rossii. Gromkie ugolovnye protsessy, 1864–1917 gg.* Leningrad: Lenizdat, 1991.

Keep, John. "1917: The Tyranny of Paris over Petrograd." *Soviet Studies* 20, no. 1 (July 1968): 22–35.

Kenez, Peter. *Cinema and Soviet Society, 1917–1953.* Cambridge: Cambridge University Press, 1992.

———. "Soviet Cinema in the Age of Stalin." In *Stalinism and Soviet Cinema,* edited by Richard Taylor and Derek Spring. London: Routledge, 1993.

Kerzhentsev, P. M. *Kak chitat' knigu?* Khar'kov: Izd. Molodoi rabochii, 1924.

———. *Kak vesti sobraniie.* Leningrad: Izd. Priboi, 1925.

———. *Revoliutsiia i teatr.* Moscow: Izd. Dennitsa, 1918.

———. *Sredi plameni. Teatral'noe predstavlenie v 3-kh deistviiakh s intermediiami.* Petrograd: Gos. Izd., 1921.

———. *Tvorcheskii teatr.* Petrograd: Gos. Izd., 1920.

———. *Tvorcheskii teatr. Izdanie piatoe peresmotrennoe i dopolnennoe.* Moscow-Petrograd: Gos. Izd., 1923.

———. *Tvorcheskii teatr. Puti sotsialisticheskogo teatra.* Petrograd: Izd. Kniga, 1918.

Kinematograf. Sbornik statei. Moscow: Gos. Izd., 1919.

Kino. Politika i liudi (30-e gody). Moscow: Materik, 1995.

Kino v rabochem klube. Sbornik statei i ofitsial'nykh materialov. Moscow: Izd. VTsSPS, 1926.

Kirschenbaum, Lisa A. "Scripting Revolution: Regicide in Russia." Unpublished paper presented at 1997 conference "Inventing the Soviet Union," at Indiana University.

Kobiakov, Sergei. "Krasnyi sud. Vpechateleniia zashchitnika v revoliutsionnykh tribunalakh." In *Arkhiv russkoi revoliutsii,* vol. 7, 246–75. Berlin: I. V.

Gessen, 1922. Reprint, Moscow: Terra-Politizdat, 1991.

Kondrat'eva, Tamara. *Bol'sheviki—iakobintsy i prizrak termidora.* Moscow: Izd. Ipol, 1993.

Koni, A. F. *Vospominaniia o dele Very Zasulich,* vol. 2 of *Sobranie sochinenii v vos'mi tomakh.* Moscow: Izd. Iuridicheskaia literatura, 1966.

Kovalev, V. A. *Raspiatie dukha. Sudebnye protsessy stalinskoi epokhi.* Moscow: Izd. NORMA, 1997.

Kovejnikov, Alexei. "Rituals of Stalinist Culture at Work: Science and the Games of Intraparty Democracy circa 1948." *Russian Review* 57 (January 1998): 25–52.

Kremlev, G. *Mikhail Kalatozov.* Moscow: Izd. Iskusstvo, 1964.

Krizis teatra. Sbornik statei. Moscow: Knigoizdatel'stvo Problemy iskusstva, 1908.

Krolov, S. *Kino vmesto vodki.* Moscow-Leningrad: Moskovskii rabochii, 1928.

Krylenko, N. V. *Ekonomicheskaia kontr-revoliutiia v Donbasse (Itogi shakhtinskogo dela). Stat'i i dokumenty.* Moscow: Iuridicheskoe Izd. NKIu RSFSR, 1928.

———. *Za piat' let, 1918–1922 gg. Obvinitel'nye rechi po naibolee krupnym protsessam, zaslushannym v moskovskom i verkhovnom revoliutsionnykh tribunalakh.* Moscow-Petrograd: Gos. Izd., 1923.

Kucherov, Samuel. "The Case of Vera Zasulich." *Russian Review* 11, no. 2 (April 1952): 86–96.

———. *Courts, Lawyers and Trials under the Last Three Tsars.* Westport: Greenwood Press, 1974.

Kuleshov, Lev. *Kuleshov on Film: Writings by Lev Kuleshov.* Translated by Ronald Levaco. Berkeley: University of California Press, 1974.

———. *Sobranie sochinenii v trekh tomakh.* 3 vols. Moscow: Iskusstvo, 1987.

Lagovier, N. *O samosudakh.* Moscow-Leningrad: Gos. Izd., 1927.

Lawton, Anna, ed. *The Red Screen: Politics, Society, Art in Soviet Cinema.* London: Routledge, 1992.

Leach, Robert. *Revolutionary Theatre.* London: Routledge, 1994.

Lenin, V. I. *Polnoe sobranie sochinenii.* 5th ed. 55 vols. Moscow: Gos. Izd. Politicheskoi Literatury, 1964.

Leonov, M. A. *Kritika i samokritika—Dialekticheskaia zakonomernost' razvitiia sovetskogo obshchestva. Stenogramma publichnoi lektsii, prochitannoi 24 fevralia 1948 goda v Tsentral'nom lektorii Obshchestva v Moskve.* Moscow: Pravda, 1948.

Levin, K. *Partiia predatelei.* Moscow: Molodaia gvardiia, 1931.

Leyda, Jay. *Kino: A History of Russian and Soviet Film.* 3rd ed. Princeton: Princeton University Press, 1983.

Lezhnev, A. "Na put' k vozrozhdeniiu satiry." *Literaturnaia gazeta* 1, April 22, 1929, 2.

Lincoln, W. Bruce. *The Great Reforms: Autocracy, Bureaucracy, and the Politics of Change in Imperial Russia.* DeKalb: Northern Illinois University Press, 1990.

Liublinskii, P. I. *Kinematograf i deti.* Moscow: Knigoizd. Pravo i zhizn', 1925.

Liudi-vrediteli. See Agranovskii, A., Iu. Alevich, and G. Ryklin. *Liudi-vrediteli. Shakhtinskoe delo.*

London, Jack. "The Unexpected." *Blackwood's Magazine* 180, no. 1090 (August 1906): 163–80.

Lotman, Iu. M. *Izbrannye stat'i v trekh tomakh.* 3 vols. Tallinn: Aleksandra, 1992.

Lunacharskii, A. V. *Byvshie liudi. Ocherk istorii partii es-erov.* Moscow: Gos. Izd., 1922.

———. *Lunacharskii o kino. Stat'i, vyskazyvaniia, stsenarii, dokumenty.* Moscow: Izd. Iskusstvo, 1965.

———. *Medvezh'ia svad'ba. Melodrama na siuzhet Merime v 9 kartinakh.* Moscow: Gos. Izd., 1924.

———. "Revolutionary Ideology and Cinema—Theses." In *The Film Factory: Russian and Soviet Cinema in Documents,* edited and translated by Richard Taylor. Cambridge: Harvard University Press, 1988.

———. *Sobranie sochinenii v vos'mi tomakh.* 8 vols. Moscow: Izd. Khudozhestvennaia Literatura, 1964.

———. "Voskresshaia melodrama." *Teatr i iskusstvo* 18, May 3, 1915, 304–6.

Lyons, Eugene. *Assignment in Utopia.* New York: Harcourt, Brace, 1937.

———. *Stalin: Czar of all the Russias.* Philadelphia: J. B. Lippincott, 1940.

Mackenzie, F. A. *Russia before Dawn.* London: T. Fisher Unwin, 1923.

Maiakovskii, V. V. *Polnoe sobranie sochinenii v trinadtsati tomakh.* 13 vols. Moscow: Gos. Izd. Khudozhestvennoi Literatury, 1959.

Mally, Lynn. *Culture of the Future: The Proletkult Movement in Revolutionary Russia.* Berkeley and Los Angeles: University of California Press, 1990.

Margolit, Evgenii, and Viacheslav Shmyrov. *(iz"iatoe kino).* Moscow: Gosfil'mofond Rossii, 1995.

Markov, P. A. *O teatre v cheyrekh tomakh.* Vol. 3. Moscow: Iskusstvo, 1976.

———. *The Soviet Theatre.* London: Victor Gollancz, 1934.

Mason, Jeffery D. *Melodrama and the Myth of America.* Bloomington: Indiana University Press, 1993.

Maximoff, G. P. *The Guillotine at Work: Twenty Years of Terror in Russia (Data and Documents).* Chicago: Chicago Section of the Alexander Berkman Fund, 1940.

Medvedev, Roi. *O Staline i stalinizme.* Moscow: Progress, 1990.

Meierkhol'd, V. E. *Stat'i, pis'ma, rechi, besedy.* Vol. 2, *Chast' vtoraia, 1917–1939.* Moscow: Izd. Iskusstvo, 1968.

Miuntsenberg, V. *Kino i revoliutsiia.* Moscow: Izd. Mezhrabpom, 1925.

Mokul'skii, S., et al. "'Strakh' v Gosteatre dramy." *Rabochii i teatr* 16 (1931): 4–7.

Muratova, K. D. "M. Gor'kii i sovetskii teatr." In *Iz istorii russkikh literaturnykh otnoshenii, 18–20 vekov.* Moscow-Leningrad: Izd. Akademii nauk SSSR, 1959.

Murav, Harriet. *Russia's Legal Fictions*. Ann Arbor: University of Michigan Press, 1998.

Neale, Steve. "Melodrama and Tears." *Screen* 27, no. 6 (November–December 1986): 6–22.

Neuberger, Joan. "Popular Legal Cultures: The St. Petersburg Mirovoi Sud." In *Russia's Great Reforms, 1855–1881,* edited by Ben Eklof et al. Bloomington: Indiana University Press, 1994.

Nietzsche, Friedrich. *The Birth of Tragedy from the Spirit of Music and The Genealogy of Morals*. Translated by Francis Golffing. New York: Anchor Books Doubleday, 1956.

Nurmin. "Protsess es-erov. (Zamechaniia i vpechatleniia.)" *Krasnaia nov'* no. 4 (July–August 1922): 270–81.

"O putiakh sovetskoi satiry." *Literaturnaia gazeta* 13, July 15, 1929, 1.

Obvinitel'nye rechi na protsesse eserov. Moscow: Izd. Krasnaia nov', 1922.

Olitskaia, E. *Moi vospominaniia*. Vol. 1. Frankfurt am Main: Posev, 1971.

Ozouf, Mona. *Festivals and the French Revolution*. Translated by Alan Sheridan. Cambridge: Harvard University Press, 1988.

Paperno, Irina. *Chernyshevsky and the Age of Realism: A Study in the Semiotics of Behavior*. Stanford: Stanford University Press, 1988.

Petric, Vlada. "A Subtextual Reading of Kuleshov's Satire *The Extraordinary Adventures of Mr. West in the Land of the Bolsheviks* (1924)." In *Inside Soviet Film Satire: Laughter with a Lash,* edited by Andrew Horton. Cambridge: Cambridge University Press, 1993.

Piotrovskii, Adr. *Teatr, kino, zhizn'*. Leningrad: Izd. Iskusstvo, 1969.

Poliakov, Iu. A., and S. V. Drobashenko, eds. *Sovetskaia kinokhronika, 1918–1925. Annotirovannyi katalog*. Vol. 1, *Kinozhurnaly*. Moscow: Tsentral'nyi Gos. Arkhiv Kinofotofonodokumentov SSSR, 1965.

Poluianov, Pavel. *Gibel' teatra i torzhestvo kino. [Pamflet.]* N. Novgorod: Tip. Nizhpoligraf, 1925.

Plato. *The Laws*. Translated by Trevor J. Saunders. New York: Penguin Books, 1970.

Protsess "Prompartii" (25 noiabria–7 dekabria 1930 g.). Stenogramma sudebnogo protsessa i materialy priobshchennye k delu. Moscow: OGIZ-Sovetskoe zakonodatel'stvo, 1931.

Radek, Karl. *Portrety vreditelei*. Moscow: OGIZ–Moskovskii rabochii, 1931.

Rahill, Frank. *The World of Melodrama*. University Park: Pennsylvania State University Press, 1967.

Reiman, Michal. *The Birth of Stalinism: The USSR on the Eve of the "Second Revolution."* Translated by George Saunders. Bloomington: Indiana University Press, 1987.

Reswick, William. *I Dreamt Revolution*. Chicago: Henry Regnery, 1952.

Robin, Régine. *Socialist Realism: An Impossible Aesthetic*. Translated by Catherine Porter. Stanford: Stanford University Press, 1992.

Rockwood, Bruce L., ed., *Law and Literature Perspectives*. New York: Peter Lang, 1996.

Rogi, M. "Puti sovetskoi satiry oshibka tov. Bliuma." *Literaturnaia gazeta* 14, July 22, 1929, 3.

Rolland, Romain. *Le théâtre du peuple*. Paris: Cahiers de la Quinzaine, 1903.

———. *Narodnyi teatr*. Translated by I. Gol'denberg. St. Petersburg: Izd. Tovarishchestva Znanie, 1910.

Roosevelt, Priscilla R. "Emerald Thrones and Living Statues: Theater and Theatricality on the Russian Estate." *Russian Review* 50, no. 1 (January 1991): 1–23.

———. *Life on the Russian Country Estate: A Social and Cultural History*. New Haven: Yale University Press, 1995.

Rosenbaum, Kurt. "The German Involvement in the Shakhty Trial." *Russian Review* 21, no. 3 (July 1962): 238–60.

Rosenthal, Bernice Glatzer, ed. *Nietzsche and Soviet Culture: Ally and Adversary*. Cambridge: Cambridge University Press, 1994.

———. *Nietzsche in Russia*. Princeton: Princeton University Press, 1986.

Rothstein, Andrew, ed. *At the Bar of Soviet Justice: A Record of the Trial of the Industrial Party Held in Moscow, November–December 1930*. Moscow-Leningrad: Co-operative Publishing Society of Foreign Workers in the USSR, 1993.

———. *Wreckers on Trial: A Record of the Trial of the Industrial Party Held in Moscow, Nov.–Dec. 1930*. New York: Workers' Library Publishers, 1931.

Rudnitsky, Konstantin. *Meyerhold: The Director*. Translated by George Petrov, edited by Sydney Schultze, introduction by Ellendea Proffer. Ann Arbor: Ardis, 1981.

———. *Russian and Soviet Theatre: Tradition and the Avant-Garde*. Translated by Roxane Permar, edited by Dr. Lesley Milne. London: Thames and Hudson, 1988.

Russell, Robert. *Russian Drama of the Revolutionary Period*. Basingstoke, England: Macmillan, 1988.

Russell, Robert, and Andrew Barratt, eds. *Russian Theatre in the Age of Modernism*. New York: St. Martin's Press, 1990.

Sadoul, Jacques. *Les SR et Vandervelde*. Paris: Librairie de l'Humanité, 1922.

Samiulenko, E. *Kinematograf i ego prosvetitel'naia rol'*. St. Petersburg: Tip. "Slovo," 1912; Petrograd: Gos. Tip., 1919.

Scheffer, Paul. "Das Klassengericht." *Berliner Tageblatt* 251, May 30, 1928, 1.

Scott, John. *Behind the Urals: An American Worker in Russia's City of Steel*. Bloomington: Indiana University Press, 1973.

Segel, Harold B. *Twentieth-Century Russian Drama: From Gorky to the Present*. Updated ed. Baltimore: Johns Hopkins University Press, 1993.

Shatrov, Mikhail. *Diktatura sovesti. Spory i razmyshleniia vosem'desiat shestogo goda v dvukh chastiakh*. *Teatr* 6 (June 1986): 3–37.

Shein, S. D. *Sud nad ekonomicheskoi kontr-revoliutsiei v Donbasse. Zametki obshchestvennogo obvinitelia*. Moscow-Leningrad: Gos. Izd., 1928.

Sheinin, Lev, and the Tur Brothers. *Ochnaia stavka. P'esa v chetyrekh deistviiakh s prologom.* Moscow-Leningrad: Gos. Izd. Iskusstvo, 1938.

Shklovskii, Viktor. *Khod konia. Sbornik statei.* Moscow/Berlin: Knigoizd. Gelikon, 1923.

Shlapentokh, Dmitry. *The Counter-Revolution in Revolution: Images of Thermidor and Napoleon at the Time of the Russian Revolution and Civil War.* New York: St. Martin's Press, 1999.

————. *The French Revolution and the Russian Anti-Democratic Tradition: A Case of False Consciousness.* New Brunswick: Transaction, 1997.

Shrag, I. "Krest'ianskie sudy vladimirskoi i moskovskoi gubernii." *Iuridicheskii vestnik* 7–8 (July–August 1877): 58–86.

Shub, David. "The Trial of the SRs." *Russian Review* 23, no. 4 (October 1964): 362–69.

Sinyavsky, Andrei. *Soviet Civilization: A Cultural History.* Translated by Joanne Turnbull and Nikolai Formozov. New York: Little, Brown, 1990.

Solomon, Peter H., Jr. *Soviet Criminal Justice under Stalin.* Cambridge: Cambridge University Press, 1996.

Solomon, Peter H., Jr., ed. *Reforming Justice in Russia, 1864–1996: Power, Culture, and the Limits of Legal Order.* Armonk, N.Y.: M. E. Sharpe, 1997.

Solzhenitsyn, Aleksandr I. *The Gulag Archipelago, 1918–1956: An Experiment in Literary Investigation.* Vols. 1–2. Translated by Thomas P. Whitney. New York: Harper and Row, 1973.

Soukhomline, V. *Les procès célèbres de la Russie.* Paris: Payot, 1937.

Ssemjonow, G. (Wassiljew). *Die Partei der Sozial-revolutionäre in den Jahren 1917–1918 (Ihre Kampftätigkeit und militärischen Aktionen).* Hamburg: Kleine Bibliothek der Russischen Korrespondenz, 1922.

Stalin, I. V. *Sochineniia.* 13 vols. Moscow: Gos. Izd. Politicheskoi Literatury, 1953.

Stalin's Letters to Molotov, edited by Lars T. Lih, Oleg V. Naumov, and Oleg V. Khlevniuk, and translated by Catherine A. Fitzpatrick. New Haven: Yale University Press, 1995.

Steinberg, Mark D., and Vladimir M. Khrustalëv. *The Fall of the Romanovs: Political Dreams and Personal Struggles in a Time of Revolution.* New Haven: Yale University Press, 1995.

Stites, Richard. *Revolutionary Dreams: Utopian Vision and Experimental Life in the Russian Revolution.* New York: Oxford University Press, 1989.

Tamashin, L. *Sovetskaia dramaturgiia v gody grazhdanskoi voiny.* Moscow: Gos. Izd. Iskusstvo, 1961.

Taylor, Richard. *Film Propaganda: Soviet Russia and Nazi Germany.* London: Groom Helm, 1979.

————. *The Politics of the Soviet Cinema, 1917–1929.* Cambridge: Cambridge University Press, 1979.

Taylor, Richard, ed. and trans. *The Film Factory: Russian and Soviet Cinema in Documents.* Cambridge: Harvard University Press, 1988.

Taylor, Richard, and Ian Christie, eds. *Inside the Film Factory: New Approaches to Russian and Soviet Cinema.* London: Routledge, 1991.

Taylor, Richard, and Derek Spring, eds. *Stalinism and Soviet Cinema*. London: Routledge, 1993.

Teatr: Kniga o novom teatre. Sbornik statei. St. Petersburg: Izd. Shipovnik, 1908.

Tenishev, Kniaz' V. V. *Pravosudie v russkom krest'ianskom bytu*. Briansk: Tip. L. I. Utina, 1907.

Le théâtre d'agit-prop de 1917 à 1932. Vol. 1, *L'URSS-recherches*. Lausanne: La Cité–L'Age d'Homme, 1977.

Thurston, Robert W. *Life and Terror in Stalin's Russia, 1934–1941*. New Haven: Yale University Press, 1996.

Tiltman, H. Hessell. *The Terror in Europe*. New York: Frederick A. Stokes, 1931.

Titova, G. V. *Tvorcheskii teatr i teatral'nyi konstruktivizm*. St. Petersburg: SLAPTI, 1995.

Tolstoi, L. N. *Polnoe sobranie sochinenii*. 91 vols. Moscow: Gos. Izd. Khudozhestvennoi Literatury, 1958.

Toporkov, A. "Kinematograf i mif." In *Kinematograf. Sbornik statei*, 44–53. Moscow: Gos. Izd., 1919.

Troitskii, N. A. *Tsarizm pod sudom progressivnoi obshchestvennosti, 1866–1895 gg*. Moscow: Mysl', 1979.

———. *Tsarskie sudy protiv revoliutsionnoi Rossii. Politicheskie protsessy, 1871–1880 gg*. Saratov: Izd. Saratovskogo universiteta, 1976.

Trotsky, Leon. *My Life: An Attempt at an Autobiography*. New York: Charles Scribner's Sons, 1931.

———. *Trotsky's Diary in Exile: 1935*. Translated by Elena Zarudnaya. Cambridge: Harvard University Press, 1958.

Tsivian, Yuri. "Some Preparatory Remarks on Russian Cinema." In *Silent Witnesses: Russian Films, 1908–1919*, edited by Paolo Cherchi Usai. British Film Institute and Edizioni Biblioteca dell'Immagine, 1989.

Tucker, Robert C. *Stalin in Power: The Revolution from Above, 1928–1941*. New York: W. W. Norton, 1990.

Udar po interventam. Obvinitel'noe zakliuchenie. Moscow-Leningrad: Gos. Izd., 1930.

Vaksberg, Arkady. *The Prosecutor and the Prey: Vyshinsky and the 1930s' Moscow Show Trials*. Translated by Jan Butler. London: Weidenfeld and Nicolson, 1990.

Valois, George, ed. *Le procès des Industriels de Moscou: Sténogramme des debats établi par le Gosisdat (Editions d'état de l'URSS)*. Paris: Librairie Valois, 1931.

Vandervelde, Emile, and Arthur Wauters. *Le procès des socialistes révolutionnaires à Moscou*. Brussels: Librairie du Peuple, 1922.

Vardin, Il. *Eserovskie ubiitsy i sotsial-demokraticheskie advokaty. (Fakty i dokumenty.)* Moscow: GIZ, 1922.

Venturi, Franco. *Roots of Revolution: A History of the Populist and Socialist Movements in Nineteenth-Century Russia*. Translated by Francis Haskell. New York: Alfred A. Knopf, 1960.

Viola, Lynne. *Peasant Rebels under Stalin: Collectivization and the Culture of Peasant Resistance.* Oxford: Oxford University Press, 1996.

von Geldern, James. *Bolshevik Festivals, 1917–1920.* Berkeley and Los Angeles: University of California Press, 1993.

V sporakh o teatre. Sbornik statei. Moscow: Knigoizdatel'stvo pisatelei v Moskve, 1914.

Vyshinskii, A. *Itogi i uroki shakhtinskogo dela.* Moscow-Leningrad: Gos. Izd., 1928.

Wagner, Richard. *Richard Wagner's Prose Works.* Vol. 1, *The Art-Work of the Future, &c.;* vol. 2, *Opera and Drama.* Translated by William Ashton Ellis. London: Kegan Paul, Trench, Trübner, 1895.

Ward, Ian. *Law and Literature: Possibilities and Perspectives.* Cambridge: Cambridge University Press, 1995.

Weber, Max. *Sociological Writings.* Edited by Wolf Heydebrand. New York: Continuum, 1994.

White, James Boyd. *Heracles' Bow: Essays on the Rhetoric and Poetics of the Law.* Madison: University of Wisconsin Press, 1985.

Williams, Albert Rhys. *Journey into Revolution: Petrograd, 1917–1918.* Chicago: Quadrangle Books, 1969.

Williams, Linda. "Melodrama Revisited." In *Refiguring American Film Genres: History and Theory,* edited by Nick Browne. Berkeley and Los Angeles: University of California Press, 1998.

Wise, Jennifer. *Dionysus Writes: The Invention of Theatre in Ancient Greece.* Ithaca: Cornell University Press, 1998.

Wolfe, Bertram D. "Dress Rehearsals for the Great Terror." Reprinted from *Studies in Comparative Communism* 3, no. 2 (April 1970).

Woloch, Isser, ed. *Revolution and the Meanings of Freedom in the Nineteenth Century.* Stanford: Stanford University Press, 1996.

Wortman, Richard S. "Comment: Theatricality, Myth, and Authority." *Russian Review* 50, no. 1 (January 1991): 48–52.

———. *The Development of a Russian Legal Consciousness.* Chicago: University of Chicago Press, 1976.

———. *Scenarios of Power: Myth and Ceremony in Russian Monarchy.* Princeton: Princeton University Press, 1995.

Youngblood, Denise J. *Movies for the Masses: Popular Cinema and Soviet Society in the 1920s.* Cambridge: Cambridge University Press, 1992.

———. *Soviet Cinema in the Silent Era, 1918–1935.* Ann Arbor, Michigan: UMI Research Press, 1985.

Zakharov, Alexander. "Mass Celebrations in a Totalitarian System." In *Tekstura: Russian Essays on Visual Culture,* edited and translated by Alla Efimova and Lev Manovich. Chicago: University of Chicago Press, 1993.

Zaslavskii, L. "Vrediteli." *Pravda* no. 115, May 19, 1928, 3.

Ziolkowski, Theodore. *The Mirror of Justice: Literary Reflections of Legal Crisis.* Princeton, N.J.: Princeton University Press, 1997.

Znosko-Borovskii, Evg. A. *Russkii teatr nachala XX veka.* Prague: Plamia, 1925.

AGITSUDY

Abramov, A. "Kak my 'sdelali' sud." *Rabochii zritel'* 22, October 5, 1924, 22.

Aduev, Nikolai, and Argo Aduev. *Tribunal: P'esa-grotesk v 1 deistvii.* Moscow-Leningrad: Izd. MODPiK, 1930.

Afonskii, V. *Sud nad gr. Zhernovoi, oblivshei sopernitsu sernoi kislotoi.* Archives of TsGALI F. 656, o. 1, d. 1927.

Agitsud nad prestupnikami. Voronezh: Tipografiia redaktsii gazety "Voronizhskoi kommuny," 1923.

Agrosud nad selianinom, sryvaiushchim posevkampaniiu. Balta: Izd. Gosizdata AMSSR, 1926.

Akkerman, A. I. *Sud nad prostitutkoi. Delo gr. Zaborovoi po obvineniiu ee v zaniatii prostitutsiei i zarazhenii sifilisom kr-tsa Krest'ianova.* Moscow-Leningrad: Gos. Izd., 1922.

———. *Sud nad prostitutkoi i svodnitsei. Delo grazhd. Evdokimovoi, po obvineniiu v soznatel'nom zarazhenii sifilisom i grazhd. Sviridovoi v svodnichestve i soobshchnichestve.* Moscow: Izd. Narkomzdrava, 1924, 1925.

Alim. "Politsud nad krest'ianinom, plokho vedushchim khoziaistvo." *Izba-chital'nia na bor'bu s zasukhou.* Moscow: Izd. Doloi Negramotnost', 1925.

Andreev, Boris. *Sud nad chitatelem.* Leningrad: Izd. Knizhnogo Sektora GUBONO, 1924.

———. *Sud nad komsomol'tsem ili komsomol'koi narushaiushchimi soiuznuiu distsiplinu.* Leningrad: Izd. knizhnogo sektora GUBONO, 1924, 1925.

———. *Sud nad negramotnym.* Leningrad: Izd. Knizhnogo Sektora GUBONO, 1924.

———. *Sud nad starym bytom. Stsenarii dlia rabochikh klubov ko dniu rabotnitsy 8-go marta (s metodicheskimi ukazaniiami).* Moscow-Leningrad: Izd. Doloi Negramotnost', 1926.

———. *Za pod"em urozhainosti i kollektivizatsiiu sel'skogo khoziaistva (Agitsudy).* Leningrad: Priboi, 1929.

Antonov, Maksim. *Sud nad plokhim krest'ianinom. P'esa dlia krest'ianskogo teatra v dvukh kartinakh.* Leningrad: Gos. Izd., 1924.

Apushkin, A., and Iu. Dantsiger. "Prestuplenie grazhdanina Tikhonova (P'esa v odnom deistvii s prologom i epilogom)." In *Antirozhdestvenskii sbornik (dlia goroda),* edited by M. M. Sheinman. Moscow: Aktsionernoe izdatel'skoe obshchestvo "Bezbozhnik," 1930.

Ardov, Viktor Efimovich. "Alimenty." *Sovetskii vodevil' (dlia klubnykh, komsomol'skikh i rabochikh teatrov)* 3 (1927): 3–9.

———. "Delo o prokhodnoi komnate." *Sovetskii vodevil' dlia rabochego, kres'ianskogo i komsomol'skogo teatra* 4 (1929): 12–21.

———. "Poltinnik pogubil (Rastratnoe)." *Sovetskii vodevil' (dlia klubnykh, komsomol'skikh i rabochikh teatrov)* 3 (1927): 20–26.

Atrashkevich, M. *Sud nad kazarmennym vorom: Instsenirovka agitsuda.* Moscow-Leningrad: Gos. Voennoe Izd., 1926.

Avdeev, Vitalii. *Sheptuny i znakhari. Instsenirovannyi agit-sud nad znakharstvom v 3-kh kart. dlia derevenskogo teatra.* Leningrad: Rabochee Izd. Priboi, 1926.

Avlov, Gr. *Sud nad khuliganami.* Moscow-Leningrad: Izd. Doloi Negramotnost', 1927.

B. A. *Sud nad "Nashei gazetoi." Instsenirovka dlia kruzhkov zhivoi gazety klubov i krasnykh ugolkov.* Moscow: Izd. TsK SSTS, 1926.

Beregite les. Agro-sud v 1 deistvii. Dlia postanovki na otkrytom vozdukhe, na liuboi plochshadke, bez vsiakikh dekoratsii. Moscow: Izd. Narkomzema Novaia Derevnia, 1925.

Boichevskii, V. et al. *Sbornik Agit-Sudy.* Moscow: Novaia Moskva, n.d.

Bozhinskaia, N. *Sud nad delegatkoi-rabotnitsei.* Moscow-Leningrad: Gos. Izd., 1928.

———. *Sud nad krest'iankoi-delegatkoi.* Moscow-Leningrad: Gos. Izd., 1926.

Dalekii, A. *Sud nad banditom. Instsentirovka-na Karel'skuiu avantiuru i uchastie v nei Finliandii (Vragi naroda pered Revoliutsionnym Sudom).* Otklik: Politicheskii otdel karel'skogo raiona, 1922.

Deev, D. N. *Sud nad zarazivshim sifilisom zhenu (Sanitarnaia p'esa).* Ekaterinoslav: Izd. Otdela Zdravookhraneniia i Dorkul'trana Ekaterininskoi zheleznoi dorogi, 1924.

Demidovich, E. B. *Sud nad gr. Kiselevym po obvineniiu ego v zarazhenii zheny ego gonorriei posledstviem chego bylo ee samoubiistvo.* Moscow-Leningrad: Gos. Izd., 1922.

———. *Sud nad polovoi raspushchennost'iu.* Moscow-Leningrad: Doloi Negramotnost', 1927.

D'iakonova, E. A. *Sud nad golovnei: Agit-komediia s 12 risunkami.* Leningrad: Gos. Izd., 1925.

Dolev, D. (Diadia Trishka). "Agitsud nad sel'rabochkomom." In *Veselaia moia garmoshka, podpevai, batratskii khor!* Moscow: Izd. TsK Soiuza Sel'goslesrabochikh SSSR, 1927.

Dubovskii, V. "Sud nad greshnoi dushoi. Predstavlenie v odnom deistvii." *Biblioteka bezbozhnik u stanka* 3 (1923–1924): 21–28.

Ershov, Art. *Za khleb, za piatiletku: Agitsud v 1 deistvii.* Novosibirsk: Sibkraiizdat, 1929.

———. *Vragi kollektivizatsii. Agitsud.* Novosibirsk: Gos. Izd., 1930.

Frolov, A. E. *Sud nad svin'ei. P'esa v 3-kh deistviiakh dlia postanovki v narodnykh domakh, domakh krest'ianina i izbakh-chital'niakh.* Pokrovsk: Glavlit no. 1060, 1928.

Gekhtman-Poliakov. "Gadiuka: Agitp'esa." In *Sbornik agit-p'es dlia derevenskogo teatra.* Moscow: Izd. Glavpolitprosvet Krasnaia nov', 1923.

Gerasimov, B. N. *Sud nad vinovnikom v umyshlennoi porche i zaderzhke knig. Instsenirovka agitsuda v pomoshch' gor. bibliotekam s metodicheskimi ukazaniiami.* Moscow: Gos. uchebno-pedagogicheskoe Izd., 1932.

Ginzburg, B. S. *Sud nad mater'iu, pokinuvshei svoego rebenka. Delo gr.*

Tikhonovoi po obvineniiu ee: (1) v prestupno-nebrezhnom otnoshenii k svoemu rebenku, povlekshem za soboi riad tiazhelykh zabolevanii; (2) ostavlenii rebenka na proizvol sud'by. Instsenirovka. Moscow: Izd. Zemlia i Fabrika, 1924.

————. *Sud nad vrachom meduchastka. (Delo zaveduiushchego Aleksandrovskim meditsinskim uchastkom vracha Sergeeva po obvineniiu ego v bezdeiatel'nosti i nevnimatel'nom otnoshenii k svoim obiazannostiam, povlekshem za soboi gromadnuiu zabolevaemost' i smertnost' detei v etom uchastke.)* Instsenirovka. Moscow: Izd. Otdela Okhr. Mat. i Mlad. NKZ, 1925, 1926.

Glebova, N. *Sud nad delegatkoi. Delo po obvineniiu delegatki Tikhonovoi, ne vypolnivshei svoego proletarskogo dolga.* Moscow-Leningrad: Gos. Izd., 1924, 1925, 1926.

Goncharova-Viktorova, N. *Korovii sud. Agro-komediia v 3-kh kartinakh.* Moscow-Leningrad: Izd. MODPiK, 1927.

Grokhovskii, Mikhail. *Delo konovala Leshchetkina. P'esa v 1 deistvii.* Tver': Izd. Tverskogo Gubzempravleniia, 1926.

————. *Sud nad zemlei derevni Golodaevo.* Tver': Izd. Tverskogo Uzemupravleniia, 1924.

Gromov, A. M. *Vinoven-li? Stsenicheskoe oformlenie suda nad muzhem, zarazivshim sifilisom svoiu zhenu.* Khar'kov: Izd. Kosmos, 1925.

Gul'binskaia, Kl. "Sud nad sifilitkom." *Rabochii zritel'* 19, September 14–21, 1924, 17–18.

Gutyr', I. G. *Kooperativnyi agitsud nad rastratchikom kooperativnogo imushchestva.* Moscow: Tsentrosoiuz, 1927.

Il'inskii, V. I., and M. G. Frenkel'. *Sud nad strelochnikom po obvineniiu v p'ianstve i nebrezhnosti po sluzhbe.* Moscow: Izd. Narkomzdrava RSFSR, 1926.

Indenbom, L. *Agrosudy. Sud nad vrediteliami, sud nad sorniakami, sud nad beskormitsei, sud nad kolkhozom, sud nad dezerterom pokhoda za urozhai i drugie; Dlia provedeniia v periody podgotovki vesennei i osennei posevnykh kampanii i na prazdniki urozhaia.* Moscow: Izd. Krest'ianskaia gazeta, 1929.

Itskov, I., and Bedrzhitskii. "Stsenarii agitsuda nad otstalym khoziainom." In *Za Urozhai. Sbornik materialov dlia provedeniia "dnia urozhaia,"* edited by I. Gelis and B. Volkov. Moscow: Doloi Negramotnost', 1925.

Kanevskii, A. E. *Sud nad Annoi Gorbovoi po obvineniiu v proizvodstve sebe vykidysha (aborta).* Odessa: Odesskoii dom sanprosveta, 1925.

Kin, D. *Sud nad razvedkoi, nevypolnivshei boevogo zadaniia.* Kiev: Izd. Politupravleniia Kievskogo Voenogo Okruga, 1921.

Klebanskii, M., V. Milov, and S. Papernyi. *Kooperativnye agitsudy: (1) Sud nad lavochnoi komissiei. (2) Sud nad domashnei khoziaikoi pokupaiushchei u chastnykh torgovtsev. (3) Sud nad rastratchikom.* Moscow: Izd. Moskovskogo Soiuza potrebitel'skikh obshchestv "Gorod i Derevnia," 1926.

———. *Sud nad upolnomochennym kooperativa*. Moscow: Tsentrosoiuz, 1927.

Kurynikha (Sud nad znakharkoi): P'esa Leningradskogo Proletkul'ta. Leningrad: Rabochee Izd. Priboi, 1925.

Kuznetsov, A., and D. Lazarev. *Agitsud nad otstalym sel'skim khoziaistvom (Instsenirovka)*. Moscow: Novaia Moskva, 1924.

———. *Sud nad khishchnikami lesa*. Moscow: Novaia Moskva, 1926.

Lebedev, G. *Sud nad trekhpol'em*. Moscow: Novaia Derevnia, 1924.

Leonov, N. "Agro-sudy." *Derevenskii teatr* 2 (September 1925): 24–25.

Letov, A. *Ne na zhivot, a na smert'*. Moscow: Arzamas, 1930.

L'vov, L. O. *Delo Medyntseva. Instsenirovka v 3-kh deistviiakh*. Archives of TsGALI F. 656, o. 1, d. 1813.

Mal'tsev, M. Iu. *Sud nad antisemitizmom v 3-kh aktakh*. Leningrad: Priboi, 1928.

Malyshev, G. D. *Kak organizovat' sud nad sokhoi. Material dlia massovoi agropropagandy*. Moscow: Gos. Izd., 1925.

Manevich, A., and A. N. Speranskii. *Obshchestvennyi sud nad pravleniem kooperativa*. Moscow: Izd. Mosk. Soiuza Potrebitel'skikh Obshch., 1925.

Maradudin, F. *Zloe delo Nikity Smirnova*. Leningrad: Gos. Izd., 1926.

Materiali dlia literaturnogo suda nad Gaponom. Petrograd: 4-ia Gos. Tip., 1921.

Militsyna, E. *Sud nad negramotnym. (P'esa dlia derevenskogo teatra)*. Rostov-Don-Krasnodar: Iugo-vostochnoe kraevoe partiinoe Izd. Burevestnik, 1925.

Mitel'man, R. M. *Sud nad gruppovodom kamenshchikom (Pokazatel'nyi sud)*. Moscow: Izd. TsK VSSR, 1930.

Naumov, Aleksandr. *Delo Giselevicha (Sud nad antsemitami)*. Leningrad: Priboi, 1930.

———. *"Za ili protiv" (Sud nad pravleniem ZhAKT'a)*. Leningrad: Gos. Izd., 1930.

Naumov, N. M. *Kto vinovat? (Sanitarnyi sud)*. Moscow: Biuro sanitarnogo prosveshchenia Mosgorzdravotdela, 1939.

Naumov, N. M., and V. N. Vladimirov. *Dela delishki. Obozrenie v 10 epizodakh s prologom i epilogom*. Leningrad: Izd. Avtorov, 1927.

Neznamov, Mikh. "Sud nad Gaponom." In *9-oe ianvaria 1905 g. Sbornik dlia rabochikh klubov i nardomov*, edited by G. S. Maliuchenko. Rostov-Don: Severno-Kavkazskoe kraevoe partiinoe Izd. Burevestnik, 1925.

———. "Sud nad kommunarami." In *Parizhskaia Kommuna. Sbornik materialov dlia chteniia i prorabotki v rabochikh i komsomol'skikh klubakh, v izbakh-chital'niakh, nardomakh, shkolakh, politkruzhkakh i t.p.*, edited by G. S. Maliuchenko. Rostov-Don: Severno-Kavkazskoe kraevoe partiinoe Izd. Burevestnik, 1925.

Nikolaev, A. *Avio-agitsud*. Moscow: Izd. ODVF RSFSR, 1925.

Obnevskii, S. S. *Sud nad Sovetskoi Rossiei ili Porfirii Titych Titov-Lord britanskoi imperii*. Archives of TsGALI, F. 656, o. 1, d. 2161.

"Obzor agitatsionnogo materiala. Instsenirovka agitatsionnykh sudov." *Vestnik agitatsii i propagandy* 3, November 25, 1920, 25–27.

Personov, I., and G. Rybinskii. "Sud nad troitsei (Komicheskoe sudoproizvodstvo v 1 deistvii)." In *Troitsyn den'*, edited by G. Rybinskii. Moscow: Novaia Moskva, 1924.

Pletnev, V. F. *Instsenirovki. Sud nad Zubatovym i Gaponom*. Moscow: Vserossiiskii Proletkul't, 1925.

"Politsud nad fashistami." *Massovaia rabota v klube*. Moscow: Izd. Rabotnik Prosveshcheniia, 1924.

"Politsud nad krest'iankoi-delegatkoi." In *Mezhdunarodnyi den' rabotnits (8-oe marta): Sbornik materialov dlia chteniia i prorabotki v klubakh, izbakh-chital'niakh, narodnykh domakh i shkolakh*, edited by G. S. Maliuchenko. Rostov-Don: Severo-kavkazskoe kraevoe partiinoe Izd. Burevestnik, 1925.

R. D. *Sud nad domashnei khoziaikoi*. Moscow-Leningrad: Gos. Izd., 1927.

R. R-t. "Sud nad neaktivnym chlenom kooperativa." In *Mezhdunarodnyi den' kooperativa*, edited by M. A. Suponev. Leningrad: Gos. Izd., 1925.

Rebel'skii, I. V. *Instsenirovannye sudy (Kak ikh organizovyvat' i provodit')*. Moscow: Izd. MGSPS Trud i kniga, 1926.

Reinberg, L. *Instsenirovannye proizvodstvennye sudy*. Moscow: Izd. MGSPS Trud i Kniga, 1926.

Rezvushkin, Ia. *Sud nad bogom*. Moscow: Gos. Izd., 1924.

———. *Sud nad bogom. Antireligioznyi sbornik*. Vtoroe izdanie. Moscow-Leningrad: Gos. Izd., 1925.

Rosliakov, P. *Sud nad podzhigatelem lesa (Agit-instsenirovka ko "Dniu lesa")*. Arkhangel'sk: Izd. p/o pechati Arkh. Gubkoma RKP, 1924.

S. K. *Kto Vinovat? P'esa. Sbornik Agit-p'es dlia derevenskogo teatra*. Moscow: Izd. Krasnaia nov', 1923.

Safonov, A. T. *Sud nad obshchinoi (instsenirovka v 3-kh deistviiakh). Delo po obvineniiu obshchestva krest'ian der. "Otstalovki" v nevypolnenii priniatogo imi pered Uezdnom Zemel'nym Upravleniem obiazatel'stva o poseve poluchennykh obshchestvom semian rzhi po vspakhannoi zemle*. Samara: Izd. Seiatel' Pravdy, 1925.

Sel'korka (Politsud). Leningrad: Rabochee Izd. Priboi, 1925.

Semenov. "Agit-sud." *Derevenskii teatr* 2 (September 1925): 14–15.

Shapiro, B., and N. Gol'dshtein. *Agrosud*. Moscow-Leningrad: Moskovskii rabochii, 1928.

Sigal, B. S. *Sud nad babkoi znakharkoi (Instsenirovka)*. Moscow: Kooperativnoe Izd. Zhizn' i znanie, 1925, 1926.

———. *Sud nad grazhdanami Ivanom i Agaf'ei Mitrokhinymi, po vine kotorykh proizoshlo zabolevanie rabochego tuberkulezom*. Moscow: Kooperativnoe Izd. Zhizn' i znanie, 1925, 1926.

———. *Sud nad grazhdaninom Fedorom Sharovym po obvineniiu v zarazhenii tripperom. (Instsenirovka suda v 2-kh aktakh)*. Leningrad: Izd. Zhizn' i znanie, 1925.

———. *Sud nad Ivanom Lobachevym po obvineniiu v p'ianstve i khuliganstve (San.-prosvet. instsenirovka v dvukh aktakh)*. Leningrad: Rabochee Izd. Priboi, 1926.

————. *Sud nad mater'iu po obvineniiu v nevezhestvennom ukhode za det'mi i neprivitii ospy, povlekshem za soboi smert' rebenka. (Sanitarno-prosvetitel'-naia instsenirovka dlia derevni)*. Omsk: Gos. Izd., 1926.

————. *Sud nad mater'iu, vinovnoi v plokhom ukhode za det'mi, povlekshem za soboi smert' rebenka. (Sanitarno-prostvetitel'naia instenirovka v 2 aktakh)*. Leningrad: Biblioteka zhurnala Gigena i zdorov'e rabochei i krest'ianskoi sem'i, 1926, and Leningrad: Izd. Leningradskaia Pravda, 1928 and 1929.

————. *Sud nad mater'iu vinovnoi v rasprostranenii skarlatiny*. Moscow: Koopera-tivnoe Izd. Zhizn' i znanie, 1925.

————. *I. Sud nad pionerom-kuril'shchikom. II. Sud nad neriashlivym pionerom. (Dve instsenirovki)*. Moscow: Kooperativnoe Izd. Zhizn' i znanie, 1927.

————. *Sud nad p'ianitsei. (Instsenirovka suda v 2-kh aktakh)*. Leningrad: Izd. Leningradskaia Pravda, 1929, 1930.

————. *Sud nad p'ianitsei Ivanom Nikiforovym*. Samara: Izd. Seiatel' Pravdy, 1925.

————. *Sud nad samogonshchikami. (Instsenirovka dlia derevni)*. Moscow: Koop-erativnoe Izd. Zhizn' i znanie, 1925.

————. *Sud nad Stepanom Korolevym (Posledstviia p'ianstva). Intsenirovka suda v 2-kh aktakh*. Moscow: Kooperativnoe Izd. Zhizn' i znanie, 1924, 1926.

Smirnov, V. A. *Dve Sily (Sud nad pabkorom). Bytovaia p'esa 1924 g., v 3-kh deistviiakh*. Voronezh: Zadonskoe Raiagentstvo, 1924.

Smontirovich, Viklog. *Pokoiniki v otpusku (Protsess Tov. Matiasa Rakoshi)*. Samara: Izd. Samarskogo Gubernskogo Komiteta MOPR, 1927.

Speranskii, A. N., and Ia. A. Manevich. *Obshchestvennyi sud nad pravleniem ko-operativa (Instsenirovka)*. Moscow: Izd. Moskovskogo Soiuza potrebitel'skikh obshchestv, 1925.

Starikovich, Stepan D. *Sud nad komsomol'tsem-neradeem. Agitp'esa v 1-om deistvii*. Archives of TsGALI, F. 656, o. 1, d. 2737.

Starko, B. *Sud nad Fordom*. Moscow-Leningrad: Gos. Izd., 1928.

"Stsenarii agitsuda nad raboche-krest'ianskoi Rossiei." In *Prazdnik Oktiabr'skoi Revoliutsii v Shkole,* edited by I. Ustinov and V. I. Krylov. Moscow-Leningrad: T-va V. V. Dumnov, nasl. br. Salaevykh, 1923, 1924, 1925.

"Stsenarii agitsuda nad T'erom." *Vecher Parizhkoi kommuny v klube. Posobie dlia rabochikh, komsomol'skikh i shkol'nykh klubov*. Khar'kov: Proletarii, 1925.

Subbotin, Leonid. *Sud nad korovoi. Krest'ianskaia p'esa*. Moscow: Izd. Novaia Derevnia, 1928.

Sud bespartiinykh rabochikh i krest'ian nad Krasnoi armiei. Moscow: Krasnaia nov', 1923.

Sud nad Ivanom Temnym. Kollektivnyi trud 4-i gruppy v 7-i Voronizhskoi shkoly Vtoroi stupeni. Moscow-Leningrad: Izd. Doloi Negramatnost', 1927.

"Sud nad kavaleristom, zarazivshim chesotkoi svoiu loshchad' i loshchad' svoego tovarishcha." In *Klub! Pomogi politruku!* Khar'kov: Izd. Voenno-Redaktsionnogo Soveta UVO, 1922.

Sud nad komarom (Instsenirovka). B.m., 1926.

"Sud nad krasnoarmeitsami za narushenie prisiagi." *Klub! Pomogi komandiru i politruku!* Khar'kov: Izd. Voenno-Red. Soveta UVO, 1923.

Sud nad krest'ianinom Medvedevym, sorvavshim vybory kandidantki ot zhen-shchin v sel'sovet. Leningrad: Rabochee Izd. Priboi, 1925.

"Sud nad Leninym." *Pravda* 83, April 22, 1920, 2.

Sud nad negramotnymi. Tashkent: Izd. Turkglavpolitprosveta, 1923.

"Sud nad Vrangelem." *Vestnik teatra* 72–73, November 7, 1920, 16–17.

Topolev, I. "Instsenirovka sudov." *Rabochii zritel'* 2, January 8, 1924, 22–24.

Trakhtenberg, V., and A. Kugel'. *Sud nad "Zagovorom imperitritsy."* Archives of Biblioteka Soiuza teatral'nykh deitelei.

Ulitin, M. N. *Sud nad trekhpolkoi.* Gomel': Zapadnoe oblastnoe Izd. Gomel'skii rabochii, 1925.

Vasilevskii, L. M., and L. A. Vasilevskaia. *Sud nad akusherkoi Lopukhinoi sover-shivshei operatsiiu aborta, sledstviem chego iavilas' smert' zhenshchiny.* Tver': Izd. Oktiabr', 1923.

———. *Sud nad samogonshchikami. Delo Karpova Tikhona i ego zheny Agaf'i po obvineniiu v izgotovlenii i tainoi torgovle samogonkoi.* Petrograd: Izd. Ok-tiabr', 1923.

Vetrov, B., and L. Petrov. *Agitsud i zhivaia gazeta v derevne.* Moscow-Leningrad: Gos. Izd., 1926.

Vilenkin, A. *Kak postavit' agitsud v izbe-chital'ne.* Leningrad: Gos. Izd., 1926.

Vishnevskii, F. F. *Da zdravstvuet trud! (Sud nad dezertirami). Revoliutsionnaia p'esa v 4 deistviiakh.* Viatka: 1-ia gos. tip., 1921.

Vylegzhanin, M. V. *Sud nad bezkhoziaistvennymi zemledel'tsami. Sel'sko-khoziaistvenniai agitatsionnaia p'esa v 2-kh deistviiakh.* Slobodskoi: Vi-atskoe Gos. Izd., 1921.

Zhemchuzhnyi, V., and Roman Veprinskii. *Politsud nad vinovnikami imperialis-ticheskoi voiny (Instsenirovka).* Khar'kov: Gos. Izd. Ukrainy, 1924.

Zubrilin, A. A. *V chem vinovato trekhpol'e. Protsess 1-go oktiabria 1923 g.* Moscow: Novaia Derevnia, 1925.

FILMOGRAPHY

(Russian title, translated title, director, year of production/year of release, studio)

Abort. "Sud nad akusherkoi Zaitsevoi" (Abortion. "The trial of midwife Zait-seva"). G. Lemberg, 1924, Goskino.

Blok interventov (A block of interventionists). 1931, Sovkinokhronika.

Bol'shaia zhizn' (A great life). L. Lukov, 1939/1940, Kiev.

Delo ob ekonomicheskoi kontrrevoliutsii v Donbasse (The case of economic coun-terrevolution in the Donbass). 1928.

Don Diego i Pelegaia. "Delo Pelegai Deminoi" (Don Diego and Pelegaia. "The af-fair of Pelegaia Demina"). Ia. Protazanov, 1927/1928, Mezhrabpom-Rus'.

Dvadtsat' shest' komissarov (Twenty-six commissars). N. Shengelaia, 1932/1933, Azerkino.

Goskino kalendar' 28. D. Vertov, 1924.

Goskinokalendar' 46. G. Lemberg, 1925.

Gosudarstvennyi chinovnik (The government bureaucrat). I. Pyr'ev, 1930, Soiuzkino.

Gvozd' v sapoge (A nail in the boot). M. Kalatozov, 1931, Goskinoprom Gruzii.

Internatsional interventov (The International of interventionists). 1931.

Istoriia grazhdanskoi voiny (The history of the civil war). D. Vertov, 1921.

Katorga (Penal colony). Iu. Raizman, 1928, Gosvoenkino.

Kino-Nedelia. Nos. 1, 3, 14, 35. D. Vertov, 1918/1919.

Kinopravda. Nos. 1–4, 7–8. D. Vertov, 1922.

Krestiane (Peasants). F. Ermler, 1934/1935, Lenfil'm.

Kruzheva (Lace). S. Iutkevich, 1928, Sovkino.

Leningradskii Goskino-kalendar' (Leningrad Goskino-calendar). No. 6. D. Vertov, 1924.

Mat' (Mother). V. Pudovkin, 1926, Mezhrabpom-Rus'.

Mat' (Mother). A. Razumnyi, 1919/1920, Moskovskii kinokomitet.

Medvezh'ia svad'ba (The bear's wedding). K. Eggert, 1925/1926, Mezhrabpom-rus'.

Neobychainye prikliucheniia Mistera Vesta v strane bol'shevikov (The extraordinary adventures of Mr. West in the land of the Bolsheviks). L. Kuleshov, 1924, Goskino.

Ona zashchishchaet rodinu (She defends the motherland). F. Ermler, 1943, TsOKS/Alma-Ata.

Oshibka Inzhenera Kochina (Engineer Kochin's mistake). A. Macheret, 1939, Mosfil'm.

Padenie Berlina (The fall of Berlin). M. Chiaureli, 1949/1950, Mosfil'm.

Parizhskii sapozhnik (The Parisian cobbler). F. Ermler, 1927/1928, Sovkino.

Partiinyi bilet (The Party card). I. Pyr'ev, 1936, Mosfil'm.

Pioneriia 2 (1935).

Po zakonu (By the law). L. Kuleshov, 1926, Goskino.

Prestuplenie Ivana Karavaeva (The crime of Ivan Karavaev). T. Lukashevich, 1929, Mezhrabpomfil'm.

Prestuplenie konovala Matova (The crime of the horse-doctor Matov). Ia. Posel'skii, 1925, Krasnaia zvedza.

Prividenie, kotoroe ne vozvrashchaetsia (The ghost that doesn't return). A. Room, 1929/1930, Sovkino.

Prigovor suda—prigovor naroda (The sentence of the court is the sentence of the people). I. Kopalin, 1938.

Protsess GUMa (The GUM affair). 1925/1926.

Protsess o trekh millionakh (The trial of the three million). Ia. Protazanov, 1926, Mezhrabpom-Rus'.

Protsess pravykh Es-erov s 8-go iiuliia po 7-oe avgusta 1922 g. (The trial of the

Right SRs from July 8 through August 7, 1922). D. Vertov, 1923.

Protsess Prompartii (13 dnei) (The trial of the Industrial Party [13 days]). Ia. Posel'skii, 1930, Soiuzkinokhronika.

Putevka v zhizn' (The road to life). N. Ekk, 1931, Mezhrabpom.

Saba (Saba). M. Chiaureli, 1929, Goskinprom Gruzii.

Sekret rapida (The secret of the rapid). P. Dolina, 1930, Ukrainfil'm.

Shakhtinskii protsess (The Shakhty trial). Eshurin, 1928.

Soiuzkinozhurnal 43 (1928), no. 1–2 (1930).

Son Tarasa (The dream of Taras). Iu. Zheliabuzhskii, 1919, Rus'.

Sovkinokhronika 18 (1930).

Sovkinokhronika/zhurnal 74 (1929); no. 10, 21 (1930).

Sovkino-Zhurnal, nos. 14, 23, 27 (1928); no. 26 (1929); no. 1 (1931).

Stepan Khalturin (Stepan Khalturin). A. Ivanovskii, 1925, Sevzapkino.

Sud dolzhen prodolzhat'sia (The trial must continue). E. Dzigan, 1930/1931, Belgoskino.

Sud idet (Order in the court), *Sovkino-zhurnal,* no. 1 (1931).

Sud nad provokatorom Okladskim (The trial of the provocateur Okladskii). 1925.

Sud nad ubiitsei v Uzbekistane (Trial of a murderer in Uzbekistan). 1930.

Teni bel'vedera (The shadows of belvedere). A. Anoshchenko, 1926, VUFKU.

Tiazhelye gody (The difficult years). A. Razumnyi, 1925, Goskino.

Velikii grazhdanin (A great citizen). First and second series. F. Ermler, 1937/1938, 1939, Lenfil'm.

Velikii uteshitel' (The great consoler). L. Kuleshov, 1933, Mezhrabpomfil'm.

Vreditel' (Wrecker). K. Bolotov, 1929, VUFKU.

Vyborgskaia storona (The Vyborg side). G. Kozintsev and L. Trauberg, 1938, Lenfil'm.

Za sotsialisticheskuiu derevniu (For a socialist countryside). No. 17, 1930.

Zagovor interventov (A conspiracy of interventionists). Ia. Posel'skii, 1930, Soiuzkino khronika.

Zakliuchennye (Prisoners). E. Cherviakov, 1936, Mosfil'm.

Zhena predrevkoma (Wife of the president of the Revolutionary Committee). A. Ivanov-Gai, 1925, Goskino.

Zhivoi trup (The living corpse). F. Otsep, 1929, Mezhrabpomfil'm and Prometheusfil'm.

INDEX

Book titles, non-English words, and page numbers of illustrations are in *italics*.
Boldface page numbers indicate extensive treatment of a topic.

*Abortion: The Trial of Midwife Zait-
    seva (Abort. Sud nad akusherkoi
    Zaitsevoi)* (Lemberg), 81
Aeschylus. Works: *Eumenides,* 7, 160;
    Oresteia, 8, 86
Afinogenov, Aleksandr, 163, 175
*Affair of Counter-revolution in the Don-
    bass, An (Delo ob ekonomicheskom
    kontrrevoliutsii v Donbasse),* 125
agitsud(y). See trials, mock
agon, 8, 26
Akkerman, A. I., 69–70, 71, 78
Aleksandrov, P. A. (defense attorney),
    32–36, 37
Alexander II, and legal reforms of
    1864, 28–29
Alpers, Boris, 153
Andreev, Boris, 77
Anoshchenko, A., 83
Ardov, Viktor. Works: *The Affair of the
    Connecting Room (Delo o prokhod-
    noi komnate), A Fifty-kopeck Piece
    Ruined Me (Poltinnik pogubil), Al-
    imony (Alimeny),* 72
"Art and the Revolution" (1848) (Wag-
    ner), 10
Art of the Theatre, The (1905) (Craig),
    11
audience participation, 57, **66–71,** 76,
    127, 188; in cinema, 24, 25–26; ma-
    nipulating, **123–28,** 166; theater vs.
    real-life, 73, 78, 93–94, 173, 191

Beatty, Bessie (correspondent, *San
    Francisco Bulletin*), 38, 39–40
Benjamin, Walter, 8, 76
Birth of Tragedy, The (1872) (Nietz-
    sche), 10
Bogoliubov, A. S., 31–32
Bolotov, K., 103
Bolshevik revolution of 1917, 4, 10,
    38, 54
Broken Pitcher, The (Kleist), 7
Brukzon, Ia. B. (theater critic), 15, 22
Bukharin, Nikolai, 44, 132, 190–91
Burkhardt, Jacob, 8

Caucasian Chalk Circle (Brecht), 7
Chernyshevskii, N. G., 34
Chiaureli, M. Works: *The Fall of Berlin
    (Padenie Berlina)* (1949), 195; *Saba*
    (1929), 82, 89, *91,* 97, 172
Chicanery (Iabeda) (Kapnist), 7
chistka. See purge
communism, 57, 150
*Conspiracy of Interventionists
    (Zagovor interventov),* edited and
    archived version of *The Trial of the
    Industrial Party [13 Days],* 170
Craig, Gordon, 11

Darkness at Noon (Koestler), 6
Decembrist uprising of 1825, 4
defective goods *(brak),* 164, 166, *167*
Demidovich, E. B., 68

Dictatorship of Conscience (Diktatura sovesti) (Shatrov), 79
Difficult Years, The (Tiazhelye gody) (1925) (Razumnyi), 82, 102
Dionysian theater, 8, 12, 13, 16, 18, 24, 65, 71, 79, 189
Dolina, P., 82, 99
Dostoevskii, F. M. Works: *The Brothers Karamazov,* 33; *Notes from Underground,* 15
drama and culture, 4, 12–13, 14, 79, 83–84; in ancient Greece, 11, 12, 86; and cinema, 4, 26, 189; and Proletarian culture movement, **16–19,** 52–53, 86, 98; in Russia, 11, 86, 89; and Western civilization, 88, 89
drama and law, 3, 4, 6, 7, 26, 49, 52, 53, 81, 111, 198n.8; in ancient Greece, 8, 9; and Western civilization, 3, 7, 9, 118, 141, 196
drama and politics, 11, 135; in Nazi Germany, 9; in Stalinist Russia, 9, 110, 132–33
drama, cinematic: as an art form, 4, 19, 20, 26, 84, 94, 134; vs. theater, 20–22, **23–27,** 83, 84, 88, 90, 92, 94–95, 161
Dream of Taras, The (Son Tarasa) (Zheliabuzhskii) (1919), 82
Duranty, Walter, 123, 210n.58

Eisenstein, Sergei, 20, 21, 24, 25
enemies of the people, 53, 74, 110, 125, 127, 161; hidden, 107–8, 111, 119, 132, 160, 182
enemies of the state, 42–43, 48, 49, 50, 51, 111, 139, 195
Erdman, Nikolai, 135, 136, 142, 155, 160, 161, 187. Works: *Mandate (Mandat)* (1925), **142–145,** 155; *Suicide (Samoubiitsa)* (1932), 136, 155
Ermler, F. Works: *A Great Citizen* (1937, 1939), 193; *The Parisian Cobbler (Parizhskii sapozhnik)* (1927), 82, **94–97,** 96; *Peasants* (1935), 182; *She Defends the Motherland* (1943), 195
Eugene Onegin (Pushkin), 23

Euripedes, 8
Evreinov, Nikolai, as proponent of theater-for-oneself, 14–16, 44, 65. Works: *The Main Thing (Samoe glavnoe),* 14; *The Storming of the Winter Palace (Vziatie zimnego dvortsa),* 15

Fairbanks, Douglas, 25
Fear (Strakh) (1931) (Afinogenov), 163, **175–81**
Former People (Byvshie liudi) (Lunacharskii), 120
French Revolution, as model for revolutionary tribunal, 38–42, 44, 49–50, 52, 209n.43
Fuchs, Georg, 11
Fülöp-Miller, René, 56

Ghost That Doesn't Return, The (Prividenie, kotoroe ne vozvrashchaetsia) (1929) (Room), 83
Glasnost, 79
Glavrepertkom, censors of, 134, 155, 164, 168, 182
Glebova, N., 74–75
Gor'kii, Maksim, 52, 85, 87, 88. Works: *Mother (Mat'),* 37; adaptation of *Mother* by A. Razumnyi (1919) and by V. Pudovkin (1926), 82; *Somov and Others (Somov i drugie)* (1941), 175
Gradovskii, G. K. (journalist), 34

Hibben, Paxton (correspondent, *Nation*), 44–45
House of Soviets, 113
Huizinga, Johan, 8

Industrial Party of 1930, trial of, 162, 163, 169
Inspector General (1926) (Gogol), 20, 142, 144
Iuvachev, I. P., 34
Ivanov, Viacheslav: as proponent of Dionysian theater, 12–13, 16, 24, 44, 65, 71, 79, 189; influence of, on Russian drama, 11–14

Ivanovskii, A., 82

Kaganovich, Lazar', 155
Kalatozov, Mikhail, 163, 164–68, 180, 187
Kerzhentsev, Platon, as proponent of proletarian theater, **16–19**, 22, 65. Works: *Amid the Flames (Sredi plameni)*, 18; *A Case of Theft (Delo o Krazhe)*, 56–57; *The Creative Theater (Tvorcheskii teatr)*, 16
Kessel, K. I. (prosecuting attorney), 32, 33, 35–36
Khersonskii, Khrisanf (critic), 149
Khokhlova, Alexandra (actress), 147
Koestler, Arthur, 6
Kolodub, Andrei, 116, 118
Kolodub, Emel'ian, 116, 118
Koni, A. F. (Zasulich judge), 32, 34–35, 71, 206n.14
Krylenko, Nikolai (prosecutor), 3; and Shakhty Affair, 112, 114, 115–17, 128, 130; and SR trial, 12, 14; and trial of the Industrial Party, 162, 163, 169
Kuleshov, Lev, 134, 139, 140, 145, 170. Works: *By the Law (Po zakonu)* (1926), 136, **145–49**; *The Extraordinary Adventures of Mr. West in the Land of the Bolsheviks (Neobychainye prikliucheniia Mistera Vesta v strane bol'shevikov)* (1924), 134, **139–42**, 170, 225n.11; *The Great Consoler (Velikii uteshitel')* (1933), 149

Laws (Plato), 7
Lemberg, G., 81
Lenin, V. I., 37, 38, 43, 119, 181
Living Corpse, The (Tolstoi), 7, 82
London, Jack, 145, 146, 147
Lotman, Iurii, 4, 5
Lukashevich, T., *The Crime of Ivan Karavaev (Prestuplenie Ivana Karavaeva)* (1929), 82, 98–99
Lunacharskii, Anatolii, 16, 52, 138, 181; as proponent of melodrama, 83–84, 85, 88–89, 94

Lyons, Eugene (correspondent, *New York Times*), 114

Maiakovskii, Vladimir, 21–22, 134, 136, 137, 149, 153, 187. Works: *Bathhouse (Bania)* (1930), 135, 136, **153–55**; *Bedbug (Klop)* (1927), 135, **149–53**; *Mystery-Bouffe: A Heroic, Epic, and Satiric Representation of Our Epoch (Misteriia-buff)* (1918, 1921), 134–35, **137–39**, 150
Markov, Pavel, 87
martyrdom, 32, 33, 34, 46
Marxist revolution, 52
metaphor, theatrical, 3, 4, 27, 121, 122, 135, 137–39, **150–53**, 154, 167
Meyerhold, Vsevolod, 19, 20, 87
monodrama, 14
Morozov, Pavlik, 116
Moscow Diary (Benjamin), 76
Moscow Nobles club. *See* House of Soviets
mythopoesis (drama as creation of myth with power to revolutionize life), 5, 12, 16, 23
mythopoesis, legal, 5, 50, 80; avantgarde, 135; in cinema, 82, 84, 108; in satire, 160; and myth of rehabilitation, 163, 180, 183, 187; in postSoviet era, 195; in provinces, 162
mythopoetic justice: in actual courtroom procedure, 111, 115, 119, 122, 128, 131, 180, 187; failure of, 160, 164; through metaphor, 137; paradigm of, 73, 78, 132, 136, 149, 161, 162, 195

Nail in the Boot, A (Gvozd' v sapoge) (1931) (Kalatozov), 163, **164–68**, 180, 187
narodnyi teatr (people's theater), 16
Neoplatonism, 11
New Economic Policy (NEP), 43, 58, 59, 80, 111, 139, 145
Nicholas II, 41, 42
Nietzsche, Friedrich, 10, 11, 14
nigilitska (female nihilist), 34, 35

Nuremberg trials, 3

Otsep, F., adaptation of Tolstoi's play *The Living Corpse (Zhivoi trup)* (1929) 82–83
Outcomes and Lessons of the Shakhty Affair (Itogi i uroki shakhtinskogo dela) (Vyshinskii), 121–22

Palen, Count K. I. (Minister of Justice), 29, 31–32, 36
Penal Colony (Katorga) (1928) (Raizman), 82
People's Theater, The (1903) (Rolland), 17, 85
Piotrovskii, Adrian (critic), 88–89
Pixerécourt, René Charles Guilbert, 86
Plato, 7, 10
Pobedonosikovitis *(pobedonosikoshchina)*, 154
poetic justice (enantiodromia), 52, 85, 97, 99, 102, 103, 105, 195
pokazatel'nyi protsess. See trials, show
Posel'skii, Ia., 81, 169. Works: *The Crime of the Horse-doctor Matov (Prestuplenie konovala Matova)*, 81; *The Trial of the Industrial Party (13 Days) (Protsess Prompartii [13 dnei])* (1931), 163, **169–75**, *171, 173*, 192
Pravda, 70, 120–21
propaganda, 5, 21, 48, 84, 88, 120, 190; in cinema, 19, 25, 94, 164; in documentaries, 163; and film censorship, 23; legal, 6, 37, 83, 84, 103, 108, 110, 111; political, 29, 43, 51, 59, 125, 128, 183; realistic, 23, 65–66, 187, 188; revolutionary, 49, 53, 54, 64, 98, 136; social, 82, 89, 97, 123; theatrical, 6, 14–15, 24, 53, 56, 58, 70, 131
Protazanov, Ia. Works: *Don Diego and Pelegaia: The Affair of Pelegaia Demina (Don Diego i Pelegaia. Delo Pelegai Deminoi)* (1927), 82, 105; *The Trial of the Three Million (Protsess o trekh millionakh)* (1926), 83

Pudovkin, Vsevolod, 83
purge *(chistka)*, 98, 99, 105, 108, 121, 154, 182
Pyr'ev, Ivan, 106, 140. Works: *The Government Bureaucrat (Gosudarstvennyi chinovnik)* (1930), 106–7, *107*, 140; *The Party Card (Partiinyi bilet)*, 163, **182–88**, *186*

Radek, Karl, 43
Raizman, Iu., 82
Razumnyi, A., 82, 102
realism, 13, 65–66, 69, 70, 72–73, 78, 101, 110, 161, 181
realism, socialist, 25, 183, 187, 190
Rebel'skii, I. V. (historian), 54
Red Truth (Krasnaia pravda) (Vermishev), 88
Revolutionary Tribunal, 38, 39
Revolution in the Theatre (1909) (Fuchs), 11
Rolland, Romain, 17, **85–87**
Room, A., 83
Rosita (Tairov), 87
Rural Theater (Derevenskii teatr), 59
Russian Orthodoxy, 52
Ryklin (Soviet journalist), 118

sabotage, 113, 116, 117, 181
St. Joan (Shaw), 7
samokritika. See self-criticism
samosud, samosudy. See self-trial
Scopes monkey trial, 3
Secret of the Rapid, The (Sekret Rapida) (1930) (Dolina), 82, 99
self-criticism, 6, 82, 108, 134, 135, 150, 154; and audience identification, 74, 76, 82, 125, 180; based on fictional reality, 193, 195; as Soviet ritual, 98, 116, 127, 136, 189, 195
self-trial, 30, 36, 49, 54, 147
Shadows of Belvedere, The (Teni bel'vedera) (1926) (Anoshchenko), 83
Shakespeare, William, 4, 8. Works: *Macbeth*, 86; *Merchant of Venice*, 7, 70, 160
Shakhty Affair of 1928, **110–19**, **123–28**, *127*, 161; as melodrama, 6,

109, 124–25, 127–28, 187, 190; in newsreels, 126; as public trial, 110, 123, 161

Shaw, George Bernard, 7, 85

Shchastnyi, Admiral, 39

Sigal, Doctor B. S., 60, 65, 66, 72, 75, 78, 90. Works: *Trial of a Mother, Guilty of the Poor Care of Her Children, Which Entailed the Death of a Child (Sud nad mater'iu, vinovnoi v plokhom ukhode za det'mi, povlekshem za soboi smert' rebenka)* (1926), 60, 68, 72, 74, 78, 90; *Trial of a Pioneer-Smoker (Sud nad pionerom-kuril'shchikom)* (1927), 67–68; *Trial of Stepan Korolev (as a Result of Drunkenness) (Sud nad Stepanom Korolevym [Posledstviia p'ianstva])* (1924), 60, 74, 78, 90

smychka (worker-peasant solidarity), 98

social class, 78, 114, 150, 178

socialism, construction of, 74, 75, 119, 153, 160, 164, 166, 189

Socialist Internationals, 43

Socialist Revolutionaries (SR), trials of 1920s, 31, **42–50**, 46, 51, 111, 112–13, 120, 126

Sophocles, 8. Works: *Ajax*, 8; *Antigone*, 8; *Oedipus Rex*, 86

Sovkino-Zhurnal newsreels, 126

spectators' involvement. *See* audience participation

SR. *See* Socialist Revolutionaries (SR), trials of 1920s

Stalin, Joseph: as director of Central Committee, 112, 122, 155; as leader of cultural revolution, 136, 161–62, 169; as movie censor, 181–82, 187, 188, 193

Stalin's Great Terror, 3, 190, 195, 197n.1; role of confession in, 5, 50, 129, 187

Stanislavskii, Konstantin, 13, 65

Stepan Khalturin (1925) (Ivanovskii), 82

Tairov, Aleksandr, 19, 87

Teacher Bubus (Uchitel' Bubus) (Meyerhold), 87

theatricality (fusion of real life with theater), 5, 10, 13–14, 15, 21, 23, 37, 44; antitheatrical, 13, 37, 39, 69, 71; in legal practice, 118, 129–31, 172; revolutionary, 10, 16, 19, 21, 23, 24, 47, 86; and satire, 135–36, 153, 154, 155, 161; as "theater therapy," 142

Thief of Baghdad, The, 25

threefold pattern, 59, 84, 107, 110–11, 161, 164, 186, 188, 189; with emphasis on confession, 108, 115, 119, 136, 143, 169, 172; with emphasis on reintegration, 83, 92, 103; with emphasis on repentance, 62, 100, 143, 169, 175

Tolstoi, L. N., 7, 36–37, 82

Trepov, F. F. (governor-general of St. Petersburg), 31–32

Trial (Kafka), 160

Trial of a Delegate (Sud nad delegatkoi) (Glebova), 74–75

Trial of a Prostitute (Sud nad prostitutkoi) (Akkerman), 69–70, 71, 78

Trial of Bootleggers (Sud nad samogonshchikami) (Vasilevskii), 71

Trial of Lenin (Sud nag Leninyn) (1920), 57, 79

Trial of Sexual Promiscuity (Sud nad polovoi raspushchennost'iu) (Demidovich), 68, 74

Trial of the Old Way of Life (Sud nad starym bytom) (Andreev), 77

trial of Vera Zasulich (1878). *See* Zasulich, Vera, trial of

Trial of Vrangel' (Sud nad Vrangelem), 58

trials: Communist Party in 1992, 195; Countess Panina, 38–40; Great Trial of Bukharin and Rykov, 190–91; Industrial Party of 1930, 58; Menshevik trial of 1931, 174; Metro-Vickers trial of 1933, 162; Moscow trials of 1936–1938, 160; 1920s, 111, 134

trials, demonstration, 37, 128, 164

trials, literary, 53

trials, mass mock, 55–59, 65, 67, 79

trials, mock *(agitsud/y)*, 67, 71, 79; as cinema, 89, 92, 100, 103, 189; as propaganda theater, 6, 53–54, 125, 140, 144, 164; scripted, 59, 64, 65, 127; use of comedy in, 72, 142

trials, model, 37, 45, 132; American cinema, 140; French Revolution, 38, 41; real-life, 109, 111–12, 113, 131, 161; Soviet, 140

trials, public, 31, 52, 99, 103, 108, 110, 113, 195

trials, show, 3, 4, 8, 15, 26, 49, 51, 127, 189: avant-garde theater, 10, 19, 27, 38, 44, 135, 160, 189; avant-garde theater, audience participation in, 49, 57, 126–27; Bolshevik, 28, **37–42**, 49–50, 51, 64, 102, 103, 108–9, 196; documentary film, 163, 168, 182, 187, 190; 1870s, **30–37**; melodrama, 84, 90, 102, 104, 106, 116, 172–73, 183–84; melodrama as model, 52, 63, 87–89, 94; melodrama, cinematic, 84, 97, 108; melodrama, legal, 79, 134, 135, 188; melodrama, revolutionary, 54, 65, 84–85; provincial, 162; silent film, 10, 94, 173, 175

Tribunal (Voinovich), 7

Twenty-six Commissars (Dvadtsat' shest' komissarov) (1932) (Shengelaia), 83

"Unexpected, The" (London), 145, 146, 147

Vakhtangov, Evgenii, 19

Vermishev, Aleksandr, 88

Vertov, Dziga, 22, 25, 169, 173; newsreel *Kino-Nedelia,* 40; newsreel *Kinopravda,* 47–49, *48, 50,* 126

Vreditel' (The Wrecker) (1929) (Bolotov), 103–5, *104*

vreditel' (wrecker, saboteur), 104, 120, 121, 122

"Vrediteli" *(Pravda)*, 120–21

Vyshinskii, Andrei, 112, 117, 123, 128, 130, 170, 172–73, 182, 192

Wagner, Richard, 10, 11

What Is to Be Done? (Chernyshevskii), 34

Woe to Wit (1928) (Griboedov), 20

Writer's Union (1932), 136

Zasulich, Vera, trial of, **31–37**, 49, 71

Zhdanov, V. A. (defense lawyer), 40